Rethinking Religion

The Living Issues
Discussion Series

*T*HE LIVING ISSUES DISCUSSION SERIES is overseen by Michael A. King and published by Cascadia Publishing House LLC (earlier by Cascadia LLC division Pandora Press U.S.) as well as sometimes copublished with Herald Press. Cascadia Publishing House, in consultation with its Editorial Council as well as volume editors and authors, is primarily responsible for content of these studies. Typically through a main text followed by materials providing affirming and critical reactions from respondents, these volumes address "living issues" likely to benefit from lively and serious discussion.

1. To Continue the Dialogue:
   Biblical Interpretation and Homosexuality
   Edited by C. Norman Kraus, 2001

2. What Does the Bible Really Say About Hell?
   Wrestling with the Traditional View
   By Randy Klassen, 2001

3. Reflecting on Faith in a Post-Christian Time (a revised and expanded
   edition of Theology in Postliberal Perspective, first published by
   SCM Press and Trinity Press International)
   By Daniel Liechty, 2003

4. Stumbling Toward a Genuine Conversation on Homosexuality
   Edited by Michael A. King, 2007

5. Theology As If Jesus Matters:
   An Introduction to Christianity's Main Themes
   By Ted Grimsrud, 2009

6. Rethinking Religion:
   Beyond Scientism, Theism, and Philosophic Doubt
   By Alan Soffin, 2011

Rethinking Religion

Beyond Scientism, Theism, And Philosophic Doubt

Alan Soffin

Living Issues Discussion Series
Volume 6

Cascadia
Publishing House
Telford, Pennsylvania

Cascadia Publishing House orders, information, reprint permissions:
contact@CascadiaPublishingHouse.com
1-215-723-9125
126 Klingerman Road, Telford PA 18969
www.CascadiaPublishingHouse.com

Rethinking Religion
Copyright © 2011 by Cascadia Publishing House
a division of Cascadia Publishing House LLC, Telford, PA 18969
All rights reserved.
ISBN 13: 978-1-931038-80-5; ISBN 10: 1-931038-80-5
Library of Congress Catalog Number: 2011007626
Book design by Cascadia Publishing House
Cover design by Alan Soffin and Cascadia Publishing House
The cover and interior: Photos by Alan Soffin

The paper used in this publication is recycled and meets the
minimum requirements of American National Standard for Information Sciences—Permanence of Paper for Printed Library Materials, ANSI Z39.48-1984.
Scripture quotations are from the King James Bible.

Library of Congress Cataloguing-in-Publication Data
Soffin, Alan, 1930-
 Rethinking religion : beyond scientism, theism, and philosophic doubt /
Alan Soffin.
   p. cm. -- (Living issues discussions series ; v. 6)
 Includes bibliographical references.
 Summary: "An atheist drawn to religion, Alan Soffin shows how to
conceptualize a "God" who is in and of the cosmos rather than also
beyond it as theists affirm. This allows Soffin and those who see value
in the path he blazes to embrace and value the treasures of religion
even while not being theistic" --Provided by publisher.
 ISBN-13: 978-1-931038-80-5 (trade pbk. : alk. paper)
 ISBN-10: 1-931038-80-5 (trade pbk. : alk. paper)
 1. God. 2. Religion--Philosophy. I. Title.
 BL473.S64 2011
 211--dc22
                    2011007626

18 17 16 15 14 13 12 11   10 9 8 7 6 5 4 3 2 1

The time must surely come when this brief passage into light that we call con-sciousness will be seen for the miracle it is, and this fragile earthly sojourn un-derstood to be the heaven of so many desperate dreams.

Contents

CHAPTER FOUR: GOD'S BODY   321

CHAPTER FIVE: CONCLUDING UNSCIENTIFIC POSTSCRIPT: TRUTH, LOVE, DEATH   397

CHAPTER SIX: RESPONSES   412

Series Editor's Preface

Alan Soffin is an unusual philosopher. An atheist drawn to religion, Soffin's project is to show how to conceptualize a "God" who is in and of the cosmos rather than also beyond it as theists affirm. This allows Soffin and those who see value in the path he blazes to value religion even while not being theistic. I found myself drawn to Soffin's wrestlings as both publisher and person.

As a publisher, the more I learned of Soffin's interests the more I came to think that his attempt to help atheism and theism make common cause made his project a "living issue" deserving serious discussion and examination of ways both Soffin's critics and those more likely to be drawn to his thought might understand his quest. This makes *Rethinking Religion* fit the Living Issues Discussion Series. To set the conversation in motion, typically books in the series include a vigorous statement of position regarding issues sometimes controversial in faith circles. Then, after a book's main text, a Responses chapter provides affirming and critical commentary.

However, I imagine it wouldn't have occurred to me to publish an atheist in the series had it not been for my own journey through such matters. I was the child of Mennonite parents who three months after I was born took me, their eldest, to begin the missionary work in Cuba and then Mexico that was to reach its close only when I was eighteen and on the cusp of starting college. What I experienced in that milieu I was decades later to summarize this way in my online seminary dean profile:

> Growing up in Cuba and Mexico as son of missionary parents, Michael A. King experienced multiple cultures and faith understandings. He learned to cherish the Anabaptist-Mennonite commitment to faithfully follow Jesus while wondering what alternate convictions another tradition might have shaped in him.

Immersion in Christian thought and life at a time his Mennonite community forbade watching TV even as he gulped down secular books and novels made him wonder what was real and true and good amid competing perspectives. . . . As a result, into early adulthood King came to question the existence of God and the validity of Christianity even while craving the divine. . . .

That history drew me to Soffin's passions. Even as I am a theist who has given my entire adult life to serving the church as pastor, publisher, and now seminary dean, I have never forgotten how questionable Christian and theistic teachings once seemed to me; I still see myself as an agnostic Christian, not in the sense that I lack faith but in the conviction that we know only fallibly, only in part, as the apostle Paul himself one described it, or, as the New Testament writer of Hebrews once famously put it, as those yearning toward a far-off country we do not fully reach in this life. My own life and thought, therefore, makes me experience Soffin as a fellow seeker.

We neither start nor end at the same place. In addition to the obvious contrasts between atheist and theist, I find the perspectivalism with which I frequently approach matters as a Christian who thinks that what we can know is shaped by the particular commitments we make to be a tendency Soffin delights (as he memorably does on p. 245) in skewering. Yet we both suspect that in pondering with rather than against each other, we draw nearer, even amid stark differences, to what we ache for. Thus though I wouldn't put matters this way, I find insight worth pondering in Soffin's statement (p. 254) that "For this reason, we say that if we have knowledge, the divine is in us—is incarnate—and creates us human. More exactly, when we attain knowledge, the divine and the human are one. *The existence of knowledge is, in this sense, God's humanity.*"

I hope readers will experience a sense of mutual enrichment as they too, now, enter this book's treasures. Reactions from authors of the Responses chapter, each quite different in view of these matters, some leaning theistic, others not, seem to me to offer such hope. They offer their diverse concerns or affirmations; they also each celebrate insights they perceive in Soffin's unusual voyage. Thus I dare to hope that in being a volume written by an atheistic writer drawn to religious faith, supported by a theistic publisher drawn to exploring the limits of what can be known, and fleshed out by responses from thinkers of various faith traditions, Rethinking Religion opens a new path in faith-related thought.

—*Michael A. King, Series Editor, Living Issues Series*

Author's Preface

MEMENTO MORI

Like most philosophers, I had always found the arguments for theism flawed. Unlike most, however, I had found the arguments for a wholly scientific worldview equally untenable. Since these seemed the only alternatives for describing what, at bottom, the human situation *really is*, religious inquiry, for me, was at an impasse.

It was the premature death of my first wife and the subsequent deaths of many friends that returned me to the subject of religion. I could neither grasp nor still the thought that they would never come again, nor could I any longer conveniently forget that soon I, too, would not exist. I set side the standard questions of philosophy and took up, once more, the question that motivates religion: "What is the meaning of our lives?" I became theologically concerned.

A CULTURE OF IRRELIGION

It was not a comfortable decision. Among philosophers, the question of life's *meaning* is regarded as jejune. The self-doubt this stirred was tempered, however, by my assessment of the current intellectual scene. Ideas were gaining credence in academic circles and beyond that plainly bore upon the meaning of human life. But they did so in ways that were destructive, intellectually as well as spiritually.

"Postmodern" philosophy and literary theory were reviving and broadcasting ancient skepticisms: The possibility of knowledge was denied. Reality was deemed a fiction—a *construction* of the human mind. Language was a barrier to truth—a *filter* that distorted our vision of the world. *Objectivity* was said to be impossible. *Evaluation* was the expression of mere preference. Texts were claimed to have no meaning other than what readers might attribute to them.

Science and medicine indirectly strengthened this attack on rationality. Advances in genetics and brain physiology spawned articles and books explaining mental operations as the product of *non-mental* causes.

It was becoming *scientifically naïve* to think that civilized development was the consequence of reasoning, evidence, moral insight, and critical reflection; none of these could have effects because none were *physical* conditions. The ideas by which we lived, and that we believed to have been thoughtfully derived, were blithely explained as the product of electrical and chemical processes.

Together, these ideas savaged responsibility. Since a free or uncaused will was scientifically absurd, a so-called "choice" could only be explained as the product of a physical brain (certainly not an imaginary *self*). But not to worry, since no choice could, be, in reality, better than another. The idea of an inherently *right* or *wrong* choice had been unmasked as an illusion.

These skeptical and scientistic theories synergistically abetted a culture driven by acquisitive self-interest. Enamored of profit and persuasion, it was a culture ready to agree that there exist no "objective" standards, no *oughts* or *ought-nots*, that might demand restraint. In thrall to endless economic growth, it was a culture with no time for the timeless, a culture so changeful nothing in it could possibly matter.

"The measure of all things" was *demand*. All else was *supply*—science, technology, art, communities, families, cities, governments, "yeah, even the great globe itself." Nothing had inherent value; nothing could command us. Evaluative terms like "good," "right," "true" or "desirable" were thought to signal only the utility of things for whatever goals we happened to have. It was a life tailor-made for skeptical philosophy.

The whole signaled a collapse not easily described. What had been lost was, in some way, deeper than intellect or morals. I can only describe it as loss of *seriousness*. The kind of meaning that lies, so to speak, in the mountains, no longer had a place. A cavalcade of psychological and economic mechanics had separated life from its roots. I thought myself a witness to the twilight of religion.

FINDING A DIRECTION

The world's religions were, it seemed, forever struggling to grasp and to express something that lay so deep in the well of life it could not quite be seen. Whatever it was, it struck the religious sensibility as something *ultimate* and, thus, beyond any possible explanation.

It was, as a developed idea, the hidden and supreme source of human guidance. It was the basis of all laws—physical, rational, moral, and aesthetic. And, as if that were not mystery enough, it was responsible for our creation.

Its names are, of course, well known: "God," "Yaweh," "Allah," "Brahman"—or, in the East, the "the Way" or "*Li*." But however it was pictured, it was *sovereign* and *external*. It gave meaning to us; we did not give meaning to it. This was, for religion, the essential direction in which meaning enters our lives.

This seemingly simple fact explained to me modernity's inherent *irreligion*. The postmodernist, skeptical, scientistic, and self-interested standpoints all insisted that meaning flowed from us into the world. It was we who decided all laws but the physical (and for some even physical law was our own logical convention). There was no meaning to life beyond what we assigned to it. We lived and died, yearned and fought for ideals and standards that had no more basis in reality, no more *right* to command or direct us, than the imaginary gods of myth.

Some may conclude that "religion" is simply a mistake; I cannot. Religion is no less a universal and continuing domain of human interest than morality, science, philosophy, history, jurisprudence, mathematics, or aesthetics. I cannot suppose the world's population fundamentally deluded.

The task at hand, then, was to elicit—from the life we already know—a conception of that *sovereign, external, creative,* and *ultimate* "something." I say "from the life we know" because (as the book argues in detail) neither I nor anyone else can lay claim to receiving a "revelation" on the subject untouched by his or her own judgment. In any case, I had no such revelation and expected none.

To rethink religion would, therefore, be to rethink what William James called "religion's object." It would be to understand in a new light that external, creative *something* that is essential to life's meaning. The book's pervasive theme, therefore, is an analysis of "God" as religion's seminal idea.

The rationale for this approach is that the *idea* of a creator-god must satisfy the deepest religious yearnings. If the ways could be specified by which the idea of "God" accomplished this end it would,

I thought, constitute a "map" of the requirements that any revised notion of "religion's object" would have to satisfy.

Whatever of religious significance that effort might uncover, the truth of it would have to be established on the basis of facts and situations with which you, the reader, are familiar. In rethinking religion, the life we live is our only sacred text.

Alas, there is no road to a responsible theology (for that is what *Rethinking* strives to be) without showing, argument by argument, why theistic supernaturalism and scientific naturalism—the two alternative accounts of what is ultimately real—are, in the end, indefensible.

The book argues that neither is consistent with life as we understand it in the offices and practices of *consequential* living—that is, when, in Gide's phrase, "the chips are down." Each is a theory purporting to explain human life. But, in explaining what lies behind that life, each, in the end, explains that life away. (Meister Eckhart and the writers of the Upanishads rightly saw that if all is a function of God's will, the life we experience is a kind of illusion, while, in similarly finding things illusory, the behaviorist, B. F. Skinner contended that what we think never explains what we do.)

Plainly, *Rethinking* is more a study than a "read." The closeness of its arguments may be more suited to the student than the general reader at whom this book is—perhaps foolishly—aimed. But what consideration of a religious framework is authentically undertaken without discipline, commitment—and fearlessness?

To the end of "spreading the word," I have endeavored to avoid specialized language, both theological and philosophical, and have confined the writing almost exclusively to arguments whose examples are drawn from everyday experience. No attempt is made to survey the literature, in large part because I think theism and scientism turn out to share the same logic and by virtue of that logic, the same faults. Their conflict is less a *war* than a family quarrel.

From the book's analysis of "God"—and "reality" as seen by theistic, empirical, and skeptical approaches—a positive account of religious significance emerges. Miracle and mystery are found within the ambit of responsible life and are accorded a non-supernatural, yet literally *miraculous* or *mysterious* status. We live ultimate reality every day, and do so in a way that cannot be explained. From the standpoint of *Rethinking Religion*, we are the universe thinking—earth made flesh, flesh made spirit.

In consequence, the idea of "God" as lawgiver and creator acquires a non-supernatural, non-scientific description consistent with the feelings of attraction, fear and awe that Rudolph Otto's *The Idea of the Holy* famously described as essential to authentic religious experience.

No doubt, for the general reader, the most unfamiliar aspect of this book is its use of *philosophical* argument. In aid of the serious, lay seeker (and. I think, those who favor contemporary perspectivist or neo-Nietzschean philosophy), the book's first chapter discusses philosophical reflection, relating it to religion and truth, and offering guidance with respect to the doing of it.

Finally: *Rethinking* swims against the current of contemporary opinion. But, so be it. The warfare "between science and religion"— between a wholly scientific version of reality and a supernatural one—has gone on too long for either one to be correct. The world may be saved by history and politics, but knowing that it has will be a matter for religion.

—*Alan L. Soffin*
  Doylestown, Pennsylvania

Acknowledgments

There are in this book more lives than can be counted. Russian grandparents who valued the education they never had. Rubin and Alice, who gave me life, love, and opportunity. Aunt Sylvia, who took a child's writing seriously. The many teachers, unsung, whose song I lend whatever voice I have. The great and dedicated minds of the University of Illinois: Frederick Will, Max Fisch, William Stanley, Othanel Smith, and all the others who kept alive the great tradition of human understanding in the middle of a vast and silent prairie. Justin Morrill, Abraham Lincoln, and the other politicians whose Land Grant colleges bear witness to the fact that once we understood the meaning of the common good. Bozidar and Milosh Muntyan, risen to professorships from an immigrant Serbian working class they never forgot. George Barnett and Elmer Eason, loyal friends whose dialogue and encouragement were as valuable for me as for the hundreds they taught. Robert Ennis, the friend whose keen mind kept before me a goal of clarity and soundness I sought but could never reach.

Byron and Leila Bozarth, second parents whose love was endlessly sustaining and whose generosity, love of literature, philosophy and music has never ceased to echo in my soul. Ex-students John Glenn, Anthony Balboni, Steven Vlam, and Dan Johnson, whose caring buoyed me in my later years. Michael Oliker, student of my university years, who brought me back into writing and publishing.

Above all, the women. Megan Bozarth, my first wife, who believed in me and who gave me more love than I deserved, who spent her life teaching and loving the very young, who brought laughter and joy to everyone she met, and who suffered the cruelty of cancer before her time and in utter contradiction of the life her work and heart had earned. Her death taught me the meaning of life. And Jean, the wife who gave me a second life, a woman whose understanding of the good in all has been, for me, transformative. A woman whose love, wisdom, constancy, and caring make better all around her. Without her counsel, conversation, and support, this book would never have achieved completion.

And Michael A. King, who was willing to take a chance.

Rethinking Religion

Chapter 1

Religion and Philosophy: Notes On Method For The General Reader

There will be those who will complain, whenever anything is shown in a clear light, that seen clearly it is no longer what they saw in darkness. For those who place value upon obscurantism, I have no argument.
—C. B. Martin, *Religious Belief*

INTRODUCTION TO CHAPTER ONE

I have written most of this book in, I suppose, an "archaic" style, hoping to focus attention on the arguments rather than on personal testimony. Mainly in prefatory material and the chapter introductions have I written in the first person. I trust the reader will forgive the distancing quality of a style that employs what is often called "the royal 'we'" instead of the politically innocent "I" and simply join me in considering the arguments.

As the title of this chapter indicates, its aim is to link truth, philosophy, and religion with a primary emphasis on what it means to think *philosophically* about religion. If you have had little or no acquaintance with philosophy, you might think of it as Olympian detachment from the pains and frustrations of daily life. Well, a certain amount of detachment is required, but only to raise the ideas by which we guide our lives to consciousness so that they may be critically examined. The task, as Socrates said, is to "know thyself."

But what does it mean to go about this task? How is it different from engaging in psychological self-analysis? And what is the point of *philosophizing* if, as is very often said, philosophy gets you nowhere—if it is true that "there are no answers, only questions"? Then, too, why make an effort to philosophize if your interest is theology or religion?

This chapter addresses these issues and, in so doing, takes up the question of what it is to philosophize and how philosophy may help—may even be essential—in arriving at a *true* religion.

TRUTH AS A RELIGIOUS IMPERATIVE

To write on religion is to risk being judged by the criteria of melodrama. However tortuous or troubled the narrative, a comforting conclusion is anticipated. Popular culture so desires *positive* or *helpful* religion, one might easily forget that religionists themselves insist that their beliefs are true and that it is only because they are true that they believe them.

Indeed, the idea that religious claims are true helps explain why even those with no motive to acquire institutional power can feel genuinely obligated to teach, persuade, or require that others believe or behave as they themselves do. The common understanding that informal religious discussions are socially risky would make little sense if religious views were thought merely to express a personal preference. Even today's congenial search for universal religious precepts intimates that what all believe is likely more *believable*, that is, more likely to be *true*.

Given the requirement of truth, to hold religious views out of habit, convenience, or utility is to dismiss the actual existence of a uniquely religious object. It is to say, in effect, that there is nothing imperative "out there" with a just claim on one's life. Those who minimize the requirement of truth belie the first attitudinal demand of any authentic religion: an unconditional seriousness which in simplest terms is the notion that things *matter* whether we like it or not, or, more specifically, that there exist independent or "natural" imperatives that can rightly transcend—and if necessary oppose—mere will, wish, or desire.

Even the vague, shopworn expression, "commitment to a higher power," acknowledges that religious imperatives are matters of obeisance not preference. Popular culture may be thrilled by charismatic preachers, buoyed by spiritual music, impressed by "miraculous" escapes and stories of extreme self-denial, but the spirit's real passage of fire comes in honestly confronting the credentials of its own devotions.

Still, the rigors of truth must not be assumed incompatible with mystery, for religion has essentially to do with things *awesome* and *ultimate*—life-shaping things whose truth can neither be explained nor reasonably denied. If an authentic religion is possible, a middle ground of ultimate truth must exist between the willful believing that is faith and the willful doubting that is philosophic skepticism.

As religions themselves understand, nothing wondrous can be false—the mysteries of authentic religion cannot be the offspring of obscurantism. A belief too vague to be fruitfully challenged, a belief so indefinite as to have no implications (and therefore no intellectual consequences that may be judged) is a belief too vague to be believed.

Indeed, the reasonable challenge of beliefs is essential to being self-possessed rather than possessed—to avoiding what William James derided as a "second-hand religious life" in which a person's religion "has been made for him by others, communicated to him by tradition, determined to fixed forms by imitation, and retained by habit."[1] It is a condition the Danish philosopher, Søren Kierkegaard, derided fifty years before James, informing his fellow Christians (with characteristic irony) that being-a-Christian is the greatest obstacle to being a Christian.[2] This emphasis on taking responsibility for claimed truth—with its implicit concern for clarity—is put forward not to denigrate the role of emotion in religion but to respect it. Intense but superficially grounded emotions are, on the whole, definitive of childhood or, in adults, of childishness. For, *intense* emotion is perfectly compatible with false or ill-considered belief, while *profound* emotion is not—which is to say that profound religious feeling has roots in wisdom.

But which religious feelings arise from sound judgment and truth and which from desire and error? This, of course, is our central problem. Quite inconveniently, the claims of theology and philosophy are not the sort that can be tested by their consequences in the realm of observable practice.

If a tornado strikes, we do not ask philosophy to test whether what we perceive is reality or mere appearance. And if we consult theology we will find that its answers will adapt to practical outcomes rather than be tested by them. So, if the tornado spares a church, it will show "prayer is answered"—for "faith brings reward," while if a church is destroyed, it will be true that "prayers are not always answered"—because "things happen for reasons the human mind cannot fathom."

The practitioners of these two disciplines do not test their claims by prediction and observation, that is, by scientific methods. Theology's reference to "miracles" as a kind of proof by observable consequences is, of course, a counter-instance. But theologically affirmed miracles are so rare they have never become part of any observational science—leaving intact the point that, as *types* of argument, theology and philosophy lack the character of practical or predictive studies.[3] It is in fact magic, not religion, which values its rituals and mysteries *solely* on the basis of their putatively practical results.[4]

So it is that the problems of philosophy and theology are condemned to the vexing, ill-understood arena of *argument*.

Here convictions and doubts swarm together in confusion. On the one hand, arguments are earnestly offered and methodically developed. On the other they are dismissed as inherently subjective persuasions. While acknowledging the problem of objectivity in argument, these essays hold that reflective thought has genuine standards and rational constraints. Arguments can be judged not only by the standard of internal consistency but also broadly and over time by the *sense* they make of a life whose aspects we already, if unevenly, understand.

Unfortunately for non-specialist readers, the requirements of ordinary living *in effect* train the mind away from an *intellectual self-consciousness of life*—a habit of thought that is useless, if not detrimental, in the conduct of practical affairs. But that very self-consciousness regarding "the nature of things" or of "the human situation" is essential for seeing the point and force of theological and philosophical arguments.

Practical activity seldom presses us to consider the degree to which tacitly acquired, but *fundamental*, notions like "necessity" or "reality" shape what we think and therefore do. Indeed, when ideas like "truth," or "an independent reality," are first considered outside any context of practical problems, they seem pointless—*mere* words.

To travel from the practical world into a seminar on "being" is to be no more prepared to judge the relevance and worth of what is said than a philosopher who visits a football huddle. Yet we press on, hoping to illuminate certain crucial—and perennial—issues, which, while normally confined to seminars, must be understood by any public who would think its religion through for itself.

Certainly, the gulf between a non-professional audience and the exacting arguments of philosophy and theology may prove only marginally bridgeable. This is the standing paradox of studies that are socially significant, yet specialized.

But it is one thing to accept the claims of scientists and historians on authority and quite another to determine one's life, and the lives one significantly touches, on the authority of someone else's thinking (hence the call for first-person inquiry by James and Kierkegaard). And though the lay public may be unprepared to thoughtfully assess religious statements, it assesses them anyway—and does so in the billions.

If humanity strives earnestly to live by what it cannot responsibly assess, then all the more reason to attempt the "impossible." On this, Emerson was clear: "whilst the doors of the temple stand open . . . and the oracles of . . . [religious] truth cease never, it is guarded by one stern condition; this namely; It is an intuition. It cannot be received at second hand." So it is that efforts must be made against the odds—by writers, readers, and seekers—in the hope that a deepened public dialogue about the nature of religion is possible.

THE PERILS AND PROMISE
OF SPECULATIVE THOUGHT

Faith, belief, miracle, God, and the nature of religion are topics of the sort whose respectful comprehension requires that reader philosophize.[5] For many, this is like being told that to comprehend a legal argument one must read it in a foreign tongue.

No doubt philosophy has acquired (and occasionally earned) a reputation as wordplay, needless abstraction, or futile speculation. Such qualms must be acknowledged and constructively addressed. Since the topic of philosophical (and theological) method generates entire books, an introductory overview cannot free it from the conceptual thicket but may, perhaps, bring it nearer the edge where its outline can be made out.

The first hurdle faced by both philosophy and theology is that the "big questions" they undertake to answer are, in a sense, too easy rather than too difficult.

One can give wrong or entirely unreasonable answers to questions about the nature of reality, mind, or truth without fear of practical penalties or emotional distress. Indeed, it often seems that the more fanciful the answer the more emotionally rewarding.

Because reassuring beliefs about, say, "freedom of the will" or "a scientific ethics," are distantly, if at all, linked to experimental evidence or practical consequences, their promulgation is as liable to irresponsible formulation as the political policies of absolute rulers. The point of Lord Acton's "power corrupts and absolute power cor-

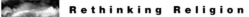

rupts absolutely" is general: immunity from negative consequences favors irresponsible decision-making. The careless engineer may witness the collapse of his bridge but a philosophical behaviorist like the late B. F. Skinner can deny the existence of mind while quite comfortably speaking his own.

The person who one week declares himself to have lived a thousand prior lives, the next to be nothing more than an evolved primate, and the next to be an organic computer puts less at risk, practically speaking, than someone who makes a bad trade in a Monopoly game.

While philosophy and theology may be at risk for cavalier conclusions because removed from practical consequences, their separation from factual testing or logical proof is not unique. Jurisprudence and art criticism are not based on scientific tests or logical proofs. They are therefore similarly open to intellectual mayhem: the so-called "legal realists" who found no *proofs* or scientific tests for justice concluded, to the delight of cynics everywhere, that "the law *is* whatever the justices *say* it is," while scientifically minded critics, unable to test for beauty, agreed that beauty must be "in the eye of the beholder"—thereby placing the aesthetic judgments of art historians on an equal footing with the judgments of children. In short, the intellectual and moral hazards of irresponsible thinking threaten any field whose conclusions are not readily called to account by logical proofs, experimental tests, or obvious practical outcomes.

But, like other "humanistic" fields, philosophy and theology are not doomed to merely fabulistic speculation. Modes of discipline exist. Consider, first, formal or "deductive" logic, which expresses the commonsense requirement that we not contradict ourselves (that what we assert we do not *at the same time* take back, as in "I am walking and I am not moving."). There is the more inclusive discipline of critical thinking—which requires, for example, that we not try to prove a point by assuming that which we are trying to prove.

There is the substantive discipline afforded by wide-ranging factual knowledge and by wisdom which, while beyond rule or recipe, is *favored* (and in part defined) by familiar habits such as self-education, self-awareness, hard work, and empathic attention to the lives of others. There is the disciplining of intellect and sensibility acquired through dialogue, communication and education—formal and informal—whose contributions are classically outlined in works like John Stuart Mill's "Essay on Liberty" and John Dewey's *Democracy and Education*.

But this reminder of the mind's disciplinary tools, however reasonable, is mere pleading for the feasibility of responsible speculation. It does nothing specifically to further it. The lay reader will find a modicum of specific advice on the responsible control of philosophical (and theological) reasoning, below, in the section "Doing Philosophy." There, philosophy's method and role in life are explored as a normal aspect of personal development. Because the position of this book roots philosophy in our experience of practical life, it is allied with *existentialism's* insistence that we live by what we profess, with *pragmatism's* requirement that ideas "work" in experience, and with *theology's* common plea that its truths make a difference in behavior.

Still, the most powerful deterrent to philosophical inquiry is the belief that it never answers questions. People do not pay philosophers to end their confusions; corporations have no staff of metaphysicians. Knowledge accumulates in the sciences, in history, in mathematics while, in philosophy, theories seem largely to repeat themselves. An ancient Greek skeptic such as Pyhrro (who denied the possibility of worldly truth) would have felt quite at home with the eighteenth-century skeptic, David Hume, whose arguments *entailed* the same conclusions, and comfortable too, perhaps, with twentieth-century "deconstructionists," who not only banished truth but denied the existence of objective meaning in texts.

The behavior of the public seems to say that if philosophy asks life's questions, theology provides life's answers. But this complementary pairing, so uncomplimentary to philosophy, may turn out to be at odds with the goal of self-possession. For if—like baffled students—people turn for answers to the back of the book by turning to what God has (putatively) said, those who find statements there (even statements that may be right) will themselves still not *know* they are right. This giving-over of self to faith or trust rather than inquiry may seem to many a satisfactory commitment—unless, of course, they have consulted the wrong book.

Surely there is something to be learned from the fact that while philosophy's language and arguments are often thought hopeless and remote, theology's equally arcane, untestable claims are not nearly so commonly decried.

Popular respect for theology survives despite theology's well-known disputes, and the remoteness of its doctrinal justifications from the language and topics of "practical life"—a remoteness no less daunting than that of philosophy. Theology and philosophy both suffer from intellectual obscurantism and a seemingly endless reworking of issues; yet, despite religious wars and historical restlessness, theology is widely accepted as a guide to understanding and philosophy is not.

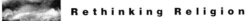

PHILOSOPHICAL THEOLOGY

Perhaps the unequal popular receptions accorded philosophy and theology delineate a fault line between the search for "meaningfulness" and the search for truth.

What we hope is true, what we need to be true—even what it would be better if true—may not be true, so that the quest for *meaning* may be threatened or stymied by what we discover to be *so*.

Theology's emphasis on the *meaningfulness* of things and philosophy's on the *truth* of things creates a relationship much like that of rival siblings. The so-called "natural" theology of the Middle Ages was, after all, *philosophy* thought capable of marking the path to God. But when theological scholars found it wandering anywhere but to another world, it was superseded by faith and revelation—by a theology whose *arguments* remained heavily philosophical but whose advantage lay in knowing by divine grace where the other world lay. As Saint Anselm fatefully and *philosophically* announced in offering a rule for rational theology, "I do not seek to understand in order that I may believe; but I believe, that I may understand."[6]

Anselm, the supernaturalist, was spared the irony of having to shake philosophic hands with his spiritual opponents—philosophers who centuries later would *agree* that thought rests on belief, but for the anti-supernatural, anti-free-will reason that beliefs are brain-states caused by prior states of the brain. On the other hand the spirit of Anselm lives in the theories of modern philosophers like Alvin Plantinga who hold that a belief (like "God exists") can be *rationally* considered "basic" to all the rest of one's thought. And because it is "properly" basic, its status cannot be rationally challenged.

In sum, philosophy and theology exhibit a substantial identity of topics and argumentation, despite being housed (typically) in separate university departments. Philosophy departments seldom argue with physics or chemistry departments but often speak to issues in theology departments.

Both theology and philosophy address the question of God's existence. Theology discusses infallibility; so does philosophy. Free will and foreknowledge are subjects of importance to both. For such reasons, these essays see philosophy and theology as having the same blood type: The claims made by one can be critically addressed by the other without any loss of relevance.

(Against this doctrine of intellectual overlap, we ought note that some *do* mark theology off from philosophy—often citing *theology's* claim that "divine revelation [is] a source of knowledge." The distinction has *historical* value. Self-described "theologians" were those who most often defended *revelation*. But even in the Middle Ages, theologians did not place the revelation argument beyond philosophical questioning.[7] Indeed, the claim that revelation is *certain* would appear to fall as much within philosophy's *theory of knowledge* ("epistemology") as a philosopher's claim that *intuitive* knowledge is certain, or that a statement is certain because it is *self-evident*.

Theological claims therefore involve philosophical assessments, however unaware of "doing philosophy" a believer may be. In claiming that God can be known through faith, theologians take a position on the relationship between knowledge and faith—surely a philosophic issue. Visions of the Virgin Mary challenge the relevance of scientific knowledge for determining the truth of observation-claims. "Original sin" is inconsistent with contemporary law and morality in which sinfulness or guilt can accrue only from one's *own* actions.

In fine, theology no less than philosophy emerges from decisions as to what can be rational and what can be real. In *Four Existentialist Theologians*, Will Herberg says of Jacques Maritain, Nicolas Berdyaev, Martin Buber, and Paul Tillich that their "central theological affirmations . . . directly reflect their ontologies"[8] That is, their views of the sacred, of God, reflect their philosophies of *Being*—their philosophical assessment of *what necessarily always exists*—be it matter, time, or a creative force.

From the philosophical side, Wilhelm Windelband's classic, *A History of Philosophy*, speaks of the constantly recurring imclination of philosophers "to view as 'Deity' the highest conception which theory has led them to use for explaining the world, . . . [giving it] at the same time a sanction for religious consciousness."[9] Even the *supernatural* no longer serves linguistically to divide theological from philosophic thinking: Contemporary dictionaries define "theology" without requiring reference to a supernatural God; a popular, Book-of-the-Month Club anthology of religious thought finds no difficulty declaring that some religions "have worshipped no God at all."[10] For these reasons, the phrase *philosophical theology* may reasonably be used to signal a special philosophic interest in which religious concepts like "miracle" (and relevant *non*-religious concepts like "knowing") are analyzed from the viewpoint of their bearing on the meaning of human life.

As we shall argue when we take up God's meaning, it is not the supernatural but *the ultimate meaning of human life* that is the controlling issue in religion. If *God's existence* could be described as not natural ("*super*natural"), yet implied nothing whatever for deciding *how* *we should live*, would God's existence be any more *religious* than cosmology's "big bang" or the (eternal, unchanging, non-material) *unmoved mover* of Aristotle's *Physics*? If not, then "meaningfulness" is the religious dog, and the *causal* role assigned to "God," the religious tail.

If ultimate meaning is in fact religion's "holy grail," and if ultimate meaning must derive from what we know to be true, then *how we think worldly truth is determined* becomes an issue of the first theological importance.

For example, the contemporary tendency to determine what exists solely by means of scientific methods consigns "good" and "evil" to the status of fictions. If only what is, in principle, scientifically testable, can be a real aspect of the world, then moral assertions, which cannot be scientifically tested, cannot refer to aspects of the world. They must therefore (falsely) *appear* to us as worldly truths or obligations—perhaps as the result of psychological or evolutionarily causes. Thus, by using *science* to rule upon what is real and what is not, we determine what *kinds* of things may or may not be used as evidence in determining "the meaning of human life."

If, when philosophy has implications for the meaning of life, we speak of "philosophical theology," the reader may wonder why biology is not "biological theology." It, too, has implications for "the meaning of human life." In fact, why can't anything we learn that has implications for the meaning of life be called "theological"? History, astronomy, physics—all have such implications, sometimes making us feel small and sometimes powerful. Here we must offer the short version of longer story. The phrase *the meaning of human life*, used theologically, has to do with ultimate meaning, with the *final* significance or point (if any) of all the activities we engage in that, of course, already have purposive, consequential, and symbolic meaning.

In a straightforward, everyday sense of "meaning," the meaning of life would surely alter for most of us if, for example, astronomy predicted Earth's demise within a year. But the "religious" significance of that demise—the ultimate meaning of humanity's end—would remain unaddressed.

For example, we might say, "things seem meaningless now," and only later ask "was humanity's time in the universe worthwhile or pointless?" The difference between astronomy's predictions of death as a fact and religion's focus on interpretation of "eschatological" fact or "the last things"—suggests the difference between what things mean *to us* (in this time or place now) and their true or "final" meaning.

Thus the poet Kathleen Norris takes religious meaning to be fundamental to self-understanding and asks of eschatology "why does it still seem to be a word that *defines* me [emphasis added]?"[11] Norris knows that things have meaning but not necessarily the *final or definitive* assessment of meaning embodied in such questions as "what was the point of us—of the many sorts of things we did—the knowing, the creating, the judging, the playing, the sport, the loving? So, astronomical prediction would likely not finalize the ultimate meaning of the life that was cut short—the role humanity played in the totality of what abides."

While the use of the phrase *philosophical theology* is intended to denote philosophy directed at satisfying the (quite radical) demands of uniquely religious concern, the reader who prefers to call these essays simply "philosophical" is invited to do so, for, in the end, any responsible "theology," must pass the tests of responsible philosophy.

In the meantime, let at least one well-known theologian speak to the relationship we say holds between the philosophical and theological interests:

> Why does philosophy use concepts and why does faith use symbols if both try to express the same ultimate? The answer . . . is that the relation to the ultimate is not the same in each case. The philosophical relation is in principle a detached description of the basic structure in which the ultimate manifests itself. The relation of faith is in principle an involved expression of concern about the meaning of the ultimate for the faithful.[12]

DOING PHILOSOPHY

Language and logic

James and Kierkegaard reminded us that *having* thoughts is easy—even thoughts we think exalted. But, once informally acquired, the thoughts that explain, justify, and organize life are not easily altered; they tend to become who we are. It is a process that anchors our worldviews in (psychological) *need* rather than *evidence*. In the extreme case, thought that is uncritically acquired and held becomes fanaticism. Here conviction waxes stronger than self—a condition suggested by the common expression "carried away" (and horrifically instanced by suicidal terrorism).

In the fanatic, forces rule; there is precious little free agency left by which to call upon the saving graces of self-criticism and educa-

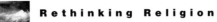

tion. What is more, the character of an over-protected idea is as liable to underdevelopment as the character of an over-protected child.

In any case, the assessment of ideas, like the assessment of persons, requires an awareness of what they *do*—and, of course, what ideas do (uniquely, though not exclusively) is *imply* things. So, to appraise what we believe, we must determine what the holding of one idea implies for others we hold or that may be brought to our attention. Only then can we master what we mean by what we say; only then can we avoid suffering from an intellectual law of unintended consequences.

But it is difficult to know what we are saying (what is implied) when we use familiar, yet seldom-analyzed, notions such as the *self* or *free will* or *moral truth* or *God*. For that reason, the goal of clear meaning has driven some to seek a universal rule for clarity that could be applied to all statements regardless of the subject matter.

"How to Make our Ideas Clear" was the title Charles Sanders Pierce, pragmatism's founder, gave to a seminal article suggesting that a statement about the world could have a clear meaning only if it entailed specific practical consequences we could observe. This single standard of "clarity" was to hold for worldly assertions whether they were about God or beauty or rightness or weather.[13] For example, the statement that wine can become the blood of Christ failed Peirce's test, since "to talk of something having all the sensible characteristics of wine yet being in reality blood, is senseless jargon."[14] (In short form: "this is blood" entails the observable consequence "this tastes salty" so, if no salty taste, then not "blood.")

To speak for a moment of ethos, the empiricist's quest for clear meaning had a spirit of hard-nosed legality about it—as if to be clear about "love," in "I love you," one must obtain from the beloved a definitive list of the specific *physical and verbal behaviors* that the assertion "I love you" entails.

The determination to eliminate empty arguments about things like "transcendent reality" and vague, often authoritarian, claims in politics and morality led some philosophers to insist on a single standard of clarity for all subject matters no matter how implausible the consequences of doing so.

For example, human life revolves around issues of *character* and the doing of right and wrong. No matter. The entire domain of moral claims was declared "meaningless" by an influential group of philosophers and physicists (the "Vienna Circle") whose "extreme respect for science and mathematics . . . and extreme distaste for

metaphysics" led them (like Peirce) to test the clarity of moral statements against the standards of clarity for scientific statements.

In essence, these *scientistic* thinkers said that if the statement "this
is ice" has meaning for science only because it clearly refers to observable properties like "solidity, translucence, and coldness," then
the statement "this is evil" can have meaning only if it, too, refers to
or entails observable properties.

But it doesn't. The reader will agree that "evil" refers to nothing
the eye can observe (nor entails anything the eye can observe). Evil
acts have no telltale look, smell, sound, taste, or feel. From the viewpoint of physical description a virtuous act cannot be distinguished
from an evil act. By imposing science's standard for meaningful talk
about *physical* subject matter on talk about *moral* subject matter (indeed, on all subject matter), the Vienna Circle concluded that when
moral claims are "clearly" understood, they will be seen to state nothing about the world, nothing, that is, about actual actions or relationships.

Of course "meaningless" moral statements are nonetheless useful since, like "whoa, Nellie!" (said to a horse), they somehow shape
social behavior. In this way, a well-intentioned but overzealous determination to find a rule for clear or determinate meaning inadvertently helped delegitimize ethics to from the 1920s through the present day.[15]

Rethinking's essays invoke no universal, highly specific standard
of clear or determinate meaning outside the context of discussion. An
idea is considered clear *enough* when we can determine the significant implications of holding that idea for the holding of others whose
meaning bears on the same question.[16]

For example, to seek the clear meaning of "miracle" we ask
whether the meaning of "miracle" requires an event that "confounds
all our previous experience" and perhaps "fills us with awe" or
whether a "miracle" must also "run counter to physical laws." If all
we mean by a "miracle" is that an event fills us with awe and confounds our experience, then there is no inherent conflict between
miracles and science (we could be speaking about the appearance of
an alien spaceship). But if miracles must be events that run counter to
physical laws, then perhaps we must choose between religion and
science.

The essential thing is that we say what we mean with enough
specificity to support or contradict other statements. Our own contradictions are diagnostically invaluable. They signal that something
we think must be in some way reformulated or else given up. (Unfor-

tunately, non-philosophers sometimes take contradictions lightly, as if the use of logic were optional; students may mention that people often say "yes and no." But of course, an everyday "yes and no" is not a contradiction; it is a provocative way of saying "yes in one respect and no in another." If "yes *and* no" were meant literally, the statement would be self-canceling, like "this is a circle and it has two corners." So, to make meaningful statements—to state *something* rather than *nothing*—contradictions must be resolved.

But avoiding contradiction or, as is it is usually phrased, "being logically consistent" is not enough to guide philosophy. Of course, philosophers and logicians are both concerned with "formal" consistency. Both insist for example, that to say "there are two things in this box" entails (commits one to say), "there is at least one thing in this box." Perhaps the most famous example of logic is that "if all men are mortal and Socrates is a man, then, Socrates is mortal." Such arguments are *logically* correct (or "consistent" or "valid") aside from factual truth. They "hold"—are *consistent*—whether or not anything circular exists or whether Socrates in fact was personally immortal. However, the philosopher's primary focus is consistency among the basic conceptions we use to interpret our lives and our world.[17]

For example: We may actually see the world as governed by a God who is said to be *necessarily* good by virtue of his very nature. Such a being cannot possibly be bad. But someone may remind us of another conviction of ours, namely, that an agent can only be deemed "good" if that agent could have chosen badly, but didn't. (The opportunity *freely* to choose between good or evil is almost universally considered a precondition for developing or practicing moral character).

Our convictions now seem contradictory. How can the conviction that God is "good" be maintained against the conviction that God could *not possibly* choose what is bad?[18] Feeling trapped, we may quickly say "well, 'good' means one thing when applied to us and another applied to God." Such a response solves the logician's problem by claiming a second meaning for "good," a meaning that makes it logically consistent to say "God is good, even though God couldn't possibly be bad." But philosophy is concerned with what we *truly believe*, not things we can make up to achieve logical consistency.[19]

We must therefore ask, "is there any *independent* reason (any separate ground of conviction) for claiming a 'second' sense of 'good'?" In saying, "God is good, but in a different way," are we expressing a genuine conviction or escaping a conflict among our convictions? One who seeks truth in a speculative field has this kind of work to do. The commitment of writer and reader doggedly to face inconsistent convictions will establish how much world-understanding, hence self-understanding, we can attain.

Philosophy and responsibility

As suggested above, the proper assessment of "humanistic" terms like *truth, mind, self,* and *knowledge* depend not upon logical acumen alone but upon an active acquaintance with the problems of life.

That is why philosophy is more closely associated with wisdom than technical brilliance. Philosophy cannot be satisfied with clever possibilities we neither believe nor could plausibly entertain, like "well, you say that's a house and that your eyes don't deceive you, but maybe we are all dreaming." Such logically possible challenges (challenges that are not self-contradictory) are *instrumentally* useful for forcing some underlying principle or idea into the open but can never be a test for truth. Were philosophy not essentially wedded to the worldly truth or justness of its claims, philosophers could assemble any set of ideas that pleased their fancy or their audience.

But the statements that interest philosophy are, finally, those that comprise a true and fundamental understanding of human judgment, action, feeling, and the world. Its touchstones are the ideas we are prepared to live by and (insofar as they affect others) for which we are prepared to accept some responsibility.

Here, curiously enough, is where morality enters essentially and palpably into speculative thought. Speculation readily becomes the arena of empty talk the Vienna Circle detested unless it is anchored in authentic convictions.

These are the things we believe when what we do counts. These are the beliefs we hope we can express should our grown children ask for the truth of what we feel—no matter how discomfiting the admission might be. The point is too seldom made: Moral seriousness is as intellectually necessary as logical acuity and factual knowledge. Used together they can move speculation toward wisdom; used apart they favor oppression, self-deception, brilliant irresponsibility, or all three.

By making conscious the concepts that organize and interpret our lives—concepts like moral properties, character, causality, being-a-person, sacredness, reality, the state, natural rights, soul, God, and the like—philosophy frees us to evaluate humanity's situation in the world.

For this reason, philosophy cannot be considered a game—neither a "word-game" nor, as some have on occasion phrased it, a "language-game." One can no more rightly "make up" meanings for terms like "self" or "reality" than one can make up legal terms when going from case to case, or redefine political terms to gain political advantage. Kierkegaard had it right when he lionized the Socratic abhorrence of "sophistry"—the attempt to win arguments by clever verbal tricks (whose analogue in serious thought is the refusal to admit inner conflict to protect belief). But these comments are safely abstract; some specific examples are in order.

It is not that the following cases *necessarily* exemplify conflict avoidance, but it is reasonable to suggest so. Consider the question, "How can an all-good God create a world in which children die of cancer?" This question has drawn both new and old answers that may with equal justice be doubted.

One new answer states that innocent children die because God "is limited in what he can do by the laws of nature."[20] Here we are to believe that God can create the laws of the universe but hasn't the power to alter or add to them. (The argument courts additional suspicion by neglecting an obvious possibility: since immunities develop without changing the laws of nature, God could add immunities to children without necessarily changing the laws of nature.)

The older, more familiar solution is that "God has a plan we cannot grasp in which *childhood cancer is required for the greatest good.*"[21] This positing of an unimaginable plan has the effect of making God's goodness logically consistent with the cancer death of innocent children. Importantly, in focusing on the plan as a logically possible way of dissolving the contradiction we are distracted from the substance of its moral implications; that is, we are distracted from having baldly to state "Children dying from cancer is good"—for none of us is *genuinely* convinced that the death of children from cancer is a good.[22]

Whenever suppositions that have little more than "logical possibility" to recommend them are used to keep factual, moral, aesthetic, or other kinds of conviction from resulting in contradiction, imagination substitutes for reason.[23] A diet of logically possible claims detaches mind from experience, that is, from the discipline of an obdurate reality. It is no accident that schizophrenics who weave fantastic yet *internally consistent* (logically consistent) accounts of things are described, with equal appropriateness, as having "lost their *minds*" or "lost touch with *reality.*"

Philosophic tendentiousness is not madness, but it apes it—by altering definitions to avoid logical entrapment, or by introducing freshly minted terms like "logocentrism" or uncommon terms like *sensums*, whose unfamiliarity beclouds their implications so as to offer few clues to their appropriateness, groundedness, or relation to other ideas.[24]

In short, the introduction of specialized or arcane terms and phrases threatens to obscure or divert an argument. The integration of ideas by which we hope to live is best served by insisting on ordinary language until clearly shown why it is inadequate and in just what way the new term enlightens us. Philosophy teeters on the edge of self-deception when it uses terms whose implications for other ideas are not embedded in common convictions.[25]

Words, mere words

Because philosophic analysis and argument typically center on the meaning of words, early encounters with philosophy often give newcomers to philosophy the feeling that its issues are merely verbal.

But words need not be "mere," for words are the storehouse of our knowledge of the world. Terms like *reality, meaning, faith, belief, knowledge, morality, truth, rationality, feeling, the natural, the supernatural*, and *the self* cannot be altered or removed from discourse without depriving argument of fundamental things humanity has learned.

The philosophic neophyte's idea that discussion is best begun by "defining our terms" inadvertently and wrongly supposes we *already know* what is critical to the subject of, say, "justice" or "knowledge" or "faith," and so can immediately pick out what needs to be said.

Similarly, some suppose that by "stipulating" meanings for key terms (making up a definition for purposes of discussion) we become *clear* and *precise*, when in fact we simply strip away the kind of *naturally accumulated connections to other ideas* that make the term important in the first place.

When guilelessly and openly employed, traditional terms of philosophic argument like "necessity" and "will" represent the great connecting nodes of human understanding. The mother who tells her child *ghosts* are "the spirits of the dead" is no more giving a mere vocabulary lesson than the theologian who insists *religion* is "a matter of faith." Soldiers who fight for *freedom* do not offer their lives to validate the dictionary.

The unity of words, thought, and action is too vast and subtle a matter for effective explication here, but it has been long and variously noted: very early on, the gnostic "Gospel of Philip" told us "truth brought names into existence in the world because it is not

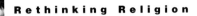

possible to teach it without names"; millenia later, the American philosopher Frederick L. Will, in "Thoughts and Things," argued that words are instrumental in, and embody, what we learn through acting in a world, so that "to develop a concept of a thing like a bird, whether it be a goldfinch, phoenix, or great roc, is to be initiated—not always well—into a complex practice which involves both men and things."[26]

Words are our intellectual ecology. They are the medium from which we extract and in which we form what we mean when clarifying our convictions. In thus emphasizing words we do not mean to ignore the defining links between meaning and *behavior*. But we cannot use a person's behavior to help us know what he or she means without making use of ideas—that is, of words in whole or in part.[27]

Movements in themselves mean nothing. We must *interpret* the point of the movements (behavior); we must understand the context, know some things, discern the goal. A horse can stare at a Bar Mitzvah ceremony forever and will never know the meaning from the movements.

Conversely, a person who insists a Bar Mitzvah is essential, yet often behaves so as to minimize the occurrence of Bar Mitzvahs, may not truly mean, "Bar Mitzvah is essential." Therefore, to know what we *mean* in expressing our convictions requires knowing both how they (or we) would *behave* if we believed (this or that) to be true and how ideas are related in discourse.

The practice of philosophic dialogue or "dialectic" progresses by uncovering ideas or situations that run counter to what we may first assert.

The procedure of questioning ourselves or others is essential for knowing not only where we do stand but where we want to stand once the implications of our initial statements have been clarified.

We might, for example, say "'truth' is any statement on which everyone agrees" but be asked "does it matter *how* everyone came to be agreed?" (The questioner may point out that "from what you say it doesn't matter whether evidence or advertising persuades them.") We may then be reminded, that "of course" method matters, and realize we can no longer simply say "'truth' is what everyone agrees on." We may dig more deeply into our sense of truth and say, "I guess what I mean is that 'truth' is what is really so, and that people will eventually see it and agree."

Dialogue sharpens thinking in innumerable ways. For example people will inadvertently state different ideas in the course of an argument while supposing themselves to have asserted only one:

"freedom *is* doing what you want" may drift into "freedom is the *right* to do what you want" and even into "freedom is the feeling of freedom."

People also state things ambiguously. When the Founding Fathers said "all men are created equal," were they making the *physical* or "factual" claim that each person has the same quantity of any attribute (such as height) or the *moral* claim that everyone should have the same rights before the law? Such confusion and vagueness is among the things philosophic dialogue helps to rectify.

The gap between *what we responsibly mean and what we first say* is what stirs the coffee in coffee-house philosophy and feeds the bull in "bull sessions." Philosophic questioning presses thought to become specific. For what we truly mean is often something we ourselves only fitfully and partly discern—ideas that are very much part of us but which we have not yet been prodded to formulate.

Philosophy as a developmental discipline

That we have a layered self is reflected in practices like retreat and meditation that purport to look deeply within, and in the Socratic/Platonic idea that our souls lived a prior life in which we learned truths that we have forgotten, but that dialectic can draw out of us. It is reflected in the experience of writing a serious letter or essay when we suddenly find that we are saying things we had not quite intended to say—things that supersede what we started to say, so that, strange as it seems, our work has shown us what we truly meant.[28]

This complementary relation between self-understanding and the *public formulation* of ideas requires that we not pre-censor our thoughts. Self-education is as dependent on openness in philosophy as it is in art when the artist steps back to contemplate a work so that the work can, so to speak, "tell" the artist what it wants to become. Indeed, the centrality of candid self-examination separates philosophy from the research disciplines and points the way to understanding its nature and the reason for its seeming futility.

Philosophy is not a research discipline on the model of history, mathematics, or biology. It is not a "factual" or a purely logical investigation from which we should expect to cull amazing true statements or "information" that is deeply counter-intuitive—so-called "breakthroughs" like learning that space is curved or that some infinities are larger than others.

The biology student is properly amazed to discover that humanity's genes barely differ from those of chimpanzees, but the student who tacitly thinks of philosophy as a *research* discipline may wrongly anticipate exciting but ill-founded counter-intuitive "discoveries" like "all humanity is self-deceived" or that "we have no knowledge of an external world" or that "nuclear physics and religion are both based on faith."

Those who anticipate astounding revelations are easy prey for splash-makers like the deconstructionist who promises *"deconstruction* subverts almost everything in the tradition [of textual theory and analysis]" or the philosophically minded geneticists whose "science" shows that humans are but tools of "selfish" genes.

Factual research, theory, and knowledge may properly upend a world whose basic factual assumptions are false. The Copernican and Darwinian revolutions were *in effect* iconoclastic. But philosophy is about a world we know very well, a world of concepts that constitute the sense-making structure of commonplace actions.

Hence, a philosophy that stands the world on its head also stands basic human experience on its head and will in due time show itself false. The British philosopher Bertrand Russell's impish announcement that "the point of philosophy is to start with something so simple as not to seem worth stating, and to end with something so paradoxical that no one will believe it" is funny because it is too often true.

Philosophy is best conceived as a *developmental* discipline—a practice in aid of conceptual maturation. One might well say that philosophy is the psychoanalysis of our ideational commitments. Like psychotherapy, philosophy puts aspects of one*self* to the test of rational integration. A change in philosophy or theology is a change in oneself at the level of life-organizing ideas.

One can (these days) engage in geological study without threatening one's self-concept, but one cannot engage either in psychotherapy or philosophy without opening one's self to the possibility of painful criticism and the requirement of attitudinal change.[29] Philosophy seeks the mature conceptual determination of self-defining ideas such as "I am fated"; "I am free"; "I can never be certain"; "I am not an animal"; "I am a spirit." The fact that its arguments continue to be revisited can therefore be understood a necessary feature of the task every generation confronts: namely, the full attainment of a uniquely human consciousness.

Conceiving what kinds of things constitute the world is, after all, part of growing up, and deciding on the nature of disparate *kinds* of things is essentially (if informally) philosophical. Engaged in living, we are at first forced to make practical conceptual distinctions. We identify *particulars* as this or that *sort* of thing (a thing that is alive, a thing that is heavy, a thing that is sharp, a thing that heats). Implicitly (again, without self-consciously "doing" philosophy) we gradually ascend to the most general relations among *kinds* of things. It is not philosophical to find that fires burn the skin, but it is philosophical to decide or understand that fires are the kinds of things cannot rationally be blamed for doing so.

We begin with me and not-me, ascend to *I*, *others*, and *self*, move on to animals and humans, causes and responsibilities, necessities and accidents, knowledge and mistakes, mysteries and explanations, love and duty, logic and emotion, reality and illusion. These are the most general distinctions we make as to the *natures* of different *kinds*.

They are distinctions whose soundness and availability to consciousness depend on the educational level of our culture, but in any case are the product of countless judgments and decisions continuously and unselfconsciously made within the flow of daily experience. They formulate *our sense of the world*.

In *psychological* development, a motivational and attitudinal framework for approaching the world grows out of countless unselfconscious yet critical "choices" we unavoidably confront in the course of mastering largely interpersonal experience. In *philosophical* development, our most general organization of reality—of the world as we find it—is likewise not constructed out of reflective deliberations or self-evident arguments. There is no momentous deliberation, no youthful seminar, no proof or set of proofs, by which our worldview is concluded. Nor is it simply willed; we do not "make it up."

Root philosophical convictions, albeit vague and sometimes inconsistent, are the most general conceptual scaffolding we acquire as, with a minimum of reflection, we make diverse kinds of things, relations, and experiences more intellectually coherent. We grow up in respect of our concepts. This developing grasp of the nature of things is, of course, no more immune from possible inconsistency, self-deception or falsehood than the outlook we develop on personal relations in the course of our psychological development.

Deliberate conceptual development or "philosophy" brings our unselfconsciously constructed notions of the nature of things to consciousness for critical review, allowing us to revisit the largely unexamined grounds we have evolved to organize and interpret life's puzzles and conflicts.

We may, for example, ask whether we have distinguished human from animal on the basis of "free will," or "awareness," or perhaps "soul"—but always we must ask what we are honestly prepared wittingly to believe in this regard and why.

Because philosophical awareness aims at giving us control over the worldview in whose ambit we have learned to live, it prepares us to take responsibility for the quality of our outlook on the nature of things. Thus it has primarily to do with attaining greater maturity and wisdom, rather than developing a more refined logical technique.

That may be why we find no child or "idiot savant" philosophers as we do idiot savant arithmeticians and pianists. Rather than despairing at the repetitiousness of philosophical arguments and perspectives, a developmental view of philosophy *expects* each generation to come upon the "problems of philosophy" anew—out of puzzles encountered in active experience and in terms shaped by the learning and the issues of its culture. Thus, Windelband:

> [Although] philosophy receives both its problems and the materials for their solution from the ideas of the general consciousness of the time and from the needs of society.[30] . . . the problems of philosophy . . . are given . . . by the inadequacy and internal contradictions of the material which consciousness presents for philosophical consideration. . . . [Hence] . . . the impression that philosophy is striving fruitlessly in ever-repeating circles for a goal that is never attained, proves only this—that the problems of philosophy are tasks which the human mind cannot escape.[31]

As extended responses to living, genuine philosophic outlooks must therefore be understood as deeply personal. But, like conclusions worked through during psychoanalysis, conclusions worked through philosophically are not personal in the sense of being *idiosyncratic* or *arbitrary*.

They are personal only in representing the ideas and feelings that actually make us up. Philosophy would have no direction were it not personal in this sense, if it did not take up the fruit of *actual responsibilities* we have carried out or acknowledged in the course of living.

Such conceptual fruits of action as "guilt," "innocence," "soul," "truth," and "the other" may be empty or directionless notions for the very young or for the sociopath, just as a twenty year jail sentence is typically a mere item-in-the-news for a reader. But for the actively engaged person—the juryperson in the courtroom—a twenty-year sentence is likely to be felt as the awful prospect it is. That is why the foundations of philosophy lie in the ideas we find necessary *when responding to the moral or "consequential" demands of action*—whether legal, artistic, scientific, or interpersonal.

Of these necessary ideas, those that are essential for making sense of the endeavors we believe we must get right constitute our notion of reality. And though our idea of reality, when consciously formulated, will likely need refining and correcting, the process of correction will be worthwhile only insofar as it continues to reflect what we experience in situations of responsibility; the task of philosophical reflection is to challenge ideas about reality without viscerally forgetting it.

Here we harken back to the philosophers of the Vienna Circle who, in this writer's view, forgot or let go of what any responsible person, acting in the world, *believes*—namely that actions really do *possess* moral properties. For, in reflecting on notions like the possibility of truth, the reality of values, or the conditions for guilt we grapple with nothing less than the way we understand our responsibilities in life.

Philosophy—no less than psychotherapy—testifies to a functional connection between responsibility and sanity, or, one might say, *morality and mind*.[32] The developmental and moral aspects of philosophy suggest why philosophic issues are intractably part of us and how "abstract" ideas can be the subject of heated debate.

Indeed, the preeminent twentieth century philosopher, Ludwig Wittgenstein, described philosophy as "logical therapy," that is, as having to do with a kind of personal change (one more narrowly conceived, perhaps, than what we have offered here). Landed in contradictions or absurdities, Wittgenstein's self-trapped "philosophical fly" is to be shown "the way out of the bottle"—freed from conceptual distortions as psychology's patients are freed from neuroses.

Whether we liken philosophy to Wittgenstein's restitutional therapy or conceive it as healthy development, the shared point is that philosophy engages *more than* our power to be consistent (what many call being "logical"), though it *absolutely depends on* being consistent. It is better described as requiring "judgment," for judgment implies a broader power than simple consistency (madness, as noted, can be quite consistent).

Therefore, philosophy, like psychoanalysis, cannot yield results for people who take it up unless they are committed to asking fearlessly what they are prepared to say and live by. As speculation, philosophy offers no hard and fast rules of discovery. Apparently *good* arguments *must sometimes be stubbornly held at bay* while honest "saving" arguments are sought; at other times good arguments *plainly must be accepted despite the discomfort of doing so*. There is no

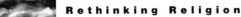 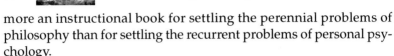

more an instructional book for settling the perennial problems of philosophy than for settling the recurrent problems of personal psychology.

Indeed, expecting to extract one's philosophy from Aristotle is as misguided as expecting to understand one's own personality by reading Freud or case histories. Nor in either field are answers secured by a few discrete arguments.

When deep things are at issue, whether they concern one's personality or one's view of reality's nature, the all-too-common demand that an argument be "proven" (*right now*! and by a single or logically clinching argument!) is as likely to prove a disguised defense against philosophical change as are the intellectualized "defenses" familiar to psychotherapy.

TRUE RELIGION

Should the reader elect to pursue the arguments that follow, it is my hope that this view of philosophy as the consistent working-through of genuine convictions will aid in refining life's experience without betraying either mystery or mind. For whatever distortions have been visited upon and earned by philosophy, no domain of fundamental human interest has been more consistently ill-served than religion.

Religion is obscure not simply on account of its content but because our schooling and our culture make and keep it so. Public discourse fails religion by making argument taboo; public schooling fails religious study by omitting it; most private schooling fails it by subordinating study to advocacy. Even "comparative religion" tends to function as toleration's sop to the avoidance of serious inquiry: Diverse claims and narratives are "appreciated" anthropologically, as *exhibits*, rather than as incompatible positions calling for further inquiry—as they would be in economics, astronomy, or any other authentically educational context.

In matters of formal and informal religious education, the banners of toleration and tendentiousness fly higher than those of truth and objectivity.

Indeed, religion—essential or useless, illusory or true—seems of all compelling human interests, the most internally conflicted. Its gods have been infinitely loving, infinitely punitive, or both; they have been multiple or single, bodied or spiritual, outside the universe or all that is the universe. Its selflessness has meant to some a life humbly offered to the needy, to others a life risked in war against the unconvinced. Thought lucid enough that we may know it "as a child," God's message has required special schooling, justified interpretive priesthoods, perpetual exegesis, and sectarian revisions without end. At its center lie mysteries "beyond human understanding" yet it reveals for humankind "the meaning of life." Deemed in fact inexpressible—mystical, ineffable—the nature of the divine or the Holy has consistently generated works and preachments that explain it, describe it, and apply it to practical life. Though insisted on as truth, religion is defended as belief; it is the only professed truth that cleaves to proper nouns, so that we comfortably accept Hindu religion, Jewish religion, or Western religion but not American physics, Mexican chemistry, or Canadian zoology.

Pronounced a matter of the most effortful faith (as in Kierkegaard's "infinite passion"), religion's truth is said also to be perfectly obvious (as in the conviction that "human life couldn't possibly have happened by accident"). Said by Judeo-Christians and Moslems to require belief in supernatural agency, religion is said by Confucians and Bhuddists to require none. Declared a creature of neurosis or merely an instrument of social control, it has nonetheless emerged and re-emerged as the avowed apex of spirit in societies of every kind and size. And in the final paroxysm of its own confusion, no message of love against hate has historically yielded so much of both.

For those who sense in modern life an underlying absence of fundamental meaning—yet fear self-deception in pursuing "God"—there may be no recourse but to shoulder the burdens of reflection and begin the ancient journey anew.

NOTES

1. William James, *The Varieties of Religious Experience*, Mentor ed. (New York: The New American Library, 1958), p. 24.

2. Søren Kierkegaard, *Concluding Unscientific Postscript* as recounted in Patrick Gardiner, *Kierkegaard* (Oxford; Oxford University Press, 1988) p. 102, where Gardiner also notes Kierkegaard's view that genuine belief is a "martyrdom," "a crucifixion of the understanding" (Ch. 5, "Truth and Subjectivity," on the struggle required for genuine Christian belief—while immensely important—is likely not for non-philosophers).

3. The implications of "miracle" are of the first importance, however, and will receive extended analysis.

4. Some will insist that practical success *is* the mark of a religious truth ("I was a drunk, now I'm sober"), but these *pragmatic* religionists will not abandon their religious claims as *false* if their faith-based efforts should fail (if their drinking resumes, or, say, if their holy war meets with defeat). Religious

proofs by "success" are arguments of *convenience* as repugnant in their disingenuousness to a Calvinist as to a secularist. Only "primitive" peoples argue it ingenuously, and that is why we describe them as conflating magic and religion.

5. The disrespectful approach *begins* by explaining religious claims away—as in "theism exists to maintain social stability."

6. Anselm of Canterbury (1033-1109), famous for the "ontological" proof of God (a perfect being would have to exist, else not be "perfect").

7. F. C. Copleston, *Medieval Philosophy* (New York and Evanston, Harper Torchbooks, 1961), pp. 4-5.

8. See Wilhelm Windelband, "The Cosmological Period," *A History of Philosophy*, vol. 1 (New York: Harper & Brothers, 1958), ch. 1, to see how philosophy arose out of the attempt to explain (roughly) how existence can be permanent while everything changes. See, also "Substance," D. W. Hamlyn, *Metaphysics* (Cambridge: Cambridge University Press, 1984), ch. 4; Windelband offers a considerably less technical discussion.

9. Ibid., p. 34

10. Jaroslav Pelikan, ed., *The World Treasury of Religious Thought* (Boston: Little, Brown & Company, 1960), p. 3.

11. Kathleen Norris, *Amazing Grace* (New York: Riverhead Books, 1998), "Eschatology," p. 12.

12. Paul Tillich, *Dynamics of Faith* (New York: Harper & Row, Publishers, Inc.; Harper Torchbooks, 1957), p. 91.

13. "Consider what effects, which might conceivably have practical bearings, we conceive the object of our conception to have. Then, our conception of these effects is the whole of our conception of the object." Charles Sanders Peirce, "How to Make Our Ideas Clear" *Popular Science Monthly* 12 (January, 1878); reprinted in *Classic American Philosophers*, ed. Max H. Fisch (Englewood Cliffs, N.J.: Prentice-Hall, Inc.), see p. 78.

14. Ibid., p. 78.

15. Geoffrey Warnock, "Logical Positivism," *English Philosophy Since 1900*, ch. 4, esp. p.44. The road is long and ironic, from the Vienna Circle's efforts to promote responsible thinking to the contemporary fecklessness of "do your own thing."

16. The impulse to ask "how do we determine the significant implications and how do we know we have enough?" is but a return to demanding a specific standard of clarity apart from the requirements of a context.

17. Philosophy's aim and methods are diverse. For the complexities, see John Passmore's "The Distinctiveness of Philosophical Reasoning," *Philosophical Reasoning* (New York: Charles Scribner's Sons, 1961), ch. 1, and his "Introduction: Change and Continuity," *Recent Philosophers* (La Salle, Ill.: Open Court Publishing Company, 1985), Despite the variation in philosophical practices and emphases, Passmore's 1985 work finds him saying that "for all the greater sophistication of method . . . it is surprising how much philosophical effort is still devoted to trying to solve problems which Plato, or Descartes, or Hume, first saw as such,"p. 13. This observation comports with our view that philosophy seeks a true, not just a consistent, picture of the nature of things that are crucial for self-understanding, such as justice, reality, mind, knowledge, and will.

18. Not God "*would not*" choose the bad, but God "*could not* possibly choose badly by his nature"—*couldn't* no matter what.

19. A sterling critique of logical consistency, *verbally* achieved, appears in John Ellis' critique of deconstructionsm; see John Ellis, *Against Deconstruction* (Princeton: Princeton University Press, 1989), last paragraph, pp. 24 into p. 25, where Ellis takes on the French philosopher, Jacques Derrida.

20. Harold Kushner, *When Bad Things Happen to Good People* (New York: Avon Books, 1983), p. 134.

21. In Moliere's play, *Candide*, the mathematician and philosopher Wilhelm Gottfried Leibniz is skewered as "Dr. Pangloss," who argues that this is "the best of all possible worlds."

22. The possible retort,"we are not *convinced* because of our ignorance (of the plan)" is weakened by the tendency to claim human ignorance *selectively* (i.e., tendentiously); for example, it is not said that we are too ignorant to be *convinced* that God is all good.

23. Of course, imagining how what you already believe might somehow be right despite apparent problems is a valid step in *conducting* inquiry; it is not a valid way to *conclude* inquiry.

24. On the role of freshly-minted expressions, see as an example the term *project* as a deconstructionist's new term for "theory" in *Against Deconstruction*, p. 3.

25. A likely example, from *The Encyclopedia of Artificial Intelligence*: "Winograd attempts to avoid spurious reification by constructing formal representations based on ontological considerations borrowed from methodological hermeneutics."

26. Frederick L. Will, "Thoughts and Things," *Proceedings and Addresses of the American Philosophic Association* 42, pp. 51-69.

27. J. N. Findlay's *Meinong's Theory of Objects and Values* (Oxford: The Clarendon Press, 1963), p. 326, succinctly makes this point against the idea that the meaning of a word *is* it use.

28. Some say these things show only that we change our statements, not that we dredge up meanings already within us; what has been said above does not establish "depth" but lets the matter rest with the reader.

29. Charles Lyell's *Principles of Geology* (1830) shook people's faith-based notions of what we are when his work entailed an age for the Earth that utterly undid the accepted biblical time frame of 8000 years.

30. Windelband, p. 13.

31. Ibid., pp. 10-11.

32. The psychopath or sociopath is not so much "bad' as *broken*; we say there is "something wrong with them"—thus treating moral incapacity as failed sanity or incomplete "mind."

Chapter 2

God's Meaning

Confronted by the most enormous fact of all, the universe. . . . we need to have the intellectual imagination of a Nietzsche to grasp how audacious and staggering is the hypothesis of atheism. For if we say the world is without a reason, then it becomes absurd, and the whole of existence, and we along with it, absurd.
—William Barrett, *The Death of the Soul*

. . . [D]espite their incontrovertible lack of authenticity, religious ideas have exerted the very strongest influence on mankind. This is a fresh psychological problem. We must ask where the inherent strength of these doctrines lies, and to what circumstance they owe their efficacy, independent as it is, of the acknowledgement of the reason.
—Sigmund Freud, *The Future of an Illusion.*

In the end, then, Christology must proclaim what it cannot explain. For it is concerned with an act initiated from beyond our world, an action which we observe . . . and rejoice in, but which we could not have predicted and cannot now profess to understand . . .
—John Hick, *God and the Universe of Faiths*

INTRODUCTION TO CHAPTER TWO

God is the truth and the way—or so theism says. If theism fails it will be because it glimpsed the way but would not tarry for the truth. What must not happen is that theism's problematic arguments lessen the prospects for religion itself.

I say this not as the person who, decades ago, delighted in upending arguments for God, but as the person who, years later, sat in

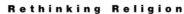

silence many times in the mission of San Xavier del Bac, and, who, in tears, heard Bach in the church of Saint Germain des Prés. Once disdainful of the search for God, I see it now as asking what we are—before we die.

The problem of rethinking religion begins with the rethinking of God. Do we really think it true that a religiously significant understanding of life depends on whether or not we, and the universe, were created "out of nothing" (*ex nihilo*) by a *will*? Are we certain that if God does not exist, human life can have no ultimate meaning?

The answer would seem to require that we know what, in the idea of a creator-god, makes "God" religion's fundamental object. Surely, the idea of a creator must satisfy criteria essential for supreme *religious* significance. If we can make conscious the foundation for God's *religious* meaning, we will understand what makes "God" *God*.

Assuming the identification of such criteria, theology would no longer be tied to the specific formulations bequeathed it by the earliest civilized thought. It would be freed to rethink the ultimate religious facts. Selective revelations, faith and tendentiously sectarian schooling would yield to publicly accessible truth; theology might, then, see a miraculously guiding reality not in another world, but in this one. To do so would be defensibly to find, with many theists, that "God," so to speak, is immanent.

For this reason, the nature of *godly* existence and the nature of *human* existence are, together, the dual themes of this chapter (as, indeed, they are of this book).

But there are obstacles to an analysis of "God." Many theists, as well as scientifically minded academics, insist that people do not believe in God for *reasons.*

The scientifically minded explain what we think and do on the basis of psychological, physiological, and genetic forces ("causes"); the "reasons" we give are but the products of those causes. Reasons are, in effect, "rationalizations" for what we need to believe. Theists, on the other hand, denigrate the importance of reasons in accepting God because religion is rooted in feelings, not reasons. Religion is a matter of the heart not the mind.

If these views are correct then philosophical theology is idle and our arguments pointless. Hence, the first responsibility of this chapter is to address the role of reasons in action and in feeling.

In this first, major section, I argue that if our reasons do not explain what we do, there is no uniquely human way of being in the world; there is only an animal way of being in the world. (The distinction is, of course, explicitly drawn in Genesis). The arguments are detailed, for what they assert constitutes the first step toward a natural religion. They find human life transcendent of physical life—as God is transcendent of physical life—and for that and certain ancillary reasons they find human life miraculous (human feelings are, for example, instances of *incarnation*). In any case, this discussion is the opening salvo in an attack upon the "ordinariness" of human life.

The second major section addresses the claim that the existence of anything-at-all can be accounted for by a creator-god. The argument against the doctrine of Creation has two aspects. The first attempts to show how the traditional arguments for God's existence do, and must, fail.

The second evolves from the first. It claims that the *persistent* use of arguments that either *do not follow* (are *non sequiturs*) or are internally contradictory strongly indicates the argument for creation is not driven by a search for true explanation but by a search for meaning. In other words, a religiously significant meaning will be had—no matter what!

In concluding this argument, I ask the reader to respond to certain options. I think the reader's own choices will show that *meaningfulness* is the operative goal of the creation idea—that creation is not a kind of extra-scientific cosmology.

The next section sets out what I term the "logic" of religion. Here I press the point that the search for God is, in motive, eminently rational. It is not *necessarily* the answer to a psychological need (Freud), or the expression of a genetic residue (Dennett). Here, the leading idea is that the search for God is the search for an ultimate context— specifically the ultimate context of humanity's actions. It is rational in that the meaning of an act depends on its context and the meaning of *all* acts depends on *the context of all acts*. If life has a meaning, that meaning can be known only if the ultimate context of life is known.

The penultimate section argues that religions cannot possibly lay claim to God's authority, and that to do so is amoral, for it necessitates denying personal responsibility. If the argument is correct, then we can never say we follow God's rules not our own.

The final section brings the descriptions of human action to bear on the description of divine action. The role of reason in explaining human action is contrasted with what "reasons" would turn out to be if all-that-exists were nothing else but the expression of a creator's will. Stated as a headline, what I contend is that our idea of what it is to be a *person* (not a creature) is *inconsistent* with the theism's idea of a creator-god. It would of course be immensely ironic if theism's explanation for why we are persons (not animals) entailed that we cannot be persons.

Included in this section is the argument that both scientism and skepticism have the same consequence as theism. This is part of showing that the dilemma—*scientific naturalism or theism*—rests on false assumptions about human action (and therefore yield the same unacceptable results).

In any case, the claims I make as to what must be the case if we are "persons" requires that *we can have knowledge*. And that requirement brings us to chapter three, "God's Humanity." For it is, precisely, worldly knowledge that many empirically minded philosophers deny. They and those who subscribe to perspectivalism and other postmodern notions see us as possessing only *belief* (ironically allying them with the "faithful" whose reliance on belief they deride).

Most importantly for natural religion, these philosophers are most emphatic (and persuasive) in denying knowledge of the good and the right and the true. For them, all normative standards, relations, and conditions are imagined or "constructed." There are no such things *in reality*. Reality is physical (and psychological, since consciousness exists). Beyond that, reality contains no norms to guide us—a deficiency remedied, to be sure, by the reception of God's Word.

Chapter 3 reconstructs the "Creation" that this chapter argues is untenable. Out of Chapter 3's critique of theism and scientism comes a natural theology in which *creation* is real, natural, yet miraculous.

GOD'S MEANING AS RELIGION'S MEANING

God-the-Creator is both the initial subject and recurring theme of these essays. Non-theistic objects of religious feeling, like the Confucian "Way," will be considered in due course.

There are substantial reasons for using the idea of a creator-god—specifically, the Judeo-Christian-Islamic conception—as a theological compass.[1] A non-natural creative agency of some kind has been long and widely accepted as religion's chief object. One can say that if a creator-god is not a primary religious object, then nothing is.

In addition, the idea of a supernatural author of existence has undergone centuries of theological elaboration so that its analysis should uncover much that a *religious* interest specifically demands.

Finally, the conception's emotional significance promises to touch the deep convictions that must be in play if speculative thought is to be properly disciplined.[2] In sum, the (Judeo-Christian-Islamic) idea of God presents us with a virtually paradigmatic religious object made rich by having addressed and, for many, resolved, issues at the center of religion's quest.[3]

God's religious significance must rest on reasons

Unlike Rudolph Otto's *The Holy* and William James' *Varieties of Religious Experience* (whose characterizations of religious attitude and feeling seem on the mark), these essays aim less to describe belief than to explore its justification.

The point of this chapter is to identify religion's defining *reasons*. On what grounds does the concept of a creator arouse *religious* rather than (say) moral or aesthetic sentiments? Why does the idea of a "creator" not arouse attitudes that would fall within *cosmology* or the study of *pre-history*? Why, in short, is God the ultimate *religious* object?

We look, as we say, for reasons, not presumed *causes* of religious belief—whether psychological, physiological, biological, or social.[4] We do not begin, as informal discussion so often does, asking what "makes" a person believe, or what familial or cultural influences account for a person's religious ideas.

This decision makes a world of difference, or rather, decides between different worlds. For, the business of doing things for reasons—reasons that both justify and account for our thinking what we think—is unique to human beings (to human "operations" or *way-of-being-in-the-world*).

It is a way of bringing forth belief and behavior that (if true) divides persons from *animals* as well as computers.[5] (Yes, whales may "sing" but not the Mozart Requiem, dolphins may play but not chess, and silverback gorillas may control group behavior but never by "divine right.")

It is only when the beliefs and action for which we normally take responsibility cannot plausibly be accounted for by our reasons—that is, when thinking is either *non-rational* or *irrational*—that we turn to *scientific* or "causal" explanation. Then we might say, "this kind of belief is genetically determined," or "this idea is the result of social conditioning, or "we are driven by unconscious forces."[6]

Still, it must be acknowledged that many estimable thinkers oppose the view that our *assessment of grounds* (our *reasons*) can really explain what we do.

Scientistic philosophers like Rudolph Carnap, Willard Quine, J. J. C. Smart, and Donald Davidson insist that *all* thinking—whether rational or not—is explicable *only* by science (assessments or reasons then become the *effects* of psycho-physical causes).[7] Davidson finds every mental event identical with a physical event, while Smart cannot believe that *everything* cannot be explained scientifically, including sensations: for him, the idea "that everything should be explicable in terms of physics . . . except the occurrence of sensations [items in consciousness]"—an idea that seems "frankly unbelievable."[8]

Since the mind we possess is, indeed, an evolved, mammalian mind, a *scientistic* approach to its workings would be entirely persuasive were it not for the fact that *in every department of practical life* what human beings normally say and, more importantly—what they mean—*explicitly contradicts* a scientific explanation by physiological *causes* (physical necessitation).

Granted, in the permissiveness of classrooms and informal gatherings, people will sometimes explain what they do as a function of "conditioning" or "the unconscious." But not so when what they say *matters*: In the context of practical activities—in the *arena of moral responsibility*—when asked why they hold their beliefs, people offer explanations that cite supporting reasons.

This is no "academic" matter. Governments stand or fall on such reasons. So do marriages and friendships. In law, criminal sentences vary depending on a miscreant's reasons. Indeed, the entire legal system explains what it does and believes by citing justifying reasons.

Thus, to state a point of method on which these essays stand or fall: When the chips are down—that is, when the context is that of *responsible, practical life*—people primarily think themselves moved to do something by the *content* of reasons which they hold to be *warranted* or *rationally sound*. (The relation between explanation by reasons and explanation by "free will" is more fully explored in Chapter 3.)

Now, it is true that the insane give *reasons* when in fact their beliefs or behaviors are actually *caused* (the reasons they give cannot plausibly explain their actions). But if it were the *norm* that reasons were irrelevant—if reasons never were explanatory—the pointlessness of reasons would long ago have been detected. We would have discounted people's "reasons" the way we discount the "reasons" very young children offer for their behavior. Reference to reasons would have faded away—just as, if *lying* became the norm, we would no longer make or listen to statements.[9]

Note, too, that when people are shown that their behavior has been determined not by their reasons, but by *causes*, they often feel deflated or embarrassed—as when a friend suddenly realizes he has helped you not out of friendship but from his need to feel approval.

So, while the *scientistic* view sees any explanation of actions by reasons ("I gave it back because my having it wasn't fair") as a kind of natural self-delusion, the practical world sees it as morally crucial.[10] Indeed, wherever someone's *character* is at issue, everything turns on the *reasons* for which action are performed.

So we maintain that in "the real world," the role of explanation by reasons can hardly be more significant.

The case against explaining what we do by reasons

Still, in fairness to scientistic views, the idea that all mental changes are *physically* caused cannot be easily dismissed. The notion that the bodily self (especially the physical brain) can undergo changes or be made to move (in any degree) by *ideas* is deeply problematic.

How can the coming-to-be of beliefs—which are in part bodily states—be explained by *non*-bodily things such as *meaning* or the *content* of ideas?[11] How can something like knowledge, which is patently *non-physical*, account—even partly—for our *behavior*, since behavior is a thing of the body which, as *physical*, operates by what science terms "causation"?[12]

To assign *any* portion of responsibility for how I, physically, behave and feel to the *content* of my thought seems like *animism*—like ascribing the wind's direction to intention.[13]

Theists, like C. S. Lewis, "solve" the mind-body problem by explaining rationality (in essence) as an instance of God's inexplicable power, while philosophers of language—like the late Gilbert Ryle— tend to say the mind-body problem is a pseudo-problem based on the misunderstanding of sentences in which "mental" terms appear, such as "intention" and "intelligence."

In any case, the position one takes on the mind-body issue shapes not only one's explanation of religion but religion's *content* as well. For, in assigning responsibility for what we do and think, variously— to causes, or reasoning, or free will, or supernatural intervention— we implicitly decide what kind of being we are ("what makes us tick").

And what we are is central to religion's definitive question, which is, of course, the meaning of life. As Michael Novak bluntly puts it in his *Belief and Unbelief*: "believer and nonbeliever disagree on what it is to be a man."[14]

In "explaining" religion, then, our philosophical method employs the same respect for reasons that is normally given them in explaining moral or "practical" activities. The rule for explaining our

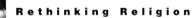

reasoning and behavior seems pretty clearly this: Under normal conditions, one's reasons ought not be discounted *unless they fail plausibly or reasonably to support the beliefs or actions in question.*[15]

Consequently, our task is to seek an explanation of God's religious meaning in the *reasons* people have for making an ultimate and sole creator the foundational object of specifically *religious* interest.[16]

We will try to understand why a "Creator" is not simply an object of interest that might fall within *cosmology* or *pre-literate history*. Should we succeed in uncovering the requirements whose apparent satisfaction gives the idea of a creator its *religious* meaning, we may find that certain traditional beliefs are not needed for their satisfaction. Theists, agnostics and atheists alike may then be positioned to answer the question raised by the American philosopher, John Dewey, in *A Common Faith*:

> What would be the idea of the unseen, of the manner of its control over us and the ways in which reverence and obedience would be manifested, if whatever is basically religious in experience had the opportunity to express itself free from all historic encumbrances?[17]

FEELINGS, MIND, AND SPIRIT

In setting out to analyze the criteria for God's religious primacy, this chapter may seem primed to deliver an irrelevantly abstract god—a god that is a "mere idea" (to use Michael Novak's pejorative phrase)—an intellectual construction that precludes "love for God as a person."[18] The concern is a fair one, and though this work, when grasped as a whole, may provide a worldview that will meet it, this issue—the issue of feeling's relation to thought—warrants early clarification, and not merely to allay apprehension.

For there exists a disastrous tendency to view religious thought as something founded in feelings apart from facts or reason. Too few believe that their feelings about God require, or are open to, any kind of critical inquiry.[19] Still fewer believe that conceptual or logical considerations might deepen their religious feelings.

This over-reliance on feeling sequesters religious ideas from inquiry, making it difficult to distinguish between the superficial and the profound, the authoritarian and the authoritative.

At the deepest level of uniquely religious concern, the idea that feelings are *internal*, self-contained indicators of the holy obscures the transcendent character of human feelings.

Human feelings rise above physiology because they are, as it were, fused with, and determined through, judgment. "Fused" is no explanatory term; it is a metaphor for a relationship between "mind" and "body" that has no physical description, and that, for the reasons that follow, we think it justified to describe as *incarnation* in the religious sense.

If, indeed, there is something holy in the nature of what we can feel, then we must consider the role of mind in making our religious feelings right.

Feelings and their object: The testimony of language

Our foray into the relationship between what we feel and what we think must traverse a narrow path. We shall not, for example, review the multiple uses of "feel."[20] We shall not lengthily explain how it may be said we *feel* an itch and also that we *feel* compassion when each is felt so differently.[21]

The point, for us, is that our spirituality is centered in our feelings (which, when actual and not imagined, show in our behavior) and that where feelings are ill-grounded or false, spirituality is defeated. With the latter point, as we shall see, traditional religions agree.

To begin, the defining feature of human feelings is that they are *about* something. They have an object. Our feelings arise, directly, in the judgments we make as to something's significance.

What we feel about the Civil War depends upon our understanding of the facts and what they mean; what we feel about our neighbors depends on what we think true of them.

The object of a feeling is the thing whose significance we suppose ourselves to be judging. That object may or may not exist. Indeed it may not be capable of existing. Nonetheless, the feelings we have— about Atlantis, Hamlet, or the Holy Grail—are generated on the basis of a judgment.

But not everything we may be said to feel arises from a judgment. We feel sensations, for example. Sensations, such as aches or stings, are explained by our physiology; their source is the body, not the mind. The bee sting we feel is not *about* anything. It is not *about* the bee; it is *caused* by the bee. The *sensations* we feel are mindless; our *feelings* are mind-dependent

It is also the case that feelings can arise from an *association* with an object rather than from one's judgment of that object. But this is a technical point, since the *original* feeling will be found to depend upon the assessment of its object.

To those acquainted with psychology, it might seem that the psychiatrist's expression, "objectless fear," contradicts our claim that feelings have objects. But in fact, "objectless fear" recognizes that the patient's feelings have an object. Its point is to characterize the *object* of the patient's feelings as in some way irrationally conceived.

So, the patient may believe, without plausible evidence, in an ever-present danger and retain that belief against any and all counter-evidence. It is the fixed and utterly implausible character of the object that allows the patient's feelings to be judged "irrational."[22]

The link between feeling and object is built into our language. To see this, one has only to assert a feeling exists while *denying* the existence of any related idea. So, if we say, "the patient feels fear but the patient has no thought of danger," we make no sense. The statement is self-contradictory because the idea of danger is *part of what it means* to speak of "fear."

William James recognized the connection between feeling and its object in his *Varieties of Religious Experience*. Speaking of presumptively "inner" states like religious love, religious fear, "and so forth," James found "religious love" to be "only man's natural emotion of love directed to a religious object" and "religious fear" to be "only . . . the common quaking of the human breast in so far as the notion of divine retribution may arouse it."[23]

As for "the religious" in general, James defined it as "*the feelings, acts, and experiences of individual men in their solitude, so far as they apprehend themselves to stand in relation to* whatever they may consider the divine [emphasis added]." James understood that neither feelings nor behavior could be identified as *religious* unless experienced or undertaken with a uniquely religious idea in mind (the object he termed "the divine").

Feelings and justification: the testimony of practice

If we examine what people actually *do* and *say* when feelings are the issue, we see that in practical, civilized life, feelings and ideas are viewed as joined. If someone announces, "I feel pained," a listener will likely ask, "what *about*?" And if the answer is "about having failed the test," or, "about having failed to help my friend," the comment that follows will likely be as familiar than the first.

It might be, "you *shouldn't* feel pained about it since no one else passed the exam," or, in the second case, "you're *right* to feel pained since one should certainly help a friend."

In these simple exchanges may be found the key features of feeling. The question, "what about?" confirms that feeling has an object. But the two suggestions—"you *shouldn't* feel pain . . . since no one else passed the exam . . . "and "you're *right* to feel pained since one should . . . help a friend" tell us more.

For these responses show that the first speaker's judgment of the object *is normally taken to explain* the speaker's pain. The *judgment* of "failure!" was *why* there was the feeling. And since a judgment is not a *physical* condition, the judgment did not *physically* cause the feeling. The judgment was—as we say—*responsible* for what the person felt. (We do not, that is, explain the feeling *scientifically*.)

Secondly, the responses underline the fact that feelings are subject to *evaluation*, even though feelings are *conditions* of the self that are in some sense "bodily" or have some kind of substance.

So, remarkably, some conditions of ourselves (our "feelings")—things in some degree *bodily*—can be judged *justifiable* or *unjustifiable* even though they are not "ideas" or "claims." (The ambiguity of "in some degree bodily" should be noted. We think our inability to break human feeling clearly into mental and physical "parts" reflects the uniqueness, the *sui generis* character, of the human mode of being, rather than confusion on our own part.)

In any case (*and this is our fundamental claim*) it would make no sense to say someone should or shouldn't feel pained for failing an exam *unless* one thought *the judgment of an object* explains the pain. The comment—"no one else passed the exam"—is plainly given in the hope that an altered judgment can engender a change in feeling.

The absolute familiarity of this way of altering feelings shows it a matter of human experience that what we *feel* is the product of thought, not physiology.

This is, of course, a position increasingly under attack by neuroscientists who see this explanation by *judgment* as pre-scientific self-deception.[24] But, it is scientifically implausible to claim that when we alter feelings by offering alternative judgments we have—unbeknownst to us—latched onto statements which, when *uttered*, act as a *physiological* causes that alter the feelings in the desired way. This is because the judgments people offer are always differently framed or uttered (drawn from an endless pool of differing possible utterances) so *no causal connections* can have been informally observed to hold between the *utterance* of a particular judgment and a change in reported feeling.

To get at this another way: It would be absurd for the respondent to *give reasons* why the person "shouldn't" or "should" feel pain at

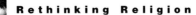

failing a test, if feelings were caused the way migraines are caused (that is: *physiologically*). Thus, one has only to imagine someone stubbing a toe on a metal table leg and being advised by a friend that they really shouldn't feel pain because, "it's not fatal," or someone giving reasons to a known psychotic as to why he or she shouldn't feeling anxious.[25]

"The extraordinary influence of the human imagination and intelligence on even our simplest emotion" was stressed by the humanistic psychologist Willard Gaylin, who argued (against *physicalist* psychology) that

> human emotions are of a different order from those of the lower creatures . . . [so that] . . . sexual desire, even when the sexual act is not a part of romantic love, is always modified by imaginative aspects of the human psyche.[26]

Only because mind and body are "fused" in the human mode of *being* can our "inner" feelings be flawed or illegitimate. That is why we ask, "how can you feel warmly toward such a phony?" or, "didn't you feel the romance in the play's final words?" or "so what if I gave to the poor because giving makes me feel important."

When the operation of ideas is reduced to the operation of brain states, human practices become the movements of an organism. Any notion of the human spirit becomes impossible. For example, if one person helps another, thinking, *This person deserves help*, and someone else helps another, thinking, *This will make me look good*, the first person's action could not be said to be morally or spiritually better than the action of the second.

This is because if people operate not by ideas but by *brain states*, then what they *think* has nothing to do with their actions—the *content* of their thought *doesn't explain* what they do. Their synapses do. It is surely mad to say "this chain of synaptic activity is morally better or more sympathetic than that one." Yet that is what we would be saying if synaptic activity (physiology) explained the behavior we morally praised. It would make just as much sense to say, "this soil is *morally* better or more sympathetic than that soil because it feeds more people."

Returning to the initial problem—the idea that the critical analysis of God will likely undervalue feeling—it would seem that the ideas and practices of humankind do not support that qualm. Quite the opposite. For if we honor and cherish what we *feel*, we must give equal care to the ideas from which our feelings (when rational) arise, and on which (when rational) they depend.

Moreover, our concern for right feelings is important not simply *for* religion but *as* religion: as we have claimed, feelings are the *substance* of spirit. It is a claim we have not fleshed out, but that we shall attempt to make clear by considering what is at stake spiritually or "religiously" in deciding whether or not to take drugs to alter feelings.

Feeling, spirit, and the religious: The testimony of philosophy

One of contemporary culture's smaller debates concerns the use of psychotropic drugs. It is a contretemps we might ignore had not Sigmund Freud's *The Psychopathology of Everyday Life* alerted us to the diagnostic value of seemingly minor disturbances.

At times, there seems little doubt that drugs have their place. No one should have to suffer clinical depression. But why not take a psychotropic to alleviate "normal," if oppressive, feelings of sadness? Indeed, why not take something just to feel happier—providing it avoids the ill effects of alcohol or marijuana and has no negative consequences on the GDP?

It is here that discomforts commonly arise. But the source of the discomfort is notoriously difficult to pinpoint. Perhaps there is no reason for it other than cultural habituation. But perhaps our feeling troubled is the symptom of an understanding too deep to be accessed in ordinary conversation.

If the latter, then a context of extreme seriousness—the sort that "sacred texts" inspire—may help lead us to unearth that concern.

Since the Pentateuch is common coin, let us consider what Abraham should have done when, reputedly, the Lord told him to kill his own son. Should not an empirically enlightened Abraham have said, "I have this horrific thing to do—killing my son—perhaps if I take certain herbs I will feel better about doing it"?

We draw back. But why?

Is it that the *difficulty* of the act would be diminished? But what of *that*? Are we saying that difficulty is a good thing in and of itself?

Or are we saying that the difficulty of the act is good because it offers Abraham "a learning experience?" (But this is not so, since we would have the same qualms about Abraham alleviating his sorrow with a drug, even if we thought Abraham would kill himself immediately after killing his son.)

So, why shouldn't Abraham have taken a calming herb, felt less distress, and killed his son—thereby obeying God while suffering less? Is it that we think God *enjoys* Abraham's pain? Clearly, the proposal to use calming herbs conflicts in some essential way with the meaningfulness of the act. But, again, how?

The imperative against palliation is not *moral* in type; we would not say it was *immoral* for Abraham to ease his suffering. Whatever the imperative is, it is *inherent*, for it is within the act itself that the (religious) significance of Abraham's experience drains away with drug palliation—even if he does what God wants (and even if, as we suggested, he kills himself afterward.)

And here one begins to see that the *way* Abraham *comes to feel reality* or "the world" is essential to his acting as a *human* agent—as essential as his having free will.

It is out if this kind of consideration that we have argued that feelings and sensations occupy different domains and thus represent different ways of being. The pain of a cut and the pain of an injustice represent entirely different aspects of our inner life.

Their spiritual difference is witnessed by the fact that the pain of a cut has no bearing on our status as a *person* while the pain of injustice does. The religious difference between these interior conditions is well understood: While a person who feels no sensations will be described as "anesthetized," a person who has no feelings will be described as "empty," "soulless," or "inhuman." Diminished sensations suggest a medical problem; diminished feelings a spiritual one.

What sets us apart from other mammals is not the degree to which we are clever. Certain advocates of "artificial intelligence" may see us as clever animals or highly adaptive, feedback systems, but even they have not (yet) managed to speak of "artificial wisdom."

The fact remains that any example of *homo sapiens sapiens*, who lacked moral feelings, esthetic feelings, and feelings of fairness and decency, would be termed—in language that is non-biological but just as *literal*—"inhuman."[27]

Thus, only in the degree to which what we feel arises out of judgment—as when we decide that justice has prevailed, or that a painting has aesthetic worth, or that a problem has been solved—does mammalian life become human life.

It is just this unbridgeable distance between what animals can feel and what humans can feel that allows Judeo-Christian religion plausibly to declare that humans have souls while animals do not.[28]

Returning to Abraham's ordeal, we can specify what is, for religion, at stake. Were Abraham's anguish diminished by a drug, the problem is not *simply* that, religiously or "metaphysically," what he felt would be *inappropriate*—for the wrong drug might produce in him the *appropriate* degree of anguish!

The problem is that what he felt would be *irrelevant*.

If what he felt reflected the properties of a chemical and not his thought, experience, or character, what he felt would be *irrelevant* to the *self* named "Abraham." What he felt would be attributable only to his body and thus could have nothing to do with his spirit (under any plausible conception of "spirit"). What he felt would have the history and status of a sensation and the story would be about an organism named "Abraham," not the human being, "Abraham."

The idea that the human spirit cannot live as *physiology* links Judeo-Christian religion with Indian religions that in other ways differ from it. In both, as one student of comparative religion says, "salvation, whether it is achieved by one's own efforts or through the grace of a god, always means deliverance from the bond that links spirit with matter."[29]

But we need not shoulder the burden of supernatural claims when common understanding supplies mystery enough—namely that even though the human spirit may require the "matter" of a body, it is, *as spirit*, saved, only when insight into the right and the good—and not *matter*—determines what we feel.

The idea that physiologically induced feeling separates the *person* from what the person feels is reflected in our treatment of people when we think their feelings and ideas are *physiologically* caused—people drunk or high on drugs.[30]

We accord what they feel no more *authority* than their sensations, which is to say, none. ("Let's see how you feel about it when you're sober!") We treat their feelings of anger or love or joy as *phenomena*, as symptoms that have befallen them; we do not seriously argue whether their feelings are *justified* because we know that a chemical accounts for them, not a judgment..

When the mind goes on holiday—which is the point of drugging and over-drinking—it is not simply that such persons are "not themselves" but that, *while in this state*, they are not anyone. It is this spiritual suicide—this fall into the world of the non-personal, the world of the organism—that nags against the persistent use of drugs.

From a *practical* or *utilitarian* and even a *moral* point of view, there is no reason relaxing or exhilarating drugs could not be regularly used if their debilitating consequences could be chemically or behaviorally managed. (Coleridge and Freud, for example, used drugs).

From the religious viewpoint, however, the situation is very different. Insofar as feelings are determined by physical causation, the "I" and the "we" are set aside. Religiously speaking, there can be no relation of "I and thou" when there is no "I."

Feelings as phenomena: are we self-contradictory?

The philosophically minded reader may have noted a contradiction. If we say "feelings" arise from judgments, then how can we talk about feelings that are produced by *physical* causes (not *judgments*)? True, but there is no standard name for what it *is* that we feel when what we feel has a *sensational* resemblance to an ordinary "feeling." People seldom, if ever, discuss these distinctions and so they have no ready place in language—no word for a *sensation of feeling* this or that.

So, calling a non-feeling a "feeling" is rather like calling a non-tree a tree—as in observing, "that tree is made of fiberglass!" Hence, in this context, calling a non-feeling a "feeling" is, in our view, a non-misleading, linguistic workaround. Still we can be more exact:

Where feeling is decoupled from judgment, we have only a simulacrum of feeling. When what we feel about something is caused by a drug or by a dream, we have a variety of sensation that *resembles* what we feel "because of something judged."

If Abraham were drugged, what he felt would only *seem* to arise from his assessment of killing his son in the same way that in a dream or under the influence of drugs or hypnosis it might seem to him he was making a judgment or that he felt a certain way.

This is not a verbal matter. There is a very real difference between dreamt judgments and actual judgments. Only our waking judgments are treated as *dispositive* or *actual* judgments.

If, in a dream, you decide you shouldn't buy a neighbor's house, and then you awake and remember the decision, it would not be a case of *changing your mind* if you decided to buy it. But if you *dreamt* decision were an *actual* decision, you would, necessarily, have *changed your mind* by deciding to buy the house.

**Feeling, spirit, incarnation:
an exercise in philosophical theology**

What we have attempted to show is that the discomfort which (still) attends the prescription of "mind-altering" drugs has to do with maintaining a *human* nature. The issue is one of survival, but not of the body, for the body requires only a *functional psychology*. It is the survival of one's uniquely *human* status that is imperiled, for that requires an "inner" life born of free mental activity.

Given that judgment and feeling are united in the being of a human, what we wish now to explore is why the issue of right feelings concerns us as human beings, indeed, why it is an ultimate concern—to borrow Paul Tillich's phrase for the religious interest.[31]

We have already noted that "not to have feelings" is to be "soul-less" or "empty." Some may think these mere "figures of speech" (the British philosopher, Gilbert Ryle, has written that when we say we feel pain at another's suffering we speak *metaphorically*). But we contend that whatever the grammatical status of talk about feelings, the reality is that we treat feelings as our inner substance.

It appears, for example, that we commonly regard what someone feels as more indicative of the kind of *person* they are than what they think. Thus someone who hates other races will be thought a bad person while one who (on the basis of some theory) thinks he *ought* to hate other races (but does not) will not be considered a bad person—and this distinction will hold even if both support the same racially relevant political policies.

Somehow, feelings are important *in themselves*, so that an education in history, art, and the sciences that enabled students to test well but left their feelings untouched would be regarded as, in some deep sense, a failure.

That our feelings are not simply psychological states is of course not easy to show. Let us try a thought-experiment. Suppose the end of your life is imminent. Suppose you feel guilt regarding certain things you have done—and suppose, also, that you are in physical pain. Which would you rather be true as you die—that you feel pain or guilt? And if dying in guilt seems the more awful, would you consider taking a drug to quell your feeling of guilt, or would only confessing it and asking for forgiveness—from a friend, a religious official, a loved one, or, yes, the silent universe—make sense?

Since we think, dear reader, you would choose confession and forgiveness, we must ask how this choice makes sense, unless you regard what you feel as something more than a troublesome *psychological* state—for which a powerful psychotropic would provide a solution. And does this choice not also say that *the substance of you is dependent on judgment and truth*—that what you feel is part of "your very soul"?

Thus our feelings seem to be ourselves in a way that our ideas are not. Feelings seem the clay and mind the armature of the self.

To be sure, our ideas are also *ours*, but unlike our feelings, ideas can be altered or rendered provisional by volition—we can set them aside, even forget them. We can directly try out new arguments; *we cannot directly try out new feelings.* In being alterable or dispensable, our thoughts are *ours* yet, in a sense, not quite *us.*

Stated in the riskier terms of a philosophical theology, the nature of our feeling-life seems a matter of *incarnation*—an embodiment no less inexplicable (hence no less mysterious) for being non-supernatural.[32] Feelings are an immediate embodiment of what we understand.

Yes, habits alter (bodily) dispositions, but through repetition, while feelings, from all evidence, alter us bodily as the direct outcome of our thinking. Something happens in our physical substance that is not, like the formation of a habit, under our control. (If physicalist language were adequate to the subject, we might speak of our "nervous system" rather than our physical "substance.")[33]

We find the transcendence that judgment gives feelings in James Joyce's *Portrait of an Artist*, when Stephen (Joyce) informs his friend, Lynch, that "the desire and loathing excited by improper esthetic means are not really esthetic emotions [feelings] . . . because they are not more than physical."[34] Joyce was notable for exploring the epiphanies of daily life and not remarkable in thinking it sacred.

And if everyday life is sacred, it may not be so odd to think that it contains the miraculous, and that among its miracles are feeling as incarnation.

In essaying the transcendence of feeling, we take seriously that in the normal course of life, our feelings—of guilt, shame, love, compassion—are not regarded as the effects of physical causes. We do not have a feeling and then wonder what physically *caused* it.

As Anthony Kenny points out, if "the relation between an emotion [feeling] and its object were one of effect to cause, then it would be only by induction and tentative hypothesis that one knew on any particular *what* one was afraid of or excited about."[35] One might feel joy watching a dance performance and but not know whether the joy was caused by one's lunch, one's companion, or the cologne of a neighboring spectator.

Surely this embodiment of mind in "feelings" may with reason be considered what tradition terms "the miraculous"—for the idea of *incarnation* asserts the "impossible" fusion of the non-material with the material.

For religion, the existence of religious facts becomes ever more perplexing in an ever more scientistic culture. Even centuries ago, Alexander Pope found "man" "in doubt to deem himself a God or beast;/ in doubt his mind or body to prefer."[36]

Incarnation has a religious importance that is universal. Religion's earliest form—pantheism—saw physical things as spiritually inhabited, while Catholicism still insists that a spiritual power transubstantiates matter in Communion.

It is perhaps no mere coincidence that the Danish philosopher and theologian Søren Kierkegaard placed incarnation at the center of religiosity. Only if the Christian believes Jesus to have been both God and man (a belief Kierkegaard himself described as "insane"), can the religious experience be genuine![37] But of course, we draw the line at literal self-contradiction.

A rationally acceptable or true religion can neither be mindless nor insane. This brief foray into mystery—the second such venture in this chapter—is but an early passage in the story of incarnation that may fairly be considered the culminating notion of this work.

For those who prefer a less speculative statement of spirit's embodiment, we think that within such august notions as Hegel's "Absolute Spirit," such honored ones as the historians' "spirit of the enlightenment," and such popular ones as the "spirit of the game" lies our present theme: *Judgments of significance can transform the materiality of the world,* making us—in our very substance—more ideal.

Feelings, spirit, and truth: the affirmations of traditional religion

In popular culture, religious participants and officials tend to focus on morality and utility, that is, on the behavioral effects of feelings. But a uniquely *religious* concern with feelings is not utilitarian. Nor is it moral, for the moralist is concerned with the relation between feelings and probable behavior.[38]

Religion's concern is with the ultimate and most meaningful *truth of fact* regarding the human situation; its statements on morals flow from that. Thus religion's specifically *religious* interest is in the *spiritual status* of our feelings—which we have argued is the status of our human substance, our "soul."

The strongest evidence that religion's first interest is in the inherent *character* of feelings (the "inner self"), and that feelings *must arise from what is true* is that religions ask how one feels about God (or "the divine"). Even among the confusions of popular theology, the peculiarly *religious* error is the failure to do things out of love, respect, or fear, not for others or for nations, but *for God*.

To state the point as a principle: Without loving or respecting what is *divine*, one's feelings may favor moral actions but are not, for that reason alone, "religious." (An empirical indicator of this non-empirical point is that ecumenists [who know they disagree about fundamental religious truths] can agree on moral principles—bearing witness to the difference between moral and religious feelings.)

In thus linking feelings with appropriate truths, religion agrees with the foregoing analysis that the worthiness of what we feel depends in large part on how truly or adequately judged is its object.

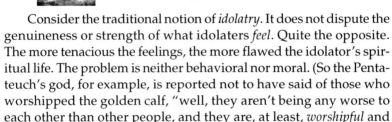

Consider the traditional notion of *idolatry*. It does not dispute the genuineness or strength of what idolaters *feel*. Quite the opposite. The more tenacious the feelings, the more flawed the idolator's spiritual life. The problem is neither behavioral nor moral. (So the Pentateuch's god, for example, is reported not to have said of those who worshipped the golden calf, "well, they aren't being any worse to each other than other people, and they are, at least, *worshipful* and what they feel is, after all, *sincere*.")

Similarly, the concept of the *cult* speaks to spiritual debasement. It is the quality of the cult member's inner life that is seen as, in itself, degraded when the object of religious feeling is too parochial or literal to be holy. Insofar as feelings of adoration are fixed as much or more upon a human leader as on God, terms like "superficial" or "perverted" may be applied to the believer's spiritual condition.[39]

Nor can the authenticity and profundity of religious feelings be reckoned apart from knowledge of their object. Authentic feelings cannot rest on self-deception; they cannot arise from reasons that would extinguish what one felt once the reasons were discerned. For example, one's unconditional love of God cannot, upon analysis, turn out to depend upon one's prospect of living forever, for then religion's real object becomes self-perpetuation and God its (conditional) instrument. (To be sure, Christianity and Islam place enormous emphasis upon eternal life, but they also insist that the first object of attachment must be God, so an important conflict of interest exists, and an issue of authenticity can with reason be raised.)

As for *profundity*, religious feeling must flow from a well-grounded notion of what is holy. Feelings cannot stem from, say, the worship of power—an object typical both of adolescent adoration and belief in magic. In such ways traditional religion suggests that feeling and commitment are neither independent of nor superior to a judgment of their object, and that a peculiarly *spiritual* price may be paid by those who take religious judgments to be easy or who think feelings or convictions justify themselves.

Even Rudolph Otto's classic, *The Idea of the Holy*, with all its concentration on feeling—in particular, the non-rational "overplus" of "ineffable" feeling in the religious response—treats feeling as qualified by its object—by what is judged to be significant. The "fearful awe" Otto found in humanity's experience of the holy is not a simple, internal phenomenon like a *sensation* of warmth. Otto viewed the feeling of religious awe as capable of evolution through "a main line of development" and therefore capable of being greater or lesser in inherent value.[40] That is to say, feelings (like "awe") are capable of *improvement*. They can be more or less justifiable—higher or lower. The movement from awe at ghosts, to awe at "daemonic forces," to awe at "the supermundane . . . which is," Otto says, "above the whole world-order" marks feeling's progression through what he calls *"higher* modes of manifestation [emphasis added]."[41] The improved character of feeling is not due to a change in intensity, duration or regularity of feelings but in what the feeling is understood to be *about*.

Feeling, spirit, and popular culture

The religious significance of the link between inner and outer is a matter of what we incarnate, of what our judgments make part of our substance. Only if what we *think* valuable really *is* valuable can the feeling or substance we derive have intrinsic value.

To be *born* into—happily participate in and love—a fascism that manages to *succeed* is, from the practical side, a perverse bit of luck, from the moral side an excusable error, and from the religious side a wasted life.

Viewed philosophically, the question of a feelingful knowledge of the Good is whether we can be one with reality. Viewed theologically, it is whether the soul can be united with God. And—to foreshadow later discussion—viewed attitudinally, the question is whether love can unite us with the world in a sense that it is, without sentiment, *religious*.

The link between inner and outer is, in any case, an issue for spiritual education in the broadest, non-denominational sense. For, as we have seen, religion affirms *absolutely* that the quality of our inner life is dependent on its object and that the object must be something not "inner" or imaginary, but "outer" or "real"—that is, something not determined by our will, wish, imagination or desire but possessed of its *own status*.[42]

"In religion," says the British theologian, H. H. Farmer, "the reality interest is paramount. Once persuade the religious man that the reality with which he supposes himself to be dealing is not 'there' in the sense in which he supposes it to be 'there' and his religion vanishes away."[43]

The point is general. Where profundity is desired, intensity is not enough. If the god you love is superficial, what you feel is superficial no matter how intensely you feel it; if the god you love is profound, what you feel is profound.

When a youngster falls in love with a star or a local celebrity, the feeling of love may be intense, but we speak of "infatuation" not love

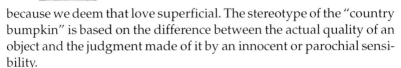

because we deem that love superficial. The stereotype of the "country bumpkin" is based on the difference between the actual quality of an object and the judgment made of it by an innocent or parochial sensibility.

That, one presumes, is why we acknowledge that the feelings derived from good melodrama (however pleasing, relaxing, or exciting it may be) are less profound than what we feel in response to tragedy or poetry.

At this writing, however, the distinction between superficial and profound experience is under attack because very idea of objective differences—in the worthiness of objects and the worthiness of judgment—is under attack. Influenced by the empiricists' scientism, by postmodern skepticism and abetted by a market-driven surfeit of novelties and thrills, the distinction between objects of profound value—those that require sustained attention, like fine art—and objects of passing or merely pleasurable value (entertainment) is becoming passé. What one feels at "professional" *wrestling* match is neither more nor less "deep" than what one feels at a performance of Vivaldi's *Gloria*.[44]

Reporting on contemporary cultural views, the *New Yorker* magazine's John Seabrook finds it widely believed among the educated— among creators and purveyors of culture—that "taste is nothing more than the ideology of the tastemaker, masquerading as disinterested judgment."[45] In scientistic and postmodern "reality," concern for the human spirit becomes unintelligible.[46] Attempts at offering "the best," or "improving" taste become baseless pretensions to superiority. What was once called "critical acumen" is now understood as "elitism."

In keeping with the tendency to replace being *valuable* with the mere fact of being *valued*, opinions on religion ape the contemporary approach to taste, so that the *intensity, persistence or extremity* of a person's religiosity proves its gravity and authenticity. Hysteria becomes religion's apogee. The strength of what one feels is respected; the content of what one thinks is irrelevant.[47] On such a principle, faith—any faith—will do, and the idea of spiritual deepening fades like a guttering candle.

Feelings and utility: the empirical reduction of spirit

We have made much of the point that feelings are considered justifiable—that they can be good or bad, better or worse. In writing for non-philosophers, there is always the need to alert readers to the presence of influential opposing views. Issues of spirit, feeling, and mind are too fundamental for us not to examine outlooks that find nothing outside ourselves to be valuable *in itself*. The most persuasive families of dissent in our view are, speaking very broadly, two: the physicalist and the utilitarian.

Physicalism is theoretical—and emboldened—made increasingly popular by experiments in which the brain is stimulated physically and the *subject* feels or sees or says this or that.[48] It takes a completely scientific view of all things human so that psycho-physical laws and conditions account for everything we think or do. Simply put, we are an organic feedback machine in no better position to say that we see what is objectively *good* than a computer which has been programmed to sort pictures by predetermined rules.

Utilitarian views, on the other hand, argue from within the practical world. In such theories, feelings can, indeed, be justified. But because values do not exist like stones and trees, the only rational way utilitarians (read "empiricists") can justify anything is to show that it is pleasurable or useful in respect to some purpose. Here we blur all utilitarian views together—Bentham with Sidgwick with Mill—because the problem is the principle of utility itself. Indeed, one has only to recall the discussion of Abraham and drugs to see that any notion of utility is somehow off the mark (consider his taking a drug on the calculation, "if I can manage to kill my son, then we both get into heaven").

There is a certain common sense in saying "if it makes me happier than anything else it is better than anything else!" It helped John Stuart Mill to ask in *Utilitarianism* "what is the principle of utility, if it be not that that 'happiness' and 'desirability' are not synonymous terms?"[49]

But, so counter-intuitive, so far from common understanding is the drift of such purely psychological "goodness," that it led Mill himself famously to declare, "it is better to be Socrates dissatisfied than a fool satisfied"—thereby denying the inherent goodness of *psychological* "happiness" by pronouncing some feelings better (more justified) than others.[50] In his impassioned remark, Mill removed goodness from the realm of psychological facts and returned the justifiability of feelings to the question of their *grounds*—that is, to judgments of the worth or rightness of what affects us. As Iris Murdoch remarked, "the ordinary person does not, unless corrupted by philosophy, believe that he creates values by his choices."[51]

What made Mill veer from psychology to judgment was the testimony of human experience and his own intellectual honesty. He

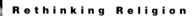

could not, save disingenuously, deny the existence of foolish or superficial feelings, nor the fact that happiness was many times unjustified. He could not bring himself to affirm or counsel that happiness be considered inherently good because it feels good—even though his theory, consistently argued, would support such a policy. And this reluctance to treat feelings *merely as manageable phenomena* confirms both their non-psychological nature as products of judgment and the importance of their status in a human life.

Our lives are rooted in feeling, in what we care about, what we dislike, what we love and what we hate, in what warms us and what leaves us cold. We are unable to let feelings be. We are unable to be no more concerned about them than we might be about a headache or an allergic itch.

Feelings thus seem to be the substance of our *person* and not (like sensations or psychoses) the substance of our *physiology*. And this in turn comports with our view that the conflict between Abraham's suffering and its palliation by drugs is a conflict between his substance as a person and his substance as an organism.

The human way of being: a reflection on the ultimate

A general point: We do not argue, simply, that if a particular action or feeling is unique to human beings we should honor or prefer it. That would lead to contradiction—for example, using and abusing atomic power would *both* be honored or preferred. We seek the essential *type* or *way* that human beings operate. Our goal is to make explicit the way of being-in-the-world (of "operating" of "working" of "making things happen") which distinguishes the *human* way from the inorganic, vegetative or animal ways.

A life of actions done for reasons distinguishes human beings *essentially*. Computers, for instance, don't have rights or responsibilities because they do not do things for reasons. Animals are not responsible beings because doing things for reasons does not apply to the ends they pursue nor to scruples regarding means they employ.

We also take it that what it is to do things for reasons—to do things one can in principle attempt to justify—is an ultimate notion of the way *uniquely human* things happen. And, *if* a way that things happen (or come to pass) is, indeed, *ultimate*, it cannot be said to proceed as it does by any process *more* ultimate!

When we try to explain the ultimate as being what it is because of something else, we cannot, with consistency, do it. For instance, "why feel deeply rather than superficially?" is on our analysis, an implicitly contradictory question, for it asks, "Why should anyone be more rather than less better grounded (more rational) in their judgments?" (Like a questioner saying, "Why should anyone ask a question?"). That is, there is no way to go deeper, to get underneath, to explain *certain* human "processes" because when one tries to explain them, one finds one cannot do so without making use of them. They are "ultimate." (And, of course, this is precisely the self-refutation scientism falls into when it explains its own explaining as an effect of physiological forces.)

"Is there an external world?" is a similarly self-stultifying question. There is nowhere to go for evidence save something external to one's opinion about it, that is, to some kind of "external world." So, the external world, like rational judgment, can have no other, stronger ground for accepting its reality.

Thus, when we confront an ultimate kind of thing, we have a vision of what, existentially, is final. And, being final, the way something is in the world cannot be explained as the way something *else* is in the world. The *aesthetic* character of a painting, for example, cannot be explained by the *physical* characteristics of the painting.

Things of a final kind cannot be re-described as other kinds of things (one way of being-in-the-world by another way of being-in-the-world). Brain physiology may explain what is *necessary* for the ability to reason; it cannot explain the *sense* of that reasoning—what makes it "reasoning" rather than blabbering.

The explanation for why a person, not a parrot, says, "two and two equals four" cannot be given by describing what happens in the brain when we think it. (We don't consult physiology to do mathematics.) On the other hand, internal events are the *only* way we can explain why a computer vocalizes "two plus two equals four." It is *only* because of its circuitry and electrical states (its "brain") that it "utters" the equation. Computer-happenings are not done *for* reasons—like "seeing the point" or "understanding." Hence, we do not remonstrate with a computer.

Because reasoning and understanding are not determined on physical principles, they have no non-mind explanation. And this defiance of explanation must hold for all things we determine to be ultimate. That is why theists refuse to explain God by non-God.

What a truth-based theology requires is a defensible *explication*—not an *explanation*—of things ultimate. And here we continue to build the case for the ultimate status of humanity's mental life.

Well-grounded *explications* of the ultimate position us better to see the implications of the ultimately real for what we choose to do.

Together they constitute a foundational worldview. It is this reference to the ultimate makeup of reality that makes religion at once vital yet unable to give proofs, causing it to walk a troubling line between wisdom and madness. Religion, in this way, touches the "ineffable."

It is in offering an ultimate context for the human story that religion exhibits another aspect of its *logic*, which might be termed *the logic of context* followed to its limit.

It happens that the meaning of things always depends on context. For that reason the meaning of human life depends upon that context of that life. The rationality of religion resides, as this chapter argues, in providing an ultimate context for human life so that the ultimate meaning of our life can be understood.

We have tried to show that feeling and judgment are inextricably bound up as the human "spirit," and that the worthiness of that spirit will depend on the soundness of the judgments it makes. The spirit that arises from false judgment cannot save the human spirit from malformation. If religion seeks the salvation of the spirit, then the judgment that gives rise to religious feelings must be right. If it seeks to know the meaning of life, its judgment as to the ultimate context of that life must be correct.

Since theism's conception of *divinity* is its concept of life's ultimate context, its concept of the divine must be the correct.

GOD'S MEANING AS CREATOR

The following analysis revolves around the divinity familiar to Judeo-Christian-Islamic belief; its arguments are nonetheless general.

What we derive from our analysis of God-as-Creator will bear upon such diverse notions as the sacredness of the Confucian Li or "way" as well as the deterministic world of Baruch Spinoza, the seventeenth-century philosopher who held that the universe itself is God.[52] But this somewhat pantheistic drift will not cause us, in the end, to ignore the counter-claim that any viable God must be "personal" in nature.

Whatever the outcome of our inquiry, few will gainsay that the beliefs most readily conceded to be "religious" tend to be those that posit or presuppose an awesome presence, awareness, or mindful power beyond the physical world, one whose origin and nature are believed (however inconstantly) to elude comprehension.

Beyond physical reality

Indeed, religious sentiment seems inexorably drawn to claims of mysterious agency or intelligence. This predilection may appear early, as in the case of Yaweh, the God of Genesis, or over time as in the case of Gautama, Bhuddism's founder, who was first thought a human teacher, but centuries later "a direct manifestation of the Supreme Being . . . the Highest One in the flesh."[53]

This disposition to ascend from natural to supra-natural realities is, we contend, as rational in motive as it is irrational in formulation. For, in moving from a less than ultimate context (the conditions, say, of a nation, today) to one that is ultimate (the conditions that are time-less), it attempts to describe the context that determines the ultimate meaning of our acts.

Otherness

We will not understand religion deeply unless we understand why God's religious meaning requires so many to suppose that God lies *outside* the domains of nature and human psychology or, as it were, lives *within* them on the model of a radiance, a presence or a power (but in any case, as something *other* than the causal domains of nature and the natural self).

By closely considering how people *most familiarly* conceive and argue for, the existence of a God—in particular, when they argue for an original *creation*—we have the opportunity to unearth the imperatives essential to the religious sensibility.

God's explanatory meaning

The attempt to understand why anything at all exists is not undertaken (save, perhaps, at the outset) to satisfy theoretical curiosity. If the explanation of the universe, so to speak, turned out to be "the action of absolutely singular, self-created field of energy," the religious impulse would be disappointed. Nothing of a specifically *religious* character would have been discovered.

The search for an ultimate origin is fraught with ambiguity. On the surface, it seems a quest for truth. But within it are choices that show religious thinkers *determined*, in the end, to find meaning. Religious thought senses (and so insists) that life must be inherently significant. At the same time, it understands that what it says cannot be false. The promise of absolute creation seems to meet the requirement of truth while satisfying the demand for meaning. It is as if to know, with certainty, the meaning of a novel, one would have to consult the author.

(God's religiously significant meaning will be found not to lie in God's office as explaining why there is "anything at all." But, of course, this remains to be shown.)

Some anomalous aspects of "creation"

For over two millennia, theologians have striven to establish that a non-physical source of intentional creation is undeniably the true explanation of "existence." Though their theorizing ignores the canons of science, it is theorizing, nonetheless.

But if the idea of a creation (whether conceived as an initiating act or as an constant activity) is an *explanatory theory*, why is its promulgation not confined largely to *theorists*—to people whose vocation is to hypothesize? Ordinary folks normally devote little time or energy to theory; they are seldom concerned to understand the expansion of the universe, galactic development, or the principles of natural selection.

And so we are moved to ask why a theory of ultimate origin has always been an issue of *popular* concern, not only for primitives, but for modern publics who—burdened with practical and familial concerns—are typically indifferent to non-practical explanatory theories. More particularly, why is it that people who would never describe themselves as "theorists" or "intellectuals" are willing to proselytize, hound, ostracize, or kill rather than see an explanatory theory of the universe's origin subject to question or rejection?

Why should an objective theory of origin—a putative assertion of *fact*—be enforced by demands for familial or ethnic loyalty—not to mention more than occasional torture and violence? Such behaviors are rare, to say the least, among the advocates of scientific, historical, or mathematical explanations. Economic and politic disputes at times resemble religious warfare, but that is because they directly propose a way of living. God's role as an *explanation* of existence no more directly entails a way of living than does the Big Bang theory of origin.

Surely, these behaviors suggest that Creation has a meaning far more important to its advocates than explaining how "existence" was *generated*.

Even if we allow that laypersons might have an interest in cosmic explanation, the manner in which Creation theory is maintained and acquired is unsuited to the life-determining implications drawn from it. Indeed, if Gallup's polling out of Princeton is to be believed, few theoretical problems are *easier* to solve than why anything exists![54]

People who would shrink from explaining the origin of continents, planets, or historical movements, do not hesitate when it comes to the origin of *everything*. Apparently, no problem of explanation requires less disciplined reflection than the problem of explaining the universe.

Nor is easy theorizing tolerated on the ground that no one really has the answer. Nine of ten people-on-the-street in America either know, or think it *rationally compelling* to believe, that a supernatural agency is responsible for there being anything at all.[55]

In addition to the foregoing *behavioral* anomalies, we find, within the pattern of argument, anomalies obvious enough to indicate that the motive is not *primarily* a search for truth. Specifically, when pressed to explain their belief in Creation, advocates will endorse *incompatible* means of arriving at belief.

Individual and institutions will say, on the one hand, that evidence and reason make belief in a creator *evident* or highly probable. They argue that "life is too *complex* to have occurred *unintentionally*," or "the universe can't possibly have existed without a beginning other than itself (hence, a supernatural "Creator"). Yet the same persons or institutions insist that, at bottom, belief in God is a matter of faith.

One cannot rationally adopt both approaches. If I believe a thing on evidence or on rationally compelling grounds, I cannot also believe it on faith. For, faith is possible only in the *absence* of knowledge or sufficient grounds.[56] To deny this is to ignore the meaning of the term *faith*. (The contention that *every* mode of inquiry—science included—rests, in the end, on faith is taken up in chapter 3.)

For example, we all recognize it would be *non*-sense to say, "Yes, here's my picture, my credit cards, my library card—this is my wallet all right. I believe it on faith." And one can only imagine a judge's bewilderment if an expert witness were to say, "your honor, the lab tests prove this is the murder weapon and, also, I believe it on faith."

It is in this respect that organized religions themselves court suspicion. While describing themselves as "faiths," they at the same time claim *knowledge* of God—citing the *evidence* of miracles, archeological finds, and *rationally compelling arguments* such as: "mind can only be created by another mind, not by matter" or "morality could only exist in 'nature' if a creator put it there."

This internally inconsistent pursuit of justifiable belief does not occur because believers are unintelligent. Rather, the self-contradicting character of these arguments is best explained by a quest for *meaning* more powerful than the quest for a *true* explanation.

What adds to dubiety of this avowedly *explanatory* quest is that, among scholars, it has long been settled that neither science nor philosophic argument can establish the existence of a first (or of a perpetually creating) cause of what exists.[57] Saint Anselm's "ontological proof," Thomas Aquinas' "five ways," and even Aristotle's "unmoved mover" are well understood to be brilliantly argued failures.

Creation, truth, and meaning

Although the idea of Creation no doubt begins in curiosity, it is not sustained by *curiosity*. What our analysis of Creation arguments hopes to make clear is that religion's aim is not to develop a *cosmology*—a history of the universe—but a *metaphysics*. That is, religion is less concerned with how the universe came to be than with what fundamental or unchangeable *kinds* of things exist ("metaphysics"). It wants to know whether such things as spirit, free will, responsibility, beauty, and goodness are *real*, not just imagined.

Religion's particular concern (to which all *Rethinking's* arguments speak) is with the ultimate reality of life's *normative* features. It is in fact ironic that a way of thinking that depends upon *supernaturalist* speculations should further the program of philosophic *realism* (the idea that physical and normative laws are real—that they exist independently of opinion and are genuinely given in experience). For the religious sensibility, the standards which guide our lives are not merely right "to us," or "right "to me," but right *in actuality*. (It is this struggle to know whether human life has a status beyond mere opinion that warrants saying, "religion is *seriousness*.")[58]

Small wonder such a vexing question—the question of normative reality—cannot be *argued* readily or even persuasively to a non-philosophic public. For, what people believe about normative reality in practice, they can be made to doubt upon reflection.

When we are in a moral situation, we seek and sometimes find the truth of obligation; when we are no longer in a moral situation we lose our grip on the moral force of such situations; the same is true with respect to physical laws, as our later discussions of David Hume will argue. Indeed, the cognitive importance of *the situation* was a great, if under-appreciated contribution of the American philosopher, John Dewey. In the domain of folk wisdom, the idea of the "ivory tower" expresses the disdain of those embroiled in everyday *situations* for those sequestered minds whose relative aloofness from practical demands allows them to doubt *without consequence*.

Once outside the moral context—and when not confronting art, fine literature, or great music—normative realities vanish like smoke.

In the abstract, normative "proofs" lose all rational basis. Given this and the contested character of "values," the idea that our guiding norms can have *independent* authority has no chance of being shown through philosophic reflection. They can be felt through preachment, art, tales of exemplary acts, and entry into moral situations such as charitable actions, but the contention—outside moral and aesthetic situations—that perhaps all our standards and ideals are "psychological" or "conventional" will gain converts as social and physiological sciences come increasingly to set the intellectual stage.

Nor is philosophy prepared for a rescue. Scientistic or "empirical" minds dominate professional philosophy. They, on the whole, emphatically reject the notion that goodness and rightness are real in any other way than *psychologically* or *socially*, that is, in being *imagined* real or else agreed upon. For them, norms and ideals lack the *testable*, practically determinable reality of physical properties. They are fictions or "constructions" that help control behavior.

For the most part, the job assumed by contemporary philosophy is that of being religion's chaperone, guarding it from exciting but misguided alliances with "ultimate" realities. Hence, no path to religiously significant meaning will come from quarters in which only what science can test should be called "real" and in which it is plausible to deny that knowledge is possible.

Thus, for popular religion—and for theologies self-separated from "philosophy"—arguments regarding life's meaning will lack the disciplining benefit of philosophic dialogue. It appears that the *philosophically* acceptable description of human life will continue to be that of scientific naturalism—an account inconsistent with the real, if problematically formulated, insights of religion.

In the absence of a reconstructed intellectual foundation, the truths proclaimed by religion will continue to be tethered less to evidence or reason—that is, to truth—and more to a vision of meaningful life that laudably, if imperfectly, it strives to secure.

The evidence that, in theism, truth is the handmaiden of meaning can perhaps best be gathered by traversing the path of its fundamental argument—the argument for an *absolute creation*.

CREATION: WILLIAM BARRETT'S "DEATH OF THE SOUL"

The late William Barrett's *Death of the* Soul argues for Creation along lines consonant with popular thought as well as traditional theology.[59] For that reason it is closer to commonplace religious con-

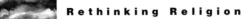

cern than more logically subtle, academic apologetics. In its conceptual ordinariness, Barrett's arguments signal what religion is authentically about (despite his claimed reliance on the seventeenth-century philosopher, Gottfried Leibniz).[60]

Barrett's work resembles our own in two respects. Like *Rethinking Religion*, it is aimed at the educated public. And, like this work, it is in great degree spurred by distress at the cultural ascension of scientism or "scientific materialism" which Barrett rightly describes as "the pervasive current that flows around all modern philosophizing."[61] (Barrett rejects, as we do, scientistic claims such as, "the mind is *really* the brain," "consciousness can be explained," or "morality is an evolutionary adaptation.")[62] Barrett's work differs from ours, however, in that its remedy for scientific naturalism develops within the confines of the dilemma: either theism or scientism.

Creation and the false dilemma

For Barrett our understanding of reality is either scientistic or theistic. We have a "scientifically" natural world with no *inherent* meaningfulness, or else a natural world that has meaning only *as a function* of God's will.

The dilemma is unjustifiable. It devalues the normative reality by which we live—seeking grounds outside the standards and conditions of value we find real in consequential activity.

This denial is particularly striking, since we do not daily "observe" God at work nor do we, daily, see people as mammals or as physiologically determined to speak and act. All the while, determining normative imperatives is something we do every day.

A world normatively understood is what we live and die for. Ordinary people do not find such standards to be matters of opinion. They understand them to be *real*, in the sense of having authority over even their own opinions. Standards are in that sense "independent" or "out there." Even those who die "for the tribe" or "our way of life" think it *in reality* good or obligatory to do so. They do not attribute the rightness of their duty to tribal opinion; tribal opinion must be "ancestrally" or "spiritually" *justified*.

A basic task of this book, throughout, is to build the case for understanding normative reality as real. At every turn we argue that the power to uncover—to be guided by and to further—that which is right and good *in reality* is what distinguishes a *human* way of "operating" (or what we prefer to describe as a human way of being-in-the-world").[63]

Rationality and truth need no proof

For most readers the question likely arises: "How can it be proven that standards of worthiness are real?" More exactly, "how can we *prove* that these normative standards and ideal states are *not* fictive—not 'subjective,' not 'personal,' not 'social'—but possessed of independent authority and therefore real?"

No argument, no conceptual proof, that objectivity is real is needed. The reason is that the demand for proof *presupposes* the existence of objective intellectual standards. If there were no standards independent of opinion, to request a *proof* would be (absurdly) to request an *opinion*.

The standard retort is that the term *proof*, when properly analyzed (that is, when understood in terms of its *behavioral* use) can be seen to mean "that opinion on which some reference group is agreed." Thus a scientific "proof" is simply an opinion on which scientists agree.

But this definition of "proof" bears no relation whatever to what we mean by a "proof." If, in actuality, we used this *consensus* criterion for "proof," a wildly successful scientific lie would—by definition—be a wildly successful proof. And if the lie were later discovered, it would, logically, *still* be true that a "proof" had been given! After all, consensus *had* been achieved and "proof" is *defined* as "the achieving of consensus."

(The philosophically inclined reader will appreciate the philosopher J. M. Findlay's critique of the idea that meaning is found in *use*.[64] The intentional meaning of a term like *proof* cannot be grasped simply by noticing its *use*. Our examples, above, of the absurdity that follows from doing so illustrate the wisdom of Findlay's counsel that when someone else is using language, the language cannot be understood "without a leap of understanding to match his leap." That is, without a grasp of what is *within*, "there can be no question of mastering the maze of his actual utterances.")[65]

Proof could not be distinguished from persuasion if there were no objective standards. Advertisements and scientific articles would have the same intellectual status. And if advertisements about drugs persuaded more people than scientific "findings" about drugs, then advertisements would have more "proof" than scientific findings.

So, rationality cannot possibly be *proven*. It is an ultimate—not because we are stumped but because we understand its status quite well. As Aristotle said in a similar vein, one cannot "seek proof of matters for which we already possess clearer evidence than any proof can afford."[66]

Looking back, what we have argued all along, and will continue to argue, is that *unless we are all profoundly self-deceived*, our actions and deliberations *must* be capable of determination by means of standards or norms whose reality—whose intellectual authority—we *discern* rather than (*necessarily*) invent.

The content of normative reality is learned not alone from teachers but from our own observations and insights. Though prophets, like Jesus, are said to bring absolute standards, the acceptance (and understanding) of the standards is as much or more a matter of seeing the moral truth in the parables as it is of accepting biblical authority. For instance, an archeologically authentic biblical manuscript in which Jesus approved of slavery would be judged apocryphal.

It is of the utmost religious significance that a normative reality exists. But for theists like Barrett, reality, whether normative or physical or simply "human"—cannot justifiably be considered *ultimate*. *Rethinking* says, "acting in the light of normative realties (the uniquely human way of being-in-the-world) is an ultimate fact of the universe." Traditional theism says it cannot be; norms must come from beyond us.

To this argument, we now turn.

The familiar argument for Creation

William Barrett's discussion of an ultimate origin is ostensibly an inquiry in pursuit of the truth. But because it is controlled by an interest in something other than explanation, his discussion proceeds ambiguously, beginning with an early appeal to evidence and logic, and shifting to what human beings *need*.

Rather lengthy quotations from his *Death of the Soul* (1986) are provided in order that theistic readers may identify with them and others find them familiar.

Early in his exposition, Barrett poses problems of *fact* and of *meaning* in a manner that fails to distinguish between them:

> "Why is there anything at all rather than nothing?" . . . is our root question. But this quest for a factual explanation quickly transmutes into a quest for meaning:
>
> It is the question of questions, says Heidegger, the existentialist, who . . . lets it lurk broodingly in the background but never comes to grips with it.[67]
>
> The question permeates more of our ordinary life than the average person is aware of. It is there in our ordinary moods

even when it is not intellectually articulated. In a moment of personal confusion or discontent, for example, we may catch a flash of our whole life and murmur, *"Why was I ever born?"* And in that movement our uneasiness may invest our whole world: *why this world, or for that matter, any world at all?* Our moods are often more total and metaphysical than we like to think [emphases added].[68]

We confront two ambiguities. The first is the ambiguity of *purpose* to which we just alluded: Are we seeking to explain existence as a fact, or are we seeking to establish that human life is meaningful?

The second is an ambiguity of *subject matter*: Barrett sets out, explicitly, to explain why there is "anything at all." But the *subject* of his explanation changes. Instead of "anything at all" (let us say, "Existence") the subject of explanation becomes *ourselves*, our *whole world*, *this world* which (even when considered together) is *less* than "anything-at-all." For example, it leaves out other worlds—most notably the supernatural "world" of God.

The shift of subject is important: If we must explain the existence of *anything-at-all*, we will face the confounding problem of explaining Existence on the basis of *nothing*. And If we realize we are trying to explain something when all we have is nothing, it is likely we will balk out of the gate.

Thus we must be, as it were, *eased* into accepting, "what might explain the existence of anything-at-all?" as a reasonable question.

The "problem" of an eternal universe

And so Barrett continues his argument in a manner familiar to us, explaining, at first, *not* "anything at all" but rather "this world"—the world we know. Echoing scholastic argument, he prepares us to find "natural" explanations wanting. He reminds us, firstly, that in "this world" things depend for their existence on something else. To wit:

All the things in nature that we know of are *contingent*. Animals are begotten, born and die; sun and moon and stars come into being through natural causes and may perish; the hills . . . are brought into existence by geological convulsions and . . . can be eroded away.

Having thus applied to "this world" the familiar rule that "everything has a cause," Barrett now enlarges his subject. Suddenly we are not talking about this world. We are talking about "anything-at all—a shift achieved" by of using abstract placeholders—letters, like "A" and "B," instead of trees and mountains:

Let us begin . . . with any particular contingent being. As contingent, *A* will have a cause external to itself, *B*. *B* in turn is produced by *C*. Etc., etc. Does the chain go on endlessly or does it have a first link, a first cause? Let us not make things easier for ourselves; let us suppose that there is no first link, that the chain is infinite.[69] But this infinite chain itself? What of it? Each link . . . is contingent . . . and thus the whole chain is itself a contingent fact.[70]

So, accepting the rule "everything has a cause" and now applying it, not to particular things, but to *everything-taken-together* ("anything at all"), we suddenly find that our normal way of explaining things has hit a wall. A world of *caused* ("contingent") things recedes endlessly into the past with no possible point of beginning. "And so we could go from chain to chain, and so on and so forth. Let us then imagine an infinite number of infinite chains. Where do we now stand? We are left with our original mystery."

Apparently the normal mode of explaining why mountains or oceans exist is *incompetent* when it comes to the "big question" of *existence*.

Why does anything at all exist? Why do all those chains, infinite upon infinite, exist at all? So long as we remain within the realm of contingent being [the world of causation], we go from link to link and chain to chain but never find an answer to the mystery of existence. Scientific explanation can only go from particular link to particular link; it can never deal with the whole [never explain why there is "anything at all"].

And so, it would appear, the limitations of physical science are exposed! After all, it can't explain where the Big Bang's matter or energy came from (a favorite argument of popular theology.) The "mystery" of existence remains.

Barrett's theistic stage is set. If there are only two approaches to explaining why things are the way they are (theism and scientific naturalism), the failure of causal explanation (scientific naturalism) means we must turn to theistic explanation.

Science falsely found wanting

Let us pause to agree it is impossible to imagine (picture, feel) things going back into time *forever*. To attempt it is to court a bad headache. But this hardly means we must seek a cause that science cannot deliver—for there is much that is true that we cannot possibly *picture*. We can imagine our death but not *being* dead; we cannot imagine the pistons in a combustion engine altering direction 180 degrees 120 times every second at 6000 rpm; we can calculate, but not *imagine*, four billion years. Yet all these things are true.

Setting aside the stress of "picturing" eternity, it is simply not true that when things are caused by other things, the resulting chain of causation *must*—as a matter of logic or conceptual consistency— come to an end. There need not be a "first cause" (a cause that is not itself caused)—or what Aristotle called an "unmoved mover." Barrett's "problem" of the endless chain of endless chains is a pseudo-problem, despite the difficulty of "seeing" it go back in time forever![71]

C. B. Martin attempted to dissolve the "problem" in his book, *Religious Belief*:

> The place to begin an infinite series [into] the future is any moment you choose after the present. The place to begin an infinite series [into] the past is any moment you choose before the present. In neither case would the series be concluded. There is no more difficulty in the idea of an infinite number of past things or happenings than in the idea of an infinite number of future things or happenings. The alternative is to say that at some time in the past things *must* start and at some time in the future things *must* stop.[72]

In short, those who find no logical barrier to supposing that an existence called "heaven" can go on forever cannot with consistency find it logically impossible that an existence called "the universe" has *gone on* forever. Infinity forward and infinity backward differ in direction, not logical difficulty. Believers ought note that they themselves do not find it impossible that heaven and God have both always existed, *sans* beginning and *sans* end.

Succinctly, then: the idea of an infinite series of causes is not self-contradictory. Hence, it does not require that an uncaused cause be inserted at a "beginning" to *render it consistent*.

Conflating causation and existence

If the reader feels there is a loose end somewhere in the Creation argument, the reader's discomfort is well-founded.

The situation in which the existence of mountains and trees (and all other contingent things) is explained by citing prior causes is one of explaining *the particular forms* existence takes. It is about how one sort of thing accounts for another sort of thing. It is *never* a problem of explaining why there are "things" in the first place; that is, it is never the problem of explaining *existence* itself (why there is *anything at all*).

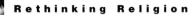

In sum: why things have the properties they do is one subject; why there are any properties at all is another subject. The search for "the first cause" conflates the two.

The simple fact is that if we explain the existence of a thing by referring to a *cause*, we *assume* that something exists or has existed—namely, the *cause*. Since a *causal* (typically, a *scientific*) explanation *assumes* something exists, *a causal explanation* cannot possibly explain how anything-at-all exists. It can't get us from nothing to something.

Therefore the "failure" of scientific or any other causal explanation to explain *existence* (the existence of *something* rather than *nothing-at-all*) is no failure but a necessary aspect of the "causal" form of explanation.

If we explain why a tree exists, we make reference to soil, to chemicals, to the sun, to photosynthesis, and so on. We *never* explain a tree or a mountain or anything else by saying "well, there was *nothing*, and then there was soil and sun and evolutionary history and then a tree."

The conflation of causal dependence and absolute existence, as in Barrett's "the hills . . . are brought into *existence* by . . . [something]" is very common. Richard Purtill's version of it (in *Thinking About Religion*) says such things as that "my *existence*, depends, for example, on the *existence* of my parents, and so on. . .[emphasis added]." It is a way of speaking that suggests our causal explanations *explain* existence rather than *assume* existence. He then accuses causal explanations of insufficiency (failure to explain existence). Science is lacking because, ". . .the series must have a beginning." What sort of a beginning? Plainly, "a thing which exists whether or not anything else exists. . . . a *necessary* being."[73] (The "necessary being" is, of course, God.)

Only by conflating the search for causes with the search for "existence" does Purtill's argument against the sufficiency of scientific or causal explanation gain any purchase on credibility. For, it would be absurd to say, "to be caused is to be caused by something else, now tell me how something is caused when there is nothing else." And that is precisely the question people ask when they ask, "why is there anything at all?" *The very form of the Creation question*, not its difficulty, *is what makes an answer impossible.*

Creation cannot succeed as an explanatory theory

We have so far not drawn all that may be instructive from Barrett's rule for rational explanation. The rule he uses is a "principle" drawn, he says, from Leibniz.

Leibniz begins . . . with this simple and familiar idea of contingent being, to which he adds an axiom, *the principle of sufficient reason. . . .* This principle states that *there is no fact without a sufficient reason why it exists and is so rather than otherwise* [emphasis added]. The principle. . . . states *the ordinary procedures of our mind* when we encounter any particular fact in the world. We ask for a cause or an explanation; *we would not be satisfied if told flatly there is no cause or reason, it just happens to be the case* [emphases added].

We have seen how the rule, "everything has a *cause*" assumes existence and cannot, therefore explain it. Here Barrett introduces a different rule for explanation, "everything has an (sufficient) *explanation*" It is different because an "explanation" need not be *causal*.

According to this "Leibnizian" rule, it is rational, always, to think something has an explanatory reason. The crucial implication is, as Barrett concludes, that it is *never* rational to say explanation does not apply—to say: "this is something that just happens to be the case."[74]

Since the scientific arm of the dilemma has "failed" to explain why anything at all exists, and since "the ordinary procedures of our mind" tell us, with Leibniz and Barrett, that *everything has an explanation*, it *must be* that existence has an explanation—and all we have left is *supernatural* agency or "God."

(It is worth pausing to sound, again, a general caution regarding how subtly these sorts of arguments proceed. Barrett has claimed that the principle of sufficient reason merely states "the ordinary procedures of our mind." This is appropriate counsel when our problems are *ordinary*—as in explaining a fire or an illness. But when we are explaining "the existence of anything at all" our subject is anything but ordinary. Indeed, it is absolutely singular. One cannot *assume*, as Barrett does, that ordinary procedures of explanation will fit extraordinary cases.)

But the insuperable problem remains. Once you gather *everything* that exists or has ever existed into a bundle called "that-which-must-be-explained," you have nothing left by which to explain it. Therefore, the only answer to "why there is anything at all" has, at some point, to be "that's just the way it is."

Indeed, unless it is legitimate *at some point* to say, "that's just the way it is," then nothing can be deemed ultimate. By definition, whatever is *ultimate* has nothing behind it that explains why it is the way it is (why it operates, behaves, appears the way it does). No doubt most people find no intellectual peace in the idea that our existence

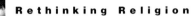

"just happen to be the way it is." We balk at the suggestion that there is no further cause or reason for our existing in the fraught way we do. It will, however, be a main argument of later pages that, when properly understood, "the way it is" *can* be understood as religiously fundamental.

Rethinking's attempt to do this is not religiously incoherent, because the same attempt is made with respect to God as an ultimate fact. God is not to be explained by something else. God therefore "just happens to be." Yet God is portrayed by theology *in such a way* as to negate the accidental (if not pedestrian) quality of "just being there."

As we shall see, theology rejects the description of God as "just happening to be" by arguing that God's "being there" is a matter of *necessity*, not happenstance. God will be described as the "necessary being." For, *without the aura of rightness, oughtness, or propriety that the notion of necessity carries*, God would have (at best) cosmologically explanatory value but not religiously significant value.

Before engaging the topic of "necessary being," we must address the Creation theory that argues God is implied by something more than the existence of stuff. This is the theory that God is entailed by an orderly, or intelligibly patterned, universe. This theory, lately famous as the theory of "intelligent design," has the additional virtue of assigning *reason* as well as power to God. It thus gives *normative* credentials to God, making God the *rightful ruler* by virtue of possessing the greatest mind.

Creation as intelligent design

Although Richard Purtill defends some of the Creation arguments that purport to explain *existence*, he is not entirely comfortable with them. He allows that, logically speaking, the stuff of existence—its "materiality"—might always have existed.

What he argues is that the universe has order and that its being orderly is best explained by the existence of an intelligent, absolute creator.

Purtill says that any "chance" explanation of the universe's order implies that what we call "physical laws" could change any minute. He argues, also, that the opposite idea—that there are "natural necessities" (physical laws of connection)—is tantamount to finding "messages" in nature that we have no reason to suppose are there.[75]

But the spine of his argument is that a scientifically "understandable" universe is impossible without an orderly universe and that there is no good explanation of such orderliness other than its intentional creation by a supreme creator. The problem for this argument is that there is a good explanation for orderliness and no good explanation for Purtill's "intelligent creator" hypothesis.

Consider, firstly, that we cannot have a notion of "stuff" or "materiality" that has absolutely no properties. (Purtill offers no evidence or reason why we should treat eternally existing materiality as stuff with *no* properties.) Despite Purtill's abstract talk of "stuff" existing, whatever exists exists *in some way* or *form* (as Aristotle long ago observed). A thing with no properties is no thing at all. (Even when we try to conceive of "nothing," we tend to imagine it as a great space, and space has the property of dimensionality.)

Now, having properties entails that whatever has them can operate one way but not another way. If mass has gravity, it cannot but be drawn to other specimens of mass. If variously sized stones fall into a rapidly flowing stream, the effect of gravity will "sort them out" so that the heavier are deposited first and the less heavy later, forming a "perfect order" of stones graded in a line from heavy to light. Without belaboring the point, properties have implications for how one thing can relate to another, just as the properties we assign to chess pieces allow some things to happen but not others.

For example, if one fills a box randomly with paper clips, pencils, balls, sticks, bit of material and so on and then turns it over smartly on a table top, slowly lifting the box from the contents beneath, one will discover a marvelous *order* in which a stick will be held in a place where *it could only be* if a paper clip was in the place it happens to be, and the light bulb will be supported by a marble and a strip of wood which, if they did not occupy the *exact* position they do, the bulb would roll onto the desktop and onto the floor. Surely these relationships were designed!

So, the very idea of *materiality* implies properties, and properties imply order of various kinds. The fact that there are relatively stable things entails stable properties exist over time. As things collide or interact, they do so in ways determined by the possibilities implicit in their properties. What results from their interactions is therefore not just a matter of "chance." Purtill acknowledges that stuff may have always existed. What he does not see is that if there is stuff, then, inevitably, a pattern or patterns of interaction will be formed ("order").

It is true that the *exquisiteness* or *complexity* of the orders we find often strike us as incredible (our own bodies, for example). Those who do not study the *details* of biological evolution cannot conceive how intricate patterns of body and behavior can be produced with-

out intention. But ignorance and amazement are no basis for metaphysics.

What we have then, are two lines of explanation. One is a matter of knowledge, the other of speculation.

We know that in the natural world orderliness results from the interaction of properties; we see a vast variety of orderly patterns produced by properties every day. The supreme Creator explanation, by contrast, is devoid of *evidence*—daily or otherwise. Given what we *know* about stuff and its properties, an intelligent creator is *unnecessary* to explain physical order.

Since we all know that properties entail patterns or "order," the argument for intelligent design has to maintain that *properties* cannot be explained except by an intelligent creator. But because there is no possible separation between creating the "existence" of things and creating "properties," the argument that God creates the properties we see as "order" reduces to an explanation of *existence*. Thus, the argument for intelligent design is but a version, one step removed, of the simpler claim that God explains the existence of *anything at all*.

Why God is ultimate

Now we turn from the argument that God can and must explain existence to the problem generated by theism's answer. As theism's *ultimate* fact, God's existence cannot depend on something that is *not* God. God's existence cannot be explained. The problem for theism lies in having to say that God "just happens to be." The abstractness, the arbitrariness, of saying "God happens to be" represents a *departure from awe* not consistent with the religious sensibility. (For the theistic sensibility, a universe that *just happens to exist* is—an "accident!")

To be religiously foundational, it will have to be seen that God is not simply an ultimate fact but that his being ultimate is, in some sense, *right*. (Religion aims, as we have said, to disclose a *normative* reality.) God's position, like that of an earthly monarch, has to be more than a matter of *de facto* power; it has to be *lawful*. Either God is the expression of a normative reality or God is just as much a *thing* as the "Big Bang." (We see this in the complaint that our existence can't be "an accident"—can't just be "the way it is.")

So, God's existence has now to have a *reason* of some kind. But, of course, no such reason is possible. The very meaning of "ultimate" entails that what is ultimate *cannot* be explained. So, if a reason for an absolute creator-God's existence is given, the argument that offers it must be self-contradictory.

The self-contradictoriness of God's necessity

The traditional way to claim God is ultimate (and cannot be explained by something else) is to say that it is God's very *nature* to exist, or "God's existence is *necessary* (it *has to be*), so that "God is the necessary being."

The phrase *a necessary being* represents the kind of linguistic adventuring against which we cautioned in Chapter 1. We have no deep sense, if we have any at all, of what is being said. When Purtill's book introduces it, he says "a necessary being is a being which always exists whether anything else exists or not."[76] But this definition allows a universe of eternal "stuff"—perhaps "ultimate particles"—to qualify as a necessary being.

Purtill disagrees, contending that

> the material universe is just a collection of things, none of which is necessary, [and] the property of always existing whether or not anything else exists is not the sort of property which can be reached by simply adding things together which lack this property. . . . we cannot get a thing that is transparent by adding together lots of things that are not transparent.[77]

The reader may recall that we have already dealt with the conflating of "things" and "existence" in which the "existence" of a particular *form* or *thing* (a tree, a cloud) is conflated with the existence of the *material* from which it is formed (stuff, energy, subatomic particles, or whatever).

We have reason, therefore, to say that *things* are "dependent" on other things for *their particular character*, but no reason, on that account, to declare that the stuff of which characteristics are made is "dependent" or "cannot exist *by itself*." (Indeed, there can be an *eternal collection* of changing things.)

Purtill says a necessary thing (which for him is God only) is something that "exists whether or not anything else exists." But this equates *necessary* existence with *solitary eternal* existence—"always existing and alone." (Of course Purtill has already said "stuff" could have always existed while not calling stuff "God" or "necessary being.") Here, the point is that there is no reason to declare what happens to exist by itself "necessary." *Indeed there could not be.*

For, if existing by "necessity" is to be more than just another *name for* "existing by itself," it has to *explain* a thing's existing eternally by itself. And to explain it, it must refer to something *independent* of it. So if "necessity" actually *explains* anything, one can no

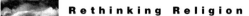

longer say of that which it explains that "it exists whether or not any-thing else exists," since there has to be a "something else"—a law of nature, perhaps—that would have to exist to make its existence *neces-sary*. And this is the self-contradiction we foretold when we stated that an "ultimate" cannot be explained without self-contradiction.[78]

Nor does it save the matter to say necessity is *part of* God (is God's "nature") and not "independent" of God. *Why* God can exist eternally is an entirely separate task of explanation—and those who claim to have answered the question are the least entitled to an answer, since it is they who insist on God's (humanly) *unfathomable* status.

Moreover, the foregoing argument still applies. If God's existence *can* be explained by his *nature*, then there is something *fixed* about God (not up to God) which means God was accorded a nature by some other, and thus greater, power.

But in the end, the movement from talk about God existing self-sufficiently to talk of *self-sufficient existence* being God's "nature" is empty. For to say something (anything) exists "eternally and self-suf-ficiently" is in fact to state its "nature." It's nature is not something extra—something more than "existing eternally and sef-sufficently."

To see this, one has only to try denying it. Try saying, "God exists eternally and self-sufficently but it is *not* in God's nature to exist." It makes no sense. It is self-contradictory to say this because some-thing's existing self-sufficiently eternally *is* its nature. How could it exist by itself if self-existence were *not* in its nature? So, explanation by God's nature is a verbal self-deception. Only if "by his nature" one really means by *necessity* is the emptiness averted. But we have al-ready dealt with this as positing a power beyond God.

God's "necessity" as God's legitimacy

When Richard Purtill faces the question "who made God?" he says that "if God is a necessary being, the question has no point: No one made God. He always existed and always will, no matter what else does or does not exist."[79]

We have already criticized the claim of "necessary being." What we here suggest is that the rhetoric of *necessity* lends God a kind of ex-istential legitimacy. Rather than merely existing in the manner of an accident—a pointless fact—God *had to* exist. God's existence is *right-ful*, either the way a law of nature is the way things *must be* or the way a moral law determines what *ought* to be. God's "necessity" functions here to turn us away from the purely factual question—why is there anything at all?—that was the justification for Creation theory *in the first place*.

The rule that "everything has a cause" or "exists for a reason" is the rule that made it seem *necessary* to posit a God. If this is a *required* rule of factual reasoning, then, since it is *we* who continue to reason (and not God), it is incumbent upon us to continue reasoning as we ought. So, if we cannot leave the universe unexplained, we cannot leave God's ultimate position unexplained.

Of course, what the refusal to explain God causally (in any normal sense) indicates is that God's factual existence is not as important as God's rightfulness or authoritativeness (his *necessariness*). And this, we shall argue, is because God's mysterious presence satisfies conditions such as the reality of miracle and of the right and good, that lie within the religious impulse.

All *factual* arguments to the effect that God is a special case suffer from the fact that there is no *independent* evidence for the existence of such a special case. Even the "evidence" that our world is beautiful, sustaining (so far), and unimaginably complex not only fails to establish a Grand Designer, but, even if that were what it rightly signified, all we would have is a designer or shaper, not an absolute Creator.

So far, we have no reason for concluding that there exists a Being whose nature is ultimate and whose *intent* or *will* directly created "Existence" or "the world we know" (etc.) Perhaps even more to the point, the difficulties of coherently describing what *sort* of being theism posits make it implausible to conclude that people believe a creator-god exists because the hypothesis of such a being constitutes a satisfactory cosmological (factual) explanation of Existence.

The turn to faith

As the intellectual difficulties accumulate, many turn from argument to *faith* to secure the meaning God supplies. From them we ask forbearance and ask them to consider, in support of this request, whether faith should exempt one from argument.

Faith, after all, is a *choice*. (If not, it can't be a virtue.) It is an act, and as an act, is as much subject to moral responsibility as any other human act. In short, faith must be responsible.

Indeed we have seen irresponsible faith—in the Middle Ages, in the time of slavery, and in the vengeful faiths of our own era. And, as noted earlier, if faith were self-justifying (even when deeply felt and behaviorally expressed) then traditional religions could not criticize faith born of cults and false prophets. For mainstream religions, the unbreakable *faith* of the cult member is precisely what harms them. Who of faith, then, can presume immunity from critical inquiry?

We have pointed out that if the universe has always existed and will always exist, then it could rightly be said that it "does not owe its existence to anything or anyone outside itself, nor does it need anything beyond itself to maintain its existence"; it is simply "its nature to exist"—all things commonly said of God (as if they could *only* be said of a god).

Nor can one defend a preference for God's ultimate status rather than the ultimate status of the universe because "some things are beyond the human mind's power to explain." For, one has already *used that mind* to think it makes sense to explain everything-taken-together and to claim there exists an unfathomable being who created all existence as well as himself and is concerned for our souls. (We later take up the retort that all this is *revealed* apart from any use of the human mind.)

Indeed, the frequency (in the writer's experience) with which the *mind's incompetence* is invoked to end arguments about what that same "incompetent" mind has *already claimed* about God only reinforces our view that Creation is not an attempt to know the factual truth but a determination to quench the thirst for meaningfulness.

Creation as the search for meaning

In light of "Creation's" explanatory difficulties, it is not surprising that Barrett gives up on *theory* and turns instead to affirmation—to faith. There will be no "first cause"; Barrett finally concedes that, yes, the universe may well have existed forever. He therefore faces the option of atheism, and it is here that we see what has motivated the entire exercise:

> 1. We can say there is no reason. But if we choose this reason we cannot do so in the style of the cavalier or superficial atheist who does not pause for a moment at the enormity he is accepting. For it is an enormity; we do not say elsewhere, of any particular fact, that there is no explanatory cause or reason, the fact just simply happens to be there; but in this case, confronted by the most enormous fact of all, the universe, we would be willing to say it just happens to be there.[80] We need to have the intellectual imagination of a Nietzsche to grasp how audacious and staggering is the hypothesis of atheism. For if we say the world is without a reason, then it becomes absurd, and the whole of existence, and we along with it, absurd. We have then to accept the absurdity of life, as some of the existentialists have spoken of it, and learn to live with that absurdity.[81]

Still, there is no logical impossibility in the atheist alternative; and we can accept it without logical contradiction, however our habits and our instincts may rebel against it. Creation is now to be believed not because, as theory, it follows from argument or evidence but because, without Creation, existence is "absurd."

Barrett's sentiment is not unusual. Friedrich Nietzsche famously cast a pall over Western culture when he repeated the claim that "God is dead." In *The Gay Science*, his "madman" (Nietzsche himself) begged to know "whither are we moving now? Away from all suns? Are we not perpetually falling? . . . Are we not straying as through an infinite nothing? Do we not feel the breath of empty space?"[82] But *unhappiness over absurdity* (or over Nietzsche's nothingness) is not a problem of *truth*—unless one defines "truth" pragmatically so that untruth is what pains us and truth whatever "works" or "satisfies."[83]

Still, suppose existence were absurd. Would it be *religious* to say "God exists" to make oneself feel better? Is God the instrument of our desires? Surely it is irreligious to say "I will worship whatever makes me feel my life is meaningful." On that rule, adults could believe in deities just as children believe in imaginary friends (without the guilelessness that excuses the young).

Barrett's philosophical train has left the rails. We are not to *conclude* at all. We are, instead, to *affirm*.

> 2. We can affirm that there is a reason or cause why all those chains of being exist. But if we make this *choice*, we have to step outside of the realm of contingent beings. So long as we remain within the sequence of contingent beings, there is no sufficient reason why the whole exists [emphasis added].[84]

This is a pragmatic argument; that is, we are to believe a proposition because we find it useful or advantageous—practical—to do so. But a pragmatic solution to a meaningless existence promises a religious tragedy of Faustian proportions. For what we wish to believe or need to believe will be haunted, always, by the question of truth as surely as it haunted Dostoevsky's student-murderer, Raskolnikov, who could not escape the truth of his guilt.

Truth cannot be held at bay forever. Over time, God can remediate meaninglessness if, and only if, God *in truth*, exists—and Barrett is dogged by the need for truth. For what reason, other than the need for *truth*, did Barrett take care to develop *detailed arguments* as to how it is God must exist?

Why, if God is a matter of *affirmation*, does he bother to insist on arcane factual claims such as that "we have to posit a being *of another order, a necessary being, the ground of whose existence lies not in another or others but in itself* [emphasis added]. And this necessary being will be what, on the level of faith and worship, the religious consciousness has called God."[85]

If truth is no issue, if a world lost to reason is to be regained by affirmation—that is by faith or *will*—then perhaps God requires no explanation. We can say, as many do, that God is simply inscrutable ("we can say what God is not, but not what God is") and that although we have no idea how God eternally exists, belief in God gives us meaning. But the burden of affirming (rather than concluding) that there is God can never be put down. For, as H. H. Farmer warned, we cannot live thinking we made God up; then we not only admit existence has no meaning but to this wasteland we add our own self-deceit in an effort to imagine it wonderful.[86]

Creation versus absurdity

Barrett claims that without a creator (an explanatory reason, or a cause for its being), existence is "absurd" and we along with it "absurd." The claim is familiar, being implicit in "we (or the universe) couldn't have happened *by accident!*"—an oft-repeated plaint that suggests any Existence that is unintended would simply be absurd.

But the term *accident* means a "chance happening," typically one that is sudden. Its use here (and abundantly, elsewhere) is, therefore, tendentious. For if the universe has always existed, calling its existence an "accident" (because *unintended*) is as inappropriate as calling the Grand Canyon "an accident" and "absurd" (because not intentionally made) or the erosion of the Allegheny mountains "an accident" and thus an absurdity. The doctor does not say to us, "You've had a nasty accident—arthritis." To call either the universe or an evolved human existence "an accident" is to misuse the English language in order to imply that reality would be absurd were it not a purposeful creation.

There is surely a hint of truth in "a world without a reason is absurd" and there is a sense, (to be later explicated) in which reasons and "the world" do have some deep connection, but if the universe has always existed, its existence is a fact—a mystery perhaps, but not an absurdity.

One sometimes hears that human life cannot have occurred by "chance." This, like "by accident," is a tendentious descriptive to apply to a lengthy chain of evolutionary interactions. The evolutionary process depends in important ways on chance occurrences (climactic and otherwise) to be sure, but the appearance of *Homo Sapiens*

Sapiens did not happen by chance any more than the orbits of the planets are what they are by chance—by tumbling into place like dice at a gaming table.

In fact, we call conditions, actions, and things "absurd" only when there *already exist* good and sufficient reasons for their properly being some other way. If a normal twenty year old has a face-lift it is "without reason" and "absurd." This is because, *normally,* there exist good and sufficient reasons for not doing it. Absurdity *presupposes* the existence of standards of what is appropriate or sensible.

A crudely painted, cliché-ridden picture hanging in a great museum would be absurd given the standards of museums and fine art. If no such standards existed, it would not be *absurd* to hang such a picture in the Louvre.[87] Finally, consider that, to be absurd, a remark must contravene the standards of sense, decency, or utility that are pertinent in a given setting of discourse. It may be odd, *but not absurd,* to make a remark "for no reason."

It follows that existence without an explanation or reason is absurd if and only if the way existences *normally* come to exist is in accordance with certain standards or reasons. But as David Hume famously pointed out, we have no experience of universes coming into being. There are no standards for the existence of universes. There is simply no reason why the absence of a prior reason for existence is inherently senseless or absurd—unless we reason in a circular way and just *assume* Creation normally happens. Rejecting absurdity, does not, however, deny that existence (rather than *nothing*) is, when confronted as root fact, capable of *stunning* us.

God's meaning as purpose

The difference between God as (cosmological) *cause* and God as *Creator* lies in the element of purpose. If God were a mindless force that produced a universe, God would be very like a "Big Bang" and would, like that hypothesized event, have no religious significance whatever. This would be true even if the Big Bang (somehow!) "created itself" or existed "by its very nature."

What we need to determine is whether an Existence or "universe" that is created on purpose *necessarily* acquires religious significance (as distinct from, say, magical significance).

(It should be mentioned that we omit a description of the way purposive explanation *prohibits* explanation by causes—why if something is done for a purpose then it is not caused. A definitive comparison of purposive and causal explanation may be found in Charles Taylor's *The Explanation of Behavior*.)[88]

Mere purpose

Suppose Barrett could prove our world was produced by an agent for a purpose that remains unknown. Would life then have meaning?

Would it be meaningful, if you lived knowing you were created on purpose but had no idea what the purpose was? Surely, the situation is absurd—even Kafkaesque. Therefore, even if Barrett could prove that a creator had some purpose for producing our world, our world would not *necessarily* be meaningful.

Irreligious purpose

Suppose we did know the purpose for which "X" or God created the world. Would our existence then be meaningful?

Just suppose, as Bertrand Russell and Anatole France have fantasized, a creator produced our world as a minor amusement Or, suppose creation was accomplished to enjoy our puzzlement, or our pain, or our fear. Now it becomes absurd to live it out because one cannot meaningfully live out a humiliation. Life has meaning, but a demeaning or dreadful meaning, which is not what we mean by "meaningful." There would be less *point* to living such a life than if existence were a fact—"without a reason."

Thus creation may have a purpose yet lack recognizably *religious* significance. Purposive creation of the sorts described might yield a mystery, but nothing sacred and or spiritually significant in the living of it. If there is awe, it would be only at unfathomable power—the demonic not the divine.

We can conclude that neither the existence of a supernatural creator with an unknown purpose, nor a supernatural creator with a known purpose, nor a supernatural creator with an unacceptable purpose would establish that life is meaningful or *should* exist.

It is mistaken to claim that "if a creator exists life is meaningful" or even that the existence of a supernatural agent or world gives *religious significance* or ultimate meaning to an otherwise purely secular world. Hence, unfathomable creative power, or unfathomable, creative, purposeful power are neither one sufficient to account for God's *religious* meaning.

God's meaning as dependent on prior meaning

By now, Barrett and like-minded theists may be aching to protest that "God would never have created existence inadvertently, indifferently, or to torture us, or to amuse himself. *That* is an idea we would call absurd!"

But it is *they* who find existence or "life" to be, in and of itself, meaningless (God being necessary for meaning). And to argue, then, that a life *in itself* meaningless or pointless must have been created by a well-intentioned God is like finding a book of meaningless scrawls and concluding that it must have an author who is wise and benign.

Others will deny the analogy. They will say, "looking at life is like finding a book of poetry, truth, and genuine morality and then inferring the magnificence of its author."

But this contention requires that we *first* find life meaningful or wonderful; life must be meaningful *in itself* or we could make no inference from it to a wise, creative, or loving source. It therefore defeats the argument that "life can be meaningful only if we know or suppose it was intentionally created."

To press the idea of independent meaningfulness: were fragments of a manuscript to fall, accidentally, into a highly poetic order, the poetic result might be meaningful, even beautiful, without the poem ever having been authored.

God's meaning—as religion's foundational object (not as a mere power or unfathomable maker)—appears, then, to derive from the values and goods we discern in existence as we find it.

Even though Immanuel Kant advanced a rather special "transcendent" argument for God, he grounded it in our own knowledge of morality, insisting that "even the Holy One of the gospel must first be compared with our idea of moral perfection *before* he is recognized as such [emphasis added]."[89]

For Kant, the concept of "God as the highest good" came "solely from the idea of moral perfection, which reason forms *a priori*."[90] Here, the reader might usefully revisit the question whether a God who hurt us or demeaned us or ignored us would, be an object of religious contemplation (much less worship). To find oneself saying "no" is to think in the manner Kant said we do, for one will have used one's idea of goodness or worthiness as a condition for assigning "divinity."

On the other side of the argument stand statements by Michael Novak, who tells us that "the reason for God's choices are beyond legitimate inquiry, in our present state. For we can know that God exists but not what he is like; we cannot read his mind, nor take a superior point of view"[91]

God's inscrutability is popular. The celebrity conservative religionist, James Dobson also dismisses our power to comprehend the mind or "plan" of God. In a book that declares our permanent intellectual abjectness (*When God Doesn't Make Sense)*, Dobson rubs it in with a chapter titled, "God Makes Sense Even When He Doesn't Make Sense," in which he rhetorically asks "if human intelligence and perception are undependable in assessing everyday reality . . . how much less capable is it [sic] of evaluating the unfathomable God of the Universe?"[92]

On views such as these, nothing we know of life can indicate what God is like or wants. That is why Novak (the serious thinker of the two) can "excuse"—nay, *extol*—the existence of pain and evil as showing very well that God's mind or intent is entirely outside our grasp.[93] We cannot possibly say God's existence makes life meaningful because we know nothing of God's intentions or "reasons."

His position must somehow explain how a God whose mind is unknowable, unfathomable (and therefore whose "character" or "personality" is unknowable, unfathomable) can function for us as the other side of a *relationship*, that is, be enough of a knowable *self* to permit an emotional, "personal," or guiding relationship.

In particular (and by way of example), we must ask how Novak knows not simply that God exists but that "one cannot please God by acting contrary to one's reflective, open conscience."[94] For, despite God's purported opacity, Novak's *Belief and Unbelief* has much say about what we ought to do in view of God's existence!

The answer illustrates the point we reiterate, which is that the meaningfulness of life is derived from what we find in life and supplies the criterion of what is divine—of what God wants or is—and not *vice-versa*. For, Novak's argument that God (credibly) exists and that God (credibly) has a certain character is based on what he finds important in human experience. To wit:

Novak focuses on the fact that humans have the power to understand what is independently the case, e.g., what is "real," and that, in addition, they have a powerful urge to do so. Hence, "our drive to understand is in harmony with the real" and "the real is the intelligible"[95] But, Novak, says, "without an intelligent source, the intelligibility of the real is a mere accident and hence unintelligible."[96]

Several things are apparent. Novak finds inquiry into the truth or "understanding" of the world to be, in his experience, immensely meaningful. Moreover, this capacity to understand would be less than wonderful if the world itself were dull and meaningless. Thus what becomes foundational is the presence in our experience of life's meaningfulness. But, alas, there comes the familiar false choice. Either a world that is intelligible for humans is "an accident" (indeed, a *"mere"* accident) or it is the intention of an external intelligence.

Again a false, indeed, tendentious, dichotomy leads to and justifies the existence of a creator.

The possibility that life in this world may be just what it seems—a wonderful and unaccountable (because ultimate) reality and thus a miraculous and holy union with existence—is out of the question."[97]

The way we develop our conception of God derives, as we have said, from what we have found, through experience and reflection, to be "good, true, and beautiful." Indeed, Novak elsewhere echoes our case when he argues that "to say God is good . . . is to say that he is the source of honesty, friendship and creativity. . . . "[98] Here, God's very worth is measured in terms of the earthly goods we know. Once again we confront the meaningful book whose glory is transferred to its putative author.

We acknowledge that many people claim life becomes more meaningful for them when they think of it as created. As the last section of this chapter will claim, this added value depends on conceiving "God" in a way that is vague or mythic rather than in terms of what the concept of a creator actually entails.

The role of inherent meaning

So far, however we have simply argued (and recounted) that Creation's purposefulness cannot be established, and that even *were* it established, it is not inherently religious and may even be humiliating depending on the purpose. We have also argued that if life is presumed to issue from a good purpose, the goodness of that purpose can be inferred only on the basis of what we have found good in life. And, finally, we have argued that if life were not in some basic, everyday sense, meaningful quite apart from knowing the Creator's mind, we would never infer that a good or wise agent had created it.

These efforts have left us without an answer to questions such as these: What is God's (uniquely religious) meaning? Why is "God" religion's object? Why does Creation make life meaningful where before—in some sense important to people—it may not be?

We know that Sigmund Freud's *The Future of an Illusion* has a psychological answer which might well be complete were the grounds for Creation no more rational than those we have considered. If there were no more rational reasons for believing in "Creation" then those we have considered, it might then be true that religion is "born of the need to make tolerable the helplessness of man" (for if "life in this world serves a higher purpose," then our suffering will be justified and even death itself will be "not annihilation. . . . but the beginning of new kind of existence").[99]

The religion Freud describes is disingenuous, in that it claims, but does not seek, the truth. It's goal is solace and a *guarantee* that all is not for naught. So, Freud tells us, with the advent of monotheism, "man's relations to him [God] could recover the intimacy and intensity of the child's relation to the father" and if "one had done . . . much for the father, then surely one would be rewarded."[100]

(It should be mentioned, in passing, that some reject talk of "the meaning of life" because the meaning of a thing lies in what it is *for*. Hammers have meaning because they can drive nails; lights because they help us see; farming because it feeds us. Thus the meaning of life must lie in what life is *for*.

But then, to have meaning, heavenly existence would also get its meaning from what it is *for* and, like earthly life, would have no meaning in itself. And, if we say heaven is for praising or seeing God, we would then have to ask "what is a life of praising and seeing God *for*?"

From this, we conclude that there can be no life of meaning if there is no such thing as *inherent* meaning. In fact, if we had no earthly experience of inherent meaningfulness, we would have no conception of "good" or "meaningful" *in itself*—and thus no way to imagine this (unknown) property as obtaining in another realm such as "heaven.")

Still, we must keep in mind that there remains something religiously unsatisfying in *characterizing* the beauty, worth, and physicality of existence as just the way it is. Religion's search for an ultimate truth about Existence is not just a search for the last truth we manage to come up with. Nor can it be *merely* ultimate. There must be something *revelatory* in what we see. *It must be a truth so deep that in realizing what it is, we realize what makes the world.*

We must, in some meaningful sense, "have found God in the world," in order, ever, to have (circularly) inferred a holy Creator from it.

But the divinity we perceive must be able to survive critical reflection. It must, in the end, be the real "God." And if whatever we know about God we must discern within life, then God's *religious* significance must derive in some way from what is miraculous *within* the life we know.

This is precisely the matter driving Chapters 3 and 4—"God's Humanity" and "God's Body"—where we explore what sense might be made of seeing "God" in life.

For we agree with theism generally, that without the element of the miraculous, neither a "God" nor anything else can have the character of the religious. Mircea Eliade, a historian of religion, is emphatic on this point in *The Sacred and the Profane:* "Man becomes aware of the sacred because it . . . shows itself, as something wholly different from the profane," that is, wholly different from natural, the physically determined, the physically causal world.[101] Thus this self-revelation of the sacred, this "hierophany," as Eliade terms it, is inexplicable in natural terms.

"By manifesting the sacred, any object becomes *something else*, yet it continues to remain itself. . . . A *sacred* stone remains a stone . . . [since] from the profane point of view . . . nothing distinguishes it from other stones."[102] (12) So the sacred ranges "from the most elementary hierophany—e.g., the manifestation of the sacred in . . . a stone or a tree—to the supreme hierophany (which for the Christian is the incarnation of God in Jesus Christ)," and so, in the being of the sacred, "there is no solution of continuity [with the natural order]."[103]

We need not rely on history to make the point. Miracle—or non-natural reality—is at the heart of sophisticated theologies.

For example, God is said by contemporary theologians to create not out of raw materials that were lying about, but by virtue of his will. God's "omnipotence" is not the power merely "to make states of affairs obtain or to actualize the possible. It is the power to cause being *ex nihilo*. . . . God's power is . . . awesome. . . . its domain is realized with its exercise."[104] Merely in thinking (willing) God brings forth Being where before there was Nothing. God is not a watchmaker who creates by means of preexisting materials. Creation is the first, and the continuing, *miracle*.[105]

Ironically, a world that can be *anything at all* because whatever it is depends on God's *inscrutable* will—the believer's world—is very like the world of the unbelieving skeptic.

It is the world as described by the most famous of skeptics, David Hume (who denied being a skeptic)—for in his world, nothing *has* to happen the way it does. Hume denies any evidence of *physical* necessity. There is no evidence of what we call "causation." Nothing *must in future be* the way it has, in the past, appeared to us, because nothing is made possible or impossible by *physical* causation. In both the skeptic's world and the believer's world, anything can happen—though to the theist the deviations are miracles, and to the skeptic they are chance.

We will examine this ironic partnership in Chapter 4, "God's Body" when we discuss *being* or *existing* and, at the close of this chapter when we consider the dire implications of both outlooks for the idea of "persons." Here we mention it to indicate how skeptical thought and theistic thought both discredit the human mind.

For theism, the mind self-deceptively sees as physical causation what is *really* God's will; for Humean skepticism, the mind self-deceptively sees as physical causation what is really a sequence of events the mind has come to expect.

And if something as robust and incontestable in practical life as *physical causation* can be "interpreted" as illusory, what chance have the necessities of moral obligation and aesthetic principle to be considered part of natural reality?

Given, in addition, every generation's penchant for skeptical challenge, *doubt* becomes the one universal sign of intellectual honesty.

But we need not rely on the authority of the fallible human mind to determine life's purpose and right practice. The rescue of objectivity is possible. If we can substitute the authority of God's mind for our own, says theism, life's ultimate meaning may be known. To this task, theism applies itself.

God's meaning as authority

The idea that we can follow God's Word *not humans'* is theology's attempt to transcend human fallibility.

If we ourselves could know what is good and right and true in the way of ends and means, knowing God's Word would be redundant; God's Word would only echo our own.

But God's-word-not-humans' theists (like secular skeptics) believe that we cannot reliably know the good and the right and the true. For them, reality is beyond us; doubts can never be securely resolved. Hence, to know ultimate truth, we must receive a word independently of human judgment. It must be immaculately received; it must be God's-word-*not*-humans'.

The special office claimed by religions and prophets is precisely this *immaculate* access to God's Word. In the words of Avery Dulles, S.J.: "The great Western religions derive their fundamental vision not from mere human speculation which would be tentative and uncertain . . . but from God's own testimony . . . from revelation."[106]

As for the Bible being authored by humans,

> it is clear that insofar as the entirety of Holy Scripture is the unique word of God . . . our authors are only God's scribes . . . charged with the duty of inscribing his law which he has dictated to them, so when compared to God they are only authors in an equivocal sense.[107]

Similarly, Karl Barth insisted God's mind can (and should) *unilaterally* determine the human mind, in that "the question cannot be whether He speaks, but only whether we hear."[108] For

> God is always the One who has made Himself known to man in His own revelation, and *not* the one man thinks out for himself and describes as God. . . . knowledge of God is a knowledge *completely effected and determined from the side of its object, from the side of God* [emphasis added].[109]

Muhammad, bringing forth the Koran, claimed to be "*no more than the mouthpiece of its revelation to men.*"[110] Moses, likewise, did not compose the Ten Commandments; he delivered them. Both were messengers. Neither presented God's Word as the fruit of wisdom, theological study, or philosophical insight.

Shaker founder Ann Lee epitomized this dismissal of the human mind when she declared, "It is not I who speak, it is Christ who dwells within me."

The idea that we can rely on "God's authority, not man's" has wide currency—certainly in America. The late U.S. Senator Jesse Helms could confidently warn his New Hampshire audience that "when . . . men no longer believe that God is in charge of human affairs, you have men attempting to take the place of God."[111] Conservative columnist Cal Thomas similarly assumed that God could be relied upon apart from human thought. Thomas rejected the "Spirit of the Enlightenment" because "it is that spirit, beginning with autonomous man rejecting God and *wisdom that does not come from the mind of man*, that has produced more deaths at the hands of governments in this century than in any period in history [emphasis added]."[112]

Even web sites advise that submitting "our fallen, finite, and fallible reason to omniscient reason is supremely reasonable."[113]

Caveat: It should be noted that recourse to "God, not man," is unlike the grammatically similar reliance on "laws, not men" in matters of political governance. The latter is a *slogan*, not a literal statement. It does not assert that laws or good government operate best when unassisted by human minds. A government of laws, not "men," insists on universal procedures and criteria for the guidance of politics and law to minimize the influence of self-interest, prejudice, and other impediments to fairness. A government of laws, not "men," aims at *disciplining* human deliberation. A government of God, not humans, aims at *transcending* human deliberation. God's-word-not-manity's is not a slogan; it it makes a literal claim.

The fallacy of immaculate communication

The problem with God-not-humanity's exhortations lies in the logical impossibility of their fulfillment. God's Word cannot enter into human life unless certified as such by a *person*.

If we *say* what we read is God's Word, or hear is God's Word, or feel is God's Word, we *take a position* on what we have read, or seen, felt, or encountered.

The statement, "this is God's Word," expresses a *conclusion*. One *decides* on the authenticity of an experience or source. It is simply not *sense* (it is self-contradictory) to assert "'this is God's word' and I haven't asserted 'this is God's Word.'"

The behavior of religions themselves comports with this view. Religions—even the most "fundamentalist"—do not hesitate to raise questions whenever a person or group claims to have received God's Word. This universal willingness to question fits the view that assertions of divine origination are *made* by humans. Even the most sincere, impassioned claims to having received God's Word are not treated by religions as *self-proving*.

The God's-word-not-man's dilemma

Thus we confront the following dilemma: either God's-word-not-man's is *unnecessary* because the human mind can know what is good, right, and true, or God's-word-not-man's is *necessary* owing to human fallibility but cannot with certainty be determined as God's due to this same human fallibility.[114]

We do not here contend that God's Word cannot possibly be known. What we say is that any claim to know it is a human claim, so that whoever may claim to know God's Word makes a claim based on the human mind. Hence the authority for claims of God's Word can rise no higher than the authority appropriate to humans.

It is ironic, surely, that officials whose religions insist on free will and responsibility should, in essence, say, with Ann Lee, "it is not I who speak." For, in saying it is God, not themselves, who speaks, they *disavow responsibility* for promulgating the chief obligations and tenets of their faith. No less ironic is that in believing that they know God's Word without relying essentially on their own minds, they fall victim to the "human self-deception" their theology sought to escape.

It is precisely this vision of displaced speakership, with its corresponding moral self-exemption, that functions as the armor of the orthodox—those strict enforcers of divine "love" whose plans for controlling (or ending!) human lives are believed by them to be immaculate directives from above. Like Clement, the first-century bishop of Rome, they find those who reject their rules "guilty of insubordination" not against religious officialdom but against "the divine master himself" (thereby deserving "the death penalty").[115]

If correct, these observations mark a watershed. On one side stand those whose exclusive and immaculate access to God's Word endows them with God's authority over human deliberations. On the other stand religious authorities whose special authority derives like all other special authorities from their (human) application to vocation. With the first stand believers who will brook no critical challenge on the ground that God has gifted them with absolute knowledge of the right and the true (a position in which absolute verdicts are passed with protestations of humility since those who issue them played no role in determining them). With the second stand believers who will countenance challenge for they claim no privileged access to God.

Counter-argument

The impossibility of escaping human authority so as to act and think entirely on God's authority has long been understood as a sticking point. So standard arguments exist to justify the claim that we can hear God untainted by fallible man. These arguments, in one way or another, assert God's power to transmit his word (intentions, rules, commands, desires) by means unimaginable to the finite human mind—that is, by miracle.

The two most popular stratagems for arguing God's immaculate communication—the "method" of faith or God's "gift of grace," and *experiential* self-evidence of *mystical experience*—posit miraculous or "divine" paths to knowledge. All claim to bypass human judgment. But mind-bypass operations must, necessarily, fail. For *any* account of how that bypass works must be devised and found persuasive by our minds.

The first stratagem claims that in religious matters, a light of faith may exist that enables us to bypass human judgment. In such cases, God grants those who genuinely trust him the ability to know his word, not in the natural way, but in a divinely enlightened (supernatural) way so that, whether because God inscrutably elects us to prescience on matters of his Word, or graces our piety with a supernatural power, we are enabled *non-naturally* to know God. Our own minds are thus presumed bypassed by a supernaturally infallible communication.

But this "light of faith" is of course God's gift, at least in the sense that it is God's *purpose* to give it. It is God's *intention* to have someone know God in this super-human way—which means the theory cannot be true *if God has no such purpose.*

Therefore to propound this theory requires that we know God's purpose—specifically, the purpose of giving us a special insight into his mind. Since the theory's task is to *establish* that we can know God's purpose, it cannot *assume* that we know God's purpose. (Arguments have no weight if they assume the truth of that which they need to conclude.)

Hence, the argument is circular—as all these counter-arguments must be. For we cannot argue that God, *by whatever means*, makes immaculate communication possible without arguing that it is God's *intention* to do so. God doesn't do things accidentally. And to know what God wants is to know his Word.

Thus, in asserting that such instruments exist as "the gift of grace" or "the light of faith" or "ineffable, infallible, wordless, "mystical" communication," it must be said to be the case that it is God's *intention* to communicate immaculately. For example, the Protestant theologian Rudolph Bultmann tells us that "if God were not *gracious*, if He did not of his own free decision turn toward men, there would be no revelation."

Bultmann's claim assumes what it must prove, for it is based on *already* knowing what God intends (and would, if he chose to speak, *say*). It attributes to God the *purpose* of granting us knowledge. But whether or not we can know God's purpose is *precisely what is at issue,* and thus what needs to be shown. We repeat: God's purpose cannot be used as part of an argument to show we can know God's purpose.

So-called "mystical experiences" fall victim to the same circularity.[116] To have such an experience is immediately to know God. The experience is said to authenticate itself. More will be said in Chapter 3.

Much is made of mystical experience and we think rightly so. But not every conclusion drawn from it is valid. For all its overwhelming force, and for all attempts to liken it to other experiences in which reality is known only through *immediate experience*—such as in art, sport, play, and sheer physicality—mystical experience carries *implications.*

For example, merely to report being in the presence of something immensely important *is to make a worldly claim.* Such a claim has implications—such as asking to be taken seriously, or denying that knowledge is achieved only by scientific method, or that one has knowledge of some sort. Mystics do not report simply having had strong *sensations*, or having had what *seem* like encounters with something.

Above all, mystical experience does not leave mystics in baffled silence. And if they could not speak of its content, we would *have no reason* to say they were "religious" mystics. Their experience could not be distinguished from that of epileptics, stroke victims, or the mentally ill. In fact, mystics claim an indubitable contact with a transcendent power—a presence that in some way *informs* them religiously. Their mystically derived claims about reality are specific enough to be *incompatible with other claims about reality*—for example, that they were hallucinating due to drugs, or that what they felt was the presence of an *immoral* force or a thrilling but *humanly unimportant* presence. Indeed, if mystical experience had no content or implications it would be as consistent with atheism as with theism.

Once again, therefore, religious significance of mystical experience lies in what the experience *says*, that is, in what it the mystics *say* it tells them. And if the mystic describes it, or what it entails, the mystic *makes an assertion*.

This assertion is not itself a mystical experience. It is a claim as to what is known as a result of having had it and it is a claim made by a human being, not a God. Enter the counter-argument: This is no ordinary person but a Holy man—someone chosen by God.

As the Moslem mystic, Al Ghazzali, said of himself,

> The prophet is endowed with qualities to which you possess nothing analogous, and which consequently you cannot possibly understand. . . . But the [mystical perception of God] which one attains by the method of the Sufis is like an immediate perception, as if one touched the objects with one's hand.[117]

But, like the "light of faith" argument, the Holy man argument is, once more, a human argument that one can achieve higher-then-human conclusions. Holy men are not "naturally" holy; divine will alone can make them so. Thus God's intent must be *assumed* in order to conclude one can know God's intent (or word). The argument *assumes the truth of what it is supposed to establish*.

Sometimes this logical point is lost in dense theological debate over criteria for holiness or having been "chosen." Among peoples, criteria for holiness have varied from (what we recognize as) insanity to drug-induced abnormal states to (in Western tradition) absolute innocence, exemplary piety, or a sudden moral reform. But the designation of such signs as "proofs" is plainly a human decision.

Because these signs are not themselves God, we could not know they were signs or proofs of divine communication unless we had *correlated* their occurrence with the revelation of God's Word.

To do this we must know how to recognize God's Word, *independently* of the signs. Otherwise we cannot conclude that mystical experience or trance or childlike innocence has anything to do with receiving the Word (not to mention its immaculate reception). We are once more thrown back on the claim that one can recognize God's Word without deciding or knowing or concluding or judging that one knows it.

The attack on logic

In desperation to transcend human authority, some deny logic applies when speaking of God.[118] We hear that God is beyond human understanding, that thought about God is exempt from all (merely) human standards—including *consistency*, which is to say, *logic*.

An example is T. F. Torrance's, "logic of obedience" which denies the argument that, *logically* speaking, we must use our own assessments when we state God's purpose. Torrance subsumes standard logic under the special "higher logic of theology." Thus Torrance thinks that even the conclusions of our abstract thinking do not really arise on the logical basis on which they seem to repose. They come from something much deeper, a certain habit or set of mind that gives these arguments their real force."[119]

As B. Hebblethwaite points out, the idea "that theological thinking has its own logic, only available within the relation of grace and faith. . . . makes theology . . . undiscussable, immune to criticism and unsusceptible of being pondered hypothetically.[120]

Torrance's approach elaborates the simplest and most popular defense against arguments that criticize statements about God as "inconsistent" or "self-contradictory." When people say "God is beyond logic" they permit themselves to say things like "God is one but God is three" or "God created himself" without having to answer charges of inconsistency or self-contradiction. "How can God create himself? He would have not to exist and then—not existing—*do* something. A contradiction? No problem; God is beyond logic.[121]

Like claims about faith and grace and mystical encounter, the claim that God is not bound by logic is, of course a (human) claim about God's capabilities—and a radically comprehensive one. For it ends any and all reflection on God's capabilities.

For example, if God is not "bound" by logic (because logic is just an agreed upon set of rules for human thinking) then God can be all good and all bad, omnipotent and impotent. For it is "only" logic (*consistency*) that says it is *impossible* to be all good *and* all bad, and *impossible* to be completely omnipotent yet completely impotent.

Plainly, if God is free from logic, then nothing said of God rules out anything *else* that may be said of God. Theology and preachment become useless. What we say of God can be true and not true of God.

The doctrine of inspiration

Theists who are sensitive to the excesses of misguided or un-self-critical believers often hold that sacred texts and the utterances of revered figures or officials may not express God's Word *literally* or *completely*, but instead contain ideas *inspired* by God. By such reasoning, those who refuse to believe every sacred text or pronouncement literally true think themselves able, *more reasonably,* to retain belief in the divine authority of much that sacred texts or holy persons say.

Nonetheless, as divinely *inspired*, such texts or words are valued only because they are thought to possess greater intellectual or moral authority than words or sources which are not divinely inspired.

The English theist, Keith Ward, is able to tell us, for instance, that when, in the Bible, God says," 'Heaven is my throne and earth my footstool,' . . . the language here is clearly symbolic," [not literal] and to declare that "the doctrine of God as Creator clarifies the metaphorical nature of much biblical language about the Divine."[122] The renowned Anglican apologist, C. S. Lewis, advises biblical readers that "the assertion that God had a Son was never intended to mean that He is a being propagating His kind by sexual intercourse." On the other hand, Lewis tells us that "the assertion that Jesus turned water into wine was meant perfectly literally, for this refers to something which, if it happened, was well within the reach of our sense and our language."[123]

Each theist brings to the sacred text reasons for stating what it truly says, *reasons for deciding* which statements were inspired and which not—and which interpretations of them state what is inspired and which not.

But if we must interpret and assess an idea's *inspired* status, then the claim of inspiration made for any Word we interpret can have no more credibility or authority than a human interpretation.

It follows that the test for a word being *literally* God's and the test for its being *inspired* by God is *exactly the same*. It is no easier to know what God said indirectly than to know what God said directly. The doctrine of "inspiration" fails to avoid the problems it sees in literalism.

In both cases, *the whole point* is to find a word having God's authority and *not man's*—for "man's" word requires no sacred text, location, or other source. There is no purpose, theistically speaking, to examining sacred writings unless one *can* distinguish God's Word from a human word. *Human* opinion as to truth and morality is *secular* by definition.

And, in neither case can the assertion that a word is God's, or is inspired by God, be made other than by a human being or possess more authority than a human mind can supply.

The attempt to speak softly of God's Word ("inspired") rather than loudly (literally true") has an analogue in the way sophisticated people prefer to describe extremely fortunate events as "providential" occurrences rather than as "miracles." C. S. Lewis makes short work of this dodge in "Appendix B" of his *Miracles*. Speaking of the idea that the unusual weather at Dunkirk which allowed the British soldiers to escape the Nazis was perhaps "providential," Lewis says

> I find it very difficult to conceive an intermediate class of events which are neither miraculous nor merely "ordinary." Either the weather at Dunkirk was or was not that which the previous history of the physical universe, by its own character, would inevitably produce. If it was, then how is it "specially" providential? If it was not, then it was a miracle. (p. 174)

So we say here of inspired texts that if inspired, they must be as much what God says and not what humans say, as in any literal "God's Word" text.

The arguments of this section on "God's authority" do not say we cannot learn much from sacred texts, from participating in rituals or listening to sermons. In fact, we say the investigation of such sources may be essential. For sacred writings and the outcomes of meditation on life and death and love represent human efforts dedicated to discerning what is ultimately meaningful. If our attitude is serious; if we are humble before fact, feeling, and reason; if our inquiries and reflections are fearless, we have much to learn from these efforts.

But, not to recognize that it is *we* who must discern what is holy means we will unwittingly worship the God that *suits our present human selves* rather than the "God" knowledge and reflection *can bring* us.

The horrors of ventriloquism
and absolute followership

Squarely faced, the idea that God's will can speak through us with no part whatsoever played by our own judgment is nightmarish. It provides no functional difference between the utterances of "prophets" and "mystics" and the utterances of a ventriloquist's doll. For, *par excellence*, the doll, like an audio recording, exemplifies what it is to broadcast the words of another while taking no position on what is said.

In pursuit of life's meaning, agreement with God must be "left to heaven." There is no presumption in *hoping* one's conclusions agree with those of an infallible mind. But, surely, presumptuousness rears its head if we say "this is the purpose of human life, and if God were to speak to us now, God would agree with me."

Unfortunately, politicians and religious leaders across the ideological spectrum seem unfazed when it comes to claiming God's authority for public policies (quite often when it comes to killing people). But this is both religiously and philosophically *irresponsible*. Whoever claims or esteems free will cannot shift responsibility for what they think and do to God.

Those who (on the God's-word-not-man's thesis) intend *absolutely* to follow a "word" that depends in no part on their own judgment must confront hard questions: "What if any given utterance or inscription or thought (etc.) denied what are to you basic and indubitable facts—such as that we move our own limbs? What would you say if 'God' urged you to censor, or punish or kill a child or a stranger—would you always do it? And what would you say if other theists deny it's His word?"

It is no minor matter to accede to a source whose statements are *always more credible than your own* on any topic that you can consider. How this hierarchical relationship differs from infantilization or the nightmare of madness is not clear. In a world that can present things unbelievable, unpredictable, and contravening of anything (or *everything*) we previously thought we knew, we have no bearings in terms of which to assess the meaning of what we are asked to say or do. We cannot even say we know that what we see is real (whatever then a term like "real" could mean).

If the counter-argument is that God will surely empower us to recognize the genuine statements and commands of God, or that nothing abhorrent or false to us would be communicated because God creates and loves reality, we would be using the same circular argument offered in support of faith and mystical experience.

That is, one would be arguing that God's Word will always comport with the important things we know are right and wrong, true and false, because God is of a certain mind, or has a certain character, or cannot but do things that are right. But by this *or any other* attempt at theological support, words that are said to have the authority of God are deemed to have it *on the authority of humans*. It can be no other way.

Meaning without God

If ultimate meaning cannot come from outside our existence, then we should find religious insight in perceptions of this world. And we do, even in Barrett and in his choice of an excerpt from the work of Immanuel Kant.

First, Kant:

> The starry heavens open before me a vista of a cosmos that broadens out into the unbounded expanse of world beyond world, system beyond system. In confrontation with that immensity, my own personal significance is diminished. Facing this universe, I am but an infinitesimal speck of matter that must in the end give back to the universe those bits of matter I have borrowed for a while. . . . On the other hand, if I turn inward to the sense of the moral law that grips my conscience, my dignity as a human person appears exalted. As a spiritual being, I seem no longer to be merely a tiny speck of matter in an indifferent universe. The moral law that commands me inwardly seems to open to a fuller destiny than that.

Then, Barrett (arguing that we are not machines like computers and so are, perhaps, spiritual beings):

> The dreamers of the computer insist that we shall someday be able to build a machine that can take over all the operations of the human mind, and so in effect replace the human person. After all, why not? There should be no "mystic" obstacle that should impede the progress of our technology. But in the course of these visions they forget the very plain fact of the human body and its presence in and through consciousness. If that eventual machine were ever to be realized, it would be a curiously disembodied kind of consciousness, for it would be without the sensitivity, intuitions, and pathos of our human flesh and blood. And without those qualities we are less than wise, and certainly less than human.[124]

Note that Barrett argues from experience to our spiritual nature; he does not argue that because the purpose of existence is "X" it follows we must be spiritual beings. His sense of the spiritual, his distinctions between mind and spirit on the one hand and mere physical cause on the other do not require supernatural premises.

And, of course, poetry speaks to meaningfulness. Consider Willa Cather's meditation on life's significance,from "Prairie Spring" (her opening to *Oh Pioneers!*) in which she virtually sings of evening, land, soil, wheat and weeds, horses and men, roads and sunsets and sky, out of which, pulsing with desire flares "youth with its unsupportable sweetness. . . ."

What then is the problem of meaningfulness? What sort of "meaningfulness" is uniquely religious, so that concepts such as creator-God, non-natural, omniscient, omnipresent, omnipotent, inherently Good—can satisfy it?

GOD'S MEANING AS ULTIMATE CONTEXT: THE LOGIC OF RELIGION

Paul Tillich viewed religion as a quest for what is ultimate, implying that, once found, what is ultimate will cast the light of meaningfulness upon existence in the deepest, all-inclusive way. He observed that

> when we speak of the world's religion, we usually think of these groups and . . . their ideas and their practical and imaginary symbols. But when we look deeper, we must say that religion is larger than this. *Religion* . . . [is] . . . an ultimate concern about the meaning of one's life and the meaning of 'being' as such also appears. . . . [125]

Similarly, in the writing of the theologian John E. Smith we find the point that *religious* meaningfulness has to do not simply with the meaningfulness of events or moments but with meaningfulness as a dimension of reality (like space and time and cause) that can be termed ultimate.

> The real trouble in connecting religion and human experience is to get a correct description and understanding not of religious experience but of the religious dimension of experience. . . . A dimension is not a determining *differentia* but a perspective or an aspect; in this case it is man as raising the question of the purpose of existence and seeking the final purpose which needs to be answered as a basis for the quality of his present life

Smith remarks that

> it is essential to an experiential approach that the question of the purpose of existence as such—the question that identifies man as the religious animal—be understood, *at the same time, as the question of God* [emphasis added]. Unless this connection is grasped, the experiential approach collapses into a psychological or phenomenological study of man and the introduction of God becomes superfluous.[126]

So let us approach experience and "God." The very *nature* of God as *God*—not simply God's particular imperatives or presumed reactions—must somehow make a life-altering difference in the *meaning* of human acts and thoughts as *"human,"* particularly "meaning" as inclusive of significance or "meaningfulness."

We have held that religion follows an objectivist logic in the manner of its *search* for meaning. Meaning is not determined from *within* us (psychologically, physiologically, genetically or as satisfying fiction) but from something possessed of an *independent* status—something "outside" us. Traditionally, it is grounded in the "truth that is God," for only what God *is* can provide an ultimate (foundational and unchangeable) meaning.

But why does knowledge of our ultimate meaning require knowledge of an ultimate reality? Is it to satisfy a non-rational, religious impulse that we agree with Smith and Tillich, saying that knowledge of our *ultimate* meaning requires knowledge of an *ultimate reality* or *God*—and that this reality be available *within* human experience (as are moral obligations, aesthetic and physical qualities)?

The answer is that we do agree, but not by ignoring rationality. Our agreement follows from commonplace, rational practice, despite the radical nature of the answers we seek. In the daylight of our ordinary lives, we follow this principle: The meaning (and, eventually, the *meaningfulness*) of an act is determined by reference to the *context* of the act. On this theology and philosophy agree. Hence, if we are ever to know the *ultimate* meaning of human acts (as a class), we must know the *ultimate* context in which human action take place.

With such knowledge, the significance of human life from the standpoint of the eternal—*sub specie aeternitatis*—would be known (which is perhaps, is what is meant by theology's contention that if the "present has any meaning it has eternity").[127]

So we say that religion's quest to know the ultimate context of human action is, in its *form* or "logic," eminently rational. This, and the idea that meaning comes from *without*, are reasons for insisting that despite egregious errors, the religious impulse has (as we have all along said) a *rational* character. Specifically, *God's meaning* as (in part) life's ultimate, relevant context—is intended to provide the basis for understanding what we do and think at the deepest level. Thus in its *motive* or *form*, the urge to know the ultimate situation of our existence—as in the theory of "Creation"—is no departure from reason.

Of course, with respect to the goal of this work, we say that if religion's requirements of *meaning-from-without* and *an ultimate, non-human context for our meaning*, were to be found elsewhere than in theism's traditional "God," then (if that "elsewhere" were miraculous) perhaps traditional theism's "God" could be congenially and fruitfully reconstructed.

But our current concern is with the importance of ultimate context for ultimate meaning, a formidable problem that, from the earliest times has be managed only through narratives.

As Mircea Eliade tells us,

> Myths . . . narrate not only the origin of the world . . . but also all the primordial events in consequence of which man has become what he is today—mortal, sexed, organized in society, obliged to work to live, and working in accordance with certain rules . . . man *as he is today* is the direct result of those mythical events, *he is constituted by those events.*[128]

It is important fully to grasp the way in context bears upon meaning. For that we turn to everyday affairs and to literature—beginning with a case in which context is misconstrued.

The comedic effect of an episode in Richard Llewellyn's novel, *How Green Was My Valley* depends on the link between context and meaning. Hugh, a Welsh coal miner's son recounts his mother's bafflement at the homework his father and he are untangling. She can make no sense of the fact that they are wrestling with a math problem that asks how long it will take to fill the bath given how many gallons are flowing in and how many flowing out through two holes in the tub. Who in the world would want to do these "silly sums" set in motion by some fool trying to fill a tub with holes? Only "a lunatic," she says.

Lunatic indeed. It is without meaning, surely, to fill *and* not fill. In the typical *domestic* context it is meaningless, pointless, incoherent, to spend time calculating the rate at which a leaky bathtub *might* be filled rather than attending first to the leak itself. But in the environing context of *an industrial world*, the problematic bathtub provides a meaningful test for minds that must quantify relationships—and the context of education for *that* world differs in its criteria of practical education from one suited to a life of domestic management.

So, actions are meaningful or meaningless depending in part on the *relevant,* actual *context.* Had industrial England been destroyed or were it under siege, learning how to solve that "sum" might have been a meaningless activity even if *thought* meaningful by the school or Hugh's father.

The phrase *ivory tower* disparages a narrow, isolated context wherein "doing sums" always *seems* meaningful to academics even when *actually* not—as when (in a wider context) a nation may be *under attack by an invader.* If we have no knowledge of the environing world and ask ourselves "is it meaningful to learn how to do rate problems?" we cannot *always* be sure of the answer. Rate problems— on a desert island, in a college-preparatory course, in a musical culture for a violin prodigy? What is the context?

The role of context in defining the significance of an action is critical. An elderly woman walks to a nearby mailbox and mails a letter. How meaningful is this act? Very little, if she does this every day. But what if she has not left her apartment for fifty years? Historical context determines meaning. On this score, one must take time to imagine what it would be like to awaken with amnesia.

The bewilderment of some citizens with respect to the meaningfulness of certain constitutionally required actions cannot be remedied in a thin historical, political and legal context. Those who wonder why freedom of speech shouldn't be denied to people who are obviously spewing hate, or why police can't wrest confessions from known criminals by means of physical threat, will not be much helped simply by reading the Bill of Rights. Democracy's meaningfulness cannot be gauged in a context of relative historical innocence or by those whose historical education was skewed, false or just a tool for passing exams.

Similarly, if the context we call "society" were *in truth* nothing more than a collection of individuals, taxation would then, perhaps, be *confiscation* or state-sponsored theft. If the societal context is *in truth* a system of interdependent agents, then paying taxes might be a moral duty.

All these examples relate *particular* actions to a wider context. But religion's subject is human activity in and of itself and thus calls for action's ultimate context.

The animating question abides: How can our actions, *whatever they are,* be inherently meaningful (*positively or negatively*) when the context of our lives is finite, when we—and (in time) our species—face the prospect of death? It is this ultimate contextual fact which religion calls us to consider when it asks, "what, is "the meaning of life?"

All along "meaning" taunts us as a kind of umbrella word, embracing *having a purpose* or, apart from purpose, simply *having significance.* We have seen that Barrett's attempt to establish the religious status of existence on purpose alone (on God's intent) was unsuccessful. Other accounts of our significance rest on the miraculous happenings. Reason, evidence, and analyses seem unable to provide an ultimate context capable of establishing human significance. (There is no miraculousness or transcendence to our arguments themselves.) Hence, *marvels*, the miraculous or fundamentally inexplicable happenings give license to imaginary visions of the ultimate context (maybe we lived before! Maybe we are part of a giant mind!). The certification of a context as ultimate becomes literary—a story is evolved that "sticks" and that purports to explain existence as we know it.

Still, in myth we see (again) that religion, far from embracing obscurity in the manner of magic, looks, even in primitive cultures, to *understanding*—to God or gods as the key to humanity's meaning. "Something cares" for us. God is *love*, for if one is loved by one's creator one's existence *must* have a meaning inclusive of meaningfulness.

But "the truth will out." And if there is no God, false belief will make us pay, immediately in the substance of the soul (if, early in this chapter, we have rightly described the religious significance of feelings)—and eventually, in the facts of living (providing, in a nuclear world, religion's extremists allow us the time).

Still, we are haunted by the need for an answer. Narratives are old as our history—they make use of all that is familiar in action and thought—but philosophical analysis is a specialty. No surprise that in its *content* and *elaborations* the idea of a God (an agent resembling us because we are made by that agent to resemble it) is, for societies, a persuasive *ultimate context.* Yes, we seek truth and our motive is reasonable but *need* prevails. We simply must, nay *will*, have what gives us meaning. Critical reason be damned, for it is, as philosophical doubters tell us, harmlessly *subjective.* Knowledge is an illusion; all is faith, belief, or mere "perspective."

We are therefore not surprised to be told by a Christian theologian that "the believer is not looking for a theoretical explanation but rather for some experience which will actually give meaning, which will endue life with significance."[129]

Yet, if the narrative of Creation is not true, then the significance derived from it cannot be genuine (which is why, in the interest of *religion*, we analyzed "Creation"). And surely, dear reader, there is something strange in betting one's life on standards of significance which are genuine *if and only if* the following is a fact: that a supernatural, self-created Being willed the universe into existence, willed us into existence, commands us, tests us, loves us, and promises those who believe and obey, eternal life and those who fail to believe, a good deal less.

Willa Cather's poem and the musings of Kant suggest what our literature, history, family life, and forays into nature suggest—that there is *something* present (in some way) that creates us what we are and that invisibly sustains our being every day of our lives. But from *within life experience* (Tillich, Smith) have we sufficient reason to say this ultimate context of living is given in the idea of a God?

How can we recognize an ultimate context? The rational specification of an ultimate context is, to say the least, a formidable question. Hegel's philosophy aimed to provide it and, in keeping with the importance of ultimate context, he considered an "Absolute Spirit" to be the ultimate content of both philosophy and religion. In addition to the problem of externality (objectivity) and absolute inclusiveness, we must face the problem of *truth*—which is why our next chapter, "God's Humanity," deals with Knowledge, Belief, Faith, and Revelation.

We seek to have a meaning deep enough to help sustain us in our struggles, though it must—*sotto voce*—be *true*. How frightening, truth. What is true may not favor us. Life is puzzling and hard. The need is deep.

For, we are born into an unknown situation—infants capable of impulse but not action. We are named, nourished, loved, protected, guided, and taught ("Heaven lies about us in our infancy," said Shelley). As children we waken to a home. But as adults we waken to a fraught and boundless world—unguided, unprotected, and apparently unloved. We waken orphans in the universe.

Thus, the journey of religion is a journey home—a journey to a context definitive of meaning and the meaningful. Do we belong here? And if we do, what is our point? *Tell us what we are.*

For such reasons we say that God's *religious* meaning is to specify our defining situation, to divulge the true nature of the human story—the ultimate context of our actions, the beginning of us and the end.

And, as the religious importance of *"creation ex nihilo"* is in providing a *true* account of how we are created *human* (in a non-human, largely inorganic, universe), surely the account of our creation must be subject to the closest scrutiny.

As our next chapter, "God's Humanity," will argue, the act of *knowing* is the *sine qua non* of our becoming *human* (of our living in a *human mode*) and that *knowing* (morality, aesthetics, logic, mathematics, law, religion, and so on) is unique to us and transcends our physical being (on Earth). And, if knowing is inexplicable but true and ultimate, then *a vindication of knowing* may vindicate, as well, religion's insistence on the transcendent, the miraculous, and the creative—and may point to the ultimate reality for which religions yearn.

Against this view of knowing and knowledge stand skepticism, scientism, and traditionally theistic theology—all of which denigrate human certitude or the hegemony of a "rational thought." The great irony is that, by virtue of what these elaborate *intellectual* efforts *entail*, the conditions essential for creating humans (as distinct from animals and things) do not exist. So, as we shall argue, below, if any one of these visions or *ultimate contexts* is true one cannot become a *person*—one must remain a creature, or at best a nonentity.[130]

GOD AND TRUTH:
THEISM, SKEPTICISM, SCIENTISM, AND THE PERSON

Theism

We have examined William Barrett's traditionalist thesis that existence is meaningless unless it was created for a purpose—that life is meaningless unless another mind has willed it into existence. Within this tradition of Creation, it is held that "God brings about the whole universe through the divine word, that is by thought and intention."[131] This is creation *ex nihilo*.

As Creator, God's will creates law (determines what cannot but happen or be so) in every domain of "law"—physical or moral or aesthetic or any other kind. His will alone *makes real* any property, norm, right or obligation. Before the existence of that will (or *outside* of its existence), there was *nothing* other than God.[132] For if there were *anything*—any law, rule, property or norm—before or outside of God, that thing would be independent of God. It would not have been created by God and would be either *unexplained* existence or else the product of another creator, before God, and, presumably, constraining of God. For example, if norms of goodness exist apart from God (are independent, not products of his will) then God, to be good, would *have to* follow them.[133]

The reader may find it interesting to search for *explanations* of how it makes *sense* to say God created things when nothing but God existed. In Brian Davies, *Introduction to the Philosophy of Religion,* one finds sixty-four pages on creation arguments, none of which explain how there is *sense* in asserting "creation" when nothing-at-all exists save a will or mind to do so ["God's will"]. Instead, one finds Davies eventually seconding an argument of the Islamic "kalam" tradition that in effect says "the universe must have had a beginning and . . . only God could have brought this about."[134] In seeing, as well, an inexplicably "orderly" universe, Brian finds "we have something for which [an] intentional explanation is legitimate."[135] But how *intending* a universe into existence makes sense (*more* sense than saying it has always existed) we are not told. Nor could we ever be. But as we have warned, "God is beyond logic," so no argument or claim can be ruled out because it lacks sense!

The point of this brief review is to establish that, when fully thought out, the idea of such a creator is (in the end) incompatible with something basic to our understanding of what it is to be a *person*.

The implications of creation *ex nihilo* are inconsistent with what we all think *required* if we are to be *persons*—that is, responsible beings, and not creatures, tools, robots, things, or animals. We speak of being a person, in a commonplace, familiar, and absolutely serious sense—one that *requires* that one's thoughts be *one's own*. As persons we will not be instruments; we want the thoughts that guide us to be (in a special sense) *ours*.

But what is it for an idea to be one's own?

If we express an idea to which someone responds, "is that your idea?" we have no trouble accepting it as a meaningful question. We have no trouble even though it is perfectly obvious that the thought is ours in the sense that it is, in fact, in our mind. And we understand there is some point to this question even if it is a fact that we *believe* the idea and a *fact* that we may act on it.

The idea is *factually* ours no less than a headache is ours. So the question, "is that your idea?" cannot be a question as to whether in fact we believe it, or in fact have it in our head.

Sometimes, of course, the question means "is that idea original with you?" and the answer will be simply "yes" or "no." But in such a case, if one says, "it is not original with me," the question may be phrased, "but is it really *your* idea?"

Here, people do not react by saying "what are you talking about? The idea has to be mine because it is in my mind as a conviction." Instead, when asked if an idea they espouse is their own, people will become somewhat irritated, especially when the idea in question has significance for the guidance of life. They require no philosophy to know (or sense) that the question speaks to the issue of their integrity or their selfhood.

It challenges their status as a responsible person. It suggests they may be someone's vessel or tool. So the question whether ideas are "our own" has not simply to do with whether it is a *fact* that we hold them.[136]

Indeed, we consider it nightmarish to suppose the content of our minds might get there outside our power to control them—to be programmed—as were the minds of workers in Aldous Huxley's *Brave New World* by genetic science and the populace of George Orwell's *1984* by mass indoctrination. When a country indoctrinates its population we pity them for thinking the ideas they cleave to are, in a humanly meaningful sense, "their own."

The techniques by which we create a robot or an adult clone are the ways we destroy or falsify a *person*. In sum, the ownership of ideas is not a physical or psychological condition, but a non-physical, *normative* one.

Our ideas are our own to the extent that we have command of them—that is, to the extent that they reside within us on the sufferance of our judgment. As Henry James observed in *What Maisy Knew*: "To criticize is to appreciate, to appropriate, to take intellectual possession. To establish, in fine, a relation with the criticized thing and to make it one's own."

The ideas in our heads are *ours* to the extent that we can assess their credibility—the degree to which they ought or ought not be believed. We must be able to recognize what counts for them and what counts against them.

Save for their connection with evidence or argument *there is no possibility of ownership* in any sense other than the psychological sense of mere *factual* possession. Put another way, without evidence or argument, there is, quite literally, nothing for us to *do* concerning an idea. It is simply "there," within us, innocent of grounds—no more ours as *persons* than a thorn or a tick.

In ordinary life we take it as essential to our status as persons that we *can* hold our ideas on a rational basis. One does not require philosophic study to feel one has been taken over, enslaved, treated as a non-person if one's guiding beliefs were the result of conditioning, drugs, neurotic forces, or the "brain-washing," "manipulation," and "false information" of indoctrinating agencies.

We pity populations whose minds have been, as we say, "controlled" for we know their thoughts are *not their own*. They have but do not own the the thoughts. They are not "responsible" for what they think. In that way they are creatures, shaped not by judgment but by forces and conditions barring bona fide exercises of judgment.

Fundamentally (that is, *ultimately*), unless we can recognize what counts for or against our ideas about things, there is no point in our having *minds*—as distinct from calculating machines, which, because they cannot know the worth of their "ideas" or "states," are without responsibility and so without any possibility of the dignity unique to a person.

Judgment, not calculation, is the essence of mind. And if being ourselves—*being self-possessed rather than possessed*—requires that we have intellectual command of our thoughts, there is a quite real sense in which it may be too little to say we have minds, rather than that we *are* minds. (We do not mean to ignore feeling, but here we speak in shorthand; see chapter three).

The issue at hand

We cannot have minds other than the kind of calculating "mind" or rule-governed machinery (computer-functioning) required for carrying out commands if the meaning and purpose of living—all statements, rules, beliefs, practices—have no ground in reality, no *independent* virtues, other than having been commanded. This is the situation we are in if there is an absolute Creator.

God's "reasons" come not only from a mind *other* than our own, but a "mind," as it were, whose "reasons" are not "decided upon" but merely *willed*. That is, we cannot possibly have substantive reasons for deciding why something ought or ought not be done or why a thing should be considered good or not, because there are no substantive reasons. There are only commands or fiats. What we call "reasons" are only what God happened to *will*.

It is not easy to think with consistency here. One's ideas of God *creating* inexorably fall back upon the way we ourselves create, wherein we notice properties, imagine improvements, consider consequences, decide what makes sense, and then make something.

We suppose God to have imagined how things could be and then (or, in the same moment) decided what among these possibilities was worthwhile or even necessary to bring into existence because it was "good" or "best" or "perfect." For example, we can imagine God as

Beethoven, having no theme in mind, then suddenly "hearing" a theme, thinking it good, and creating a composition that uses it.

But God doesn't *hear* music, God *wills* (let us say) sound, and God doesn't *perceive* whether it is a good bit of music but decides what will be labeled "good" sound or "music." Beethoven existed in a world of sounds, instruments, traditions, audiences, compositional experience in terms of which things could be imagined and judged. But God exists in nothing and makes absolutely everything for no reason because there are no reasons for God to consult (no way things sound, for example) that *pre-exist* to indicate to God what must be done or can be done for things to sound "right")

God makes up, wills, what is right—which is why, for example, William of Ockham declared that "by the very fact that God wills something, it is right for it to be done."[137] (God is under no pre-existing obligations.)

What we typically (and persistently) forget is that an *absolute* creator confronts a *nothingness* in which there are no standards of beauty or goodness or anything else—no beautiful things, no ugly things, no "nature," no morality, no physical laws, no stuff or norms of any kind.

We repeat: If God is the Creator of all that can be said, in *any* sense, to *exist*—if God is the Creator of all realities—then in creation there is God and *nothing else*.

No prior creator left ideas or things or standards for "our" Creator to perceive or reflect on. God has nothing with preexisting qualities or properties to think about. Creation *ex nihilo* is an idea whose extremity we cannot easily picture or keep in mind as we think things through.

We imagine God reflecting (whether instantly or not) on such things as birth or free will or judgment or planetary systems, but one does this only if these things *already have* their own independent qualities, properties, or implications to force considerations about them. In addition, one does this *in terms of* one's standards of thinking (whether logical, moral, scientific, aesthetic, etc.) God doesn't confront the beauty of something in his mind because there is no beauty, as standard or as fact, for him to confront.

In sum, an *absolute* creator cannot think. This is because an *absolute* creator has nothing to think *about* and no *independent* standards for thinking rightly. (And here we can appreciate why notions like "Brahman" are so vague.) If standards for right thinking did *exist*, and if aesthetic qualities did *exist* and if moral qualities did *exist* and if physicality did *exist*, then our Creator *did*—at Creation—have the wherewithal to think and decide and create. But then, the existence of these already-existing things (like the universe itself) would remain *unexplained*. If they were used by God to decide on a good or perfect "creation," then another creator is needed to explain how *they* came to be. And so it must go.

The *absolutely radical* nature of an absolute creator was not grasped even by scholastics who spoke of God's perfection when the standards for perfection could only be whatever standards God willed—there being no *independent* standard by which to evaluate *God's* "choices" and say "yes . . . anyone capable of knowing the truth can look at his choices and see they are perfect."

The Pentateuch's *wordings* (like those of all other "creation" myths) reflect the human model—the watchmaker or craftsman or author or artist or magician model—telling us that God looked on his work and "*saw* that it was good."

Indeed, *the following arguments will be unintelligible if one cannot shelve the human model for creating.*[138]

Let us rephrase and expand. God does not learn what is true or good or right by experience, by imagining or by "looking around" because God *makes up*—from nothing-at-all—what will be called "good" and "true" and "right." Therefore these rules and properties and qualities cannot have been willed *because*—or "on the ground that"—they were good and true and right.

For example, God did not say "mountains! Let me imagine them. Oh yes, I see they are beautiful, let's have them." For mountains cannot *have* beauty until beauty is an existent, until it is a reality. And since the Creator alone wills all things, the "reality" of *beauty* cannot exist unless willed to exist, and it cannot be a property of mountains unless *willed* to be a property of mountains.

Because God *makes reasons by fiat* rather than *follows* reasons or evidence, no *supporting* reasons *exist* for the reasons and evidence he gives us. There is no independent substance or independent grounds for commending them that led God to see he had to acknowledge them. (That's what *we* do when we determine what is right or true.) Hence there is nothing about them that can be cited to *justify* following God's rules or statements. That is, there is nothing about *the reasons themselves* for us to consider. Such reasons as these justify the observation of the British philosopher, Simon Blackburn that it is "very hard to understand how something can become true just simply by being commanded."[139]

They are "good" reasons only because God labeled them "good"—for they were not *already* good (before God's willing) so that God needed only the wisdom to see that, "yes," they were.

Because, then, of what is entailed by absolute Creation, to live a life according to a (literal) God's will is therefore necessarily to follow orders without any reason other than to do it. We must remember that *any* reason we give has the status of a "reason" *only because* God willed that it be "a 'good' reason." Thus there is never, *at bottom*, any other weight behind—any other authority for—a reason than that it was willed by an Absolute Creator. Again we say: If reasons and evidence had *their own, independently compelling intellectual force*, then even God would have had to obey them—and who, we repeat, would have created them?

To be sure, many have reasons for following God's will. They may say, "God is good, God created me, and God is infallible, *therefore* (reason) I should follow God's orders." But though at first this seems plausible, indeed, natural and familiar, in the end one cannot usefully say this. It is undermined by the radical, seldom thought-through implications of creation *ex nihilo*.

For these very reasons offered to justify obeying God have weight only because, and insofar as, God *willed* that they have weight—*and for no other reason.* God willed us to find such reasons "good" or "compelling" (otherwise, to repeat, they would be good and compelling *on their own*, independent of God's willing them worthy and real, and therefore would have as great a claim on God as on us).

Therefore, when one says something like "I should obey God because God is good" one is saying, "I should obey God's will because of something else God willed."

Absolute creation means mindless obedience

To obey God (to "obey God's Word") can only amount to accepting commands or statements that have no reason for compliance other than being commanded. Because their basis lies only in will, there exist no reasons or grounds that may be examined to decide to obey God's Word—*or to justify anything else one may wish to decide.*

And without the countless things that in life we use as reasons or grounds—things we perceive and judge and test, like someone's behavior or reasoning, or something's harmoniousness or randomness, something's efficiency or inefficiency or something's ideal character—we have no basis on which to make an idea our own—to possess it rather than be possessed by it.

One cannot possess one's ideas if ultimately all one can do is accept or reject an idea for no reason. (Risking tedium, we point out that it does no good to say God created, say, a beautiful place, and that you

judge it beautiful and thereby *make up your mind* to spend time it—
and that is an idea or plan you *own*. For there is no such thing as
beauty (over ugliness), only the will to call something "beauty" and
the will that our bodies respond to it.

Some might say of obeying God without grounds that there is a
special purity of obedience that transcends rational considerations,
since this obedience is a sacred, not a secular act. (It is the kind of se-
questering or "privileging" of the religious most famously found,
perhaps, in Søren Kierkegaard's "leap of faith" which was avowedly
religious precisely because it involved contravening rationality.)

Absolute creation homogenizes all thought

But the idea of willing to believe in God *for no reason* whatever—
especially when willed *against* what we ourselves are convinced is a
reason—makes it impossible to assign that willing to the particular
sphere of *religion* rather than any other.

For willing, sheer willing, *apart from independent reasons*, is willing
pure and simple. It is not academic willing, not artistic willing, not
nationalistic willing, not religious willing (and so on). If one wills
pure obedience only in the case of belief in God, one must have reasons for the differentiation, and then the willing rests on rationality,
on consistency, not on pure, universal obedience.

Skepticism and scientism contra the person

It is equally essential to see that another worldview, another
stance toward ultimate reality, is incompatible with criteria for being
a person. Religion's passion to know the ultimate context of human
activity is aped by two literally different, yet effectively identical,
worldviews: skepticism and scientism. Of course both deny they
have anything to do with metaphysics (the ultimate nature of things).

Skepticism says we cannot know the world. Scientism says we
can know the world—but only through the methods and concepts of
physical science. But, when human thought and culture are viewed
through the lens of physical science, the resulting picture of mind and
culture entails skepticism—hence their effective sameness.

When scientifically explained, the products of the human mind
are attributed to causes—not reasons and not meanings. Immaterial
or "non-physical" things cannot "make" or cause anything to happen. We cannot explain what we do or say by referring to reasons and
meanings.

Like feedback machines run by *cause and effect*—caused "minds"
are no more able to "know" things or "realize" or "understand"

things computers are.[140] Hence, scientism becomes skepticism.

First skepticism itself:

The ability to know reality has been denied by thinkers as separated in time as Pyrrho of fourth-century Greece and James Ellis of contemporary America. Pyrrho (and others) began a long tradition of saying we cannot compare our ideas of reality with things-in-themselves—that is, things as they are when we are not looking at them or thinking about them ourselves (things untainted by a perspective on them). So, we cannot know how things really are.[141]

Ellis (whose *Against Deconstruction* brilliantly "deconstructs" it) denies knowledge subtly, holding, for example, that objectivity and subjectivity are a false dichotomy. But, in the end, Ellis says "there is no piece of knowledge such that its complete objectivity can be the occasion of an inner conviction . . . [in the knower] . . . that he could not possibly be mistaken."[142]

Skeptical views such as this will be critically examined in Chapter 3. Here we simply say this is not true. Ellis knows he wrote a book; that he knows it is incontrovertible and objectively the case. That Ellis worked at a university is known by Ellis in a way that is also incontrovertible and can be stated with absolute and complete objectivity.

Once they deny that we can know the physical world, skeptics have no problem denying the independent status or "reality" of nonphysical "worlds." The rules or standards—the norms—by which we distinguish rationality from irrationality and meaningfulness from meaninglessness are, for skeptics, not real in the sense of having independent status (and a claim, therefore, on all thought).

Even norms governing physical inquiry—norms of inductive validity essential to science—can and have been denied any independent imperative status. Whatever force they may have is deemed the outcome of our own decisions to make them so—nothing else. In consequence the reality of (even) physical properties—known through the use of such norms—can be denied.

Hume, for example, admitted that his theory of knowledge entailed that no knowledge of a world outside our own consciousness was possible, while the philosopher Ernst Mach insisted that reality or "the world" is a construction—a useful fiction.[143]

Therefore, skepticism and scientism, *no less than creationist theism*, deny the existence of evidential grounds or probative arguments that can justify human purposes or ideas. That is, nothing exists, in reality, that is independent of and evaluative of our own wishes, desires, demands, or mere imagining.

Without *independent* evidence or *independently normative reasons or norms*, the question "is that your idea?" can only be answered *psychologically*: "yes, I have it in my head," or "yes, it's mine because I believe it." There is no way, under these methodologies and worldviews, to escape from the mind's confines when it comes to supporting or discrediting ideas.

Where, in theism, God simply makes things up, in skepticism humankind simply makes things up. For both there is no independent material or ground by which the mind can chasten or improve itself. There be no such thing as *learning*! There is nothing "out there." It is all "in the head." The mind has no means for becoming its own master, that is, for taking responsibility for what it concludes or decides or feels.

The "war" between creationist theism on the one hand and scientism and skepticism on the other, is, therefore, at the deepest level, a family feud. One can only choose between sheer willfulness in the infinite, supernatural domain, or sheer "willfulness" in the finite, natural domain.

In neither case has one any recourse to the processes of judgment that distinguish control from lack of control in respect to what one believes. Without such processes of judgment, one cannot own one's life. One cannot become one's own person—or, as we have said, a person rather than a creature or thing.

Scientism's role is identical in effect but different in form. We have mentioned the incompatibility of a programmed mind or a genetically determined mind with a mind that is its own master. Scientism sees the processes of judgment moving from idea to idea by virtue of physical causation. Psychology as science explains why we think what we think by reference to causal forces like anxiety states, or genetic impulses or dispositions, and other causal factors.[144] But if one's thoughts are determined by causation of the physical or psycho-physical sort, then there is no center of control, no independent "self" that may be said to manage what we think.

The conflict between causation and responsibility is widely recognized. Popular culture is no stranger to it. Stereotypically, "liberals" are willing to consider that a crime may have resulted from causes beyond the criminal's control—a violent childhood and a history of social rejection, perhaps—while "conservatives," granting the forces of childhood and society insist that, in the end, we are not caused to do things but elect to do them. One cites causation with its entailment of non-responsibility; the other admits causal elements but asserts free (uncaused) will and thus, responsibility.

In any case, we all think it good to help others. But a completely *scientistic* account would explain our idea not as derived from investigation and perception—or born of experiential knowledge and moral insight—but as the unavoidable result (given our initial brain conditions) of a chain of causation that produces what we call "helping" behavior in the presence of those we call "needy." The thoughts we think (if we think at all) are themselves eruptions in consciousness that are aspects of the causal chain; they themselves, as *ideas*, cause nothing (they may cause things, as thoughts—if we consider thoughts to be states of the brain).

There is no difference in such a reality between the principles that determine the way a computer operates and the way human minds operate. As we have said, scientism talks about "artificial intelligence"—but as we have also said, the artificial intelligence movement (and there *is* a movement) doesn't talk about "artificial wisdom"—yet.

If all reality is describable by science, then one cannot meaningfully say, in an ordinary way, "this is what I conclude," for, strictly speaking, what would be true is "this is what my brain concludes"— or "this is what I conclude but I could never have concluded anything else" (I had no choices), or "this is what my brain concludes and I can't specify all the causes that made it so."

"Responsibility" is meaningless here (until radically redefined by scientistic and skeptical types to give it a *new*, scientistically or skeptically adjusted meaning!) We cannot be "responsible" for causes we neither know of nor understand; nor can we be responsible for the chains of causation that began when we were born.

Indeed, since scientistic theorists can only describe how scientistic ideas have *happened to them* (by the same causal principle that acne or headaches happen to them), they cannot even take *responsibility* for holding or defending a scientistic theory.

Because they cannot claim knowledge but can only report *convictions* (factual dispositions to perceive, speak and act in certain ways), they are as we have said, skeptics—self-defeated by their own skeptical implications.

So it is that as scientism prospers in a techno-scientific, market-driven culture, people speak less of their convictions and understandings than of their "belief-systems" (read "software program"). If someone asks, "are those ideas your own?" there is only one answer unless you are lying—"of course they're my own; they're in my head aren't they?" Issues between education and indoctrination disappear, if there is no *objective* difference between well-grounded instruction and ill-grounded instruction and no *objective* difference in worthiness between manipulating a child's mind or informing a child's mind.

The requirement of grounds and understanding to make ideas one's *own* is utterly irrelevant when ideas are caused rather than grounded—when they result from forces and conditions, not meanings and rational considerations.

The "belief-system" advocate who ignores research and reason can comfortably say, "why bother thinking"—it's simpler just to believe straightaway." (For, an ungrounded belief cannot be made better by supporting it with more, but equally ungrounded, beliefs.)

Thus, the idea of the *person*—the responsible self—depends absolutely on the possibility of knowledge. And with this reference to truth's creative power—for we are saying it enables us to be more than machine, more than animal. . . . to be *human*—we move to consider the nature of knowledge, belief, faith, and revelation, hoping to show in what sense knowledge may be seen both as a miracle and as an aspect of what we seek when we seek both our purpose and a oneness with God.

NOTES

1. Some will fear the choice courts bias. Fair enough, if objectivity be not disallowed. But, in this writer's experience those quick to charge bias also hold that bias is inescapable because *one* view is not *all* views (which makes the charge of bias as useful as the charge of using language. (The retort that the charge encourages bias-reduction is inconsistent; see Ch. 3).

2. Ch. 1, "Truth, Religion and Philosophy."

3. Karen Armstrong, in a *A History of God*, says God has been conceived both variously and *incompatibly*. But, as her book is the history of an *idea*, not a *word*, there must be a meaningful "family resemblance" among God-ideas despite literal differences.

4. The term *cause* here refers to *physical* causation, understood as physical *necessitation*. But "cause" has other meanings as in "the price caused me to change my mind" where "cause" means "a sufficient *reason*."

5. Which is why, dear reader, I am writing and you are reading.

6. See Sigmund Freud's example in *The Future of an Illusion* (Garden City, N.Y.: Doubleday Anchor Books, orig. pub. 1927), pp. 44-45, wherein Freud argues for the irrationality of certain religious ideas before suggesting what *causes* them.

7. For example, Rudolph Carnap spoke of "constructing finally all of science, including psychology, on the basis of physics," see "The Methodological Character of Theoretical Concepts," p. 74, in *Minnesota Studies in the Philosophy of Science*, vol. 1, ed. Herbert Feigl and Michael Scriven (Minneapolis: University of Minnesota Press, 1956), pp. 38-76. See also the work of W. V.

Quine (*From a Logical Point of View*) in which all mental activity, including, knowing, is explained by physical concepts.

8. J. J. C. Smart, "Sensations and Brain Processes, in *The Philosophy of Mind*, ed. V. C. Chappell (New Jersey: Prentice-Hall, 1962).

9. Some might argue that "reasons" could be understood as *signs* (the way dark clouds are signs of rain), but if exponents of such a theory tried to give reasons for their theory, they would only be telling us what *signals* their belief in the theory; they would not be telling us what *supports* or *warrants* it.

10. Historians tend to be in touch with "the practical world": see, for example, William Dray, *Laws and Explanation in History* (London: Oxford University Press, 1957), pp. 124-126, which emphasizes explanation by reasons. See also pp. 152-154 on "rational necessity" as explanation, though here, when he says reasons *can* be called "causes," he doesn't mean *physical* causes.

11. "Bodily state" is vague; belief, like habits, have inertia; mind cannot directly control them, hence *embedded* or *bodied*.

12. We have no interest in dissolving the problem by denying the necessity in causation; causes do *make* things happen.

13. As a type, this error seems to be what the British philosopher Gilbert Ryle called a "category error," wherein things that "by definition" (as it were) cannot possibly interact are said to do so. (like explaining a tire failure by reference to pronunciation of its brand name). See Gilbert Ryle, *Mind*.

14. Michael Novak, *Belief and Unbelief* (New York: A Mentor Book, The New American Library, The Macmillan Company, 1965), p. 113.

15. People who say that talk about God need not meet the tests of plausibility or reason (because God's doings are above reason) exempt themselves from *any* charge of irrationality. But for that very reason, they can never support or deny other things attributed to God by appealing to rationality or irrationality of whatever may be attributed.

16. "Metaphysics"(roughly) asks for the most general and ultimate features of reality. See Richard Taylor, *Metaphysics* (Englewood-Cliffs, N.J.: Prentice-Hall Foundations of Philosophy Series, 1963), pp. 1-2. And (more advanced) D. W. Hamlyn, *Metaphysics* (Cambridge, UK: Cambridge University Press, 1984), pp. 1-10, esp. p. 8, par. 2.

17. John Dewey, *A Common Faith* (New Haven: Yale University Press, 1934.), p. 6.

18. Michael Novak, p. 109; also Martin Buber's *I and Thou* affirms the personal approach to God.

19. This attitude poses problems for religious education; a God outside evidence cannot be supported by evidence, which makes religious "education" a misnomer; the appropriate terms would be "indoctrination" or "training."

20. For an excellent, comprehensive analysis of feeling ("emotion"), see Anthony Kenny, "Feelings," *Action, Emotion and Will* (London: Routledge & Kegan Paul, 1963), Ch. 3, pp. 52-75. For initial differentiations, see pp. 52-53.

21. See, for example, Gilbert Ryle, "Feelings" in *Aesthetics and Language*, ed. William Elton (Oxford, UK: Basil Blackwell, 1959) pp. 56-72; note pp. 58-59.

22. The idea that some beliefs, like belief in God, can be rationally held quite apart from evidence has been advanced by the philosopher, Alvin Plantinga. His view is addressed in Ch. 3, "God's Humanity."

23. William James, *The Varieties of Religious Experience* (New York: New

American Library/ a Mentor Book, 1958; orig. "The Gifford Lectures 1901-2), p. 40.

24. For the general physiological approach: see Antii Revonsuo, *Inner Presence* (Cambridge, Mass.: MIT Press, 2006) which argue that consciousness works causally; see also P. S. Churchland and T. J. Sejnowski, *The Computational Brain* (Cambridge, Mass.: MIT Press, 1994) for similar arguments which see neuroscience and/or biology explaining what we think as *physically caused*.

25. Psychiatric therapy does use talk to alter feelings that are in some degree "fixed" or "stuck," that is, which are physically (neurologically) caused, but this is said to be useful only because of "transference," a process of psychological attachment that, is neurologically rooted and thus "causal" and which allows psychological bonds to be broken when combined with certain ideas. There is no doubt that this process is shrouded in mind-body issues that may, perhaps, never be fully clarified.

26. Willard Gaylin, *Rediscovering Love* (New York, NY: Viking Penguin, Inc., 1986), p. 92.

27. All people today are classified as *homo sapiens sapiens*—i.e., the *sapiens* variety of the species *homo sapiens*.

28. One can love the attitudinal beauty or religious universality of religions that attribute souls to animals, but since their adherents typically eat animals and not people; the idea of "soul" is a matter of appreciating the link between living, perceiving beings while withholding recognition of the gulf. "Western" religion is unbalanced the other way.

29. R. C. Zaehner, "Introduction," in *The Concise Encyclopedia of Living Faiths,* ed. R. C. Zaehner (Boston: Beacon Press, 1959),p. 18.

30. To philosophers: I simplify here. Feelings remain connected with judgment but drugs or physiological causation can and do produce conjoined "judgment" content with feeling-sensations or state. The *structure* of human feeling is mimicked rather than arising out of "in touch" or rational judgment. So, "seeing" involves an object, but drug-induced seeing only mimics seeing.

31. See, for example, Paul Tillich, *Dynamics of Faith* (New York: Harper & Row Publishers, 1957), p. 44. "The fundamental symbol of our ultimate concern is God." The question as to whether "ultimate concern" was *psychologically* ultimate or *conceptually* ultimate plagued Tillich till the end.

32. For neuroscientists ready to see thought as driven by brain conditions, the notion of incarnation is sheer nonsense.

33. This need for the nervous system is an empirical conclusion. Whether the idea of the self requires a physical body *conceptually* is another matter; this writer thinks not, as against Terence Penelhum's *Survival and Disembodied Existence* (London: Routledge and Kegan Paul, 1970), see esp. ch. 6, "Incorporeal Identity."

34. James Joyce, *Portrait of the Artist as a Young Man* (New York: The Modern Library, 1928), p. 241.

35. Kenny, p. 73.

36. Philip Clayton, "In Whom We Have Our Being," in *Advents of the Spirit: An Introduction to the Current Study of Pneumatology,* ed. D. Lyle Dabney and Bradford E. Hinze (Milwaukee: Marquette University Press, 2001), p. 173.

Alexander Pope, An Essay on Man, Epistle II.

37. Søren Kierkegaard,*Training in Christianity*, trans. Walter Lowrie (New York: Oxford University Press, 1941), p. 84.

38. Of course religions are concerned with behavior, but they are *uniquely* concerned only with what behavior signifies regarding *religious* belief. E.g., "can you believe and not give to the poor" or "believe and not pray?" etc. If one's primary concern is with the *morality* of what one feels, then one need only be a moralist; there is nothing specifically "religious" in this.

39. It may be sensed that in cults, feelings are neurotically or psychotically generated so that one's very humanity is at stake—as noted in discussing Abraham and drugs.

40. Rudolph Otto, *The Idea of the Holy*, trans. John W. Harvey (Oxford: Oxford University Press, 1967; orig. published Oxford University Press, 1923), p. 29.

41. Ibid., pp. 28-29. Otto's claim that God (the object) is "beyond our apprehension and comprehension" can be misleading, e.g., in being "supermundane" the "mysterious object" is already in part comprehended; the best clue to "ineffability"

42. Strictly, without knowledge about things there could be no hallucinations or fantasies or dreams. On this, see Frederick L. Will, "Thoughts and Things," in *Pragmatism and Realism: The Later Essays of Frederick L. Will*, ed. Kenneth Westphal (Lanham, Md.: Rowman & Littlefield. 1997), pp. 1-19.

43. H. H. Farmer, *Towards Belief in God* (New York: Macmillan Publishing Co., 1947), p. 176

44. For a powerful discussion of the superficiality that attends the attribution of value to subjective or personal enjoyment, see G. E. Moore, *Ethics* (New York: Oxford University Press, 1965; orig.pub. 1912), p. 102. It ends with an assertion of "self-evidence" against subjectivity or "pleasure" which we take to show not the impotence of Moore's argument but rather the profundity of the issue as "human" vs *non*-human.

45. John Seabrook's *Nobrow* (New York: Vintage Books, 2001), p. 24 (echoes of Thrasymachus in Plato's *Republic*).

46. See Alan Soffin, "Recollecting Honor" in *Images of Youth*, ed. Oliker and Krolokowski (New York: Peter Lang, 2001), pp. 200-221, esp. pp. 202-204.

47. Apropos this point, a film featuring the beating, torturing, but not the ideas, of Christ broke box office records.

48. This amazements flow from technological renderings of the brain and from the specificity of causation. It seems forgotten that the whole world understands what alcohol makes us say or do—proof that human thinking is a chemical process!

49. *Utilitarianism*, in J. S. Mill, *Utilitarianism, Liberty, Representative Government* (London: E. P. Dutton & Co., 1910), p. 395.

50. Ibid., p. 9.

51. Iris Murdoch, "The Sovereignty of Good over Other Concepts," in *Existentialist and Mystics*, ed. Peter Conradi (New York: Penguin Putnam Inc., 1998), p. 380.

52. See Herbert Fingarette, *Confucious—The Secular as Sacred* (New York: Harper & Row, Publishers, Harper Torchbooks,1972) and Baruch Spinoza, *Ethics*.

53. But this pantheistic drift will not cause us to slight the counter-claim that any viable God must be "personal" in nature. Whatever the outcome of inquiry, few will gainsay that the beliefs most readily conceded to be "religious" tend to be those that posit or presuppose an awesome presence, awareness, or mindful power beyond the physical world, one whose origin and nature are believed (however inconstantly) to elude comprehension. Indeed, religious sentiment seems inexorably drawn to claims of mysterious *agency* or *intelligence*. This predilection may appear early, as in the case of Jaweh, the God of Genesis, or over time as in the case of Gautama, Buddhism's founder, who was first thought a human teacher but centuries later "a direct manifestation of the Supreme Being . . . the Highest One in the flesh

54. "Why does anything exist?" may be too simply framed as a question to merit the appellation "theoretical," but we take as presumptively the case that any plausible answer to such a question must ascend to the level of a "theory."

55. George Gallup organization, "Basic Beliefs," 1993, p. 18.

56. Faith is fully discussed in ch. 3, "God's Humanity."

57. Strictly, a first cause or "unmoved mover (Aristotle)—Aquinas saying that argument could establish *that* there was a non-natural (non-contingent) reality which must be God, but not *what* that reality ("God") was like. The latter required revelation.

58. Forbearance, dear reader, we shall not in the end give short shrift to love.

59. William Barrett was chairman of the philosophy department at New York University, an editor of the *Partisan Review*, and a literary critic for the *Atlantic Monthly*.

60. Leibniz is famous, philosophically for his *Monadology,* which proclaimed a "pre-established harmony" among the ultimate constituents of reality. We are not concerned with whether Barret follows or deviates from Leibniz' chain of reasoning.

61. William Barrett, *Death of the Soul: From Descartes to the Computer* (Garden City, N.Y.: Anchor Press/Doubleday, 1986).

62. His *The Illusion of Technique* and *Irrational Man* pursue the anti-scientistic theme.

63. It is considered archaic to argue as to "human nature" but (to drop names) we think Plato and Aristotle were right in this.

64. J. M. Findlay, *Meinong's Theory of Objects and Values*, 2nd. ed. (Oxford: The Clarnedon Press, 1963), p. 326.

65. Ibid. p. 326.

66. Aristotle, *Physics* Bk. VII, Ch. 3.

67. Martin Heidegger was a student of "Being" famous for his Nazi affinities, obscure phraseology, and, for many philosophers, his brilliance! Despite his arcane terminology and subject matter, he did appreciate the reality revealed in everyday affairs.

68. Barrett, pp. 28-29

69. Of course it wouldn't have been "easier" to have one chain and a first cause if contingent things "must have a cause external to [themselves]. It would have been self-contradictory.

70. Actually, the parts of a thing can be contingent while the while is not,

because of the parts' contingency, contingent. Thus a necklace had links dependent on each other. But the necklace as a whole, or thing, is not *therefore* dependent on something. (This is the part-whole fallacy. E.g., each part of a chain may be round, but the chain itself can be not-round, i.e., straight.

71. The issue is clouded, too, by the idea that everything we encounter or know about has a beginning. But no beginning we have ever encountered began from *nothing*.

72. C. B. Martin, *Religious Belief* (Ithaca, N.Y.: Cornell University Press, 1959), p.148.

73. Richard Purtill, *Thinking About Religion* (Englewood Cliffs, N.J.: Prentice-Hall, Inc.), pp. 53-54.

74. The principle that "there is no fact without a sufficient reason why it exists and is so rather than otherwise" is circular or "empty." For, by definition, nothing could exist as it exists if there were *insufficient* reason for that to be the case.

75. See in Richard Purtill's *Thinking About Religion*, pp. 55-56.

76. Ibid., p. 54.

77. Ibid.

78. For an objection to this argument, see Jeffrey Brower, "Simplicity and Aseity," http://web.ics.purdue.edu/~brower/Papers/Simplicity%20and%20Aseity.pdf

79. Purtill, p. 55.

80. Barrett treats the universe as if it were "a particular fact" of the sort we normally explain or might try to explain. But "the universe" or "the whole" or "existence" is the *fact that* there are facts, it is not a "fact" in the particular or ordinary sense. We see this in realizing that there can be no facts of any sort left over to explain it. Being all there is, it cannot be explained by something *else*.

81. Ibid., p. 30

82. Friedrich Nietzsche, *The Gay Science*, trans. Walter Kaufman (New York: Random House, 1974; Vintage Books, 1974).

83. Often, but not always, William James' form of pragmatism conflated utility with truth; in his *Pragmatism"* (New York: Longmans Green. 1908), p. 76: "The true is the name for whatever proves itself to be good in the way of belief. . . ."

84. Barrett, pp. 30-31.

85. Ibid.

86. This writer cannot comfortably proceed without a personal remark. I write, necessarily, for those who have the good fortune of time and good health and who have elected to explore the issues of religious truth. Few have the luxury of doing so. But, like you, dear reader, I have seen the pain and need of those who lose loved ones and would never dispute the solace they no doubt require, nor do I disrespect their feelings. But true religion requires the long view. We must prepare. For all the struggle it involves, we all face death, and for the true religionist, it seems no preparation for life's end to have lived a falsehood.

87. Without standard expectations, the "Dadaist" movement could not have created "absurd" art; see also Martin Esslin, 3rd. ed., *The Theater of the Absurd* (New York: Vintage Books, 2004).

88. Charles Taylor, *The Explanation of Behavior* (London: Routledge & Kegan Paul, 1964), ch. 1, "Purpose and Teleology"; esp. pp. 17-23.

89. Immanuel Kant, *Grounding of the Metaphysics of Morals*, trans. James W. Ellington (Indianapolis: Hackett Publishing Company, 1981), p. 21.

90. Ibid.

91. Novak, *Belief and Unbelief*, p. 146. It is interesting that Novak qualifies God's inscrutability by saying "in our present state"—suggesting God's reasons might be known in a heavenly afterlife—but if God's will *is* his "reasons" we can only know that the existence of what we call "evil" and what we call "good" will never be more justifiable than being what God willed.

92. James Dobson, *When God Doesn't Make Sense* (Carol Stream, Ill.: Tyndale House Publishers, 1997), p. 43.

93. Novak, especially pp. 111-112 and p. 146.

94. Ibid., p. 155.

95. Ibid., p. 125.

96. Ibid., p. 125

97. That knowing is indeed miraculous is the "politically incorrect" contention of chapter three.

98. Novak, p. 143.

99. Sigmund Freud, *The Future of an Illusion* (Garden City, N.Y.: Doubleday & Company, Inc., 1963; orig. pub. 1927), pp. 28-29.

100. Freud, *Future*, p. 31.

101. Mircea Eliade, *The Sacred and the Profane*, trans. Willard R. Trask (New York: Harcourt Brace Jovanovich, Publishers; a Harvest/HBJ Book, 1959), p. 11.

102. Ibid., p. 12.

103. Ibid., p. 11.

104. James F. Ross, "God, Creator of Kinds and Possibilities," in *Rationality, Religious Belief and Moral Commitment*, ed. Robert Audi and William J. Wainright (Ithaca: Cornell University Press, 1986), pp. 315-334.

105. Recall that "nothing" is not an *empty space*—and may be best "envisioned" by trying to imagine the inside of a point.

106. Avery Dulles, S. J., *Models of Revelation* (Garden City, N.Y.: Doubleday & Company, Inc., 1983), p. 3.

107. John Wyclif, quoted in Ian Christopher Levy, *Scriptural Logic, Real Presence, and the Parameters of Orthodoxy* (Milwaukee: Marquette University Press, 2003), p. 83.

108. Karl Barth, trans. G. T. Thomson, *Dogmatics in Outline* (New York: Harper's Torchbooks, 1959) p. 23

109. Barth, *loc. cit.*

110. H. A. R. Gibb, "Islam" in *The Concise Encyclopedia of Living Faiths*, ed. R. C. Zaehner (Boston: The Beacon Press, 1959), p. 178.

111. John L. Kater, *Christians on the Right* (New York: Seabury Press, 1982), pp. 10-11.

112. Jim Castelli, *A Plea for Common Sense* (San Francisco: Harper & Row Publishers, 1988), p. 133.

113. Triablogue.blogspot.com 11/13/2004

114. Any suggestion that people who can know (recognize) what is good would know it *faster* through God's Word must contend with the vision of life

as God's intended testing or learning-and-developing ground.

115. Elaine Pagels, *The Gnostic Gospels* (New York: Vintage Books, Random House, Inc., 1979), p. 34.

116. Ch. 3 deals with the idea that all knowledge claims are circular (making circularity is a pointless charge).

117. James, *The Varieties*, p. 311.

118. Logic is about consistent argument. To say logic doesn't apply to God is misleadingly to say.

119. In Frederick Ferré, *Lamguage, Logic and God* (Chicago: University of Chicago Press, 1981 orig. pub. Harper, New York), p. 78.

120. Brian Hebblethwaite, *In Defense of Christianity* (Oxford, England: Oxford University Press, 2005), p. 59.

121. It seems not recognized that this means "*I myself* am beyond logic"; that is, "I need not argue consistently when I talk about God."

122. Keith Ward, *Religion and Creation* (Oxford: Oxford University Press, 1996), p. 9

123. C. S. Lewis, *Miracles* (New York: Macmillan Publishing Co., Inc., 1960 [orig. pub. 1947]), p. 80

124. Barrett, pp. 160-161.

125. Paul Tillich in D. Mackenzie Brown, *Ultimate Concern: Tillich in Dialogue* (New York: Harper & Row, Publishers, 1965), p. 6.

126. Vincent M. Colapietro and John E. Smith, eds. *Reason, Experience and God: John E. Smith in Dialogue* (New York: Fordham University Press, 1997), p. 12.

127. Paul Tillich, *The Religious Situation* (New York: Meridian Books, 1956), p. 35.

128. Mercea Eliade, *Myth and Reality* (New York: Harper & Row Publishers, Inc., 1963), p. 11.

129. Ward, *Religion and Creation*, p. 119; see pp. 113-114.

130. Of course, if true, nothing can be argued at all, or said, for animals cannot "do" reasoned argument; like Ludwig Wittgenstein, we say what we "cannot" say and "throw away the ladder." See Wittgenstein's *Tractatus.*

131. Keith Ward, *Religion and Creation*, p. 9; see also pp. 292ff.

132. God is generally said to be "outside time" or "time irrelevant" so terms like "before" are frowned upon. Hence we say "outside of" God's willing, not just "before" God's willing. For convenience, and because it changes no arguments, we tend to describe God as acting in time.

133. Aquinas said God' s moral laws were not arbitrary because God already had an idea of human nature from which certain rules of behavior would follow and other not. But Aquinas did not, and could not, claim God was *bound* to this conception of human nature. God could envision anything God opts to envision.

134. Brian Davies, *An Introduction to the Philosophy of Religion*, p. 75; Davies explores many "has to be a beginning" arguments.

135. Davies, *An Introduction*, p. 119.

136. A point made by F. H. Bradley and implicitly seconded by Mary Warnock who, paraphrasing Bradley, allows that "it is, in fact, not merely a tautology that a man's acts are his own." See Mary Warnock, *Ethics Since 1900* (London: Oxford University Press, 1960), p. 4. Bradley's point is that acts ex-

press one's whole character, but this could not be important if the only difference between acts was that they were atomistically or wholistically produced; clearly "character" is something created out of judgments and choices
fro which one can be held *responsible*.

137. F. C. Copleston, *Medieval Philosophy*, p. 133

138. Irony is surely the rule of life. When arguments attack the idea that
God exists, we are repeatedly advised that God is utterly unlike us and operates for reasons and in ways way we cannot possible conceive. When God is
accepted, the explanation of his ways and powers turn out to be enough like
the ways and powers of mankind to be widely and readily understood.

139. Simon Blackburn, *Truth* (Oxford: Oxford University Press, 2005), p.
43.

140. Computers may have "memories" but not nostalgia (frogs as well);
computers may calculate but are never wise (frogs as well . . . recall the accurately calculated tongue-flick).

141. See A. A. Long, *Hellenistic Philosophy*, 2nd. ed. (Berkeley: University of
California Press), p. 84 and pp. 87-88.

142. John Ellis, *Against Deconstruction* (Princeton: Princeton University
Press, 1989), p. 123.

143. See Leszek Kolakowski, *The Alienation of Reason* (Garden City, N.Y.:
Doubleday & Company, Inc., 1968) for a history of Positivism (which, while
"scientism," strictly, is nonetheless effectively skeptical).

144. As "science," psychology doesn't allow explanation of thought by
meanings or reasons or understandings—the categories of practical existence—but by causes and effects such as "anxiety reduction." We do not
mean that the mind cannot be overdetermined by causes and properly studied, then, scientifically. We say this is not always the way the mind works.

God's Humanity

Confucius saw, and tried to call to our attention, that the truly, distinctively human powers have, characteristically, a magical quality. His task, therefore, required, in effect, that he reveal what is already so familiar and universal as to be unnoticed. What is necessary in such cases is that one come upon this "obvious" dimension of our experience in a new way, in the right way.
—Herbert Fingarette, *Confucius—the Secular as Sacred*

Thus I live in the world rather as a Spectator of mankind than as one of the species."
—Joseph Addison, *The Spectator*, no. 1., London, 1711.

"The mind of man cannot be enlightened permanently by merely teaching him to reject some particular set of superstitions. There is an infinite supply of other superstitions always at hand."
—Gilbert Murray, *Five Stages of Greek Religion*

INTRODUCTION

This is the chapter on which the reinterpretation of religious "facts" turns. Either there is a natural, knowledge-based foundation for uniquely *religious* facts or else exemplary religious facts like creation, miracle, incarnation, and revelation will continue to rest, at bottom, not on evidence or reason but on the will to believe—that is, on *faith*.

This may not trouble some, but without a basis in knowledge and reason, the institution of religion will continue to be diminished by the hegemony of science, by philosophical critiques, and by societies increasingly organized around acquisitive self-interest and the allure of technique. As a vital human concern, religion ought not continue to suffer from the perpetuation of human beings' earliest speculations regarding the nature of reality and the manner in which knowledge is acquired.

The truth of uniquely religious facts is regarded by religions themselves as essential. That is why religions so vigorously defend the existence of "supernatural" facts. If there are no *uniquely* religious facts, then there is nothing to distinguish religion from ethics—save morally instructive parables and exhortations that are, in themselves, secular. (One might think that Confucianism proves religions can be nothing more than moral codes, but as Chapter 4 shows, the "Li" or "the Way" has more by way of mystery than a collection of moral injunctions.)

The chief theological contention of this chapter is that knowledge, when fully understood, supports the reality of uniquely religious facts. Specifically, I wish to argue that knowledge is a bridging of mind and matter that is *in principle* a mystery—hence, a *genuine* mystery—and that through *knowing* we mammals—we "homo sapiens sapiens"—are *inexplicably* created "human." Mahatma Ghandi may well have sensed this when he declared, "truth is God." In any case, what I suggest is a reinterpreted but no less miraculous understanding of the traditional "Creation."

I wish also to assert that knowledge is, literally, *incarnation*, for in *the act of knowing*, the *incorporeal* truth of things becomes *effective* in the corporeal beings that we are. Indeed, this conception further illustrates what I mean by religious facts resting not on faith but on evidence and reason. What I contend is that the traditional, religious "fact" of God (or Gods) walking the Earth in human form represents an early insight into the *strangeness of knowing*; so that knowledge *miraculously* comes to us—but from godly visitations.

And, indeed, knowing *is* strange. If it were not, there would be no history of skeptical attacks on knowledge beginning in the Hellenic period and achieving full flower in our own. Knowledge is strange (to put it as succinctly as possible) because knowledge of worldly truths cannot be *logically* proven, yet worldly knowledge purports to state what *cannot possibly* be false. That's why you can't say, "I know it's true but maybe it's not." Nor, when we know a thing, is there any physical feature of our brains, utterances, or behavior that distinguishes our knowing a thing from our merely believing it.

That is why positivism, anthropological relativism, and a recrudescent Nietzchean cynicism all see knowledge as nothing but *be-*

lief. "Knowledge" and "truth" have fallen on hard philosophic times. "Truth" has been demoted to the status of an honorific tag hung on whatever we believe; "knowledge" has been derided as the term we use to justify imposing our beliefs on others.

All culture is infected. The journalism that mediates between social fact and the citizen's impression of social fact tells its audience that "objectivity" is impossible. "Truth" becomes "an expression of your perspective" (or "belief-system"). The democratic necessity of governance by an informed (not brainwashed, not mislead) citizenry is undercut by the contention that humans can never know reality.

Consequently, for cultural no less than for religious reasons, the first task of this chapter is to defend the idea that knowledge can be had—that objectivity is real. To that end, I address *the basic intellectual strategies* by which knowledge is denied—with special attention to the arguments of empirical philosophers against the reality of right and wrong, that is, against evaluative *knowledge*. In the course of these critical deliberations, I argue, as did Immanuel Kant, that if we have knowledge then there must be free will, confirming theism's insistence that free will is a reality. (The reader unacquainted with philosophy should be alerted that in arguing for the reality of moral and aesthetic knowledge and for free will I argue against the most vocal, perhaps dominant, tradition in philosophy—sparing it no more than I spared supernaturalism.)

This chapter is not easy. I would not attempt to draw the religious seeker into the close, philosophical arguments by which my conclusions are reached were it not that only through active engagement can their significance be *felt*. Only by *working these arguments through* can one find, in the religious vision they imply, the emotional substance that religion demands.

I make no argument against wordless, religious feeling: the sight of vast landscapes, the dappled light of late afternoon, the face of a loved one asleep. But moments of great wonder and awe, while *religiously foundational*, also presage and encourage ideational development. The simple folk melodies that justly and deeply touch the heart are not demeaned but further realized by the larger works brought forth from them.

In any case, one must *live* the arguments if emotion is to grow from what intellect discerns. And so, this chapter invites you into an ancient field of battle. In facing the assault of skeptical challenges, I hope you will find yourself beginning to *doubt* that knowledge of reality can be had and, yes, to *feel* that worldly knowledge-claims can have no justification, and that knowledge is *impossible*!

Feeling this, should you later come to see that worldly knowledge is *presupposed*—is unavoidably assumed—by everything we think, then, perhaps you may see knowledge as the foundational miracle it is. (And "miracle," here, is argued strictly on the basis of *traditional* theistic standards.) I believe that only when its "impossible" transcendence of the physical domain is fully grasped can the religious significance of knowledge come alive. Only then might one be willing to agree that in *knowing* is the word become flesh, and that the presence of the word in flesh may be understood as God's humanity.

A religious vision of the human situation builds upward from the miracle of knowledge. *Knowing*, for example, makes us *responsible*, and responsibility distinguishes the animal from the human. Here, the unbeliever seeks support from Genesis!

In the tale of the Garden, the Tree of Knowledge is linked to responsibility and then to being human. However shakily, it tells us that what Adam and Eve know is the condition of their responsibility. It would not "parse" for God to have said, "you didn't know what you were supposed to do but, nevertheless, I'm going to punish you." Later, Adam "names" (has dominion over) the animals that—lacking knowledge—have not Adam's responsibility. The story implies that no being is responsible who is without knowledge, and that no being can deny responsibility who possesses it.

The role of knowledge in creating us *human* is thus intimated in our earliest attempts to understand the meaning of uniquely "human" life. It is, nonetheless, with some trepidation that I commend this lengthy chapter to you, hoping you may find the journey worthwhile.

RELIGION AND KNOWLEDGE

Our dependence on the "other"

If, as we say, religion hopes to find that the universe is not merely our location, but our home, then it must tell us how we came to be and what we are. And if we are more than our own psychology—as in every walk of life respect for standards and for truth implicitly affirms—then we are indeed, a form of life in *some* real sense "created" above, if continuous with, the life of animals.

But this unique status is possible only if norms and knowledge are aspects of the world. Norms and knowledge must be *complements* and not inventions or "projections" of the mind, as philosophic doubt would have it.

We transcend the animal only if, "epistemologically"—that is, with respect to *knowing*—the world can impress itself upon us (albeit not by simply stamping truths on passive minds, as when statements are explained as *God's*-word-*not*-humanity's.

If life's meaning can be more than self-satisfying fiction, it must be true that "things can guide us in our epistemic endeavors, if we have the good fortune and wit to discern their guiding signs."[1] It must be true that "they can, nudge us, frustrate us and so prompt us to bring our conceptual and linguistic practices into conformity with aspects of the world which we at the time may only dimly recognize."[2]

As muscles develop only where the world offers resistance, the mind, too, develops only where the world resists the mind's internal play. A dreamer who has never been awake has no more "mind" then a kaleidoscope.

And, while it is well understood that our bodies *exist* only by absorbing and reworking the world, it seems little noted that the mind *exists* only insofar as, in a very different way, it absorbs and reworks the world.

Still, people have an underlying sense that the nourishment of soul and mind depends on a source outside themselves. The sense that we depend on something "other" finds expression in traditional theism. According to its narratives, life's meaning comes from without. Something independent creates and informs the thinking being. In a word, "God"—the multifaceted reality that exists independently of us—enables us, through the various domains of *knowing*—to recognize, and thus be "given," the *law*.[3]

In claiming, as we do, that, from the standpoint of a philosophical theology, reality fills an otherwise animal humanity, we are not forced to deny the importance of free will and responsibility. Quite the opposite.

Free will and responsibility would be pointless in a world where whatever we might think or do could not be distinguished in value or truth from anything else we might think or do.

Free will and responsibility become irrelevant if rightness and goodness and truth can make no *independent* claims on us.

Indeed, the very possession of intellect would be useless if nothing independent existed to inform, challenge, and test it.

The religious interest is, surely, to know and live an ultimately meaningful life—a life that transcends—even as it incorporates—our animal nature. But one cannot sanely love and commit to a world one cannot possibly know. Indeed, to love a world one entirely invents is, in effect, to love oneself.

That is why, if the philosophic doubt of knowledge is justifiable, religion collapses, becoming either an entertainment, an instrument of social control or inexpensive therapy.

In this way philosophic doubt (not agnosticism or atheism) becomes the most profound enemy of religion. The skeptical outcome of philosophic doubting blinds us to the union of body and spirit that the activity of *knowing*, alone, effects, and to the union thus implied between spirit and world—the union for which religion yearns.

Knowledge, belief, faith, and revelation

As may already be apparent, this chapter is pivotal for all we write. If we are wrong about the nature and implications of knowing, we are wrong about practically everything else we hold to be of religious or philosophical significance.

Against skepticism, we shall argue that knowledge cannot be coherently denied.

And we shall argue, beyond what we already have, that without the existence of *knowledge*, the very idea of a *mind* cannot be affirmed. Without knowledge, the term *mind* can have no sense other than as a container of sensations and images.

The union of knowledge and mind is, we think, *metaphysically* fundamental in declaring *the nature of a relationship ineluctable and irreducible.*

(Love is of course essential or foundational for religion and human life.[4] But it is not foundational of *transcendence*. Love can embrace evil as well as good, the foolish as well as the profound, and when untouched by appraisal, hardly differs from animal love; therefore to say the knowing *mind* is foundational is not to minimize love but only to insist on the conditions necessary to liberate love's goodness.)[5]

We will analyze knowing from the viewpoint of philosophy and state the outcome from the viewpoint of theology.

Our basic contention will be that *knowing*—like Existence and like the gods of theism—is unique (*sui generis*) and miraculous. Inexplicable yet true, *knowing* (by virtue of its nature) is *creative of Being*—specifically the *human* type of Being. Such knowing is a way of being in the world that is neither idea nor body but instead, irreducibly, uses both.

We do not say, "synthesizes" both. The use of "synthesize" may suggest an understanding of the way this happens. We think it *ultimate*, hence inexplicable.

These brief, formulaic descriptions of knowing and its implications are, unhappily, abstruse, but humanity is, of itself, a very strange thing—having emerged out of stardust and comets.

Phrased in language appropriate to religion, *knowing* is the transformation of material reality by non-material reality—the physical by the notional, the corporeal by the incorporeal.[6]

Knowing parallels theism's miracle of Creation in that something without a *physical* existence transforms and elevates that which, otherwise, would have only a *physically determined* existence—and does so simply by virtue of what it *is*. Thus *human* being emerges from *physical* being, whether the latter is conceived as "animal" or as chemical and electrical processes.

Knowing can therefore, in our view, be fairly described as an "unmoved mover"—a moment of insight or completion that, *merely by occurring*, creates a new form of Being—one that transcends (is not determined by) bodily, or physical *cause-effect* determination.

And in this inexplicable "union," shall we say, of idea and body (this galactic surprise wherein an animal asks what is right or true), we find the *religious*—the *miraculous*.

It is this idea of miraculous transformation (or "becoming") that infuses the theism's idea of "God-become-man" with its peculiarly religious character. Indeed, for Søren Kierkegaard, the *identity* of God and man in Christ is the key to Christian religion.[7]

We do not say the physical and the ideational are the same—a pure self-contradiction. We say only that they operate on different and incompatible principles that *somehow* find expression in the kind of felt understanding that constitutes a human existence. We may be blindly "fudging" things, but these seem the unblinkable facts of the matter, and though it is *not* an argument, still, we are encouraged by the puzzles of physics in which, for example, light behaves sometimes as a particle sometimes as a wave.

God's humanity—"God's" human form—is found in mind's *dependence* on the body. In *knowing*, "God becomes man" for what would otherwise be merely a body now *incorporates* truth.

God's humanity is truth mundanely realized. One might say that human divinity is, conversely, also made true by this "union," but we do not say it. There is too much animal in us to say it; it is more accurate to speak of a "divine spark." And this (though not well thought out at this writing) may be our only "original sin"—and not a "sin," really, because not our doing.

But all this is foreshadowing. One step at a time.

Is our talk about "God" reductionist?

It may seem that these arguments amount to a redefinition of "God." If they were, we could hardly criticize (as we have, and will, philosophers who consider ordinary language misleading with respect to reality and who therefore define its terms to fit the philosophers' conceptions of reality).

When (in our discussion of knowing) we argue as *fact* that something non-material enters into and transforms something otherwise merely material, we do not say that is what theists "really" mean by "incarnation."

We understand that in standard theistic usage, a non-natural agent becomes a natural agent while (miraculously) remaining what it was. What we contend is that *incarnation* and *knowing* share religiously significant characteristics or "criteria."

Assuming that knowing has the character we say it has, then one kind of Being (the evolved, physically determined species, homo sapiens sapiens) can be transformed into a *normatively determined* "species" by incorporating, *ideationally* and *affectively*, a different kind of Being—reality or, in a sense, "God." (We are created by the witting grasp of truth.)

These philosophical formulations are abstract, but what they refer to is familiar. Anyone who has had the good fortune to see an infant become a child and a child a "person" can recall that these stages involve a suddenly increased grasp of the human and physical world and a correspondingly increased degree of selfhood The way of being of the infant and the child is, in these periods, transformed.

The incarnation we speak of is implicitly acknowledged when we accord special value to the expert or the artist or wise person because we know they possess (have incorporated) aesthetic or factual or moral "information" and have become different in their person (not personality) through their mastery of it—"mastery" making it one with the self.

We implicitly acknowledge the metaphysical character of incarnation every time we want our children to find pleasure in the "better" things or "higher" appreciations. And we recognize it in ourselves when we find it of absolute importance that something we had read or been told (say, regarding our national history) was false (even if it had been, in fact, enjoyable to read or hear it—indeed, worse if we had enjoyed it.)

In *theistic* incarnation (physicality) "dust" can, by God's non-physical *willing*, become human. In the *non*-theistic version of incarnation, "dust" can by *knowing* become human.

In both cases, a multi-faceted reality (whether willed into existence by God, or an existence that simply is) enters into the being that is an animal (homo sapiens sapiens) by virtue of knowing (either by revelation or inquiry)—thereby creating us responsible or "human."

We take it that this embodiment—considered as a general taking in or mindfulness of reality—involves the taking in of what must be and thus of law and thus of what theism envisions as "God."

In both theistic and secular discourse, a transformation takes place in which disparate kinds of being are "somehow" synthesized. And in both cases the transformation is held true but *in principle* inexplicable ("in principle" meaning that the knowing *cannot possibly* have a scientific explanation).

Thus, both supernatural and secular theology assert the miraculous—the inexplicably transformative and elevating.

It is our argument that these are precisely the elements that give "God becoming man" a peculiarly *religious*, as opposed to a *superstitious*—or *magical*—character. Indeed, without the criterion of elevation that knowing, alone, provides the blending of a non-natural being with a natural might well elicit talk of demons, and not religious objects like "God."

For such reasons, we claim not to redefine theism's "incarnation" but to tease out its religiously significant principle.

We aim to rethink what makes it "religious" for people (rather than demonic or magical) when they suppose that God becomes one of us and "moves among us" or that God's creates us out of dust. On that basis, this chapter's claim that knowing is, in a religiously significant sense, *incarnation*, must be tested against the ordinary person's sense of what constitutes a phenomenon *religious*—or *literally miraculous* rather than magical or merely astonishing.

(This we do when we take up the "impossibility" of knowledge and C. S. Lewis' account of "miracles.")

In any event, we do not attempt to redefine religious terms in ways acceptable to *non*-religious interests such as the scientific or the therapeutic. Rather, we look to the criteria that, in our view, make god "God"—or "the divine"—religion's fundamental object.

We ask what it is about the God-idea that makes God sacred or "religious" and not (simply) a moral exemplar or dominating power (noting, always, that God as power must be "higher" not just "perfectly good" or "an absolute power").

Epistemology and religious experience

To grasp what it is to *know* is to awaken to a phenomenon no less mysterious, no less awesome, than what Rudolph Otto referred to in *The Holy*, as experiencing of the *"numen"*—a complex feeling of love, fear, and awe called forth in contemplation of the creative force, or "the divine." For when we see knowing clearly, we see it as a transaction that reveals the laws that constitute whatever is *real*—that makes things *resistant* to us—to will, wish, desire, need, intend, and so on—obduracy making them what they *are*.

(The "revealing of laws" is an archaic notion not in the mode of modern philosophy. Chapter 4, "God's Body," argues that whatever we consider real always partakes of *necessity*—hence "law.")

The problem for a philosophical theology is one of reawakening—of what has been called "re-enchantment." For how can we awaken to a miracle that is *commonplace*?[8] The *interdependence* of world, mind, and truth is so pervasive and continuous that what we call "knowing" seems to us no more remarkable than breathing or eating.

The same failure of appreciation hounds language. We marvel at the cell phone and satellite communications but never at the fact that sounds and marks can allow separate minds to be as one in thought. Oblivious to the amazements in us and around us, we, too often, fall victim to *manufactured* wonders—beguiled by gurus, indecipherable poesy, or the escapist promise of "alternate realities."

Save for the work of specialists, *knowing* seldom merits a remark. (We repeat Frederick Waismann's arch observation: "fish don't know that they are wet.")

To awaken to what we are, we must reexamine perception and inquiry from the standpoint of those who challenge our ability to access reality. We must see on what grounds brilliant minds, in all ages, have found themselves forced to conclude what no one amid life ever concludes—that we know nothing whatever about the world.

It must at the same time be confessed that if, in the flow of practical life some were honestly to state that they didn't know whether they were sitting in a chair or dancing on Mars, or whether torturing babies is wrong, they would be considered either drugged or "out of their minds" (an expression more profound than its ready employment suggests).[9]

But (most) philosophers are not insane! Their doubts about knowledge are not *actual* or *felt* doubts. Their "doubting" is based on the impossibility of justifying knowledge claims by dint of reasons. Putting it everyday terms: human beings have no *proof* that they can know reality; they have no logically certain proof of worldly certainties. So, knowledge-claims are held illegitimate by *rule*, namely, "It is always rational to doubt that we know (a thing)."

The efforts of philosophers to uncover the credentials of knowing as a human power arise from a genuine puzzle. How (they ask) can humans claim to know when, in fact, humans are fallible? What can distinguish so-called "knowledge" from *opinion*, "truth" from error?

Quite inadvertently, philosophic doubting can serve the religious interest. For the reasons philosophers offer against the possibility of knowledge only highlight for consciousness how "impossible" are the hurdles that knowing overcomes.

Skepticism's arguments show that what we overcome, we overcome inexplicably. And that is part of why we assert (*pace* philosophical disdain) the *miraculous* nature of "knowing."

By seeing knowing as skeptical thinkers view it, we are made to ask, "how can knowledge be?" and the answer—tellingly, we think—must, in the end, parallel "God's" famous answer: "I am."

Knowledge and error

To proceed, we must be clear that *if* we know (not *claim* to know), then we cannot possibly be wrong. "Not possibly wrong," is entailed by the term, "knowledge."[10]

We can see this when we try to deny it. If someone said, "I know it is so, but just possibly it may not be so" we would ask the person, "Do you know it or not?" The statement is self-contradictory.

"Knowing" entails "not possibly wrong as to truth." If we think a statement could just possibly be false, we say we *believe* it, or *think* it, or *feel* sure about it, or that it's *probable*—but not that we *know* it.

All skepticisms rest, implicitly or explicitly, on the point that worldly error can never be *proven* impossible. This lack of proof is taken to show that there is no rational way—no intellectually justifiable way—to eliminate all challenges to a knowledge-claim about worldly things.

Suppose I say something as plain as, "I *know* am brushing my teeth." The skeptic can say, "you may be deluded, hypnotized, in a trance and not know it." If I say, "but I'm not any of those things. Just look at this toothbrush, smell the mint, feel the wetness," the skeptic can observe that claims about toothbrush, foam, and wetness are all of the same type as the claim to know one is "brushing one's teeth."

If I say, "So what?" the skeptic will tell me that, "you cannot establish that you can know about the world by claiming to know other things about the world. That would be circular reasoning."

Typically, as we shall see, the skeptical challenge is couched in rather more imposing language. In philosophy, skeptics do not quibble over observable facts like toothbrushing. More to their taste are theoretical entities like sub-atomic particles and dark matter.

So we find one expression of skepticism saying: "the data of experience" [things we can observe] always leave scope for more than one explanatory hypothesis, and which one is to be chosen cannot be determined by experience."[11]

Here the aura of erudition can distract the non-philosopher from confronting the radical nature of what is being claimed. The statement entails that *no matter how much we study the world* we can never *know* why anything happens.

We can never be *certain* (not possibly wrong) that what we observe is explained, say, by the motion of molecules. Maybe an unknown force explains it—not molecules: "which one [explanation] is to be chosen cannot be determined by experience." In other words, you cannot prove as a matter of certainty that nothing else explains what you think you've explained.

Suddenly, we face an impasse. We can't give *evidence* that we know any particular thing since, to have force, the evidence must be (or rest on) knowledge, not belief or guesswork. And we can't say the evidence is *knowledge* since that is what we have to prove.

Defeated by the skeptic, we pull back: "Alright, I can have no *proof* of brushing my teeth, or *proof* that I do it as a choice, so, I suppose it's possible for me to be deluded, but I'm just certain I'm brushing my teeth, and doing it on purpose . . . I mean, for all practical purposes, my assertion is justifiable or, if you like, warranted, or, well . . . for me, *it works*."

And indeed, because we cannot *prove* that that we *cannot possibly* be wrong, and because the term *knowledge* seems unlikely to fall out of use, many philosophers decided knowledge cannot mean what people think it means. They therefore suggested that the word *knowledge* can make sense only if we understand it to mean "warranted assertability," "justifiable belief," "that which works" or "satisfies."[12]

What unites these and other re definitions of "knowledge" is that they no longer require that worldly knowledge-claims be not possibly wrong.

For, claims that are *warranted, justifiable, satisfying or useful* can be so even if they are false. It makes perfect sense to say, "I had every reason to think it, but it was false" or "what I said was justified by the evidence, but I later found out it was false."

Therefore, and crucially: when "knowledge" is redefined as what "works" or "satisfies," *truth* becomes irrelevant.

For instance, false ideas can *work*: "I chased the evil spirit out of the radio by banging on it, so now my radio works." And false ideas can satisfy: "I know my dead mother spoke to me because my life improved when I followed her advice."

In keeping with the "scientific" spirit of much philosophy, these *utilitarian* interpretations of "knowledge" make knowledge a matter of psychological or else, practical, satisfaction. And if knowledge is defined as some form of satisfying belief, then (because neither satisfaction nor belief are mysteries), suddenly neither is "knowledge!"

Empirical philosophy's noble—but in its zeal, ideological—program for demystifying the world is thus served, and knowing becomes anything but a miracle.

But for the religious impulse (which, for all its flights, remains rooted in the categories of practical life—that is, in such kinds of things as *free will, truth, moral reality*)—"knowledge" is still what the person-on-the-street understands it to be—a thing that, if possessed, cannot possibly be wrong.

Small wonder that against the denial of knowledge, many have sought its guarantee as the gift of a revelatory, supra-human "God."

Logic, knowledge, and reason

Of course, there is one kind of "knowledge" philosophers typically have no wish to redefine. That knowledge is not about the world but about *consistency among statements*.

For instance, if you *say*, "success is certain," you *know* you can't also say, "failure is possible." If you state, "this person is my father," you know you can't rationally state, "I am older than this person." If you state that something is circular, you know you can't state that it has two corners. If you state all pianists are persons, you can't, from that, conclude that all persons are pianists. Nor can you sensibly ask whether, if is Wednesday, the following day might also be Wednesday.

So, in formal logic and mathematics, when you state something, then (given what you have stated) there are other statements you cannot make without erasing, denying—that is, "contradicting"—your first statement.

The nature of contradiction was alluded to in chapter 1: if you state that something is so—for example, "Z is a circle"—then, if you also state it is not so—saying, "Z has corners"—you have taken back with the second statement what you stated in the first " In the end, you state *nothing*; you cancel out what you said.

(That is why one cannot say, "God is beyond logic, if by "logic" is meant "consistent reasoning"—for to utter a self-contradiction is not to state anything. If God says, "love is always good" and also "love is always bad," then [even] God hasn't stated anything.)

In short, in the fields of logic and mathematics, we can identify conclusions that *cannot possibly be wrongly drawn*. We can have *knowledge*—but only about what can be concluded from other *statements*. In logic, the *necessity* of a conclusion has naught to do with the facts of the *world*. A hypothetical skeptical challenge, "maybe a circle will be found that has one corner," fails through self-contradiction. It contradicts the definition of "circle."

But when the skeptic talks not about *definitional* entities like *geometry's* circles but about the *world* and says "you may not be brushing your teeth right now," the skeptic utters no self-contradiction. The worldly arguments of skeptics can be absurd, utterly implausible— yet not self-contradictory. And if not self-contradictory, they cannot be *necessarily* rejected. (Technically: *worldly* claims are "contingent"; their truth is contingent on, dependent on, the way the world is. Purely logical claims are termed "analytic" not "contingent"; their "logical truth"—their validity—depends only on the content of definitions, as in Euclidian geometry.)

We belabor what for many may be obvious because the ideas of "knowing" and "rational reasoning" have been (and seem implicitly to remain) *based* on what it is to "know" when drawing logical and mathematical conclusions. "Rationality" and (logical) "proof" went together. Hence, the term *rational* has often been tied to the standards of argument about *statements*, even when arguments are about the *world*, not statements.

But for a century or so, the idea of "rationality" or "reason" has expanded to include the worldly reasoning of scientists (who don't settle things by logical necessity). Despite this, many still question that science's testing of hypotheses by observable outcomes can yield knowledge of physical *laws* (necessities). For them, physical laws can't describe the way things *necessarily* operate because only *logic* establishes "necessity." They live by the logical model, "explaining" physical laws as just convenient ways of thinking to generate predictions.

Of course, even less capable of fulfilling the demand for "proof" are the conclusions we reach in morals, aesthetics, and religion. Far more than in science, the way we think in these domains is described as "non-rational," "non-cognitive," or "emotional"—the idea being that *feelings* and *comprehension* are entirely separate elements.[13] (Chapter 2, of course, found feelings fused with comprehension.)

So long as logic and math define "reasoning," the fact that worldly or *contingent* claims cannot be *proven* becomes a popular solvent for all worldly claims, including the moral, aesthetic, or religious ones by which we live—as in "no on can prove slavery is bad" (or "prove Cezanne is good art," or "prove life is holy," etc.).

(Later, we shall speak to the vast over-simplification the "logic" model encourages with respect to arguments over values and worldviews. It is a prejudice that hangs on. As F. L. Will remarks: "The thought that . . . the governance of practice [standards of the good and the right] could be both rational and deeply rooted in practice has not been much favored in modern philosophy.")[14]

The gap

Skepticism lives in the gap between *evidence* and *conclusion*—a gap not present in *logic*. In logic, if you say, "*All birds are black, and swans are* birds" then you must conclude, "all swans are black." Otherwise you contradict having said, "All birds are black, and swans are birds." (The conclusion—all swans are black—is already "contained" in the premise. *No gap.*)

But in *worldly* claims the "premise"—the evidence—is logically separate from the evidence or "premise." There is a formal logical gap. So, if you say, "All the birds I've seen are black, and a swan is bird," you can still say, "some swans may not be black." The link between *evidence* and *conclusion* is not "locked up," not logically necessary as in formal logic. The gap lacks "logic" and thus, as noted above, it cannot be bridged by "reasoning" (rational inference).

And yet we *constantly* bridge the "gap" between evidence and worldly conclusion. Since, skeptics say, it can't be rationally bridged, that is, by reasoning, or "rational inference," by what means do we move from our evidence to our worldly conclusions?

Well, if it can't be reasons or evidence that (we say) leads us to a conclusion, we can only say one thought "precedes" another thought. Now we are treating thoughts as *facts* not *reasons*. Therefore the movement from evidence-thoughts to conclusion-thoughts must be explained like *any* sequence of facts—scientifically.

Thus psychological "forces" or "causes" bridge the gap. Nietzsche saw the gap filled by an unconscious "will to power" (philosophers wanted their views to rule over others'). Karl Marx thought historical laws governed our conclusions about economics and rights.

Sociobiologists now fill the gap with genetic and other physiological determinants, neuro-scientists with electro-chemical forces, anthropologists with forces of socialization—just so long as the gap between our reasons and our worldly conclusions is filled by a process *accessible to physical science.*

So it seems that *at the very point where we use evidence to reach conclusions about the world,* what we do is not rational but physiological or psychological. (Unless "rational" is redefined as, say, "the way of thinking that is culturally or socially approved"—so that on an island restricted to the insane, "rational" might be thinking the insane approve.)

In any case, the point is this: the enabling fact of philosophic doubt is that reasoning about the world is not secured by logically necessary steps. And if worldly claims lack logical certainty, how can we say they are knowledge—that they cannot possibly be wrong? On this rock, skepticism founds its church.

THE SKEPTICAL CHALLENGE

Skepticism

Selective skepticism is the essence of good sense. If we hear of a free cure for cancer we are skeptical; we *feel* doubtful. But if the cure costs thousands we may take the trouble to investigate it. Our doubts arise or diminish as we assess each claim's credibility.

Of course, some people doubt less selectively. They are inclined to doubt almost any claim they hear. Their skepticism expresses an *attitude*. Doubt is something they bring. They are semi-detached, as it were, from situational particulars.

Philosophic skeptics, on the other hand, are detached absolutely from what they doubt. Their "doubting" has nothing to do with how they feel about particular claims, nor does it express an attitude.

Their rejection of knowledge-claims is based entirely on theoretical considerations. It is not that knowledge-claims might not state what happens to be true. Rather it is that we cannot know that they are true. Claims to *knowledge* can never be justifiably asserted. Therefore they can always be doubted. One can never justifiably claim to know the way things are "in reality."

Because their skepticism is the outcome of theorizing and not of doubts they feel in particular situations, it is somewhat misleading to refer to their denial of knowledge as "doubting." Still, the expression "philosophic doubt" is generally understood as holding that no worldly claim can be certain (knowledge cannot rationally be claimed).

This policy of universal doubt (which we here refer to, simply as "skepticism") can be, as in the case of scientism, implicit rather than avowed.[15]

When implicit, that is, when it is not overtly and plainly the denial of worldly knowledge, it can infiltrate popular culture—insidiously relieving social practice of its obligations to objectivity and making of "the true, the good and the beautiful" a quaint, outdated hope.

Were skepticism offered explicitly, its insistence that "we can't know *anything*" would be greeted (may we say) with skepticism.

But indirect skepticism has been successful. The late Paul Tillich opened his final lectures by expressing an "uneasiness about the victory of relativism in all realms of life and thought today"—a victory that seemed to Tillich "total."[16] From anthropology's cultural relativism to pop-Freudian, neurological, and other scientistic explanations, non-conscious forces are said to explain what we come to believe. Insofar as these theories venture to describe all minds, they imply that whatever we consider real or true are, in essence, those things we (or our bodies) *need*—are *determined*—to feel true.

So popular has this sort of psychologizing become that the denial of objectivity is now less a theory than a social convention.[17]

Sophisticated and unsophisticated alike will tell you that everyone is biased—meaning not that we all have some biases, but that thinking itself is unavoidably biased. In fact, dear reader, you may already have had the experience of being asked not for your opinion but (in all innocence) for your *bias*—that is, for your not-quite-true, not-quite-fair version of the truth.

Unfortunately, when a culture accepts a scientistic view of its own mind (especially when absorbed unconsciously) it can easily suppose objectivity to be of reach.[18] There was a time, not long ago, when an admission of bias was a confession of systematic error; today it is simply good manners.

The cultural invasiveness of skepticism will be noted as our argument develops. What follows is an effort to *join* skepticism in showing why knowledge can never justifiably be claimed—why it is impossible rightly to claim, "this is true."

Empirical skepticism

Empiricism is a family of philosophic theories that says worldly information comes only from experience—where "experience" means only what the five senses deliver.

Early empiricism spoke of "experience" as *sensations* (presumed to be received from the five senses), while later empiricism spoke less of *sensations* and more of *sense-observation* or *sense-perception.*

In our view the later, sense-perception, way of speaking retains a fundamental loyalty to earlier talk of sensations, since it maintains a similarly "five senses" view of what we experience. For example, the common claim that we experience beauty or experience evil is false for any empiricism, since "beauty" and "evil" are neither given in sensations nor visible to sense-perception (sometimes phrased, simply, as "observation").

Since our aim is to feel the force of philosophic skepticism, we propose a generic stroll down empiricism's garden path.[19]

Along the way, someone remarks that he sees a large tree. A philosophically minded acquaintance admonishes the observer, urging him to exercise greater intellectual responsibility.

"Strictly speaking, you do not see a tree, but only one side of a tree. The other side is blocked from your view."

Respectful of intellectual rigor, the observer feels justly chastened and agrees that the reformulation "I see one side of a large tree," is indeed, strictly speaking, a more accurate, more intellectually responsible, formulation than his first one.

Eventually, the philosopher adds that, "of course, strictly speaking, you do not see one side of a large tree, but only bark—the wood itself being out of sight."

It soon becomes apparent that strict adherence to accurate description calls for an even narrower claim: "Of course, strictly, you cannot see bark," says the philosopher, "you can see only a grayish surface, since the bark's thickness, and other dimensional properties that make it bark, are not directly observable."

Here, the observer's continued dedication to justification and accuracy forces him to agree that, "of course, what the eye sees directly is color and shading, not the 'surface'—strictly speaking—of anything."

The observer has finally realized that to say he "sees bark" requires not just looking but *inferring*—that is, *thinking*—and that the same is true even for saying he sees a "surface." After all, being a *surface* requires being the outermost layer of a *body*, and strictly, you can't see that what you are looking at is actually *part* of something and not just something that appears immediately adjacent to something else you may see.

Therefore, those who hold to the highest standards of truth and accuracy will always state their perceptual tree-watching claims in language such as "I see areas of grayish, brownish, and thin dark lines, and I infer from these things the existence of an object that I call a 'tree.'"

The observer in the woods has finally realized that the "correct" way of describing things entails that he can never actually *see* any thing at all; he can never see a three-dimensional *thing*. The claim, "I see a tree"—or "a truck," or "myself"—is always false.

For what the eye sees—as when seeing a mirage—is the *look* of things, say, the *appearance* of a lake, which is the sort of thing one has in one's awareness even when there is no lake—no dimensional thing—present at all.

Here the *scientific* viewpoint is confirming of empiricism. The eye, after all, when it "sees" is a retina excited by light waves. The consequence is that a color or shape (or, for hearing, *sound*, or for touching, *feel*) appears in our awareness.[20]

It is only by taking the additional step of inferring (when we say, "a tree is in front of me") from sensations introduced by our senses, that the grayish patch and the brown lines can be said to be tree bark. And to infer from sensations in awareness to things in a world is not to "see" but *to use one's mind*.

Thus, only by virtue of hypotheses we generate about an independent world—a dimensional space in which there can be trees—do we say that the stimulation of retinal cells has anything to do with dimensional "things." (This hypothesizing is what skeptics call "speculation" or the "construction" of reality)

Now we realize how much we have taken for granted. We see that human beings cannot rationally (justifiably) claim to see *truly*, or observe truly, the things that are in the world.

We necessarily must infer "things" from what appears in our consciousness (in the form of color sensations or flashes or buzzes or pressures). We *imagine* what might be causing them to appear in our minds (like "trees" and "leaves" out there in "space"). Do we *know* what is out there? How can we? The only evidence we have is what we find "in our own heads."

Thus, the British empiricist, John Locke looked into his mind (like a scientistically inclined observer "observing" himself), and in *An Essay Concerning Human Understanding* (1690) found only his own sensations and ideas. He therefore "realized" that if we stick to the facts, it is the content of our minds that we know by experience and *not* the contents of the world. "Since the mind in all its thoughts and reasonings, hath no other immediate object but its own ideas . . . it is evident that our knowledge is only conversant with them."[21]

The most influential empirical skeptic of them all, David Hume, came to the same conclusion for the very same reason (while insisting he was not a skeptic). Said Hume,

> As to those *impressions* ["sensations"] which arise from the senses, their ultimate cause is, in my opinion, perfectly inexplicable by human reason, and it will always be impossible to decide with certainty, whether they arise immediately from the object, or are produced by the creative power of the mind, or are derived from the Author of our being.

The reference to the "Author" was Hume's way of saying "think anything you like" about what may cause your impressions—for Hume was an agnostic, posthumously famous for his anti-theistic, *Dialogues Concerning Natural Religion*.[22]

This skeptical scenario (in which all we can perceive are phenomena inside us) seems fated to arise wherever reflection flourishes. Greek (Pyrrhonist) skepticism, for example, claimed that we "cannot get at objects independently of sense-perception, and sense-perception provides no guarantee that we apprehend things as they really are. *Objects in themselves are therefore not available* to test our sense-perception [emphasis added]."[23] As his pupil, Timon, wrote, "that honey is sweet I do not postulate, but I admit that it appears sweet ("I have a sensation of sweetness").[24] In Sextus' "sceptic school," the perception of an object meant simply "its impressions on the senses.

Twenty-one centuries later, Immanuel Kant, striving to answer Hume's skeptical narrative, implicitly accepted Hume's (and Pyrrho's) idea of "experience" with its unavoidably skeptical implications. But his *Critique of Pure Reason* explained our *experience* in terms not of sensations alone but sensations organized within categories of thought such as *time* and *space* and *number*—"categories" which are supplied *by the mind itself.*

(Categories come "from the mind" because we do not get categories like *numbers* or *time* from our senses or within sense-perception, yet we employ these categories. We cannot, for example, say something as simple as, "dripping water is slowly staining that rug" without making use of categories such as number, cause, time, or space.)

Because Kant accepted the idea that the *substance* of experience is "sensations"—and because his "categories" are *products of the mind*—he was, ironically, forced to agree with the narrowly empirical Pyrrho, that we can never have experience of (and thus knowledge of) things as they are *in themselves* (in Kant: the *"ding an sich"*).

Steeped in empiricism's "sensation" version of experience—and supplying the interpretive ideas (categories) it lacked by finding them in our own minds—Kant could not fully overcome the idea that reality in itself could be known unfiltered by our mind's pre-existing "categories."[25]

And, surely, *it is of no small religious import* to be told by inquiring minds that our perception is unsuited to seeing the world as it really is—the world we normally suppose to be perception's subject—the very world which, for theists, is its intended subject!

Because the empiricist view of experience reflects well-known facts regarding the five senses (how the enclosed brain receives impulses from their being excited) its primacy in picturing "experience" remained unassailable.

A hundred years after Kant, we find Franz Brentano (philosopher and ex-priest), claiming, in *Psychology from an Empirical Standpoint*, that perception of a supposed world is "misception"—an illusion (*Warnehmung ist Falschnehmung*). Similarly dubious, the twentieth century positivist, Ernst Mach, argued that the whole question of whether what we experience in awareness as "qualities" or "elements" or "impressions" have any status in existence (outside our awareness) is "meaningless."[26]

Thus, while the empiricism's arguments have become more sophisticated, its *subjective* or psychology-dependent conclusions have remained the same. Mach found the question of whether our impressions have external references "meaningless" for the same reason Pyrrho did, namely, that we have no *self-independent* way to see whether the sound or the color in our consciousness is independently real (we cannot step outside our own senses).

(Art lovers may note that given Mach's and Pyrrho's view of reality it is *meaningless* to have an art competition since there is no way to know the judges are judging the same image.)

Still!—what of all this? Aren't scientific accounts factually true? Doesn't science alone verifiably describe the operative *facts of human perception*? As late as the twentieth century, was not this identification of scientific knowledge with all worldly knowledge proclaimed by influential philosophers such as Ludwig Wittgenstein in England and Willard Quine in the United States?

And doesn't it remain a fact that *between* what we think of as a world and whatever world there may actually be are *opaque* conduits called "nerves" by which we claim (somehow) to *see* external things? Impossible!

Hume's indirect deconstruction of the world

On the title page of his *Treatise of Human Nature* (1739), David Hume declared his work "an attempt to introduce the experimental method of reasoning [*the empirical methods of science*] into moral subjects."[27]

Like most post-Newtonian thinkers, Hume was decisively impressed by the ability of scientific thought to grasp the hidden workings of the universe. Francis Bacon's earlier vision of empirical discovery had in spirit proven right; there was indeed a "New Method," an observational, non-traditional approach to inquiry that might well change the world. Hume's *Treatise on Human Nature* aimed to carry that method forward.

Since knowledge (to be "knowledge") cannot possibly be wrong, Hume needed to find a foundation in experience that could not possibly be wrong. Looking into human experience as if a third-person observer of that experience, all he could find that was *certain* were our sensations. This is because (Chapter 2) sensations contain no ideas.

That which we directly sense (like a bright flash) involves no ideas—no inferences, no speculations. "Experience" of this kind cannot possibly be mistaken. For example, if you "see spots before your eyes (as we say) then you have a sensation of spots and there can be no doubt about it. If a noise erupts in your head (in your "awareness") you cannot possibly be mistaken that a sensation of noise occurs. Only the certainty of our sensations seemed able provide an experiential basis for *knowledge*.[28]

Thus, Hume opens the *Treatise*,

> All the perceptions of the human mind resolve themselves into two distinct kinds . . . *impressions* and *ideas*. . . . The perceptions which enter with the most force . . . we may name *impressions*; and under this name I comprehend all our sensations, passions, and emotions as they make their appearance in the soul [the mind]. By *ideas* I mean the faint images of these in thinking and reasoning. . . . [29]

That is, *impressions* are what we sense *apart from any thoughts*—they are certain.

"Ideas" are what we "remember" of the sensations we had. Of course, it is precisely this *"scientific"* picture of "human experience" that told us we couldn't, "strictly speaking," see a tree (or any other external object).

Empiricism as metaphysics

One may fairly say that the irony of the empiricist perspective on knowledge is epitomized in Hume's philosophy. For, the implications of his "scientific" philosophy could hardly have been more inimical to science.[30]

This is most notably true with respect to our idea of physical causation wherein we think one thing *makes* another thing necessarily come to pass (that one state of affairs is sufficient to necessitate the occurrence of another). This principle of physical necessitation is of course at the center of our metaphysics (our notion of a world's "nature")—of things that, as it were, "go their own way" or have certain consequences whether we like them or not.

Hume's reason for denying causation follows from his view of experience. When we observe one billiard striking another we only experience sensations—sensations of circular areas, colors, and sounds and blurs.

Nowhere in this kind of "experience" does a sensation of *necessity* appear. There is no such thing as a *sensation* of causing or making or necessitating: "When we consider these objects with utmost attention, we find only that one body approaches the other and that the motion of it precedes that of the other, but without any sensible interval [one ball hits the other]. It is in vain to rack ourselves with further thought and reflection upon this subject."[31]

"If we go any further and ascribe a power or necessary connection to these objects, *this is what we can never observe in them. . .* [emphasis added]." From whence, then, comes our idea of causation or physical necessitation? We "must draw the idea of it [the impression of it] from what we feel *internally* in contemplating them [emphasis added]."[32]

It turns out that what we "feel internally" is the *expectation* that what we have seen occur over and over again will happen the same way next time. Having seen one thing follow, regularly, on the appearance of another, a habit of expectation builds that that makes us feel, "this *must* happen" (we feel the first thing *causes* the second thing to happen). Causality is not a feature of the world, says Hume; it is a *psychological artifact*.

And, indeed, we never directly experience (in later empiricism, *observe*) necessity. We may have a sensation of pressure when lifting a weight, or of pain when a needle enters our skin—but not "necessity."

And this, we suggest, is *the same mode of thought we will encounter when we consider the empiricist's account of* moral *necessity or "obliga-*

tion." Moral laws or necessities will turn out to be no more accessible through experience than physical laws or necessities.

For empiricism, generally, the idea that physical laws exist can never be proven; the conviction that the hammer that struck our thumb *caused* it to compress (and hurt) is a kind of self-deception. By Hume's reasoning, Isaac Newton's stunning unification of earthly and heavenly motions was in fact a clever mathematical formulation of the patterns in Newtown's own consciousness.

Physical laws, so-called, were not laws (as there is no causation) and, even as "principles," were not about the world at all.

Here we see epistemology's *metaphysical* import. It is nothing less than the world destroyed. The so-called "forces" of nature *force* nothing to occur. If a woman pushes a baby carriage, she does not *make* it move. That means "the real world" operates the same way motion picture imagery operates, for in a movie, the woman's movements and hands that we see do not *make* the baby carriage that we see *move.* The movement of the woman and the movement of the carriage simply happen together. One doesn't cause the other.

So "reality" is like a movie, but projected in mental space by humanity's genetically programmed imagination.

Hume's way of thinking, with its complementary account of reality, has seemed factually irrefutable. Leszak Kolakowski recounts the French "conventionalist" philosopher Le Roy's view that "a scientific fact is a convention [made up by agreement]."[33] When speaking about electricity, scientists may say that

> "the current runs through the wire.". . . But sensory experience discloses no *flowing* of the current. All that we actually observe are such phenomena as shifts of the galvanometer needle, flashing bulbs . . . [etc.] . . . [so] the expression "the current runs" is no more than a summing up of the given phenomena, a convenient linguistic tool, not the description of an actual process.[34]

The parallel with a Humean account of colliding billiard balls is plain, even though, as we have noted, this later empiricism talks of "observation" and "sense-perception" rather than "sensations."

Thus, by denying all necessities, whether physical or moral or aesthetic, *empiricism deconstructs or dissolves the reality experience discloses in the activities of practical life.*

Skepticism undefeated

But are we not criticizing Hume and empiricism in a circular manner? For example, we complain that his view of experience entails that we cannot actually look directly at the world. But this complaint simply *assumes* the contrary position, namely that we *can* look at the world.

And when we look, as Hume did—and as brain physiologists today do—at the working of our minds as a series of mental *events*, how can we possibly claim that we cannot be deluded about such things as a "reality" outside us?

Does not our so-called "knowledge" rest on what we *believe*, or, as some have said (and still say!) on *faith*? So. Skepticism seems nicely positioned to survive.

Perspectival skepticism

The second family of skeptical theories doubts knowledge-claims by analyzing how we think. It is concerned with the *logic* of our judgments, not the facts of our experience.

Perspectivism reminds us that when we draw conclusions about the world, we always make use of ideas about *what is so* and about the *right way to reason*. For example, the simplest conclusions about what we perceive assume such things as that our eyes are in roughly the same condition they have lately been, that we are wide awake, that the light on what we see is normal light in that situation.

And when we draw conclusions about complex things like the value of democracy or the size of the universe, the assumptions that determine our conclusions can hardly be enumerated.

Since can't draw conclusions without using ideas and norms of reasoning, we cannot help but interpret the world in terms of one perspective or another.

What makes this conclusion *skeptical* is that there is no way to get outside one's perspective to see whether it leads one to the truth. There is no way to justify the probity of the perspective one happens to use.

Surely we cannot use a perspective to justify itself. One does not establish a witness' credibility by asking the witness whether he or she is credible.

Therefore, to conclude that a perspective is justified, we must avail ourselves of a second perspective in terms of which to judge the first. But that second perspective will not yet have been justified. Its justification will require yet another perspective. So the attempt to justify our perspectives fails because it can never end.

There is no empirical argument here—no reference to worldly *facts*, whether social, psychological, or genetic. Simply by looking at the *conceptual* structure of our reasoning, we see that the bases on which we determine worldly truths have no justification beyond the fact that we happen to use them.

We conclude that we can never *justifiably* lay claim to worldly knowledge. We can never say we *know*; we can never say we cannot possibly be wrong about any worldly claim.

Here, the reader may appreciate the safe harbor offered by various *pragmatisms* that dispense with the quest for truth (as "truth" is commonly understood). Rather than seek an *intellectual* justification, they seek a *practical* justification—a justification on the basis of utility. Justifiable perspectives are those that, broadly speaking, "satisfy" us or "work" for us.

Some pragmatisms simply redefine "truth" so as to make it a matter of what satisfies us. "Ideas," said William James, " . . . become true just insofar as they help us to get into satisfactory relation with other parts of our experience."[35]

So, for example, the choice of the Copernican over the Ptolemaic view of Earth's relation to the sun has been described as a choice based on the satisfactions afforded by the Copernican theory's "simplicity"—that is, its *convenience*. The Ptolemaic view requires more assumptions than the Copernican view to predict the apparent motions of the stars.[36] Were complexity more *satisfying* than simplicity, we might have retained the Ptolemaic theory and said the sun revolves around the Earth.

Once we concede that our perspectives are beyond intellectual justification, whatever we find it *useful* to call "real" is all the reality we can ever seek. The entire project of *knowing* the world, the past, ourselves, becomes, at best, an exercise in entertaining fiction or, at worst, a speculative detour from *getting things done*.

The world we say we "take into account" is really a world we *construct*. We invent, rather than discover, the world.

Perhaps no effort to declare reality *constructed* was more aggressively advanced than by the broad "deconstructionist" movement whose perspectivism powered one of the twentieth century's last skeptical tides. Not just worldly facts but the *meaning* of texts were declared unknowable.

The deconstructionist movement acknowledged the existence of language (which requires that meanings exist and can be known), yet it had no problem rendering its meanings entirely subjective: Robert Crosman, for example, asked, "Do Readers Make Meaning?" and answered that "a poem really means whatever any reader seriously believes it to mean"; Stanley Fish declared that when "two critics . . . [have] . . . opposing interpretations. . . . clearly there is no basis for deciding between them. One cannot appeal to the text, because the text has become an extension of the interpretive disagreement that divides them."[37]

For such thinkers, it is impossible to escape one's interpretative perspective and therefore to see statements for what they *actually* mean.

Cultural relativism

There is another road to the conclusion that our perspectives are never (objectively) justifiable. Rather than reason from the structure of our judgments (as perspectivism, proper, does), the movement called "cultural relativism" looks at the way our perspectives are learned and maintained. Its conclusions are putatively *empirical* rather than *conceptual*.

Cultural relativism emerges from the findings of anthropology. For cultural relativism, the startling degree to which human perspectives diverge and the degree to which any change in them is resisted, shows they are neither intellectually justified nor open to correction by evidence or argument.

This divergence and resistance among human perspectives is explained scientifically, by reference to psycho-social processes (mechanisms) rather than by grounds or reasons. What reasoning there is, takes place within the assumptions that comprise the perspective.

Growing up in a culture, we (unavoidably) absorb from our elders a basic outlook on what constitutes reality and rationality. That perspective becomes part of our identity. We do not choose it. As it becomes, "who we are," it becomes a psychological necessity. Nothing basic in one's perspective is acquired by objective inquiry or critical reflection.

Cultures evolve these perspectives in the course of surviving. Beliefs are adaptations for survival—not *truths*.[38] (Adaptations shape the mind as they shape the body.)

The anthropological evidence for this outlook is compelling. Different peoples have divergent beliefs about the world and the way human beings should behave in it, and their beliefs surely resist change by evidence or argument. The counter-claim that our ideas can come from knowledge of the world is therefore seen to lack factual confirmation.

Thus, the seminal anthropologist, William Graham Sumner, in his influential *Folkways* of 1906, confidently pronounced that, "rightness is merely the expression of a learned perspective." Anthropologists like Franz Boaz, Ruth Benedict, Melville Herskovits, and others, similarly taught that moral judgments, for example, are not based on knowledge but express a psycho-socially acquired cultural perspective.

As a consequence of anthropology's popularity, the authority of science, and everyone's acquaintance with stubbornness and self-serving belief, cultural relativism gained a cultural foothold. It became a mark of sophistication to say that "moral" means, "strictly speaking," moral *for us* or moral *for them*.

An advocate of "universal human rights" could (and might still) expect to hear that "belief in human rights is just a Western idea." And anyone resting a case for worldwide vaccination on scientific evidence may still be cautioned by a college student that scientific medicine has no universal validity because "science is valid for some peoples but not others."

The mind comes to be described as a "belief-system"—a terminology more suited to machines than agents. Even now, disagreements may be ended by politely referring to the "fact" that "we have different belief-systems," which is rather like saying we are determined by different software programs.

But cultural relativism is not a strictly scientific doctrine. The argument that *if* cultures radically differ in their assumptions, then *none is right* is not a scientific conclusion but a *philosophical* one.

The argument takes a position on the criteria for determining truth—whether moral, factual, or esthetic. It is an intellectual assessment not a factual test.

From the "fact" (not always true) that groups think incompatibly, it concludes that no one of them can be known to be right. But, plainly, if everyone in a room disagrees and cannot be moved by arguments, it simply does not follow that no one in the room is right, either with respect to belief or in resisting change.

Therefore, although cultural relativism purports to rest on an account of the way perspectives develop (as artifacts of environmental *adaptation*), in truth it rests on a *non sequitur*, namely that sustained disagreement entails the nonexistence of possible truth.

The popularity of cultural relativism owes much to social idealism. It promised to end ethnocentrism and colonialism. But in throwing out the bathwater of cultural hubris, it threw out the baby of truth.

But wait—by what right do we speak of truth?

Is it not obvious that people interpret the world in a manner that reflects the culture of their upbringing? And is it not the case that their perspectives seem, on the whole, impossible to change? And does this not show their ideas to be instruments of *identity*—of psychological security and social stability—rather than of truth?

In other words, if everyone in the room disagrees and no one changes through argument, it may not follow as a matter of pure logic that no one is right, but doesn't it strongly suggest that no one can lay claim to being right? By what means can anyone claim knowledge?

And what about you, dear reader, and this writer, as well—this Western quasi-Platonist, this advocate of a knowable reality and sometime language analyst—of whom the philosopher, Kai Nielsen would likely complain,

> Even now, there are philosophers who want to be ontologically serious. They tell us we need to see the world rightly, and to do this we must work out a fundamental ontology that will display the most basic features the world must have. . . . It seems to me that people who think this way have learned nothing from history. It is far too late in the day to think something like this.[39]

Perspectivism rampant

The idea that perspectives are *conceptually* barred from intellectual justification is no longer restricted to the academy nor limited to "postmodern" or "deconstruction" fads. It is a shibboleth of popular and academic culture.

One can turn to semi-popular works such as, *The Survival* of *God in a Scientific Age* in which its scientist-author declares that the scientific perspective has no justification other than faith and so no right to speak of what is real:

> The scientist must . . . have faith in the validity of logic and of his percepts as basic tools for constructing his models of the universe. It is this faith upon which all scientific knowledge is based, and it is this limitation which restricts scientists to discussing models of reality, rather than reality itself.[40]

Similarly, the biologist, Paul B. Weisz, writes that

> neither the scientific nor the religious interpretation is the truer. If the theologian argues that everything was made by God . . . then the scientist will argue back that chance chemical reactions created men with brains, including those theological brains which can conceive of a God who made everything. The impasse is permanent, and within their own system of communications the scientist and theologian *are equally right* [italics added].[41]

We cannot "get out of our own skin"

Academic thought remains a lively source of perspectival skepticism. The anthropologist and epistemological theorist, Richard Shweder, draws on T. S. Kuhn's widely quoted *Structure of Scientific Revolutions* in support of perspectival theory. There, major changes in the theoretical models of physics are attributed more to changed psycho-social conditions than to scientific considerations.

Shweder approves of Kuhn's view that there is *no way to say what exists apart from our assumptions*, He approvingly references Kuhn's argument that "there is no . . . theory independent way to reconstruct phrases like 'really there'; the notion of a match between the ontology of a theory [*what it says is real*] and its 'real' counterpart in nature, now seems to me elusive in principle [explanatory paraphrase added]."[42] That is, *no match can be had between what a theory says exists and what really does exist.*

"The rub, here," says Shweder,

> seems to be that the mind has no way of getting beyond the skin. . . . [43] It becomes impossible, in principle, to separate what is mind and what is reality, to say how things would look from "nowhere in particular," or to guarantee that all minds will conjecture in the same way or that any one description of what is out there is the only way to make sense of that which arrives at the surface of the skin.[44]

To know reality as it is, we must see it "from nowhere in particular"—free of any particular perspective. ("As God knows" might be the relevant phrase.) But we cannot be nowhere-in-particular.

These views carry forward much in Friedrich Nietzsche's thinking. Nietzsche was the preeminent proponent of both an empirical, that is, a *psychological*, "perspectivism" as well as a proper, conceptual one. No one has more vividly or influentially argued that we create rather than report, the world in which we live, than the "bad boy" of nineteenth-century philosophy.[45] Philosophy, Nietzsche warned, "always creates the world in its own image; it cannot do otherwise."[46]

The very ideas of truth and of objectivity were for Nietzsche a snare.[47] Guided by what he deemed the (philosopher's) *will to power* (an empirical claim), a philosopher's conclusions were always *interested*, not *disinterested*; they were subjective not objective.

Philosophy was determined by psychological preferences: "Behind all logic and its seeming sovereignty of movement, too, there stand valuations or, more clearly, physiological demands for the preservation of a certain type of life."[48]

Linguistic perspectivism

The passion of Nietzsche's rhetorical style cannot be well conveyed in the fragments we extract. Nor can justice be done to the full range of his thinking. For us, the point of primary interest is not Nietzsche's psychological theories but his most influential conceptual claim, namely, that language determines our perspectives.

For Nietzsche, we are "inmates" (as F. L. Will phrases it) of our linguistic systems. Language is not a freeing instrument that makes possible true statements. For Nietzsche, it is, rather, a conceptual cage: "we cease to think when we will to do so without the constraint of language. . . . Rational thought is an interpreting according to a schema that we cannot throw off."[49]

Language, then, does not *mediate but intervenes* between us and the environment. The imperatives of our language determine our thoughts as to how things really are (the view that surfaced in the latter twentieth century as "deconstructionist" or "postmodern").

For Nietzsche (as commentator John Richardson says),

> truth as *correspondence* is impossible, because reality can be "viewed" by the subject only through a "representation" [*Vorstellung*], a stand-in for the object. . . . But the translation into this other realm [the "realm" of our interpretive, linguistic framework] inevitably changes and distorts.[50]

For example, the physicist, Arthur Eddington, once argued that common objects like tables are really not solid (since they consist mostly of space between atoms). But for people serving coffee, tables are solid.

So whether realities are *solid* or *mostly space* depends on the whether you are using practical language or scientific language. The table *in itself* is not "really" solid or "really" mostly space. The reality one lives by appears solely to depend on one's language

This seems particularly plausible when it comes to the issue of moral truths. Is an unborn a "fetus" or a "child?" If a "child," then to abort for practical reasons is to "murder "; if a "fetus," then to abort for practical reasons is a "medical procedure" or a "choice."

Are morally repugnant thoughts "sins," or can actions alone be *sins*? When are sins real? It depends on how you use the term *sin*. Reality is defined by your language.

How do we think of "intelligence"? Gilbert Ryle says "intelligence" lies within our activities (writing intelligently, driving intelligently) rather than in the quality of any mental activity before, or responsible for, "intelligent" or "unintelligent" activity.

But most people say that intelligent activity is *brought about by* intelligent thinking that *controls* behavior—especially since we deem ourselves *responsible* for that behavior. Does the way we use the term *intelligence* make it an attribute of our minds or of our activities? Does our language, rather than our knowledge, determine our vision of reality?

Everything seems to depend on our perspective: the inner use of language by which we represent the world to ourselves as well as others.

Linguistic perspectivism was featured by George Orwell in his novel, *1984*:

> The purpose of [the language] "Newspeak" was not only to provide a medium of expression for the world-view and mental habits proper to the devotees of "Ingsoc" [English Socialism], but to *make all other modes of thought impossible*. It was intended that when Newspeak had been adopted once and for all and "Oldspeak" forgotten, a heretical thought—that is, a thought diverging from the principles of Ingsoc—*should be literally unthinkable.* . . . [emphasis added]

Before Orwell, in linguistic science, the Sapir-Whorff hypothesis (strong form) proclaimed that language determines thought, so that "The fact of the matter is that the 'real world' is to a large extent unconsciously built up on the language habits of the group."[51]

As Richardson says of Nietzsche's perspectivist view, "it's the nature of reality that it can never be mirrored or matched [in our language and thus in our minds]."[52]

The inability to mirror reality introduces the foremost proponent of Nietzschean, linguistic perspectivism, the philosopher, Richard Rorty. Few have said more plainly that what we call "reality" is determined from the inside, not—as both objectivity and religion require—from the *outside*. (Of course what we *mean* by "determined from the outside" must in time be made out.)

For Rorty, "notions . . . like 'hard fact' and 'matters of fact' are absurd, 'unfortunate relics of metaphysical thought'. The idea of 'an objective public world which is not of our making . . . [is] no more than out-dated rhetoric.'"[53] "[Rorty's] idea of '*something which is what it is apart from language, apart from any description*' is that the whole idea is but a 'pseudoproblem' [emphasis added]."[54] As Rorty sees it, "A pragmatist must . . . insist that there is no such thing as the way the thing is in itself, under no description, apart from any use to which human beings might want to put it."[55]

Here we see repeated Kant's view that we can never see how things are in themselves, that is, as they *really* are apart from what we *think* they are. Kant's "categories" and Rorty's "language" are both creations, as it were, of the human mind (not discovered *through experience*).

In *Contingency, Irony and Solidarity*, Rorty insists that his main interest is the relation between truth and large-scale perspectives, rather than truth and single sentences like "the cat is on the mat." These perspectives—or "worldviews"—he calls "vocabularies."[56] "Vocabularies" is a word well-suited to supposing that *thoughts* can comprehended wholly internally and *linguistically* (as if what a "thought" is can be understood without any mention of *referring* to anything outside the thought itself).

Rorty has it that such vocabularies as that of "Romantic poetry, socialist politics or Galilean mechanics" did not change because new truths overturned old ways of thinking or supported new ways: "Europe did not *decide* to accept [these new vocabularies]."[57]

Instead of changing by virtue of objective argument, the adducing of worldly evidence—or even by will—"Europe gradually lost the habit of using certain words and gradually acquired the habit of using others."[58]

In support of this striking thesis, Rorty might challenge the reader to recall the evidence or arguments the reader has specifically employed to arrive at the reader's life-directing "judgment" that democracy is the best political system (and perhaps worth dying for).

Most will find precious little they can cite representing rigorous, comprehensive comparative study or extensive empirical inquiry. Rorty might then with satisfaction reiterate that people acquire their political ideas and commitments the way they acquire habits of dining, dressing and socializing.

After concluding that changes in the way we view the world are nothing more than changes in *habitual speech*, Rorty makes a statement which epitomizes the difference between perspectivist philosophy and a religious outlook. "The world," Rorty says, "does not speak. Only we do."[59] (Note: this does not parallel our statement in Chapter 2 that "*we* speak, not God." Ours was about the *source* of statements; Rorty's metaphor is about their *basis*.)

We must be clear why for Rorty (as for all perspectivist theorists) "truth" is not something "out there" but is rather a creation of our own. Rorty holds that "truth *is a property* of linguistic entities, *of sentences*."[60] (And, emphatically, that "sentences are elements of human languages, and human languages are human creations.")[61]

Of course, this is not what people ordinarily mean. They do not suppose that in seeking truth they are seeking the property of a sentence. A "true" statement *corresponds*, we say, to reality. ("That truth is a matter of the relation between words and the world is a trite but central point," said the renowned British language analyst, J. L. Austin.)

But the reason why truth, for perspectivism, must be a property of language is that if "truth" were the property, not of sentences *per se* (as Rorty insists) but only of those sentences that *correspond to reality*, we could never assign the property "truth" to our sentences unless (defying perspectivism) we could check our sentences against *reality as it is in itself*.

The whole point of perspectivism is of course to show why this is not possible. Once again, popular culture absorbs this skeptical outlook through "popular" philosophical anecdotes. "Einstein proved that everything was relative," "Quantum mechanics shows that all events are matters of chance," and "the Heisenberg principle of uncertainty tells us that all events are uncertain or can't be accurately measured" (a problem, indeed, for anesthetists, construction engineers, and conscientious chefs).

The essential point remains that we "can never get out of our own skin," never step outside the encircling wall of our sentences (thoughts) to see what is "out there" *entirely apart* from our *opinion* of what we are seeing.

And since we have to *think* to *know* then, in Rorty's words, "there is no standpoint outside the particular historically conditioned and temporary vocabulary we are presently using"[62] and therefore no "outside" or "objective" statements we can employ "from which to judge this vocabulary." "Consequently, "we have to give up on the idea that there can be reasons *for* using languages as well as reasons *within* languages for believing statements [emphases added]."[63]

But if we give up reasons *for* the language we live by then how can one sort of thing we say about the world be any more or less rational then any other thing we might say?

The answer is that it can't be. According to Rorty, we must "give up the idea that intellectual or political progress is rational, in any sense of 'rational' that is neutral between vocabularies."[64]

Locked within a perspective embodied in a vocabulary—and with no access to an *independent* standpoint outside that or any other vocabulary, all we can do is use words *persuasively*.[65] All we can do is come up with new, more attractive ways of describing the world. And if we win someone over to our vocabulary, then we may, if we wish, hang a tag on our (merely) preferred way of talking on which is written, "true"—or "right" or "rational."

That is why, for Rorty, general evaluative terms like "truth" and "rationality," have no descriptive implications. They do not add to any argument. They are empty. Terms like "truth" and "knowledge" and "rightness" do no intellectual work. They are "honorific."

The situation resembles that of arguments over God's Word. Without clinching empirical evidence or purely logical proofs, religious disputants attempt to gain agreement by means of *persuasive* descriptions. If they succeed in getting agreement—if they create "solidarity" in Rorty's terms—they hang a tag on the agreed-upon ideas that reads: "God's Word."

So, to seek "the truth" or "what is right" or "God's Word" is to impose no particular responsibility on the conduct of an inquiry or argument. Rorty makes this point when he says,

> From our point of view, explaining the success of science, or the desirability of political liberalism by talk of "fitting the world" or "expressing human nature" is like explaining why opium makes you sleepy by talking about its dormitive power. . . . To say that. . . . Newton's [vocabulary] gets at the truth about the heavens, is not an explanation of anything. It is just an empty compliment—one traditionally paid to writer's whose novel jargon we have found useful.[66]

(Note: Rorty's term *useful* seems as *normative* an expression as "truthful" or "fitting the world." If so, he himself is using "useful" as an "empty" term.)

Plainly, where truth is, at bottom, a function of what we decide to say, argument can be nothing other than persuasion, and a successful result can be only *belief*. It cannot be *knowledge*, not in what Rorty considers the old *Enlightenment* or *rationalist* sense (the *common* sense) wherein we see reality for what it is.

Moral and aesthetic skepticism

If philosophy can "doubt" the possibility of scientifically acquired knowledge, the doubt of moral and aesthetic knowledge seems almost an afterthought.

There are no proofs, tests, or sense-perceptible *evidence* by which the alleged moral character of an act or the aesthetic value of a work can be in any degree established.

No such avenues to verification exist because goodness, rightness, relevance, beauty and so on are not "out there" in the way that "physical" or "factual" characteristics solidity or movement are typically acknowledged to be.

Where *in the world* do we locate "goodness" or "value" or "worth" in an act, a relationship or an object?

We can see the knife but not the moral wrongness of its wielding. We can see the lines, colors and shapes of a painting, but not the "beauty" or "aesthetic value" that is said to lie in those lines and colors and shapes. And in the matter of written texts, we can *see* the writing but not, for example, the *aptness* or *relevance* of it.

And if there are no qualities or properties that in any sense exist independently of our opinions—to which terms like *good* and *bad*, *better* and *worse*, *apropos* or *inapropos* can refer—then there are no evaluative *facts*, certainly no *moral facts*, for the wise to have *discovered*. Thus, the fundamental view of most philosophers is that moral and aesthetic terms are in no way descriptive of reality.

Consider the descriptive term *killing* and the evaluative term *murder*. For example, we don't say our soldiers *murder* enemy soldiers. We say they *kill* them. "Killing" is a descriptive term, not an evaluative one.

If a witness testifies that "a man was *killed* with that rifle," and adds "in fact, he was *murdered* with that rifle," most philosophers will say the second statement adds no new facts—no *information* about the event—to the first description of what happened.

The evaluative sentence, "the man was murdered" may, on the page, look like the descriptive sentence, "the man was killed with a rifle" (it has the same grammar), but, in fact, say empiricists, it is not descriptive at all. Onlookers who saw the killing and thought it was *not* a murder *observed* precisely the same facts—the same world, the same reality—as onlookers who thought it *was*.

This picture of our relation to reality represents a watershed for religious and philosophical conceptions of the human situation.

Behind all skeptical interpretations of evaluative terms like good or *right* or *beautiful* or *appropriate* stands the empiricist version of reality. In that reality only physical and psychological (or psycho-physical) properties *exist*.

Against the background of the empiricist's *physical* world—the world of sense-*observables*, of the ways that things *function*, of *predictions*, *consequences*, and *measurements*—those who would speak of *moral knowledge* face the problem of explaining the meaning of "good" such that there can be good *in the world*.[67]

Because ordinary people, unlike most philosophers, feel that goodness and badness *exist* (and so are, somehow, properties of acts and relations in the world) some empirically minded thinkers—those who believed or respected the common view—sought to identify what worldly property it might be that "good," for example, might refer to.

But, given their empiricist idea of *reality* (noted, above) they could only locate "good" if "good" could be defined as some kind of physical or psycho-physical fact.[68]

Thus, the empirically minded moralist, John Stuart Mill, defined "good" in term of a psychological property—"happiness"; the greatest good being the "happiness of the greatest number."[69] (Others have defined "good" factually or "empirically" as "that which maximizes the probability of human survival" and others as "whatever is pleasurable.")

The possibility of moral and aesthetic truth

Enter, the British philosopher, G. E. Moore.[70] Moore challenged the idea that we can define "good" as a physical, or psycho-physical, property. He pointed out that no matter what "natural" property (like *pleasure*, or *survival*, or *happiness*) was proposed as "the *meaning* of the word *good*" one could *always sensibly ask* whether that natural property *was* good."

And, if we can always sensibly ask of a fact—like "happiness" or "survival"—"Is it good?" then that fact cannot mean the *same* thing as "good." If it meant the *same* thing, the question would be as senseless as asking, "Is a circle circular?"

But, because it is always possible *intelligibly* to ask, "Is survival good?" or "Is pleasure good?" (and so on), utilitarians like Mill, who defined *good* in "factual" terms, were, according to Moore, committing "the naturalistic fallacy"—a phrase Moore coined for the error of defining "good" in non-evaluative terms, like *pleasure*, *survival*, or *happiness*.

Hence, even "supernatural" facts—like the fact of *being willed by God*—cannot *define* "good." Thus, if someone says, "God willed it" it would be intelligible (linguistically coherent) to ask "But, was what God willed *good*?"

Indeed, it would be *empty* for theists to argue "what God wills is always good" if "good" simply *meant* "what God wills."

Moore was not denying that facts like pleasure, happiness, or survival were or could be good. He was only pointing out that facts cannot *define* the word *good*.

In fact, Moore was rare among modern philosophers in not being a moral skeptic. He thought morality could be objective—that there could be moral truths, that moral knowledge was possible. He simply challenged the empiricist's version of reality—of what can exist independently of our thinking it exists. "Good" Moore said, refers to a "non-natural" property—a property radically different from the physical and psycho-physical properties which alone populate the empiricist's "reality."

The plausibility of Moore's approach can be *suggested* by considering that if we see a blue and a yellow pencil on a table, the blue of one and the yellow of the other *is sense-perceptible*, but not something else that is *also true*, namely that he *number* of pencils is *two*—for "two" is a number, and numbers are not sense-perceptible.[71]

The reader is not alone in being unsure as to just how numbers may be said to, (in some sense) "exist." But to analyze the matter directly would at this juncture be impractical and perhaps unnecessary. The complications would be many.

For instance, Robert P. Sylvester's work on Moore (from which the example above is drawn) speaks of *good* existing by "exemplification" and as "ingressing" into reality—*special usages and terms* that, in our view, obscure a conceptual impasse that has eluded clarification.[72] For now, it may suffice to suggest that Moore's handling of *good* need not be a merely verbal exercise. There may be a sense in which things that are not physical or psychological can have an independent status in the world.

The logical barrier to evaluative truth

An equally consequential obstacle to the idea of moral knowledge was introduced two centuries before Moore's "naturalistic fallacy" (*Principia Ethica*, 1903). This impediment to moral inquiry surfaced as a nearly incidental observation in Hume's *Treatise of Human Nature*. Just as he denied knowledge of *physical* necessity, Hume also denied knowledge of *moral* necessity. However, this time he did not argue (as he could have) that we have no impression or sensation of moral necessity.

Instead, Hume made a chastening observation about deductive inference. He argued that how things ought (morally) to be cannot be concluded (deduced) from the way things are (or will be). So logically impeccable was his case (below) that his point—"what ought to be cannot be inferred from what *is*"—has become a staple of moral skeptics. Said Hume,

> In every system of morality. . . . the author proceeds for some time in the ordinary way of reasoning, and establishes the being

of a god, or makes observations concerning human affairs [all claims about what *is* the case]; when of a sudden I am surprised to find that instead of the usual copulations of propositions *is* and *is not* [instead of continuing to talk of what is and what is not], I meet with no proposition that is not connected with an *ought* or *ought not* [I find him talking about what ought or ought not be]. This change is imperceptible, but is, however, of the last consequence [explanatory phrases added].[73]

Simply put: "How," Hume asked, "can you possibly draw an *ought* conclusion from premises that have no *oughts* in them?" From the premises "this *is* a child" and "this child *is* hungry" one cannot validly conclude, "this child *ought* not be hungry" or "this child *ought* to be fed." That is, from factual statements such as "people hate" and "hate brings sorrow," the "ought" statement "people *ought* not hate" does not follow.

The point is a logical one. Deductive logic tells us that one cannot have in one's conclusion elements that are not already in one's premises. It is invalid, therefore, to draw an ought conclusion from non-ought premises.

Yet, people draw ought conclusions from *is* statements every day! "Your child is starving (therefore), you ought to feed him" or "if that's your child, then you have obligations toward her."

But as formal logic, Hume's point is irrefutable. Moral conclusions cannot be validly deduced from factual premises.

(Perhaps when people draw moral conclusions from facts, they are always *covertly* employing an ought statement; still, they could not have *deduced* it from worldly facts).

But this problem has a familiar ring. We confronted it in a different but related form when we encountered Hume's denial of causation—of what, given physical laws—ought to happen. Hume said that from what *is* (from what *does* happen) one could not conclude what, physically speaking, *ought* to happen due to physical necessity.

Now we confront the same thing with respect to what, morally speaking, ought to happen.

The gap between grounds (premises) and conclusions as to worldly truth was what opened the door to skeptical arguments against factual truth. For example, from a past tense premise, "this has always happened" you cannot validly derive "this *will* happen."

In fact, worldly ("contingent") claims are not made through pure deduction. A human judgment must bridge the formal logical gap between evidence and conclusion. This is the gap we said enabled all skepticisms. It is the gap between grounds and conclusion that scientistic minds fill with psychological, physiological, or genetic causes that purport to explain how we reach conclusions when formal logic alone (deduction) cannot get us there.

It would seem, then, that no matter what people ordinarily think, moral conclusions cannot be rationally inferred from the facts of the world. That is why Hume—who believed in morality!—explained it as arising from feelings—in particular, from the sentiment of *sympathy*—rather than from perception (that is, from knowledge, from "seeing" the right). Of course sympathy can not explain where the idea of "obligation"—of *ought* to help rather than *wanting to* help—comes from.

But, if moral oughts cannot be rationally derived from an assessment of life's actual characteristics—and if claimed divine revelations must, unavoidably, be *judged* divine or not divine by us—then we seem consigned to moral skepticism.

Yet, in practical life, we are not moral skeptics. Indeed, the very attempt to adjust moral judgments to changing factual conditions can raise cries of false, "situational," ethics.

People think there are moral truths. As Iris Murdoch remarked, "The ordinary person thinks that some things are really better than others and that he is capable of getting it wrong"[74] And as G. E. Moore insisted, when the ordinary person says "an action is right," that person "certainly does not mean merely that that we *ourselves* have a certain feeling toward it."[75]

But if we cannot rationally, validly, derive what *ought* to be or what is *good* from the way things actually *are*, then we must all be gravely mislead.

Small wonder, then, that supposing no evidence or tests for good and evil, people look to a source beyond this world—to a law-giving God—whose will alone might make moral principles and attributes "real." As Simon Blackburn frames the dilemma: "what kind of reality could 'laws of justice' be supposed to have, if they are neither God's commands on the one hand, nor those of human beings on the other?"[76]

Thus, from the truth that goodness and badness cannot be physically observed, cannot be scientifically established, and cannot be formally deduced from what exists, skeptical theories flow in a perpetual stream. And on what basis can we say they are wrong?

What perhaps we do not find in the empiricist's picture is, in a curious sense, the human mind as it actually works. In particular, there is no room in empiricism for *insight*. Presumably, to talk about insight is to speak either of magic or of nothing real at all.

But the work of science in designing experiments can only come from the *insight* that some things make other things happen. Without that idea (which is not sense-perceptible, of course) that some things *make* others happen—the result of insight, not training—controlled experiment would be absurd, indeed unintelligible. It would be like controlling for those who stand and those who sit at a roulette table in an attempt to predict what number or color will come up.

Galileo, Newton, and Einstein did not observe more regularities or take more field trips than other thinkers. They considered what *is*, and came up with the necessities that explained what is.

We think the situation the same in morals and aesthetics in this regard. Insight into what ought to be, into moral necessity, is a function of intelligence in a sentient human being. "Seeing" things can be more than sense-perception and more than formal logical comprehension.

But all this is denied by skeptical theories of morality. Since we cannot (and, in our view, need not) review all the inhabitants of the ethically skeptical universe, we shall examine just a few in an effort to make clear why *knowledge* of good and evil is judged "impossible" by so many distinguished minds.

Because the question of moral, aesthetic, or religious truths is central to human life and yet elusive with respect to argument, we shall present the skeptical view and then criticize it, so that its elements will not require refreshing, in detail, at a later point.

Morality as emotional expression

Technical differences aside, such empirically minded philosophers as C. L. Stevenson. A. J. Ayer, and Paul Edwards, consider terms like *good* and *bad* to be linguistic vehicles of emotional expression whose function is to promote the same feelings or attitudes in others.

Evaluative words like *good* and *evil* and *beautiful* are therefore said to have "emotive meaning"—not "truth asserting" or "descriptive" meaning. They are, in C. L. Stevenson's words "magnetic."[77] To a significant degree (perhaps entirely) evaluative language is seen an instrument of social control.

Of course these evaluative terms have influence *only* because (as Iris Murdoch and G. E. Moore insist) people ordinarily think such language *can* state truths.

The *emotivist* interpretation of moral language reflects both Hume's insistence that what ought to be cannot be concluded from what *is* and the empiricist idea that "evaluative" or "normative" terms like *good* and *right* refer to nothing that can be observed by means of sense-perception. The *good* of things or their *rightness* is nothing "out there." Thus, empiricists like A. J. Ayer "shared Hume's basic conviction that value is not part of the world."[78]

Morality may express our feelings and get others to feel as we do, *but the distinguishing moral element*—the assignment of moral goodness and badness to actions—is now "revealed" as an expression of our psychology. It is the product of reaction, not contemplation, reflection, or inquiry. (Expressions such as "feelingful insight" or "moral perceptiveness," for example, would be considered hopelessly vague and quite beyond the pale.)

When the British philosopher, C. E. M. Joad, criticized this emotivist version of a moral response, he asked how "does a uniquely *moral* quality come into play if morality is just positive or negative feeling?" Why—if the *feeling* aspect of moral response is simply *positive or negative feeling*—are not our feelings of revulsion at, say, tooth-pulling also considered moral revulsion?

The American emotivist, Paul Edwards' rejoinder was that emotivists do not say morality is the expression of "just *any* sort of feeling or attitude."[79] It is the expression only of "*certain* emotions or attitudes, such as *approval* and *disapproval* [emphasis added]."[80] (But since we "approve and disapprove" home decorations, "approval and disapproval" cannot distinguish our "moral" emotions or attitudes.)

Emotivism has its variations. C. L. Stevenson's early version of emotivism treated the meaning of "good" as like the "*meaning*" of "hoorah!" (and "evil" as "meaning" Ugh!). Edwards' later version says, instead, that evaluative terms like *good* and *evil* do have objective reference, that they are in a sense "defined" by those factual features of the world to which persons or groups apply the words.

This says the *objective* meaning of the word *good* lies in its reference to whatever *facts* we approve of.[81] For example, when a person is asked, "what do you mean by a *good* car?" the person may refer to objective (factual) features like high gas mileage, safety, pleasing lines, passenger capacity, and the like. That, Edwards says, exemplifies the way in which "good" has an objective meaning. (This view resembles "cultural relativism" where the good and the bad are defined as those things approved of by each group or "culture.") In defense of the idea that he can define the word *good* in this way, Edwards tells us he can successfully define a "good" person as someone who is "truthful, loving, gentle and free from envy or malice."[82]

Edwards' argument is that these well-understood criteria explain how *good* is "definable in concrete situations." (Edwards claims this shows his position to be in keeping with G. E. Moore's proof that good has no single definition. But Moore's point was that it had no definition, whether single, multiple or open-ended).[83]

Edwards' "proof" that he has defined the word *good* is that one would never really ask whether "a truthful, loving, gentle . . . etc. person is a 'good' person. (In short, it seems contradictory to deny such a person is good.)

However, as the reader may have already surmised, *truthful, loving, gentle,* and free from *envy* or *malice,* are characteristics that already entail (contain the idea of) "good" or "bad."

For example, "truthful" doesn't mean "always states what is true" (like telling a bedridden person who asks, "you will die in a week') but rather, tells the truth *appropriately*—that is, when it is *good* to do so. That is the reason why these characteristics seem able to "define" *good*; they already entail (contain) the word *good*. Since they "contain" it they *use* it; they do not define it.

Emotive skepticism and fundamental moral judgments

Of primary importance however, is the way Edward's analysis affects what he—and everyone else—regards as "fundamental" moral judgments. These are the judgments of greatest interest to religion as well as morality. They are the judgments of things we think right or wrong *in themselves*. For example, causing pain to others for amusement is wrong *in itself*. Stealing simply to enrich oneself is wrong in itself.

For Edwards, however, it turns out that these fundamental moral judgments amount to nothing more than emotional reactions—pure and simple.

Non-fundamental judgments of good *people*, good *cars*, good *houses*, and so on rest, as Edwards has insisted (above), on *reasons*— where "reasons" are the worldly facts that define for us what we will call "good" in each situation.

But *fundamental* moral judgments make no use of such reasons. Edwards explains:

> When Muriel said "It's just that stealing is wrong" and when Voltaire exclaimed "It is just wrong to convict an innocent man" they were primarily concerned to indicate their stand or attitude. Moreover, they were concerned to indicate that their judg-

ment did stand on its own feet, that it did not require to be followed by a sentence beginning with "because."[84]

And so, "their judgments had *emotive* meaning only. . . . Muriel . . . might easily have said 'I just abhor stealing, *that's all.*'"[85]

To clarify: When we say something is wrong *in itself* we do not say it is wrong because of something *else*—some other thing—some objective reason or "fact" like "it hurts" or "it threatens society."

If we think stealing wrong in itself, we do not say "stealing is wrong because it weakens the social order" or " because it makes people sad" (even though we may think that in fact it is also bad for those reasons).

No. Fundamentally, stealing is simply wrong—wrong in its very character as a type of act (like enslaving someone); it is wrong in *being* the demeaning or negating of the "other."

And, according to Edwards, his analysis of a basic moral judgment as a judgment *"without reasons"* (because "good" or "bad" are not defined in terms of worldly facts) is "the intrinsically most plausible account of what a human being is doing in such a case."[86]

If Edwards is right, then our most fundamental moral judgments are *simply* emotional reactions and, as reactions, do not describe moral realities.

Emotivism's inescapable skepticism

Unfortunately, Edwards' distinction between a purely emotional, "fundamental" moral judgment (where a thing is good or bad in itself) and an objective judgment that a thing is good or bad for (one or more) factual reasons, is a distinction without a difference. For, unless his "objectifying" *factual* reasons are good or bad *in themselves*, they can never function as moral (or any) evaluative *reasons*. To wit:

Suppose we do not claim "stealing is bad *in itself.* Suppose, instead, we evaluate stealing *objectively* (not just "emotionally"), and say, "stealing is bad for the reason that 'it weakens the social order.'"

Now, "weakening the social order" can only be a reason why stealing is bad if "weakening the social order" is bad. But why is this weakening bad?

Perhaps it is bad in itself. But things bad in themselves represent the "fundamental moral judgments" that Edwards' emotivist analysis portrayed as *purely emotional.* And, clearly, Edwards cannot term moral judgments "objective" if the reasons they rest on are purely emotional.

Edwards must instead say "weakening the social order" is bad for a reason—that it is "bad because" of something else.

But to do the job, this "something else" will have to be something bad. And, as we now see, it will have either to be bad in itself (so "purely emotional") or bad for (another) reason. Thus, giving "objective" reasons is a process that can never reach a rational conclusion.

(Sometimes it is argued that giving reasons leads to no infinite regress because, as a practical matter, people eventually stop demanding more reasons—either of others or of themselves. But neither exhaustion, insouciance, nor ennui seems good reason to claim objectivity.)

Edwards' analysis of moral judgment entails a dilemma that negates moral objectivity, and with it, the possibility of moral knowledge. In the end, on his theory, the judgment, "it is intrinsically wrong to gratuitously kill other people" is simply an emotional outburst (early Stevenson) or an expression of one's personal disapproval (Edwards). Nothing more.

Our most basic moral judgments turn out to be paradigms of ungrounded emotionality while ordinary people look upon them as life's foundational *"knowledge* of right and wrong."

In the spirit of demystification that is at once the strength and the weakness of empirical philosophy, Edwards tells us, in a summation, that "there is nothing very puzzling about the origin of ethical terms" (this, in the face of longstanding metaphysical disagreements regarding the nature of morality!).

We are told that ethical judgments "are convenient ways of doing several things at once. They serve to refer to certain qualities or features [like "stealing disrupts the economy"] to express the speaker's moral attitude ["I don't approve of stealing"], and in several cases also to commend a certain attitude or conduct to one's audience [you! disapprove of stealing!]."[87]

Viewed this way, it passing strange that such ethical judgments should ever have puzzled philosophers or driven others to explain them by reference to God! Striking, too, is that ethical judgment, on this view, has nothing to do with a unique way of thinking—a distinct domain of rationality—as is the case in science or mathematics.

In describing moral judgment as a combination of certain attitudes and attempts at social control, emotivism opens moral judgment to complete explanation by the sciences—social, psychological, and biological. Within its scientistic understanding of moral experience, ordinary notions of "moral insight," "moral perceptiveness," or "moral sensitivity" have no place.

Moral judgments as prescriptions

Not all implicitly skeptical views of morality emphasize emotions and attitudes. The British philosopher R. M. Hare's account of moral judgment rests on a conceptual analysis of moral language.

Hare contends that puzzles about the nature of morality stem from linguistic misunderstanding. We are simply unclear as to what it is we are saying when we say a thing is morally good or bad—or is a moral obligation or a moral right.

Moral language is *evaluative*. And evaluative language exists to *tell us what to do*. It is, in Hare's terms, "prescriptive." Moral language, he says, is prescriptive because morality is about what people *do*:

> If we were to ask of a person "What are his moral principles?" the way in which we could be most sure of a true answer would be by studying what he *did* . . . the reason why actions are in a peculiar way revelatory of moral principles is that *the function of moral principles is to guide conduct.* The language of morals is one sort of prescriptive language. And this is what makes ethics worth studying: *for the question "What shall I do?"* is one that we cannot long evade [emphases added].[88]

The contrast is with *descriptive* language. Descriptions do not tell us what to do. They tell us *what is the case*. Of course, descriptions can be used to guide us. If a road sign says, "bridge out" we will likely turn around. But the guidance of behavior does not explain the existence of descriptive language. For Hare, it does explain the existence of evaluative language. And so, according to Hare, *prescription* is entirely the point of moral and all other evaluative speech.

It should be noted (for later comment) that the way our use of evaluative language affects others is, in Hare's view, by telling us directly to do or not do something. In this he differs from emotivists who say evaluative terms like *good* affect the behavior of others by "influence" or psychological causation.

By thus distinguishing morality's *telling* or *informing* us what to do from the sort of non-rational, influential processes of propaganda and advertising, Hare seems to acknowledge something rational or "objective" in the idea of morality.[89]

Prescriptivism's moral skepticism

Nevertheless, Hare's analysis leads us into the same skeptical universe as emotivism. In neither theory can evaluative terms *describe* qualities or aspects of the world.[90] And because they do not, they can be neither true nor false.

The idea that moral terms are essentially prescriptive—that they tell us to *do* a thing—seems reasonable when we think of statements like, "one ought to be truthful." But *prescription* seems a less appropriate term when we say things like, "slavery is evil" or "torture is immoral" or "love is good." Surely, few would comfortably say that when we tell someone a given act is evil, we are not describing that act but are just telling them (and everyone else) not to do it.

Why do people think "love is good" is descriptive of love—that love's goodness is a fact just as slavery's evil is a fact—if evaluative statements are really prescriptions?

Hare answers, firstly, by acknowledging that we call things good or bad, but on the basis of "standards of value" such as "slavery is evil" or "love is good." And, of course, these *standards of value*—or, in moral matters, *moral principles*—are the *reasons* (as he terms them) that we offer for saying a particular act is good or bad.

But, secondly, and crucially, Hare says, we use these standards *over and over*. As a result, they become so familiar through habitual use, they *feel* to us like facts. "People who have acquired very stable standards of values come to treat value-judgments [like "slavery is evil"] . . . as purely descriptive" (when they are not).[91]

We are thus mislead by the descriptive force which moral judgments acquire, through the general acceptance of the principles on which they rest."[92]

> If they are accepted sufficiently long and unquestioningly, they come to have the force of intuition. Thus our ultimate moral principles can become so completely accepted by us, that we treat them, not as universal *imperatives*, but as matters of *fact*; they have the same obstinate indubitability [emphases added].[93]

This psychological phenomenon "is quite sufficient to account for the feeling we have that, when we appeal to a moral principle, we are appealing to something that is there already."[94] Hare's explanation of our self-deception concerning the reality of moral necessity or *obligation* echoes Hume's explanation of our self-deception regarding physical necessity or *causation*. Recall that Hume argued that when people see B *always following* upon A, they are mislead into thinking that A *causes* or *necessitates* that B occur. According to Hume, the idea that A *causes* B to happen is merely a projection onto the world of our *feeling of expectation* [our habit of expecting] that B *must* appear.

Neither Hume nor Hare can find *necessity* in the world because empiricist epistemology can neither observe necessity directly nor test for it directly. And this is true whether that necessity is moral (obligation) or physical (causation).

Thus, we see, again, that theories of knowledge have as their complement a view of what is ineluctably or ultimately *real*. They have a "metaphysics"—however much empirical epistemologists may decry metaphysics.

Indeed, in our view, these tough-minded, secular theories of knowledge and reality may pose as much a challenge to reason in science and morals as any theory of "revealed" knowledge with its complementary supernaturalist metaphysics.

Moral language as prescriptive language

Hare's reasons for insisting that evaluative language is not descriptive focus on the way we use language. The empiricist assumptions we attribute to him are not the basis on which he explicitly builds his linguistic case.

In a representative argument, Hare examines a parson's application of the word *good* to a parishioner's character. Although it will turn out that the parson's use of "good" has some factual ("descriptive") meaning, the descriptive element will not be the primary one:

> When a parson says of a girl, she is a good girl . . . we can form a shrewd idea, of what *description* she is; we may expect her to go to church, for example. [Note: this is what Edwards called the objective part of morals, the "description" of fact that he termed "reasons."] It is therefore easy to fall into the error of supposing that by calling her a good girl the parson means simply that she has these descriptive characteristics [going to church and other *behaviors*]. . . . It is quite true that part of what the parson means is that the girl has these characteristics . . . [but] . . . he also *means to commend her* for having them; and this part of his meaning is *primary* [emphases and explanations added].[95]

Hare's point is that if "good" (or any other evaluative term) merely *referred* to facts of the world—as in, "she attends church regularly"—we would not be *commending* any particular stance toward those facts by calling them "good."

We would only be *mentioning* facts like churchgoing when what we want to do is commend them (to ourselves as well as others). So, when the parson says she is "good," he is not describing facts ("she regularly goes to church") but *telling us* to go to church regularly.

Evaluative terms have "a special function in a language, that of commending, and . . . they cannot be defined in terms of other words which themselves do not perform this function; for if this is done, we are deprived of a means of performing this function."[96]

In furtherance of his case, Hare points out that it would be senseless for people from divergent cultures to *argue* about what is good, if "good" simply referred (by definition) to certain facts. If people of divergent cultures can argue about what is good,

> it is because in its primary evaluative meaning "good" means . . . [no particular facts] . . . but is in both languages *the most general adjective of commendation*"—the result being "that . . . [a] missionary can use it to teach . . . cannibals Christian morals.[97]

Arguing, further, that evaluative terms do not *describe*, Hare points out that *good* "can be applied to any number of different classes of objects. We have good cricket-bats, good chronometers . . . good pictures, good sunsets, good men."[98] When it comes to evaluative terms "there is no common property . . . recognizable in all cases."[99] (For example, in aesthetics, an evaluative term such as *beautiful* does not refer to a set of physical characteristics.) Thus, when looked at (*by an empiricist*) as a descriptive term, *good* is an empty vessel.

So, simply put, *value terms* like good and right and appropriate and rational *are* not descriptive of anything in the world. Hare can say (in concert with emotivism and the bulk of philosophic opinion) that although we may convey the meaning of "red" by pointing to a colored surface, we cannot convey the meaning of "good" by pointing to a feature of the world.

(Nor do evaluative terms describe inner facts. "Good" does not refer to a special inner feeling. If it did, Hare points out, then, when we *felt* a thing was good it would, necessarily, be "good." But few believe that if a thing feels *good*, it necessarily is good.)

Moral principles as reasons

We agree with Hare that evaluative language makes sense (is *rational*) only on the assumption that you have a reason for your judgment (that you are *not* simply "blurting" or "emoting"). Hare is right in saying that "it . . . always makes sense, after someone has said . . . [something is good] . . . to ask, "What is good about it?"[100]

For Hare, the *reason* why something is evaluated one way or another is a "*standard* of the good"—the sort of thing in morals we would call a "moral principle."

So we might say to a teacher, "it's bad to keep the whole class after school when only a few misbehaved" and our *reason* might be the moral principle (or "standard of the good"): "the innocent ought not suffer" or "it is morally bad that the innocent suffer."

But this is the sort of standard or principle that, in Hare's view, refers to or describes nothing actual. Thus it cannot be said that an act which punishes the innocent has *in reality* any particularly moral character or quality. Because they refer to nothing real, moral principles or standards that we offer as reasons are neither true nor false!

Reasons and truth

But here is another oddity. If a principle like "persons are of infinite worth" were not *co*nsidered a truth, why would anyone think it was a reason for acting one way rather than another? It seems senseless to say, "human life is of infinite worth" (or "great" worth) is not a truth, but it is the reason why I refrain from violence."

Surely reasons for actions are not reasons unless they are offered as true.

Hare has explained the tendency offer moral reasons as truths as a self-deception. Moral principles are internalized through habitual use and projected onto the world as a kind of fact.

Holding to Hare's account, if we were enlightened in respect of our moral principles, then with respect to the principle of truthfulness, we would say, "the reason why people should be truthful is because I have always believed we should." The search for moral wisdom would be the search for our own habits.

If Hare is right, moral gravity is an unwitting charade.

But our behavior is, in moral matters, considerably more subject to the consideration of reasons for continuity or change than Hare's analysis suggests.

Indeed, the very reason we *ask* "for a reason" (to which Hare insists we are always entitled) is that we intend to *pass judgment* on that reason.

How do we imagine we can pass judgment on a reason—a standard of value or moral principle—if the moral, the obligatory, nature of such a reason is not concluded from worldly evidence? What is there to think about if what *ought* to be cannot be concluded from *is*?

For moral principles to function as reasons, they cannot be opaque to judgment. And the earnestness and persistence over time that attaches to arguments about principles makes it plain that no one thinks them unconnected to worldly evidence concerning their goodness and badness, their rightness and wrongness.

It should be mentioned that Hare does assign an element of what he calls "descriptive" meaning to evaluative judgments. But what judgments "describe" are the principles used in them—not characteristics of the world on which evaluations might be based.

According to Hare, "to know the *descriptive* meaning [of any evaluative judgment like "the girl is good" or "the car is good"] is to know *by what standards* the speaker is judging."[101] The "descriptive" meaning of "morally bad" in "torture is morally bad" might therefore be the principle, "hurting people to get information is bad."

But this is surely wrong. No one thinks that when they say, "torture is evil," what they are describing (insofar as they are describing anything) is the *principle* they use and not the *practice* they condemn.

Our critical arguments (we reiterate) are based on what we claim to be ordinary moral understanding. Hare can say, "well, 'ordinary understanding' is wrong" or—the more difficult thing—"moral principles can state no moral truths." But that is what he must say, outright—which is why, in Chapter One, we said philosophy requires integrating one's *convictions* (and why the reader's worldview is—like the writer's—always on trial).

The strangeness of moral obligation

What then, of moral force? What is the unconditional, non-practical, life-shaping, soul-shaping "ought": the *ought* of moral obligation?

To his credit, Hare did not conceive moral judgments emotively—as mere feeling-reactions or outbursts that have a certain social utility. He realized that moral judgments are somehow serious— that they seek to be more objective, more rational that. But then, wherein lies their peculiar force? What is it to be morally obliged? *This is the crucial moral question.*

If worldly evidence does not determine what we ought *morally* do, what can it be that *requires* anything of human beings? What can call for the unconditional obedience of morality?

From whence comes the idea that there are principles of action to which we are beholden—not by fear of punishment or out of practical calculation but *absolutely*, even at the cost of our happiness or lives?

As the theologian George I. Mavrodes observed, moral obligation—the peculiarly *moral* sense of *ought*—is "absurd" in what he terms a "Russelian world" (the *empiricists'* world of sensations, of psychological conditions and proclivities subscribed to by the British philosopher, Bertrand Russell)—a world of "causation," limited to *physical* facts.[102]

What Mavrodes termed "the queerness of morality" is the strangeness of undergoing burdens and pains in obeisance to moral necessities if reality is composed solely of physical and mental facts. The "Russellian" world is a world in which moral necessities simply don't *exist*.

For Mavrodes, God's will offers an answer: "Christianity. . . . provides a view of the world in which morality is not an absurdity."[103] But Hare does not attribute the *imperative* force of moral obligation to God's will, to worldly evidence or to psychological causation. So for Hare, other sources of the *requirements*, the *demandingness*, of moral governance must be found.

That moral principles command us

Setting aside, for the moment, the question of where moral obligations come from, let us consider Hare's contention that once we have them, moral principles oblige us—directs us to do something— by *commanding* us to perform specific acts.

One might well think otherwise. One might think (as we argued, above) that a moral principle like "truth-telling is morally good" obliges us—directs our behavior—by *informing* us of an obligation that is truly ours.

But this route is not open to Hare; moral evaluations, for him, are not informative (they do not *describe* anything). The only way they can direct our behavior is by *telling us* what we must do. Thus, for Hare, it is essential that the acceptance of a moral principle be the acceptance of a command: "[any idea that] 'ought-sentences are *not* imperative and . . . [do not] . . . entail imperatives'. . . . strikes at the root of my whole argument."[104]

Hare does not say that a moral principle can be *defined* as a command (he is too much the grammarian, and too aware of Moore's "naturalistic fallacy" to make such a claim). Instead, moral principles *oblige* us to do things us by *entailing* commands. That is, commands follow *by logical necessity* from principles.

In sum: On Hare's analysis, we are obliged to behave in specific ways by moral principles because moral principles (like "lying is morally bad") entail (logically necessitate) commands (like "don't lie to this person!").

There is surely an element of truth in this. We all understand a complaint like, "how can you say it's wrong, and then go ahead and do it?" But there may also be an element of untruth, for when we acknowledge what we *ought* to do, we don't take ourselves to have been *commanded* to do it. Indeed, the whole point of morality is to *know* what we ought to do—not to be *told* what to do—not even by ourselves.

Moral obligation and the human situation

We now devote close attention to this question of whether princi-ples entail commands because nothing is more central to a grasp of the human situation than explaining *why* humans do things.

Acting out of moral obligation—and against self-interest—is, as Mavrodes clearly saw, a puzzle of the very first order. What is there about a moral "ought" that *moves* us? What bridges the gap between a principle and a decision to perform a certain action?

For the empiricist, it cannot be that we act because we perceive the moral necessity of the act (as expressed in the moral principle). The denial of moral truths follows from empiricism's epistemology. Nor, for Hare, do moral principles move us to act by psychological in-fluence, that is, by *causation.*

So, why, in the light of a moral principle must an act be done?

It turns out that, according to Hare, the reason we must perform particular actions is because the command to perform them follows *logically* from the moral principles we accept.

Hare claims that when you accept a moral principle—an "evalu-ative judgment"—the *command* to commit a specific act follows from it by *logical necessity.* (That is the only kind of necessity open to an em-piricist) Put in lay terms, a moral principle like "lying is bad" *contains within it* as part of its meaning, a *command*—namely, "do not lie!"

So if you accept the principle "lying is bad" you have *already* ac-cepted the *command* not to lie in this or that situation.

But there is no *proof* that moral principles are the sort of principle that entails commands (like "do not lie!"). Hare, after wrestling with this issue, declares that he will "get over this difficulty in the only possible way, by making it a matter of definition" that assenting to a moral principle is assenting to a command.[105]

Hare's decision is not quite arbitrary, since, as we have said, logi-cal entailment is the only kind of necessity left to an empiricist who has rejected psycho-physical causation yet wishes to explain why, in the light of a moral principle, a particular action is necessary.

And so he proposes "that the test, whether someone is using the judgment, 'I ought to do X' as a value judgment or not is, 'Does he or does he not recognize that if he assents to the judgment, he *must also assent* to the command 'Let me do X'? [emphasis added]"[106]

Hare insists the connection is one of logical entailment: "princi-ples of conduct entail particular commands. *The entailment is rigorous* [emphasis added][107] But Hare's way with moral obligation will not do. And if it fails, the whole subject of moral obligation reopens, and we must think once more upon the nature of reality.

For if the imperative force of moral obligation cannot be explained as supernatural, as physical, as logical, or, derived from worldly evidence, what are we to say of its reality? Whether obligation is or is not *real* determines whether we are humans or just uniquely clever (if fantasy-driven) animals.[108]

The problem for Hare is that if commands were really *entailed* by principles, then, logically speaking, rejection of the command (as we shall argue) would entail rejection of the moral principle. If this is so, then the violation of one's own moral principles becomes impossible! And if it is so, we will be, as we have said, returned to metaphysics, returned to confronting what we think about moral reality.

Let us, firstly, be clear about *entailment*. Entailment posits a strict logical connection between statements.

For example: suppose we accept the statement, "S is a straight line." If we understand the verbal meaning of "S is a straight line," we know that we must also accept the statement "S has no curves." That is to say, "S is a straight line" *entails* "S has no curves."

If we accept "today is Monday" it is a matter of logical necessity—it is entailed—that "tomorrow is Tuesday." If "there exist three apples" is true, then "there exists more than one apple" is also true." In a sense, the second statement—the entailed statement—is "contained" within the first.

In these examples we see that the acceptance of the first statement—"there are three apples"—requires the acceptance of the entailed statement—"there exists more than one apple." But this means one cannot reject the second *without also rejecting the first*. For example, if we reject "there is more than one apple" *then* we reject "there are three apples."

So, if the command to do a thing is tied to a moral principle by *entailment*—if the moral principle "one ought to be truthful" entails (contains within it) the command, "tell the truth!"—then, if we *reject* the command, "tell the truth!" (saying "I'll lie, anyway") we reject the moral principle itself. We reject "one ought to be truthful," we don't, that is, *disobey* it.

Hence, under Hare's doctrine of entailment, because the rejection of the command rejects the principle that entailed it, we can never violate our principles! For one cannot violate principles if the failure to follow them "automatically" *cancels* them.

But of course our principles *can* be violated. If this were not so, there could be neither hypocrisy nor guilt.

Indeed, in law, under the principle called the "M' Naghten Rule," one is guilty only if, when the crime was committed, one *knew* that what one was about to do was wrong (one accepted that it was wrong). Therefore, in the law, it must be possible to accept a moral principle and yet *not* choose the action is prescribes.

Put another way, it has to *make sense* to say, "I believe I ought not have done it, but I decided to do it anyway."

This "merely technical" flaw (like many others in, for instance, emotivism and utilitarianism) is symptomatic of hugely consequential conclusions as to the nature of reality and human life.

Here the error is symptomatic of denying that humans *can come to see* the moral necessity of a principle of action—and out of that *perception*—that *understanding*—rationally conclude that a particular act *should* be done.[109]

Analogously, (as we have noted) in physical matters, it was denied by empiricism (as it was denied by theism's William of Ockham) that humans can come to see the necessity of a physical sequence—and out of that perception—that understanding—rationally conclude that a particular event must occur.

Talk of "moral perception" is denigrated by empirically minded philosophers who see it as "mysticism," as vacuously positing a "sixth sense," or an inexplicable (hence "empty") power of *intuition*. Insightful decision-making or what might be termed *uniquely human perception* has been ruled out because the *reality* of moral necessity has been ruled out.

If sense perception is the only medium through which reality can be perceived than there is no goodness or badness, rightness or wrongness "out there" to be understood.[110]

However, if we turn to practical life—to situations where actions will affect human beings—people do, in fact, think they can discern principles that express moral truths. They employ distinctly *perceptual* and other terms of worldly *inquiry* when discussing the status of moral principles. They use expressions like "I see that it ought to be done" or "it's clear that I ought to do it" or "I've come realize that we ought to help."

And this language of *perception*, of *discovery*, is not a grammatical quirk, a mere manner of speaking. People really *mean* that they *see* something—that they *realize* something moral or immoral about something in the world. Whether people pray for guidance or hope to make the right decision, *reflection* and *contemplation* appear, universally in practice, to be very much in order.

Here, the very briefest of suggestions as to how one can "reflect" on a moral principle and *see* why it ought to be followed: Why is lying morally wrong (or, why is truth-telling a moral principle)? One consideration may be that when one lies, one cuts oneself off from others; one severs a relation of trust. These things are *part of* lying; they are not separate effects. They are *aspects* of what lying *is*, not just *consequences* of it.

And, as we shall argue, additionally, in Chapter 4, they are qualitative and real and visible only within the medium of feeling—which is why poetry, novels, and concrete accounts of human situations are instruments of moral enlightenment.

Fiction may be a curious resource, but we stand with Mark Twain, whose Huckleberry Finn struggles to decide whether he is obligated to turn in his friend, the runaway slave, "Nigger Jim" or to refuse. As a boy, Huck decides he will not turn him and therefore will "go to hell" for doing what the fugitive slave law and his white, southern culture says is the wrong thing. But it is clear that Huck has seen the humanity of this "three fifths of a human being," and realizes that it cannot be right to follow the law in this case.

Twain's story exemplifies what it is to think about the world morally and to achieve a moral insight higher than law or opinion.

Of course there is always concrete reality:

> There were no seats on the plane, only three rows of litters, five high, all filled with badly wounded and dying soldiers, most of them still kids themselves. I was strapped to my litter, as they were, but my mother, brother and sister were ambulatory.
>
> The thing I remember most vividly is the soldiers screaming in pain and crying out for their mothers. My mother went up and down the aisles holding their hands, stroking their brows, giving them sips of water. My sister helped light their cigarettes. Many of them were amputees. Some had no stomachs, some had no faces.
>
> The soldiers in the litters above and below me both died, blood dripping from their wounds. Many other soldiers died while we were in the air.[111]

But for empiricists like Hare, there is nothing in the world to perceive—nothing, in any meaningful sense, to *see*. That is why Hare was driven to wring moral necessity out of *logical* necessity (entailment).

Still, empiricism's strength must be admitted. We have no empirical tests for moral necessity.

The justification of moral principles

Of course, Hare, like everyone else, harbors a sense that what we *learn* from life is somehow important for deciding on moral principles. But, because "evaluative judgments " do not *describe* any part of life, life can supply no *evidence* for or against any one of them.

And since Hare, like Hume, thinks one cannot conclude what *ought* to be from what *is*, the very idea of learning how one ought to live from the way life actually is becomes a logical impossibility.

It is not surprising, then, that instead of telling us, in his usual, exacting way, just how a moral principle or "standard of value" is justified, Hare shifts his attention from logical analyses to vague generalities and the informative potential of religious narratives.[112]

By framing the problem of moral justification as one of "complete" moral justification (below), Hare unjustifiably raises the bar of argument and is able to skim over details that his skeptical framework cannot accommodate. The resulting aloofness from specificity allows him to suggest that prescriptivist morality *somehow* arises cognitively, or intelligently, from experience:

> A complete justification of a [moral] decision would consist of a complete account of its effects, together with a complete account of the principles which it observed, and the effects of observing those principles—for, of course, it is the effects (what obeying them in fact consists in) which give content to the principles too. Thus, if pressed to justify a decision completely, *we have to give a complete specification* of the way of life of which it is a part. This complete specification it is impossible in practice to give; the nearest attempts are those given by the great religions, especially those which can point to historical persons who carried out the way of life in practice [emphasis added].[113]

None of this is justifiable within empiricism. "Completeness" cannot be an issue since not even a million facts of life support or negate moral standards that, scientifically viewed, can claim no truth.

One must keep in mind that although one can justify a principle—or anything—on *utilitarian* grounds (such as self-interest, pleasure, security, survival, happiness) utilitarian justifications are not moral in type; they can show something is *useful* but not that it is *obligatory*.

Hare is, nonetheless, sensitive to the charge of moral skepticism and defends his position against the idea that it renders moral principles groundless. He imagines someone who, after receiving a complete justification (per above), "still goes on asking 'But why *should* I live like that?'"[114]

Hare answers that he has specified *all* the (purportedly) justifying facts so that "We can only ask him to make up his own mind which way he ought to live; *for in the end everything rests upon such a decision of principle* [emphasis added]. "[115]

This view may at first seem harmlessly obvious—telling the questioner that he has to "make up his own mind." But its baldness reflects the skeptical emptiness beneath. Hare cannot give such advice as "look again" or "acquire more experience," or "feel what (a principle) means between people" or "as given in novels, poetry, or history." He cannot suggest there may be morally relevant evidence in confronting poverty or wilderness or social exclusivity firsthand.

Hare is left, at bottom, with *choice*. In saying "in the end everything rests upon such a decision of principle," Hare is either harmlessly saying "choices rests on decisions," or else he is claiming that the *basis* for selecting moral principles is one's choosing them and not one's "experience" or inquiry into their nature.

Thus we find Hare throwing up his hands: "He has to decide whether to accept that way of life or not; if he accepts it, then we can proceed to justify the decisions that are based upon it; if he does not accept it, *then let him accept some other, and try to live by it* [emphasis added]."

Surely this rather crisp challenge makes sense only if, in "living by" one's principles, one can learn something about the moral adequacy of one's chosen principles. But, because we *presumably* cannot derive oughts from what is, we cannot *learn*—cannot get value-relevant *information*—so Hare's challenge can only be a *psychological*, not a moral, one: "try living that way and see if you like it—see if it is painful or pleasant" (see how it goes in the Russellian world Mavrodes rightly rejected).

Finally, Hare denies that his analysis is implicitly skeptical—that it makes moral choice arbitrary. But his argument seems beside the point:

> To describe such ultimate decisions as arbitrary, because *ex hypothesi* everything which could be used to justify them has already been included in the decision, would be like saying that a complete description of the universe was utterly unfounded, because no further fact could be called upon in corroboration of it. This is not how we use the words "arbitrary" and "unfounded." Far from being arbitrary, such a decision would be the most well-founded of decisions, because it would be based upon a consideration of everything upon which it could possibly be founded.[116]

It is true that if you consider everything that might possibly bear upon a decision, your effort at decision cannot be fairly described as "arbitrary." But if moral oughts cannot be concluded from worldly facts (from what *is*), then life presents nothing to consider—and if moral principles cannot, as a last resort, be based on their *utility*—then a decision as to moral principle can *only* be arbitrary.

Moral skepticism and the golden rule

In a later work—*Freedom and Reason*—Hare continued his attempt to square prescriptivism with the ordinary person's conviction that moral truths exist. Not just any moral principle was acceptable. Like so many others, from Rabbi Hillel to Immanuel Kant, Hare specified that moral principles be decided by (loosely speaking) adhering to the "golden rule."

To properly decide the moral law, one must put oneself in the other person's shoes. One must "identify" with the other. One has to imagine oneself as in another's position and imagine that the moral principle in question applies to oneself (as that person in the person's situation). If you can accept the consequences of acting on the principle *thus imagined*, you can, then, decide if the principle should be a moral law. For, *a moral law must apply without exception to all humankind.*

(We omit arguments as to whether we really can know the preferences of others by imagining we are "identifying" with them, and commend to the reader Bernard Williams' critique of Hare's "identification" criterion in Williams' *Ethics and the Limits of Philosophy*).[117]

Our question is this: why *should* we go through any such identification procedure at all before deciding whether to universalize a rule of action?

Surely it is not just to comport with the *linguistic convention* that for the rule to be called "a moral principle, it must be something we intend to apply universally. We think, instead, that in practical life, this identification with others has a *substantive* point. The reason for "putting oneself in another's shoes" is to help *perception*.

When we ask a child whether he or she would like another child to take his or her toys, we are asking the child to picture a situation—to see life from the angle of one whose toys are about to be taken. And if moral principles cannot be validly concluded from considering "what *is*," then all we are doing is manipulating the child's emotions to achieve the behavior we prefer the child have. (There is nothing cognitively relevant for the child to "see.")

In seeing actions from the other's point of view, one positions oneself to *recognize* something one might otherwise not recognize. If we ask someone who is habitually late to imagine in detail the other person's wondering and waiting after having striven to be on time, we are positioning the habitually tardy person to *appreciate* the facts of someone's having-to-wait.

And these consequences for others are features of lateness no less *real*, no less "out there," than the features of an alluvial plain. Similarly, it is one thing to contemplate torturing an enemy and another to contemplate a loved one, or yourself, being tortured. Quite literally, one may see the reality of it—the facts—for the very first time.

And if the *heuristic* rule "decide only on moral laws for others that you would apply to yourself" involves "taking in" facts, then you must be looking at what *is* to determine what *ought* to be.

Hence, we maintain that unless life presents a moral testing ground—a moral reality—the demand that any moral principle must be applicable in the same way and the same degree to all human beings is a mere linguistic convention and the "universality" of moral principles nothing more than a lexical requirement.

Indeed, the idea that there are things of a sort that we *must* all unconditionally commit to doing—whether we like them, prefer them, gain advantage from them, are burdened by them, or could escape them—constitutes the foundational moral *insight* (the kind of insight scientistic thinkers view as a morality's basic *illusion*).

Moral truth and human being

As "insight" is *seeing a truth*, then, if moral insight exists, there must be a moral reality—a kind of worldly or "actual" necessity called (variously) "obligation" or "duty" or "the good." And the perception of that reality can be the *reason* why one behaves a certain way.

In the second book of Plato's *Republic*, the Ring of Gyges provides a thought experiment that challenges the idea of moral reality. The ring confers invisibility on its wearer.

One of Socrates' questioners, Glaucon, takes the "Russellian" or empiricist view of reality and thus of human beings: Anyone wearing the ring could steal or ravish with impunity and would be crazy not to do so. Pleasure, satisfaction, impulse-release are real and are all.

Socrates speaks to the self-destruction of doing so, which turns out be the destruction of the mutually supportive powers that together *constitute* the state, and the good and, eventually, God.

The essence of his argument is that once the good is recognized, to violate it is to oppose one's self, to dis-integrate, insofar as one's self is a *human* self. For only a human can see what ought to be. Therefore, to act a pain/pleasure driven form of life is to prefer the animal mode of being to the human mode of being that transcends it.

This is less an argument than the presentation of a picture; it attempts to depict what is *as* it is. It is an attempt concretely to describe our *being*. It offers a *religious* context for thinking about what one ought to do. That is why the religious importance of acting on morally directive reasons is more concretely (and thus more effectively) suggested by literary works, as in, for example, Aldous Huxley's anti-utilitarian *Brave New World*.

In Huxley's brave new world, social order is maintained *internally*. Not, however, on the basis of moral perception but on a basis of genetic programming. People are programmed from birth to behave in certain ways. Moral reflection plays no part.

This is, of course, precisely how animals, and, in principle, plants, maintain their "social" order. Huxley's "argument" against a physically necessitated life is *qualitative* and so requires *portrayal*—a recourse to first-person *experience*.

As accounts of feral or severely isolated children suggest, moral insight arises within the experience of social practices. Morality is about relationships. Therefore, it is *concluded* within experience even though it is not concluded *deductively* from *statements* about experience or arrived at by scientific experimentation. (This point—that rational thinking can be broader than deductive or scientific reasoning—is explored in our final critique of philosophic doubt.)[118]

So we say that without specifically moral *insight*, without the moral perception that scientism denies, one cannot have a recognizably *human*, as distinct from an animal, mind. And if this is true, moral insight takes its place as one of the basic (unanalyzable) insights that constitutes a "human" mind.

Further, we are saying that moral insight is insight into a *type* of *necessity* and is no more a fantasy than mathematical insight and physical-science insight into *logical* necessity and *physical* necessity. The religious importance of necessity is, in the view of this work, *ultimate* (which is why, in Chapter 4, "God's Body," we focus on the point that "the creator-god" is a promulgator of *laws*).

The universality of obligation is the disclosure of the moral realm—no different and no less inexplicable (ultimate) than the moment when noise becomes language, motions becomes causes, and items become numbers. The notion that the universality of moral laws is morality's first truth is something we feel, grasp, recognize.

Imagine, dear reader, if you will, a moral principle with exceptions. Imagine that "humans ought to eschew violence, except for the

Jones family"—or William Smith, or America, or Protestants, or those with I.Q. scores over one hundred fifty. One needn't be a theologian or philosopher to sense the absurdity of this.

(To those who say there have been and are people who make such exceptions one must say there are those who deny the reality of repeated scientific experiments and others who think they have actually traveled in their dreams. That is, without a certain level of sophistication and worldly knowledge, all argument is smoke).

And when we say to declarations of moral privilege, "that's not right!" we are not complaining about word usage. We are not saying "you can't use the term *moral* to describe that self-serving decision" because the word *morality* entails saying that "the same rules of action apply to all." (We are talking about a particular and real kind of *ought*.)

Our complaint is *substantive*. We mean, "the *truth* is, that's not morally right (that ought not be)." And this, we say, is the original moral *insight*. It is the grasp of something that sociobiology cannot accept as insight but must attribute to evolutionarily selected brain-function (not *understanding* or *reasoned learning*)—something they never say about their field's own "insights" which, on their own theory, must be accounted for socio-biologically.

In sum, it is absurd to explain the ability of moral language to influence the behavior of a *single* individual because it can influence *multiple* individuals. (Hare, for example, suggests that morality's force derives from the fact that we *believe* it applies to "all humans" and cannot be escaped.)

Indeed, the requirement that moral principles be applied universally makes it a more difficult system of control by commands than a system tailored to specific social needs in specific situations. The targeting of specific persons or groups by commands and influence is familiarly known as the exercise of *power*. It is social control by *de facto* "leadership"—the system of tyrants, efficiency experts, self-serving politicos, and animals. Flexible, convenient, and effective, it could hardly be more unlike morality. (And the idea that it can never work *lastingly* awaits refutation by new technologies of mind control—profit-minded media, anxiety-driven education, and psychotropic drugs.)

Doing the right thing rather than the desired thing—even against one's advantage or life—is, for psychological, mammalian, or "empirical human" a form of madness. It is more than merely "queer" as Mavrodes put it. It is "mad" because it denies utilitarian reason (As Glaucon claimed in the tale of Gyges' ring, above.)

Doing what is right against what one wants or desires violates the rationality of survival, of power, of ego, or physical pleasure and the avoidance of pain. No doubt, as is often observed, morality provides internal social controls, so that social order can be maintained free from the unmanageable burden of constant policing. But unless we are the self-deceived, organically determined creatures E. O. Wilson's genetic explanation of ethics says we are, our respect for moral principles—principles of "ought" and "ought not"—remains a mystery.

Hare's prescriptivism is satisfied to say that morality's purpose is *to tell us what to do*. But Hare can supply no reason for insisting—as he did out of obvious moral concern—that we are *told* (by moral language) rather than *caused* or "influenced" by it (a feature Hare said distinguished his view from emotivism). He cannot supply an *objective* reason unless he thinks that in being told we are being *informed*. There is no reason for preferring *telling* people what to do over *causing* (influencing) them to do things if there is no truth at stake.

That is, unless choices *can* be guided by the specific, imperative force of *truth*, human action can be nothing *other* than influenced or caused.

Hare's reliance on moral language as the language of command reflects the same empirical skepticism that leads theists to conceive morality as *telling*—where, of course, it is God who tells, not humans . Still, what is *told* is only what God *wills*, not what God finds *already* true—and so is not instructive because of what it helps us *see* (as in the writing of art critics).

We have seen Hare attempt to align his moral theory with ordinary thinking by suggesting the relevance of religious visions to moral outlooks. Presumably, religious narratives avoid "arbitrary" moral judgment by providing a kind of ultimate basis for formulating moral principles. But without the possibility of *insight* into what humans ought to do—without the perception of moral facts—Hare has no basis on which to differentiate exemplars of *social* leadership (power, influence) from exemplars of *moral* leadership (truth and moral teaching)—which is the very point of *religious* narrations.

It is hardly a unique rebuttal of our critique of emotivist and prescriptivist moralities to maintain that we "project" or imagine moral *rightness*—for *necessity* (of which moral obligation is but one kind) has been denied in every domain of understanding in which humans claim to "see" realities. The denial of necessity is the stock in trade of empiricism.

Thus, in *science*, with Hume and "conventionalists": we "see" no necessities so the "law" of gravity is a mere projection or convenient

assumption. Thus, in *morality* with Hare: the truth of "slavery is evil" is a mere projection. Thus, in *history* with postmodernists: history projects present viewpoints onto an unknowable past. Thus, in *literature* with deconstructionists: the "meanings" we see are projections onto "texts" that have no meanings of their own (nothing in their sense is *necessary*).

Once more, we have found philosophy arguing that what ordinary people *think* they are doing, they cannot possibly be doing—and this with respect to nothing less than the basis for assessing and directing their lives. Once more, the existential vision that governs practice has been taken to the woodshed of philosophic doubt and made to confess its self-deceptiveness.

Morality's question and the importance of language

Why be moral?

"The function of moral principles is to guide conduct" [and] "the language of morals is one sort of prescriptive language. And this is what makes ethics worth studying: for the question 'what shall I do?' is one that we cannot long evade."[119] Thus, Hare explains morality as answering the question, "what *shall* I do?" But is this right? Is not morality's germinating question, "what *should* I do?"

The difference is crucial. "What *should* I do?" asks for advice, for directive information, it does not ask to be *commanded* what to do.

"What should I do?" is a request for information as to what choice, broadly speaking, is right—and is therefore concerned with what is the case, with truth, not commands. For that reason, it cannot support a prescriptivist account of moral language.

The issue between *shall* and *should* is therefore not grammatical. At stake is the logic of moral judgment and the role of worldly truth in that judgment.

"What *shall* I do?" asks only that a choice be settled. It does not *require* advice or information as means for doing so. *It asks about a future fact* (a choice)—which means it does not ask about what is right or proper or necessary.

We can see this because it makes sense to say, "I know what I *should* do, but I wonder what I *shall* do? Knowing what I *should* do is knowing what is proper or best to do. But knowing what I *shall* do is independent of the issues of rightness or propriety called for by *should*."

And that is why "what shall I do?" can always be *fully* answered by a *command*. "What shall I do here?" "Pay the bill!" And if one is wondering what one will do—by a *prediction*: "What shall I do? Hmm, I suppose I shall face the music."

The fact that *shall* is about future *fact* while *should* is about what is *right* shows that despite his efforts to avoid the "naturalistic fallacy" Hare committed it.

By selecting as morality's basic question, a question that requires nothing normative to answer it, Hare treated a question that asks for a fact (what shall I do) as a question that asks for what is good (what should I do). And, defining *normative* expressions (like "good") in *factual* terms (like "happiness") is of course, Moore's "naturalistic fallacy."

Importantly, it was by starting with the normatively neutral "what shall I do?" that Hare was able plausibly to speak of morality as, essentially, *telling people what to do*—as commending (in emotivism) or commanding (in his "prescriptivism"), rather than as *informing* them with respect to what is good or right.

Still *should's* connection with *ought*—especially with moral *ought*—remains to be shown. For the question, "what should I do?" often seems to ask for the *means* I should use to reach my goal. For example, if someone says, "this faucet leaks; what should I do?" it seems the answer—"you should call a plumber"—is complete.

Why, then, do we insist that "What should I do?" is always a question implicitly connected to the *obliged* choice of actions?

We can begin to see why, if we revisit the "faucet" problem, but this time in a non-usual world in which plumbers are racially discriminatory in their hiring. In this situation, "what should I do about my leaking faucet?" might well bring the answer, "fix it yourself" or "let it drip (until equal opportunity is established)."

What this shows is that the answer to a *"should"* question *will always depend upon ideas of what is right or correct*—upon "normative" considerations.

The reason why the normative character of "should" may go unnoticed is that, in typical situations, assumptions about what is right or good are tacitly shared. Questions of value or rightness often fail to come up. Means are then recommended with an eye to the purely factual. But not always.

Thus, to "What should I do about the cold in here?" the response, "You should set the thermostat higher" may seem only about facts, about how to achieve a goal. But a knowledgeable conservationist might answer differently: "Put on a sweater; don't waste energy."

Because *should* is about what it is right to do, answers to a question like, "What should I do, my car is in the shop and I have a meeting out of town?" can reflect very different values. Thus, you should: "Take the train," says the conservationist friend; "Borrow my car," says the relative; "Rent a limousine, this is a real opportunity," says the social climber.

Should is always a normative term—even in science—though not always because of a *moral* norm. When a scientist uses "should" to state what *will in fact* happen, the implication is that "by rights" it should happen. That is, a scientist who says, "the flame *should* extinguish when the oxygen runs out" is saying so because of *physical* norms or "laws." But if the scientist knew nothing about laws governing oxidation, the scientist would more likely say, "in a while, the flame will go out . . . it always does."

And, what is more, if the scientist said "it *should* go out," we would ask, Why? And without some reference to physical laws, the scientist would have no answer.

So what should happen, even in science, is a matter of what we have a *right* to believe will happen. The normative character of "should" is as apparent in matters of physical fact as in matters of human choice.

It is because the *should* question is an unbounded question about what it is best or right to do that it opens the way to moral considerations. Human activity is always subject to moral judgment, so asking what one should do implicitly opens the door to moral judgment (on top of other kinds of evaluative judgment).

That is why the *should* question makes sense only if there can be a *reason* for the answer. It makes no sense to say "Of the many things you *could* do, here is what you *should* do, but I say this for no reason." To this, one would surely respond: "if you have no reason for my doing it, why did you say I *should* do it instead of just *telling* me to do it?"

Should without a reason makes no sense, while, as noted, *shall* can be fully answered by commands or predictions.

Adverting to our prior argument that the reasons we offer for actions are reasons only if offered as truths: "What should I do?" makes sense only if the world can offer truths *that are normative* in character such as "love is a better *kind of thing* than hatred."

And this is to say that "What should I do?" is a sound question only if value-skepticism is wrong.

Morality, reasons, and human being

Since any act involves means and ends, to say someone should choose a particular means is to agree they should choose the end it produces. It is to be complicit in accomplishing that end. So, the question "what should I do?" opens the *entirety* of an act to *direction by moral and factual reasons*.

Still, "Should I?" makes sense only if it is true that human activity can be accounted for by the reasons offered to explain it. Otherwise moral and factual *reasons* are irrelevant to what a person chooses to do; the explanation of the choice must then fall to physiological or psychological causes (the determinants of the scientistic or "Russellian" self).

Much about the strangeness of human life is buried in the simple notion that *reasons can account for* our choices. This is important because a reason can be more than a *thought*. It can be, or can rest on, *knowledge*.

No one would care about reasons—about reasons for going to war, or for choosing a vocation—if reasons never reflected worldly knowledge. *For we seek reasons only that we may choose the right or better thing.* And if we could not know the soundness or truth of our reasons, then *having* reasons would yield no advantage over having *none at all.* Reasons disconnected from knowledge would be useless as thoughts in a dream. Doing things for reasons is not doing things for *thoughts.*

The fact is that we *judge* each other on the basis of the reasons for our actions. Whether someone helps us for gain or out of caring is, in a sense, *everything*—for, in life, our reasons tell us who we are. And—as the role of reasons in answering the "*should*" question shows—these reasons must include claims that are evaluative or "normative."

(Indeed, if normative reasons could not account for—could not truly explain—the conclusions people draw, then it would be senseless for value-skeptics to offer reasons for their skepticism, since their reasons would not explain the positions they take.)

So the importance in our lives of reasons constitutes a kind of revelation—not just with respect to the importance of evaluative knowledge, but with respect to what the use and centrality of reasons tells us about our nature.

Is it not *religiously foundational* that a creature (a physical organism) can be moved by its internalization of the world, by knowledge of it, not by brain-events or "thoughts" wholly internal to the organism?

Unless we are all deluded, the grasp of what is true and right can explain the behavior we display. For example, a shout of "fire!" is typically explained by referring to the breakout of a *fire* and the danger it poses to people, not by the *thought* of it in a person's mind (which would be the explanation if the shout was the result of a hallucination).

If what we think and do can be explained by reasons—by normative considerations that commonly (not always) embody or rest on knowledge (are informed, not *conditioned, physiological, or imaginary*)—then the human way of being in the world differs in type from the way other living forms are determined.

The recognition of this inexplicable mode of existence is recognized and poetically framed in sacred writings that portray it as a mystery (the mystery it genuinely is)—as when physicality or "dust" is made to live and understand by the unfathomable power of a god. Formed of the dust of stars and comets, yet we are no longer driven in their mindless manner, no longer moved, as they, by *causation* but instead by reasons, by knowledge whose existence depends on the physical yet cannot be explained by it.

And this, we maintain is the common understanding of the matter. The physically transcendent way we come to act and think is, every day, implicitly acknowledged: in ordinary life. For, when we are thought to be *caused* we are deemed *not responsible*.

Thus we are: "not guilty by reason of *insanity*"; we are not guilty of *blinking* (but we are of *winking*). We are not held responsible for our behavior in Tourette's syndrome, psychosis, drugged-behavior, hypnosis, or brain-probe-induced-behavior. These cases are distinguished by being thought *caused*. Thus regarded, they are viewed as lying outside the condition of free-will-and-responsibility that distinguishes us from "organisms."

(A challenge noted: The American philosopher John R. Searle has argued that a scientific ("causal") explanation of our knowledge-claims need *not* conflict with our knowing what we claim. If this is right, then—against this writer's view—a conclusion can be explained by causation yet still described as "freely chosen" or "done for a reason (based on knowledge)." On this view, determinism (the physical causation of all events and conditions) would be compatible with free will. It implies I can responsibly decide something is true even though the processes of the brain and nervous system cause me to think what I think.

A response is in order but must be brief. Searle recounts the "strictly speaking" argument of what we termed "empiricism's garden path" (wherein light waves reflect into the retina and neurons discharge in the brain and we say we "perceive a tree"). He then says it doesn't follow that if my perception (of a tree) is physically caused, then "I don't see the real world."

But his supporting argument (and we quote it, with some misgiving, from a work rich with insight and valuable arguments) is this: "The fact that I can give a causal account of why I believe that two plus two equals four (I was conditioned by . . . my first grade teacher) does not show that two plus two does not equal four."[120] However, this argument does not support the compatibility of determinism and rational choice.

It is true that a *caused* idea of what is seen or uttered can also be a *true* idea of what could be seen or uttered—in that lies the value of computers. (A person or a computer can state something true by accident.)

Our point is that if Searle and all humans were always "conditioned" or "*caused*" to say what they say (or picture what they picture), then, like computers, they would be in no position to determine whether what their internal mechanisms (brain cells or "software") produced happened also to be *true*. The reason Searle can plausibly say he *knows* what the conditioning argument "does not show" is that in it he drops the parenthetical statement that he was "conditioned" to say that two plus two is four.

In the course of discussing reasons and evaluations, we have sometimes spoken of "imperatives." This is because if a reason could not point toward a choice—if it did not guide, if it had no imperative *aspect*—there would be no reason to say it *explains* a choice.

If reasons possess an imperative or *guiding* aspect, does this imply a new "determinism"—that our actions and conclusions are not quite ours but are merely *given* to us? Hardly. We are not speaking of force or brute "influence." It is the *perception* of a reason's worth that allows it to guide us, thus making the reasons we accept *our own*. Without reasons that *commend themselves to judgment*, what moves us would make us less a *person* than a creature—explained by notions and feelings not made by us our own. We would be possessed, not self-possessed. (See section "Theism, Skepticism, Scientism, and the Person" in Chapter 2.)

Hence, we say that *only* if Searle is not "conditioned" can the assessment of "two plus two" be *Searle's* and not the product of Searle's synapses. Turning again to the life we live, we acknowledge the directive impetus peculiar to ideas when we speak of "the weight of evidence."

Useful here may be an adversion to Rorty's declaration that "the world doesn't speak to us" (one metaphor deserving another). The idea that the world doesn't speak to us is belied, even turned on its head, by the way people across walks of life speak about "evidence" or "fact," saying "the facts *tell us, point to, say, indicate, inform us, speak to* (*the point*), *reveal, show*"—not to mention that "an honest person must *face reality* or *listen to the facts*." But one never hears things like "I show, we construct, we determine, (etc.) what the evidence says."

Add to this that artists say the materials of their work speak to them, that writers say their characters speak to them, and that people often say a situation of need cries out to them, and the world's vote on the metaphor best suited to describing the world's relation to us is "*directive or imperative force* one hundred; Rorty zero."

Throughout this discussion of the nature of human *being*, it must be kept in mind that a reason is not a physical thing. (*Reasons* can be contradictory, but *things* cannot—they can be incompatible but not contradictory.) So: *a reason's directive force is not a physical force* and its *pointing is not spatial pointing*.

As "vague," "mystical" or merely "radical," this assertion demands a full stop: everything we have to say depends on the claim that there exists a *non-physical directive "power"* and that the ability to discern it is part of what we mean by "having a mind."

And since any idea of non-physical power or force remains a lively issue in "the philosophy of mind" or "action," we must attempt, however rudimentarily, to further clarify and explicate our view.

In this discussion, ideas must be distinguished from *thoughts*— something practical understanding allows but is not often required, explicitly, to differentiate. It must be clear that *ideas*, of which our *reasons* are one kind, are not objects, not psycho-physical things: In the realm of mathematical thinking, the idea of "zero" does not depend on zero thought, nor *infinity* on endless thought. The number *two* is twice as big as the number *one*, but the *thought* of two is not twice as big as the *thought* of one. When we do arithmetic we deal with ideas, that is, with *numbers*, not with *thoughts of* numbers.[121]

"Thought," we suggest, is the medium of ideas. "Thought" is a name for the fact that ideas are *organically bodied* or "incarnate." Analogously, oil paint is the medium of visible aesthetic qualities and sound waves the medium of songs—art, itself, representing, *par excellence*, matter shaped by spirit or feeling-idea.

Similarly, when we "fight for *democracy*" we fight for an *idea* of how to live. The *thought* of a democracy can be achieved by reading about it. So, to speak of "the force of an idea," is not to speak of the force of a mental *event* or *condition* like a *thought* or a *brain-state*.[122]

The puzzle, of course, is how a *physical* brain can support—or be essential for—a sequence of *ideas* whose relation to one another is not determined *physically*.[123] Immanuel Kant assigned us dual selves on account of this seeming impossibility—an *empirical* ("bodily" or "physical") *caused* self and a *noumenal* or *uncaused* self that—as un-caused—had a free will. The dual classification did not ameliorate the incongruity.

In Kant's view and our own, our manner of being can never be explained (much as the existence of *something* rather than *nothing-at-all*—can never be explained.)[124]

In our view, *human* being differs from *physical* being only if changes in human behavior can be explained in a way that is concep-tually incompatible with the way we explain changes in the physical world. We therefore agree with theists that humans are a unique form of being. (One might say there is a kind of human "physics.") How-ever, we think it no advance in understanding to explain one thing we cannot explain phenomenon by positing another (divine exis-tence) that we cannot explain.

We say, then, that an *effective* human rationality is a way of being-in-the-world in which ideas *as* reasons can actually *explain* why *mate-rial* (physical and psycho-physical) changes occur. (And, we reiterate, ideas can explain *because they can actually represent what is true or real*. Otherwise they would be mere imaginings—they would just be thoughts. They would be internal phenomena like sensations or im-ages that could only explain things the way brain activity or electrical potential explains things—*causally*.

Events come to pass by different modes of operation. As philoso-phers like to say, blinking and winking are essentially different, or, as we might say, when a baby stuffs a ballot into a box and a voter stuffs a ballot into a box. The way we suppose things actually happen in the latter case is incompatible with things happening entirely physically. Not so in the case of the blinking or the case of baby.

And if our *physical* being supports a *rational* way of being—a way of being that cannot be *explained* by the physical basis it requires—then an effective rationality would be, *in principle*, inexplicable, but true. It would constitute *transcendence*.

So, yes, the fact of *effective rationality* in which what is *right* and what is *physical* (through the mind and the brain) work (inexplicably) together in a "person" may with reason be described as a natural mir-acle—and constitutes another way of describing the previously mooted miracle of *knowing*.

(Non-philosophical readers are well advised that this talk of mir-acles—even natural ones—is anathema to mainstream philosophy where right thinking is often equated with demystification. Civiliza-

tion owes its existence to that criterion—but has the world no genuine mysteries?)

Free will

Of course reasons must be acted on if they are to explain an action. And so, the issue of free choice—more specifically, *free will*—is
unavoidably engaged. The relationship between reasons that explain
our choices and a free will that explains our choices cannot be left unaddressed.

"Free will" is almost as often disputed in philosophy as it is affirmed in religion and practical affairs. We can now either attempt a
book within a book (as if we haven't sinned on this count already) or
else reduce the issues to what we consider basic, and hope we do not
say too many things by fiat.

A free will is a will whose choice or action is not predetermined.[125] "Not predetermined" means this: if we could rewind time
so that the conditions of a choice (conditions inside and outside the
person) were *exactly what they were when the choice was made*, it would
have been *physically* possible for a *different* choice to have been made.

It is, in our view, of the very first importance to note that free
will—so defined—requires only that, physically, we "could have"
chosen other than we did. "Free will" requires that the physical properties of the brain do not restrict our choice to outcomes predetermined by those physical properties. For those properties operate by
bodily necessities beyond our direct control.

Some philosophers deny that causal determination of the will
renders it unfree.[126] But determinism makes it impossible sensibly to
speak of what we "could have done." The British philosopher, J. L.
Austin's essay, "If's and Can's" is definitive on this point.[127] (In
essence, it says that: if "I could have" (*done otherwise*) meant, "I could
have *if* conditions had been different" then—because conditions
weren't different—it follows that "I could *not* have." Therefore, a deterministic interpretation of the statement, "I could have," entails the
contradictory statement, "I couldn't have."

The merely negative fact that our will is not psycho-physically
predetermined does not explain the coming-into-the-world of a *particular* choice—or *particular* conclusion. Simply put, we do not learn
what free will is by learning what it is not.

Nor do we learn—simply by denying psychological determinism—why free will is *important*. After all, as previously noted, the
physically determined life of insects and bacteria "works"—they survive and may well out-survive us.

A note: By now, this unfolding of thoughts may (once again!) seem to readers unacquainted with philosophy unduly scrupulous or "technical" But our topic is the nature of human action—the very manner of our being-in-the-world. In "unpacking" what "morality" requires (as people understand that term in daily life), we must examine the logic that drives theism's story—the story of a creature *extracted* from *physical nature* by something (God) transcendent of physical nature. So, we proceed.

The idea of human responsibility requires that we *ourselves* be the cause of our actions, and not something *part* of or *different* from ourselves (from "the self"). Consider that the statement, "I did it" implies the possibility of blame while "the devil made me do it" does not (being no different from saying, "my muscles made me do it" or "my brain processes made me do it"). And that is why, if—like the unfortunate "Manchurian Candidate"—we learned that our brain cells had been engineered to produce a given decision we would say, "I didn't *really* do it" or "*I* didn't do it."

Recently, Sam Harris, in his popular book on religion (*The End of Faith*), dismissed the idea that our choices are anything other than (psycho-physically) determined:

> Free will is actually more than an illusion (or less) in that it cannot even be rendered coherently *conceptually*, since no one has ever has described a manner in which mental and physical events could arise that would attest to its existence. Surely most illusions are made of sterner stuff than this.[128]

Once more, we see the theme: "It can't be explained, so it can't be true."

Thinking scientistically, Harris discounts the idea of individual responsibility because "it has long been obvious . . . [that] . . . either our wills are determined by prior causes, and we are not responsible for them, or they are the product of chance, and we are not responsible for them."[129] Harris then suggests that we can see this by looking inward:

> What most people overlook is that free will doesn't even correspond to any *subjective* fact about us. . . . apparent acts of volition merely arise spontaneously [whether caused, uncaused or probabilistically inclined, it makes no difference] and cannot be traced to a point of origin in the stream of consciousness. A moment or two of serious *self-scrutiny* and the reader might observe that *he no more authors the next thought he thinks than the next thought I write* [emphasis added].[130]

Thus, Harris suggests we *might* be responsible and have free will—if we *authored* (decided) what we should think. But that cannot be, given his account of thinking. To author or decide on our thoughts is to *think* about them and, according to Harris, thinking is not under our *control* and "just happens" without having any "point of origin." Therefore, authoring, because it is thinking, can no more be "ours"—under our control and free—than the thinking he suggests authoring could control.

Why this confusion? In our view, Harris (like anyone else) has internalized the common understanding of authorship in which it makes sense to speak of authoring as a form of deciding freely, hence responsibly, what to say. (Harris does, after all, live a real life.) But his scientistic outlook has led him to seek causes for thought and thus to counsel that we view our own thinking from the third-person stance of a scientific observer. And so, of course, he can find neither causes nor an author (a *self*)—for the same reason Hume could find neither causes nor a self. (The hunter cannot hunt himself.)

By discounting his first-person self, and adopting the stance of *spectator* toward his own mind, he sees his thoughts as mental facts, going by like traffic, and is forced to admit that thinking is a kind of automatic process (as yet unexplained) that no "self" controls. On his own argument, Harris did not author his own book and was not responsible for what it said (since either he was physiologically unable to have written anything else or what he wrote he wrote by chance).

But we agree with Harris that the mere absence of causation is not "free will" (chance action is not "free will"). For, if we could do something we are not physiologically caused to do, and which we have *no reason whatever* to do, we could never comfortably refer to it (conceive of it) as something we "willed." *We would not know what to say about it.* Perhaps we might ascribe (uniformatively) it to an "impulse."

Sometimes coffee-house philosophers attempt to show that choices can be freely willed by "arbitrarily" picking up (say) a pencil from a table rather than (say) a cup which happens also to be on the table. The thoughtless grab for one thing rather than the other is represented as a *pure act of will*. It is pure because even the grabber doesn't know which thing he or she will pick up.

But this thought-free grabbing is done for a *reason*. The *arbitrary* (groundless) grabbing of the pencil rather than the cup—groundless even for the one who grabs it—is done for the reason of showing that "the will can be free."[131] The *act*—the thing willed—is one of *demonstration* in which mindless grabbing plays only an instrumental role.

The grabbing itself is not *willing* (pure or otherwise). The grabber intends for the grab to *just happen*, and a behavior that just happens is not possibly a behavior that is willed, since accidental doings cannot be willed doings.

Thus, what the grabbing case shows is that there is no such thing as exercising one's "will" *for no reason whatever*—any more than we would say we exercise our will when we have no direct control, as when a behavior or a thought moved by brain-impulse or reflex or some other physiological cause ("free association" is achieved by *letting go*—that is, by not willing). Otherwise the exercise of a free will would be a *mindless* exercise and could not be distinguished, even in oneself, from being *caused* (moved by something beside *oneself*).

In striving to make conscious what the practical mind implicitly grasps, we join arguments at least as old as Kant's, who in 1785 already saw what we have attempted to argue.

In our view, he, too, said that will is an aspect of mind or "rationality" and that *self*-determination meant being caused by the self and not something *not* the self or "alien"—which is the fate of physical things:

> Will is a kind of causality belonging to living beings so far as they are rational. *Freedom* would then be the property this causality has of being able to work independently of *determination* by alien causes; just as *natural necessity* is a property characterizing the causality of all non-rational beings—the property of being determined to activity by the influence of alien causes.[132]

So, saying someone's will is "free" is a way of saying that the reasons the person cites for the choice are not "rationalizations"—are not irrelevant (due to the choice being predetermined by psychological or physiological causation).

Thus, we are prepared to argue that freedom of the will depends upon making a choice for a reason. Further (to pick up the theme with which we began the section, *"Morality, reason and the human being"*), we hold that the best *evidence* that the reason really does explain the choice is the degree to which the reason is *sufficient* for the choice.

This description recalls the biblical statement that "you shall know the truth, and the truth shall make you free"—an observation whose theme is metaphysically consistent with our own in respect of the condition for having free will—and is consistent, as well, with the secular insight that sees indoctrination and censorship as inimical to that will.[133]

It also tracks with everyday practice. For example, if one person shoots another for the *claimed* reason that the victim ignored him when he said, "how are you, today?" we judge it not to be the "real" reason. It is insufficient; in this case, absurdly so.

And, in the absence of some other, self-interested reason like "knowing the person wanted to kill me," we begin to explain the choice as *caused*—as not a "free choice" or a "real" choice but as behavior that looked like a choice but was the inexorable outcome of paranoia or some other kind of causation.

At this point the question of cultural influence comes into play. Perhaps, in a given culture, impoliteness may be considered rational grounds for killing! Unfortunately, we cannot here explore all the challenges a full consideration of free will must meet.

We suggest, however, that there are closed or totalistic cultures and that their methods of upbringing and maintaining social cohesion *really do* block insight into reality, and therefore really do limit the freedom of their members. In short, we would argue that there are forms of upbringing in which reasons are fixed, or embedded, psychologically—typically, by being emphatically tied to *personal identity*—so that, though they are given as "reasons" they function outside the reach of rationality and are disguised causation.

In this way, whole societies can be built on rationalizations such as being a chosen people, living under a divinely chosen or inspired ruler, or being the manifestation of a master or super race. For us the main point is that even in politics the role of free will is implicitly understood to be evidenced by acting on sufficient reason.

Indoctrination, brainwashing, and state control of information are all generally acknowledged to threaten individual freedom. It is not simply that these instrumentalities limit physical access to facts and ideas. It is that they make individuals into the puppets of those who control information. They use people "as means merely" (in Kant's derogating phrase) because the use of reasons by which people operate as *selves* or "persons" has been arranged, falsified by severe limitation or outright lying.

What we sense in decrying indoctrination and censorship is that the "reasons" of indoctrinated or informationally sheltered persons have the status only of belief—not knowledge. So their reasons, so-called, cannot function as reasons must if they are to have "free will."

And this general condemnation of indoctrination, censorship, and bias—a condemnation not limited to philosophers—supports our dual contention that "the best *evidence* that the *reason* really does explain the choice is the degree to which the reason is *sufficient* for the choice" and that the will is free to the extent that choices are grounded in good reasons.

A final comment on the reality of human freedom (and thus what we claim is its miraculous nature). The will's freedom cannot be known through information dependent on the senses; that is, no "facts" can prove there is an uncaused will, so it cannot be empirically known.[134]

Kant says free will must be *assumed* by rational persons since it cannot be *known*.[135] We prefer to say that to recognize "rational persons" is to recognize free will.

Uncaused behavior can only be known if there is such a thing as rational thought. And if there is not, then the arguments in which we engage are merely vocalization.

That is why it is a joke to *argue* with computers or parrots and unthinkable to upbraid those we judge to be deranged. The operative principle is that the very idea of meaningful speech and thought presupposes responsible action, uncaused action—free will. And if this is true, then free will is not dependent on one's point of view but is prerequisite for *any* point of view that is rational.

Put another way, free will *cannot be coherently denied*, for the denial is credible if—and only if—the denial can be explained by reasons, and neither physiological nor psychological causes are reasons.

Because morality makes sense only if we are responsible for what we do, and because a free or responsible will depends upon the sufficiency of our reasons, for a rationally compelling morality to exist, we must be able to evaluate reasons for their *sufficiency*.

So, morality cannot be a matter merely of fastening onto ("choosing") principles. There has to be moral knowledge. There has to be a way to judge the sufficiency—the credibility, the truth—of reasons for what we *should* do.

A reason for what we should do or conclude must be compelling—not in isolation from other reasons but as the *clinching consideration* within the background of interrelated reasons that comprise the substance of our thinking. (Here we echo John Dewey on the *situation* of knowing and Hegel on civilized thought as a kind of great situation expressing the evolution of Absolute Spirit.)

To say that many arguments remain is of course a considerable understatement. Nonetheless, we feel constrained to venture some remarks that have a bearing on moral reality and the religious significance of morally relevant facts.

We want to emphasize that if reasons are essential, the only plausible basis for deciding what it is *right* to do in the world must be what the world *is like*. And this implies that, against the words of Hume, we can only conclude what ought to be from what *is*. If we cannot, then morality can be as justly the fruit of ignorance as experience.

For this reason, we second Iris Murdoch's philosophic lamentation:

> Why has it been so readily assumed that the stripped and behavioristic account of morality which the modern philosopher gives is imposed on us by philosophical considerations? I think this is because the anti-metaphysical argument and the logical argument have been very closely connected in the minds of those who used them with a much more general and ambiguous dictum to this effect: *you cannot attach morality to the substance of this world* [emphasis added]. And this dictum, which expresses the whole spirit of modern ethics, has been accorded a sort of logical dignity. But, why can morality not be thought of as attached to the substance of the world? Surely many people who are not philosophers, and who cannot be accused of using faulty arguments since they use no arguments, do think of morality in just this way? They think of it as continuous with some sort of larger structure of reality, whether this is a religious structure, or a social or historical one.[136]

But, not only must we learn from the world, we must learn from it what has *necessity*. As we have argued, we cannot know what we *should* do from learning only what we *might* do. And this would be our fate if our reasons revealed nothing *necessary* for us to do. And whatever is necessary, morally, is the moral law.

So, if we learn from a guiding world, we live instructed by the world as lawgiver, not as power that determines us. To say we have been "struck by a stone" can mean either that we have suffered a blow or found evidence of a geological truth. The world informs us as to *what must be* (both morally and physically, as Kant said).

What we have been saying, about reasons, will, and morality, is that knowledge of the world—the power to have the world inform us—is what transforms us from species to persons, from animal to human. This inexplicable relation between thought and world—if such a relationship exists—is, we wish to argue, in a literal sense, *miraculous*.

KNOWLEDGE AS MIRACLE

Our theological assertion that knowledge is miraculous rests on its being (in a way we have not yet specified) "'*impossible*' yet true."

Indeed, we have argued that this "impossibility" drove people like Descartes and Pascal to God as the guarantor of truth.

But if knowledge is only *apparently* impossible, its existence is only apparently a miracle, and our talk of *miracles* may be mere hyperbole. However theism's traditional miracles face the *same* problem of being "impossible but true." For that reason, both may rely on the same credentials. In any case, we have made large and questionable claims on credit that we must now try to make good.

Miracles and the impossible

Why should something that is *possible* be capable of doing more than astonishing us? Why should certain happenings lead people beyond amazement to God—to the idea that another, *non*-natural world exists?

Our first question is whether miracles have in fact occurred. The Christian apologist C. S. Lewis insisted that miracles are possible. He understood that they do not do what is *literally* "impossible" (if a thing is impossible, by definition, it cannot be). He must therefore claim, as he does, that miracles do not violate physical *laws*. This departs the common view, expressed by Samuel Johnson, that "although God has made Nature to operate by . . . fixed laws, yet it is not unreasonable to think that he may suspend those laws [in a manner] . . . advantageous to mankind."

Lewis rejected the suspension argument because he understood that if there really were physical laws, then certain physical relationships would be *necessary* relationships. And, to say a relationship is necessary is to say it cannot be otherwise. For example, to say a chain is unbreakable is to say it necessarily will not come apart. If it breaks, then it was not unbreakable; its holding together was not necessary.

So, if we say physical necessities exist, and also say, "God suspends physical laws," we contradict ourselves. We would be saying, "God makes what cannot happen, happen."

So, to make miracles non-contradictory, Lewis had to argue that "laws of nature" do not describe physically *necessities*. Instead, physical "laws" describe what has been observed to happen. They are *generalizations*.[137]

In the tradition of Hume, Lewis declared that

Mere experience . . . cannot tell us whether the thing [anything] is possible. Experiment finds out what *regularly* happens in Nature."[138] The business of science is only "to tell us what normally occurs."[139] Therefore, miracles violate no laws and offend no science. They are events that run "contrary to the natural course of events."[140]

This is surely a diffident characterization of such occurrences as virgin birth, the sudden death of all Egypt's first sons, and Mary's return from the dead to address six children in Fatima, Portugal. [141]

Something is missing. The substance of miracles does not lie in their rarity. In fact, they need not even run counter to the "natural course" of events, where that means *what regularly happens*. For, if God *regularly* created worlds like ours every day, or each day brought someone back from the dead, each event would still be considered a miracle.

And so we are returned to the traditional notion of "suspending" natural laws in hopes of uncovering what it is about miracles that makes them "miraculous."

As yet, we have not yet mentioned that miracles must be (as Johnson's view suggested) *beneficial*. Miracles are never the work of Satan or evil spirits. Language is clear on this.

Were God to create a bad event, it would not be called a "miracle."

However, beneficence is not a sufficient condition for miracles—even when combined with rarity. Even if our Earth were the only life-supporting planet in the universe, it would not be, on that basis alone, a miracle.

The task remains to specify what it is that gives certain amazing and beneficial events the miraculousness that bestows *religious* significance.

When he addresses this issue, Lewis does an about face. It turns out that, after all, nature *does* operate according to necessities: *Miracles reveal the existence of another world* because "Nature" (Lewis' name for the *physical*—the cause-and-effect—universe) *cannot* produce such occurrences. Lewis advises us that, "In calling them miracles . . . we mean that, left to her own resources, she [Nature] *could never* produce them [emphases added]."[142]

But if Nature is "whatever happens," Nature could produce *anything*. Only if Nature has *necessities* can Nature have limits. Only if there are physical laws can Lewis know what Nature *cannot possibly* do. Lewis must therefore deny his original contention that "laws" describe only "regular connections" ("observed uniformities") to claim that certain events *require* a source outside Nature.

We are now at a critical impasse. Miracles must, it seems, point elsewhere—*must reveal another order of Existence.*

There must be a reason to say that Nature, *alone*, cannot account for them, that they come from "outside" the world of *non-intentional cause-and-effect*.

But, as Lewis himself pointed out, it would be self-contradictory to claim miracles are "outside" Nature in the sense that miracles suspend natural laws.

So, what is it to be *outside* Nature? What is this revealed realm?

Miracles and mind

Lewis provides us with an example of something outside cause-and-effect Nature. It is the phenomenon we have been touting all along. We and Lewis agree that rational thought proceeds according to principles entirely different from those that govern the behavior of the physical world.

Because Lewis holds, as we do, that "worlds" are defined by *the principles that govern their operation*, Lewis assigns the rational mind its own realm, a realm he calls, "supernature."[143]

Lewis finds, as we find, that in the world of practical affairs—the world of social responsibility—when people think the principles of the *physical* world (causation) have governed mental events, they consider *rationality* to have been negated.

Thus Lewis observes that people "always assume, in discussions about morality, *as in all other discussions*, that the other man's views are worthless if they can be fully accounted for by some non-moral and non-rational cause [emphasis added]."[144] (Think of the expression "blinded by hate" or the expression, "that's the alcohol talking.")

This is precisely the point made by Kant to which we made reference while arguing that rationality is essential for free will.

Miracles, mind, and God's will

On these grounds, a parallel exists (if not an identity) between the workings of God and the workings of mind in satisfying the *minimum* conditions for a miracle: *the operation of mind is no less undetermined by nature* (by cause-and-effect) *than the operation of "God's will."*

A parallel exists as well in the requirement that a miracle be beneficent. And this beneficence, to be religious in import, must amount to something more than practical assistance. Specifically, miracles must help us in a way that signals help from outside nature.

Miracles are a sign of God's presence, in the sense that they imply *reality* or "the universe" is in harmony with our *human* kind of existence.

When things occur that are outside mere physical powers and that help us achieve what is good or right, we are assured that despite nature's mindless silence and implacable caprice, we nonetheless belong in it—and that our being here can have purpose.

But *knowledge*, as the foundation of rationality or mind (as we have argued) carries much the same message—not by *willing* our purposes but by revealing what we *ought* to seek by revealing what *is good and right*. In support of our purposeful conflating of *God* and *knowledge*, we think it relevant that a miracle's revelation of God is thought by theists to be the revelation of a *mind*—of an effective intelligence.

We have already confessed the possibility of our own self-contradictoriness in blithely accepting that matter can "somehow" give rise to or set the conditions for the emergence of *mind*—something that operates in an essentially different way. We regard this position as facing the facts—as not denying them because we cannot conceive explaining them.

In that regard, we cannot let pass theism's contention that mind—unlike God—can be explained. For theists like Lewis, mind becomes a miracle because it is accounted for by God's will—just as all existence is to be accounted for by God's will.

Since we think mind must be seen as an ultimate form of being, and not the expression or effect of some other way of being, it is important to see why Lewis' argument fails.

Rationality and God's will

Lewis argues from the existence of human "Reason" as "supernature" to its status as a creation of the "Supernatural," that is, the mind of God.[145]

For Lewis, God's mind is needed to explain our mind because the physical world's cause-effect principles cannot explain rational thinking. As he says, "when you are asked to believe in Reason coming from non-Reason . . . you must cry 'Halt!'"[146] For him, that which is physical cannot produce that which is not. So God's mind creates our mind.

But, on the other hand, Lewis argues that a non-physical God created physical nature. This needs evidence or else is inconsistent.

If that which is not mind cannot be conceived to produce mind, then, as argument, that which is mind (or, certainly, non-physical) cannot be conceived to produce what is not mind.

Lewis' refusal to allow that mind may be an ultimate constituent of "reality" traces back, in our view, to the religious framework from which he happens to be arguing. In that framework, there is, as Augustine said, really only one miracle, and that is the miracle of Creation, the direct and immediate realization of God's will (particular miracles being instances of that process).

But, as we have argued, above, the idea that pure "will" can be the source of "reason" mind, or anything else, is not a coherent notion. Without being grounded in reasons, "will" (will, alone) is simply a force; it cannot be distinguished from impulse or even the arbitrary status of a chance occurrence.

And if it literally makes no sense to speak of an agent's having a "will" apart from the agent's rationality, then to explain the *existence* of rationality by citing God's "will" is to *explain* rationality by assuming a *prior* rationality. This is like saying: "How can light exist? Because another light exists."

So Lewis' explanation of the human mind as miracle—the mind that he calls "supernature"—not only violates his own rule that unlike principles cannot produce one another, it also assumes what it purports to explain.

An additional problem for a Lewis' theistic explanation of rationality is that it can't explain rational thinking as the *mirroring* of God's "rational thinking." The reason is that God cannot think in any sense of "thinking" that fits what we mean by "rational thinking." Rational thought must adhere to standards of right inference and be guided, in the main, by knowledge of reality. But God (as noted in Chapter Two) created "existence" out of nothing-at-all (*creation ex nihilo*) so there could be no independent standards that God had to meet to think "rationally." God's doings are *pure will*. Whatever God wills is (by definition) "right" (so to speak). And since God also knows all that that can possibly be known, God cannot *inquire* or *reason* or *conclude* or *critically reflect* since these activities presuppose the possibility of error or ignorance. So Lewis cannot successfully explain "rational thinking" on the principle that it reflects God's "rational" thinking.

And if the arguments about the meaning of "will" (above) are right, then, because *God's* will makes use of no *independent* reason or evidence, God's "pure will" is not "will" at all. (The counter-argument says talk of God's will is just *analogous* to "will" as we mean it. But this is like saying wealth and poverty are analogous because both are economic conditions.)

The absolute *independence* of God's putative "will" from rational standards—the "standards," so-called, being nothing more than whatever God wills—was something both Calvin and Luther recognized. As Luther phrased it:

God is he for Whose will no cause or ground may be laid down
as its rule or standard; for nothing is on a level with it or above
it, but *it is itself the rule for all things.* . . . What God wills is not
right because he ought or was bound so to will; on the contrary,
what takes place must be right because he so wills it [emphases
added].[147]

(Again, Chapter 2 examines the conflict between this kind of Creation theory and the idea of being a "person.")

Here we see, once more, the underlying sameness of theism and
its presumed antithesis, scientism. Both insist that mind, or human
rationality, must be explicable (can't be an ultimate phenomenon)
and proceed to explain human judgments as the effects of something
other than those judgments.

In theism, rational standards are the effect of a reason-free "pure
will"; in scientism, they are the effect of reason-free *physiological
causes.* For each, what we perceive to be right or good or beautiful or
true has been predetermined by a power that lies outside our own
judgment.

At bottom, the idea that the standards of rational thinking can be
explained is necessarily self-defeating. It commits one to explaining
one's own thought by reference to something that is not one's
thought. It makes reason the handmaiden of non-reason.

Through the same doubting of human experience, even *physical*
reality is doubted and explained away. Thus, what we think we know
as physical reality is really just the manifestation of a will that
"makes" the "physical" appear to us as it does. If God wills something else, "all that is solid melts away"—the world's objects being no
more solid, no more what they are in themselves, than the objects in a
video game. Clarifications that explain the existence and the ways of
mind or matter reduce them to something other than, in experience,
we know them to be.

Neither theism nor scientism can face the possibility that physical laws and normative insight—matter and mind—are ultimate substances. Neither can allow that nothing else explains their existence
and that we stand, vulnerable and responsible, in the presence of a sacred finality.

Reasons, we have argued, sustain our human life. Thus—it
seems—the question arises: Must not reasons stand behind everything that exists? Humankind—far from being fundamentally irrational—shows itself in religion, myth, and science to be relentless in
pursuit of reasons—but able, also, when the ultimate looms, to tell it-

self a story or keep seeking, in order not to know it *already* sees "the face of God."

Just why the inscrutable action of a *will* seems religiously essential is an issue we reserve for Chapter 4. Yet creation by will is something miracles are thought to prove. For Lewis, miracles are "what this universal story is about."[148] To theologian Richard Purtill, they are a kind of essential evidence: "Can miracles be explained as due to powers less than God? If the answer . . . is no, then we are forced to grant that miracles give a strong argument for the existence of God."[149]

The striking fact about all this *reasoning* and purported reliance on evidence is that, in the end, that which is said to explain—namely, God's self-existent nature and power to create by will alone—is admitted to be beyond human conception. But instead of giving pause, the self-confessed inability to form any conception of how will creates the stuff of mind and nature is taken to confirm, rather than diminish, the credibility of the theory. The very failure to explain is itself explained by reiterating the theory's own claim that an unfathomable creative force exists. Anselm's faith in logic seems long gone.

Knowing and the criteria for "miracles"

We thus conclude, regarding miracles, that:

When a miracle occurs, something happens in the physical world that cannot be directly explained by the physical world (by cause-effect).

When there is a miracle, the hegemony of physical necessitation is ended by the intrusion of rational governance.

When there is a miracle, a realm is revealed that is outside "Nature" as the realm of cause-effect.

Finally, miracles show that *the physical may made to conform to the good* (did not the Israelites need to cross the Red Sea, and the sick need to be healed?).

In sum, miracles instantiate creation. A miracle brings the reality of the right and the good into a physical "reality" that, left to its own cause-and-effect devices, cannot produce it.

In theistic tradition, "Creation" guarantees our existence as a unique, or not-entirely physical type of being (e.g., "we were given souls"). Miracles function as signs, confirming—as the adult confirms for youth—that we really are what we think we are. We are sentient, normatively governed beings, able to see "the good, the true, and the beautiful" that only a transcendence of the physical makes possible.

We have already criticized the attempt to explain miracles by positing yet another miracle (that God "self-exists").

Our aim is only to explain what make miracles a metaphysical wonder. It is to say that a miracle is a stunning mix of worlds that confirms what we are—and that the seminal miracle is the miracle of creation—the emergence of something unlike the physical universe.

If knowledge exists, it may be seen to create us human. If knowledge of the world is what, as this chapter, *in toto*, describes it to be, then we can say it is an actuality that allows us to transcend our own physicality—to escape total explanation by cause-effect.

It is in knowing that *reasons acquire both point and bodily existence,* and is is through knowing that bodily life can be *altered by reasons.* (No doubt knowing emerges by degrees through evolution, but neither chimpanzees, dolphins, nor parrots debate war, criticize poetry, argue about euthanasia, create ballets and quartets, research the causes of disease, or debate forms of government.)

Only through knowing can what is good and true and beautiful be found in an otherwise physical universe and by our devotion and our needs, alter a *physical world.* The fact of knowing is an intercession in the physical world—or, if one prefers, an "emergent" fact—no less transforming, no less inexplicable than the "miracles" of theism. For without the transformation effected by *knowing,* we are mechanisms, animals, organisms only. Without knowledge, even the theistic idea of a miracle's "benefit" *cannot be confirmed.*

In thus characterizing an inexplicably transformative "knowledge," we approach but do not reach (or would be mistaken if we did) the self-contradictory belief in the miraculous that Kierkegaard required for a *genuinely* religious commitment.[150]

Kierkegaard's faith in what he himself called a self-contradictory or "insane" miracle (the idea that Jesus was a God-man), put rational thought in the service of effortful faith or sheer will. "There is neither in heaven, nor on earth . . . nor in the aberrations of the most fantastic thinking, the possibility of a (humanly speaking), more insane combination.[151]

Rationality had to be sacrificed; one had to have faith. It was a matter of will.

This insupportable notion we understand as Kierkegaard's insistence on the *absoluteness* of religious passion. It is the absoluteness that marks it religious or "above all other passions"—the proof being that it is above one's own reason!

We suggest (in response to that Kierkegaardian quest for which we feel a wrenching affinity), that it calls upon a passion that is absolute to live in the light of what is true. It requires such a passion to face *what is so* against the weight of failure, disappointment, injustice, and death. Indeed, we think the shortest definition of *uniquely religious passion* is the commitment unflinchingly to live by the truth.[152]

Kierkegaard erred, in our view, religiously, insofar as he counseled obedience not to truth, *per se*, but to a *particular* truth, namely to the Christian claim that Jesus was a God and a man *at the same time.*

It is not, we suggest, the (Christian) *content* of the commitment that is crucial for knowing one's commitment is *religious* but the *form.* (Kierkegaard does not even argue the content; he is not satisfied with historical evidence or theological proofs. The emphasis on these is, for him, the cant of popular Christianity.)

It is simply the *form* of that belief—its "insanity," its admitted self-contradictoriness—that makes for unqualified, nonpareil, absolute, and total religious faith. By believing in what is logically impossible, one denies one's own mind, and achieves—in a single, terrible, blow—proof that one's religious commitment is absolutely selfless. One gives up the mental powers that normally sustain one.

In this "madness" we see a certain depth. We view it as restating, with Kierkegaardian ferocity, a thing required by any true religion, which is obedience to the demands of ultimate reality.

Since an ultimate reality with ultimate demands cannot—because "ultimate"—be *explained*, it appears to Kierkegaard that to accept something as ultimate is to leap beyond one's mind (the "leap of faith"). It is to relinquish mind as hubris, to live without an explanation, to *feel* the inexplicability of "God"—to grasp, to *live*, that God simply *is*.

But if *human* status can be achieved only with obedience to what is *true*—and not to the awful "forces" or "needs" to which circumstance subjects us—then selflessness begins and ends in *knowledge*— that "impossible but true" union with the real on which the human mind depends. Kierkegaard's willed attack on his own reason as true religious passion seems, ironically, not selflessness but a covert self-concern that echoes the self-assaulting, self-disdaining attitude of the flagellant.[153]

For us, selflessness is giving oneself over to the truth. It is to accept not contradiction but that which inexplicably exists. And if we realize that knowing *exists*, but can be neither proven nor explained, knowing will *look* to the observing eye much like what Kierkegaard found in the God-man: a stunning, inexplicable truth to which we owe our perilously transcendent status and which burdens us with responsibility for the right and the good.

KNOWLEDGE

If it is true that knowledge creates us human, arguments against the possibility of knowledge are arguments against our nature: Pyrrho's skepticism, which said we could know "neither truths nor falsehoods," had the outcome, for those who adopted it, of "speechlessness."[154] The Humean empiricism of "the garden path" imprisoned us within our own awareness; perspectivism "proved" that language and ideas are what keep us from the truth; evaluative skepticism told us that moral truths are fictions.

Viewed through the skeptical lens, the only difference between human life and animal life is that animals have no illusions.

Knowledge cannot be philosophically undone

The question of whether one does or does not know a thing is a *factual question*. Knowing a thing is (like seeing a color) a fact of first-person experience. Like the terms *seeing* and *perceiving*, the terms *knowing* or *knowledge* have no sense without a reference to something independent of the content of our consciousness.

If knowing and seeing could be understood without reference to anything independent of consciousness, they would have to be phenomena generated by the brain alone—like sensations or the familiar "spots before your eyes." And if knowledge referred to nothing more than a fact or condition within consciousness, it would never have been doubted by philosophers.

So the question, "Is knowledge possible?" is not to be answered by formal logic; logic asks only whether one statement follows from another; its subject is *consistency*, not truth. Philosophers do not reject "knowing" or "knowledge" because these concepts are logically self-contradictory.

And if the existence of knowledge is not a question within logic, it can no more be *settled* by philosophical arguments than can the existence of visual perception.

Knowledge has no foundation

Philosophy's quest for the foundations of knowledge failed because knowledge itself is foundational, not because there is no knowledge (comes then the inevitable echo: "But *how* can that be?"—"No, it cannot be!").

The reality of knowledge cannot be established by logic, but neither can it be established by evidence. Whatever evidence we offer would have to be something we can *know*, so to offer it is to *assume*, not provide, the answer to the question "Is there knowledge?"

Knowledge is therefore the prerequisite for any worldly inquiry; it is foundational.

But demands for explanation will not end: "How is knowledge acquired in the first place?"

We have seen that it cannot be constructed out of things we do not know—that is, out of *less than* what we know, such as belief. (A belief, by definition, is a conviction that might prove false.) We can't establish a proposition that cannot possibly be wrong on a foundation of propositions that we say might be wrong. But still we hear: "Surely, knowledge cannot simply *appear*!" (Again, knowledge seems "impossible.")[155]

To this continuing objection we say that, nonetheless, nothing can be conjectured, investigated, or believed by a mind that is absolutely ignorant. Lacking a single scrap of knowledge, we can develop no further knowledge (and no probabilities).

The archetypal denial of knowledge is found, of course, in the decision of René Descartes' to doubt all knowledge. His failure to establish knowledge from a hypothetical state of total ignorance is well known, and his eventual recourse to God as the guarantor of knowledge speaks eloquently of the impasse his universal doubting entailed.

As for the objection that it is "giving up" or is "mere mystification" to say knowledge is *foundational* (ultimate) and cannot possibly be explained, we counter that neither the existence of anything-at-all can possibly be explained, nor can consciousness (*pace* Daniel Dennett). And if consciousness and the existence of things are not to be *denied* for want of explanation, perhaps knowledge need not be denied for that reason either. This kind of acceptance seems wise, particularly since we could not possibly discuss existence or consciousness unless these things were *known*.

The futile search for a foundation

Many have thought our "realist" attitude toward knowledge merely opens the door to such dubious, unverifiable knowledge-claims, as having talked with the dead or gotten orders from God. And, yes, countless honest claims to worldly knowledge have been false—not to mention dangerous or deadly. But, in the end, it must be asked: How can *falsehoods* be determined by persons with no knowledge?

Nonetheless, many thinkers have insisted that knowledge-claims require a foundation. If knowledge is some sort of witting or conscious realization that a given claim is true—*that it cannot possibly be wrong*—then there must exist some factual criterion to guarantee its presence.

On this assumption (as noted above) Descartes launched his foray into doubt. The strategy was simple: try doubting *all* claims to knowledge and then readmit (as "knowledge") only those claims that rest on a foundation that excludes any rational doubt.

Descartes' exercise in the universal doubting led him to discover what he thought was a foundational criterion. He reasoned that "I am doubting! Doubting entails a doubter; therefore, I must, necessarily, *exist*!" By this circular route he thought he had proven at least one worldly fact, namely, his own existence. ("I think, therefore I am"). What this "proof" also revealed, he said, is that the criterion of knowledge is the "clearness and distinctness" of an argument or "proposition." (Of course, his effort was doomed from the start since—as argued above—the presence of knowledge is a *factual* matter, and facts cannot be established by *arguments* alone.)

Others have sought a lesser factual criterion, one that is *necessary* for knowledge, though not *sufficient*. The prime example is the empiricist criterion for knowledge: One cannot claim knowledge unless what one claims (or what *follows* from what one claims) can be detected by one or more of the five senses. For example, the proposition that the universe is expanding might be true—might be knowledge—because it entails facts (like changes in the lines on a spectrometer) that the senses can discern.

(It was on the basis of a *necessary* criterion—the empiricists' *sense-perceptibility* criterion—that Hare and Edwards said *evaluative* claims could not be knowledge.)

There have been other factual criteria for knowledge: William James spoke of *satisfaction*, the British "idealists" spoke of *coherence* among one's propositions, and others have offered psychological criteria, like *consensus* or a *consensus of rational persons*.

But all attempts at finding *factual* foundations for knowledge (whether sufficient or necessary) must fail. For they require the linking of two different things—the *factual criterion* and the *fact of knowledge*. And, to be different facts (things not linked logically or by definition), they must be defined independently of one another. But if knowledge can be identified *independently* of its supposed necessary or sufficient criterion, then a criterion for knowledge is unnecessary. Thus, any search for a foundational fact—a criterion for knowledge—*presupposes* that knowledge can be recognized without one.

For this reason, it is conceptually impossible to establish knowledge on the basis of anything that is not knowledge. Hence, if we do have knowledge—if we are capable of knowing—then *knowledge*, and nothing else, is foundational ("basic," "rationally ultimate").

Although we contend that knowing is basic and emerges as an ultimate (inexplicable) fact like consciousness or the physical universe, we do not mean to suggest that it arises in contextless snapshots, or by dedicated staring. Rather, it emerges within a context of physical activity, social interaction, and linguistic development as numberless insights or moments of recognition (terms of exposition, not explanation, since both "insight" and "recognition" presuppose "knowledge").

The coherence theorists have at least the right metaphor. The certainty of knowledge comes into being *in a context of connectedness*—a situation more like a web than a building (which rests on a "foundation"). John Dewey's description of inquiry's "situation" in which not everything can, at the same time, be in doubt is, in our view, essentially right. We agree that "we never experience nor form judgments about objects and events in isolation. But only in connection with a contextual whole.")[156]

Indeed, as Hegel, Dewey, and lately, F. L. Will have pointed out, we gain knowledge on the basis of socially and linguistically embedded practices and judgments. What currently we know is the fruit of centuries of interpersonal, practical, and theoretical activity. Galileo and Newton could not have come to know what they did, had they been living in a hunter-gatherer tribe. As Will puts it,

> Galileo did not simply stare . . . [through his telescope] . . . at those oddly moving lights . . . like a child marveling at the shifting lights in a kaleidoscope. He tried to understand these lights from the point of view of the astronomy and physics available at his time, following a complex set of technical practices of thought and action available in or appropriate to these branches of learning: practices of observation, calculation . . . and practices embodied in a complex technical language.[157]

Knowledge is foundational for mind

Knowledge is the foundation of what we call rational thought (what Lewis calls "Reason").[158] If one can't say anything is true, one can't say anything at all. (Re: the speechlessness of certain Greek skeptics.)

As we argued when claiming that the value of reasons for behavior depends upon knowledge, what people mean by "rational" thought about the world can never be considered "rational" if theorists restrict "reason" and "reasoning" to the forming of logical consistent arguments. The rationality of logical and mathematical arguments cannot be determined entirely apart from any knowledge. For, to recognize the consistency of arguments, one must know what a given argument *says*. One cannot conclude—even from "If P then Q," that "not Q, therefore not P" is valid just by *believing* one knows the meaning of these expressions. One must *know* what has been stated.[159]

Knowledge is so intimately woven into all we do that the depth of its foundational role eludes appreciation—as for example, that without it, there would be no sense in explaining our behavior by reasons.

The point implicit there (to be further probed here) is that the very notion of our *inner* "mind" depends for its meaning on an *outer* world. The passage of thoughts within us cannot be identified as rational unless they are can be used to state true things about the world or making valid inferences. And this is to say that the distinguishing condition of mind is its dependence on types of knowledge.

Too often the mind is conceived as a container, but its interior parade of images, sensations, and thoughts is *mind*, not because of this *inner* activity, but because of the inner activity that *incorporates* the world so as to permit reflection on what it incorporates. Without knowledge there is no "mind."

If our thoughts could not successfully refer to what is the case in the world, we would not explain having this or that idea because of "the ways things are"—that is, because certain things are true.

If the explanation of our ideas returned us to a locus within our heads, then our "thinking" could not be distinguished from our *dreaming*—indeed, not even "dreaming," for the only dream "facts" we can describe involve people, talk, situations, artifacts, and so on—things that are in dreams only *because* we have knowledge.

As we have insisted, if what is "in our heads" is not explained by what we *know*, the only way to explain their effect is by *causes*—psychological or physiological. But then "mind" is discounted. As C. S. Lewis observed, people consider judgments "worthless" when they can be explained by causes rather than reasons.

Frederick Will's essay, "Thoughts and Things" also argues—though in far greater detail and substance than we can venture into here—that the operations we call "thinking" are not possible without knowledge of a world outside consciousness.[160]

In considering our brief sketch of his argument, it may be helpful to recall to mind the vague images and half-thoughts we often experience upon waking. These are "thoughts" that "lead nowhere." They have no implications and cannot be assessed. For them we can find no words and never could. If these tongue-tied moments were standard, we would not have what we call "minds." (Thinking depends on things that behave dependably.)

Will argues that mind and world cannot be conceptualized separately. He declares the "Cartesian" (and Humean) approach to thinking mistaken in supposing that thinking can be carried on using only on the mind's own material—that is, simply by *imagining* this or that. In Will's words, "Thinking is an activity we engage in not only in the world of things, but by means of the things of this world, supported and sustained by them."[161]

Although our own argument is similar, we do not pretend to match the depth and subtlety of Will's approach; we can, however, give a sense of it. Will rejects the idea of ideas as visual *representations* of the world. The mistake concerning mind's relation to the world stems from the idea that the medium of our reasoning—our thoughts about things—gets into our heads the way an image of the world gets onto a piece of film. It is as if our ideas about the world came (as Hume said) through impressions—as if "the development of . . . representations [of the world] is . . . the production in the medium of thought of facsimiles, gossamer replicas of the things represented."[162]

To paraphrase: We are on the wrong track if we imagine our thought of, say, "a stone" to be a mental image of it. It is wrong to start with a picture of the stone safely in mind, and then, like Descartes (to use Will's example) begin to think about its truth or falsity.

When we wonder whether it is granite or basalt, or whether it is one million or one billion years old or four billion, the mistake lies in thinking that it is only these *latter* questions have to do with worldly truth.

For the mere image of a thing, far from being "worth a thousand words," says nothing. It does not present the *idea* of anything. One has only to recall seeing photographs taken with an electron microscope (perhaps of an atom's shadow, or the lines of a crystal's structure) to understand that if one knows nothing at all about microscopes or atoms or crystals one can make neither heads nor tails of what one *sees*.

So the first thing known must be the stone itself. It must be known that there is a "something" that has a definite character so that we can ask further questions about it. If it didn't "hold still"—if stones weren't a certain way and not some other way, if they reacted to actions utterly unpredictably—we couldn't frame any questions about them. We would have no *thing* ("*no*thing") in mind to think about or with. There would be no "subjects" of inquiry. As Will puts it,

> If we suppose the beginning items of knowledge to rest upon some foundation independent of thought [like a sensation], how is it possible for thought to expand knowledge beyond these admittedly restricted first steps? [interpolation added][163]

What we miss if we conceive of our ideas are copies or representations of things "out there" is what we *know about* those things we see.[164] (Will doesn't speak of *knowing* the world; he speaks of being "informed" by the world or receiving "information"—which, if it is not the reception of knowledge, is surely not the reception of "information.")

Putting the crux of the matter perhaps over-simply, to be able to think, the things about which we would think must behave in a manner that allows us to draw inferences about and from them. Among Will's examples of a world that would prevent thinking is the case of the bizarre goldfinch described in the work of J. L. Austin. Austin asks us to contemplate a goldfinch that "'explodes, or quotes Mrs.Woolf, or what not.'" In such a case, Austin says (and Will agrees) we do not know what to say. "Words fail us." Are we thinking about a bird, or a bomb, or feathered person?

To carry the example forward, if the world were, from the very onset of one's consciousness, like a kaleidoscope or a dream, there would be no way to think. Even the most "unrealistic" cartoons depend on the way things are in fact. The character who walks off a cliff into the air and who falls upon realizing he is walking on air can amuse only those who know the simplest truths.

If the cartoon character morphed into a light beam and the cliff into a patch of green color, and so on, there would not be enough "known" to allow our "strictly inner" imagination to operate.

In essence, if things happened utterly unpredictably—either all the time or without warning—there would be no such concept as that of "a thing." We would be in the infant's world of William James, which he described as a "buzzing, blooming confusion."

What we labor to make plain is that there is no way to speak about an outside world once *mind* or *thinking* is defined in terms restricted to what may located inside one's head—that is, *psychologically*. This was illustrated earlier by the embarrassments of Locke and Hume, who admitted that if all we know are the sensations or "impressions" that appear in our awareness, we cannot know whether they have a source outside them. We cannot rationally claim to know there is an external world.

But, of course, idea of an "external world" is not a "construction"—not a piece of ungrounded guesswork. There is no way human beings, *aware only of sensations*, can say "let's construct something we will call a 'world' that will not be visible to us, but will be treated as the cause of our sensations"—as if words like "construct" and "world" and "cause" could come to a mind that has encountered only patches of color, lines, shapes, and areas of brightness and darkness.

That is why Will could conclude his essay on thoughts and their relation to things by saying one cannot frame a *problem* of knowledge without an acquaintance with knowledge.

> The Problem of Induction [the philosophical question as to how we can know the way things work in the world] is this: that upon the view of things embodied in this celebrated Problem, anyone who *has* this problem must already have solved it [interpolation added].[165]

And we would add that one cannot frame the problem of knowledge without reference to mind, and that anyone who understands the term *mind* must already have solved the "problem" of knowledge. (Impressions and sensations are not *thoughts* and there is awareness but not mind without thoughts. But there are not *thoughts* without *things*.)

Knowledge as linguistically foundational

The last point deserves its own treatment. If we have never known an external world, we can have nothing in our language that *affirms* we can know it—but on that account (*contra* skepticism) there could be nothing in our language that *denies* we can know it.

Even an agnostic of the world could not meaningfully use the word *world* without some knowledge of it.

Terms like "knowledge" and "world" or "out there" or "reality" are essential to talk about experience, indeed, to *have* experience (as we and Will have been arguing).

In a similar vein, if we never knew *color*, words like "red" or "tints" could never arise. And if we never knew truth, the denial of truth could never arise. Skepticism is, linguistically, self-refutational.

Certain terms are indispensable because their denial is the denial of rational discourse. They are part of the idea of a "rational" thinking. A term like *God*, however, is not such a term. One can deny God rationally. The term *God*, unlike *knowledge* or *truth* or *world*, is not a prerequisite for rational discourse.

Miracles and contradictions

Even if all forms of skepticism fail because they make use of the knowledge they deny, still, they cast light on the strangeness of human existence. They give us reason to doubt that mental union with the world is possible. In so doing, they make us aware of what *knowing* unaccountably overcomes.

In the end, however, they reveal themselves to be inconsistent. And (as we insist) they must, since no purely conceptual argument can establish the impossibility of knowledge.

Empiricist skepticism redux

Consider the impossibility of knowledge on empiricism's "garden path." There, the observer could not possibly perceive a tree—or, for that matter, any dimensional object. It was troubling because the philosopher's description of how perception *physically* proceeds was true. Physically speaking, the brain *does* receive only electrical impulses, so that if the mind is the brain, the mind is always in the dark. Given this obstacle, how can we possibly *see*?

However, in order make his case, the (Humean) philosopher made use of the *object language* of science—the language of light waves, nerves, meter readings, precipitates, and the like—which are essential to science but which his skepticism had put beyond the reach of perception and knowledge.

So knowledge is "impossible"—but possible. The skeptical argument "shows" why knowledge of an external world is "impossible" even as its arguments assume it is possible.

Perspectival skepticism redux

Perspectivism argued that the statements we make about the world can never be justified by argument and can never be checked against reality. Any justifying argument for a perspective must rely on yet another perspective. Justification never ends. As for our so-called "knowledge" of the world, it depends on the perspectives we happen to have—on *particular* methods, rules, and beliefs that we can never "step outside" to ascertain whether the conclusions they deliver are really true.

Thus, the force of the perspectivist argument lies in pointing out that we have no independent check on our own minds. We can't look at reality *as it is in itself* apart from our ideas about it.[166] Therefore, any attempt to *verify* what our minds tell us about the world will rest on what our minds tell us about the world. Our arguments will be circular. Our ideas can never "mirror" nature, as Rorty says. Knowledge cannot be claimed.

But perspectivists somehow, know a great deal. What is this "world" of which they speak and whose properties we can never know? How do they know what it is for an object to have a "property?" How do perspectivists know there are other people and that there is more than one perspective? How can they know that "out there" are minds beside their own?

However, beyond all else, perspectivists must—self-contradictorily—know one worldly truth. They must know as a matter of fact that there is no perspective some of whose conclusions have turned out to be true. That is, they must know the *fact* that no one knows the truth about any aspect of the world.

For, *it doesn't matter* that we use premises and methods we cannot justify by an argument. It *doesn't matter* that we cannot perceive the world without using our own ideas. These things are not proof that we do not know the truth.

For example, it is absurd to say that I cannot possibly know that I have dropped a heavy object on my bare toe because I use a particular standards of perception and have a particular set of beliefs. This is because *knowing something* is, as we insist, a matter of fact, not conceptual proof. No purely *logical* argument—no argument from ideas alone—can prove anything, positively or negatively, about the existence of a *fact*.

And since it is fact whether we know, or do not know, a thing, no philosophic argument can prove knowing is impossible.

Moreover, if the use of perspectives is unavoidable, and if the use of any one perspective (of many possible ones) entails the absence of any *objective* standpoint, then perspectivism itself is in no position to claim an objective argument.

Once again, knowledge is deemed "impossible" (since we cannot check the human mind for its ability to possess it)—yet possible!—according to perspectivism's own claims to truth.

Evaluative skepticism

We have seen that when modern empiricism *does* accept the possibility of worldly knowledge, it takes the physical sciences as its only possible source. The result is the denial of normative or "evaluative" knowledge-claims—claims regarding what is good, right, beautiful, appropriate, relevant, and the like (normative characteristics such as being "good" or "right" or "relevant" are not visible to scientific or "sense" perception).

Because it draws on the authority of science, the popularity of evaluative skepticism seems only to grow—at least in the "industrial" nations. Thus, in *The Atlantic*, a mainstream magazine, sociobiologist Edward O. Wilson enlightened readers regarding the bogus nature of moral knowledge: "'From the perspective of the natural sciences, they [moral principles] are no more than . . . the behavioral codes that that members of society fervently wish others to follow and are themselves willing to accept for the common good.'"[167] Moral judgments are psychological dispositions determined largely by genetic causes; dispositions and genes are things science can study.

So, moral and other evaluations have no possibility of being *true* statements. Evaluations are nothing more than expressions of what we like or approve according to standards which themselves rest on mere approval or preference. Hence, knowledge of good and bad, right and wrong, beautiful or ugly, relevant or irrelevant, appropriate or inappropriate is deemed *impossible.*

However, the "impossibility" of evaluative knowledge is offered by evaluation-skeptics as the *right* philosophic position—having been determined by the *right* kind of thinking and, on that account, able to declare *false* and or *badly* reasoned, those (mistaken) ideas about goodness and badness that govern courtrooms, political discourse, and informal education in which families discuss *morality* with children.

And, if evaluative skeptics counter that "all they are doing is expressing their preferences or commendations," they contradict the implicit claim that they are offering a *theory*—something that claims a *higher* (more important) status than a personal preference or recommendation.

"Philosophies" and "theories" are constructed to be right rather than wrong, to be more rather than less *rational*—*better* to believe than not to believe—or else what are they? A thinker's preferences and commendations, if not objectively better than those of another, is nothing more than material for the thinker's biography.

Hence evaluative knowledge is deemed "impossible" because not scientifically testable—yet possible, if the theories *against* evaluative knowledge are, indeed, *justifiable, right,* or *more rational* than their contraries.

(No small thing, also, that evaluative skeptics condemn the great mass of humankind to foolishness. For people say they do things because they are *right*; they honor and respect those whom they think do things because they are the *right* thing to do. Yet, if "right" *means*, essentially, "what I like or approve of," then humanity honors and respects those who do the things they like to do or approve of doing!)

Still, evaluative skepticism rests on a troubling truth: we can test for the existence of things we perceive by means of our senses, and, indirectly, for entities (like molecules and light waves) that explain what we *sense*; but we cannot test, directly or indirectly, for the existence of goodness, rightness, propriety, or beauty—their presence cannot be detected by the senses (even thought their reality is claimed within the course of first-person experience). How we learn what is good, bad, right, appropriate, or beautiful *from experience* remains a question that taunts our conceptions of reality..

The third-person fallacy

When, in the first edition of the *Spectator* (1711), the essayist Joseph Addison declared, "I live in the world rather as a Spectator of mankind than as one of the species," he inadvertently echoed the fundamental attitude of philosophic doubt (whose internal contradictions we have just discussed, above).

Addison's professed third-person stance toward first-person living was a literary conceit. But for philosophic doubt it was a policy— a policy of alienation. In what sense alienation is perhaps best suggested narratively:

A reporter from another galaxy is assigned to describe human activity. As an alien, the reporter can describe that activity only from a third-person vantage point. The reporter encounters a golf match. "His" account reads as follows (translation by the author):

"I am prepared to give you a description of an activity that Earthlings call 'golf' or 'golfing.' I assure you I have been scrupulously *objective*, that is—entirely uninvolved—in the activity I am about to describe.

"In golfing, individuals or groups walk or drive about, on low, green plant material, carrying or carting containers of sticks with a variety of right-angled ends on them. They then place a white sphere (or 'ball,' they call it), either on the green plant material or on a very short wooden support and each, in turn, strikes a sphere with one of the long sticks until it falls into a hole. Each time the sphere falls into a hole it is taken out of the hole. They then hit it again until it falls into another hole from which, again, they retrieve it. They do this anywhere from nine to eighteen times. They make records of these events and talk and drink and leave. Earthlings often spend a twelfth or more of their daylight period doing this. They seem to think it is an activity of value, but, to an objective observer, none is evident."

Like the alien reporter, the philosophic doubter makes third-person surveillance foundational. And, like the alien reporter, the doubter supposes, fallaciously, that only from outside *existential* situations—situations of first-person *activity* (from sport to science, to morality, to sexuality, to art) can a *disinterested*, hence *dispositive*, judgment be rendered on claims of truth, validity, or value. Only the disengaged can be objective.

A philosophical critique of knowing never has a basis *within* the experiential situation of a given type of inquiry. The doubting of particular kinds of knowledge does not begin when philosophers act as scientists, moralists, or art critics, but only when they assume a stance of external criticism—only when they follow the traditional claim that "philosophy is queen of the sciences."

To be sure we often take a third-person stance toward *particular* (first-person) judgments. We may doubt what we said or did or thought when *involved* ("Was I wise to take that job?") But unlike the alien visitor or skeptical philosophers, we never (*per impossible*) stand back from our first-person self *absolutely*. We will ask "Was that statement true?" but not, literally speaking, "Is anything I think true, *true*?" We do not, if sane, think we are God looking down on merely human claims of "truth."

But as *philosophic* doubters we are obliged to discount our own experience—to suppress entire aspects of ourselves as if, indeed, we were alien visitors. (Here, we remember with despair the emotivist view that when a person says the Holocaust was evil, that person is expressing an a-rational, *emotional*, reaction that in no sense expresses a *rational judgment*. Only those standing outside first-person experiences (outside what Dewey would call a *moral situation*) could find no problem in declaring that experience of evil "illusory.")

In practice, we take the spectator's dispassionate stance *selectively*. We take it toward *particular* elements in our initial judgment or experience—elements we suspect might benefit from reconsideration (as in "reasonable doubt"). And the practice of (third-person) reflection on our first-person judgments makes sense only if there *can* be objectivity and truth, for otherwise we would have no reason to do it. Hence a third-person reflection on first-person judgment so sweeping that it leads to a counsel against objectivity and truth is, once again, a self-defeating effort.

So, the notion comes to pass illegitimately that "objectivity" precludes "emotional" *involvement*, and that only if we approach first-person judgments with no prior ideas in mind—no "perspective," no "assumptions" about the subject matter of that judgment—can we judge first-person claims *dispassionately, neutrally, objectively* (which is exactly what Descartes did when he set aside all first-person judgments of truth).

By this third-person standard, every truth-claim must be judged from *outside* the experience that gives the notion of *truth* its substance. The doctrine of "reasonable" doubt becomes a permanent license to doubt (as in: "how do you know you're brushing your teeth," or "seeing a tree?")

But something is, strangely, overlooked. A spectator's third-person stance on someone else is, of course, a first-person stance for the spectator and must express the spectator's own criteria for good judgment (or else be an arbitrary opinion). The idea that there can be an experientially immaculate way to judge first-person inquiry is a fallacy of self-exemption.

It is only the latest form of the third-person fallacy for postmodern thought to say, "yes, that's the whole point. There is no third-person, neutral vantage point from which to determine what is true. That's why we deny both objectivity and truth." Fleshed out a bit, the argument says that "any judgment must employ particular ideas, assumptions and ways of reasoning and not *other* ideas, assumptions and ways of reasoning, so a person's reasoning is never free to be neutral or 'objective' on any topic and therefore no one can legitimately claim to know what is true, valid, or worthy."

But this argument is made by a person. And this person apparently thinks himself or herself able to take a third-person, *objective* standpoint on the implications of having to use one idea, assumption, or passage of reasoning *rather than another* (that is, on the way any mind has to work!)—such that he or she can determine something *true*.

It is an ancient fallacy to suppose one can *stand back from the grunt work of worldly inquiry and from Olympus declare the truth that humans can claim no truth.*

Hume's approach to human perception, for example, assumed that the "experimental" (scientific) method stood outside the self-deceptions of first-person experience, providing an *objective* approach to what people called the acquisition of "knowledge."

Similarly, if first-person perceivers thought they saw trees, the third-person, scientist-philosopher explained what they *really* saw (again, from a vantage point *outside* first-person experience). (How Hume knew about other people's awareness, or that their minds "copied" sensations, was not subjected to scrutiny—nor was scientist-philosopher's ability to *see* his companion and *see* that trees were dimensional.)

The irony of philosophic doubting is that in attempting to escape dogmatism and minimize fallibility, both secular and theistic thinkers deny finality to the only stance toward subject matter (the standpoint of first-person experience) by which knowledge can possibly be found.

Both try, impossibly, to escape the famous "finiteness" or "self-deceptiveness" of human judgment by accessing a source outside and "above" it. above" it. Secularists think they do it by following an objective science; theists think they do it by reading or receiving messages from God. And the "war" goes on—skeptics and theists driven by the same hyperbolic doubt, the same denigration of experience.

So, rhetorically w ask, Is there nothing religiously significant in viewing the human aspect of "creation"—the realm of thought-feeling, of minded experience—as a snare and a delusion?

Doubting "doubting"

Doubts that do not arise from "first-person" engagement with the subject matter are not doubts but *policy*. Such "doubting" of claims within a subject matter can never be ended by further inquiry into that subject matter. Third-person doubting of first person inquiry is therefore "intellectual" in the pejorative sense.

It has no root in the existential situation of inquiry. It is not *felt* within the inquiries it doubts. It is in that way akin to pretense—*and a pretend doubt can have only a pretend solution.*

When juries are admonished to determine guilt "beyond a reasonable doubt," the doubt is considered "reasonable" only if it arises from the subject matter of the trial. If a juror doubts the defendant's guilt because "no one can know the truth," the court will not consider the doubt "reasonable."

Descartes did not engage the world to determine which of his ideas might be true. He "resolved to pretend that everything that had ever entered my mind was as false as the figments of my dreams."[168] He therefore had no subject matter into which he could inquire.

It was only when he stopped thinking *about* the making of judgments and—in the first-person—made one, that he was able to know anything. This he did when he took a first-person stance toward himself. Then, of course, it was possible to know something! He knew very well he was doubting (he was thinking), and if thinking, then existing. (And as we have said, the whole world of his experience played into what he knew—for a notion like "doubt" assumes an acquaintance with "truth" as does "existence" and *as does the proper use of the pronoun "I" which presupposes knowledge of "a person"*—none of which things can be known by introspection involving no knowledge of a world.

Consider the denial that we can know physical laws (physical necessity). In the century preceding David Hume's *Treatise*, the Anglo-Irish chemist, Robert Boyle, determined that that the volume of a gas must vary inversely as the pressure ("Boyle's *law*"). Hume's *Treatise*, in effect, denied the law.

What Hume did *not* do was go into the laboratory and run tests in which he varied the pressure of gases to see if they might be induced to do something else. Hume's "doubt" of the necessities asserted by science did not arise out of his own scientific experimentation or scientific thinking about the laboratory reports of others.

Since scientists *engage with the world* to develop and support what they claim, Hume had to suppose he had a better way than science to determine what may rightly be claimed about the way the world works.

Scientists find necessities when they work just as golfers find value when they play, but neither Hume nor the alien reporter found either necessity or value. From a third-person standpoint, they couldn't.

Aside: the theistic reader who is still aboard may think religious inquiry is similarly self-sufficient, and no doubt it is. But there can be bad religious inquiry just as there can be bad scientific inquiry—and much theology, as we have argued, suffers from internal inconsistency (and inconsistency with convictions that are not inherently religious such that what it is required to have one's "*own* ideas").

The philosopher on the garden path never doubted the claim "I see a tree" in the first person. Like Hume, he never looked. He never said, "how can you say that when you only glanced at it?" Instead he said, "you only see one side of a tree."

But since that is precisely what you *do* see when you see a tree, he wasn't (in saying that) doubting the statement "I see a tree." Not having looked *for himself*, the philosopher lacked the guidance of a genuine doubt about seeing a tree.

The problem at hand is an existential one—for *doubt* is as tied to the issue of *truth* as knowledge. To doubt is to feel something may not be *true*, to feel one may not *know* it. Because the scientistic philosopher *felt* no doubt regarding "I see a tree," he had no *reason* for questioning it. And to lack a reason is to lack any *guiding consideration—to have no*

standard of relevance—by which to determine what an appropriate question might be.

We might say that the philosopher was in the same *location* as the observer but not in the same *situation*.[169] The observer was in a situation of *perceiving something*; the philosopher was in a situation of commenting on *the situation of* perceiving something.

Similarly, the perspectivists who denied the possibility of known truths did not express doubts about—did not find trouble with—particular propositions. When Rorty said truth, as the property of a sentence, was man-made, and hence a kind of fiction, it was not because he doubted particular sentences like, "Rorty teaches at a University."

Nor did Shweder doubt the rational grounding of quantum mechanics because there is evidence against it. Rather, he said, with Kuhn, that no theory can be compared with an independent actuality. And since his "doubt" of quantum mechanics' truth did not arise from finding fault with its claims but from a third-person stance toward inquiry, there was no confrontation with the world that might constrain or guide his speculations on its credibility.

The same narrative fits evaluative skepticism. Neither Edwards nor Hare reported doubting that slavery was bad, or doubting that hostility is morally preferable on the whole to kindness. Neither one reported investigating moral situations. Neither one said "I doubt that it's good to foster slavery—and here are my reasons—for example, it is painful, there is no recourse for unfair treatment, the recompense is inadequate," and so on.

From a standpoint outside the discipline of actual moral involvement it was easy to say, "unless we can see the goodness or badness of slavery the way we can see fields and slaves, then neither the goodness or the badness of slavery exists." And this was said as if it would not be morally insane to say "I don't see the badness in slavery, but let me get my binoculars. Perhaps you're right and I can make it out."

Only someone as distanced from a moral situation as the alien reporter was distanced from a golfing situation could doubt the reality of goodness and badness because *moral claims can't be established the way we establish physical claims.*

Professor Will makes a parallel point about doubting *scientific* claims because they fail to meet *deductive* claim standards:

> When, in setting out to appraise the claims to acceptance of any pattern of scientific procedure, *one first excludes all these processes from consideration* and seeks a form of 'proof' altogether separate and independent of them, one has surely set for oneself . . . [a] . . . trap. [emphasis added][170]

The nature of reality cannot be settled by an approach that pretends (as if it were the mind of God) not to require an engagement with it.

This was Kierkegaard's point when he insisted on what he called "subjectivity"—*personal engagement with the world*—in contrast to what he considered Hegel's aloof (third-person), purely conceptual, philosophical system-building. Kierkegaard's "subjectivity" is what we prefer to speak of as a "first-person" stance toward the world, which is ("in the end") to believe in philosophy only what one can believe in the conduct of life's practice.

And precisely this issue bedeviled Hume. His philosophical policies led him to conclusions he could not, in the context of practical living, believe. In the *Treatise*, he expresses relief at the way "nature" works in social living to make his conclusions seem unreal: "It is happy . . . nature breaks the force of all skeptical arguments in time, and keeps them from having any considerable influence on the understanding."[171]

The fact that his philosophical methodology yielded conclusions that practical, responsible living caused him, genuinely, to doubt, never led him to reconsider his methods or assumptions.

Knowledge of "things in themselves"

Let us consider, at long last, the perspectivist theme that one can never know reality *in itself*.

For Rorty, the "idea of *'something which is what it is apart from language, apart from any description'*" is that the whole idea (of an independent reality) is but a "pseudo problem [emphasis added]."[172] "'A pragmatist must . . . insist'," Rorty says, "that there is no such thing as the way the thing is in itself, under no description, apart from any use to which human beings might want to put it.'"[173]

Here we see repeated the views of Kant and Shweder to the effect that that we can never see how things are in themselves, that is, as they *really* are apart from the way we *think* they are. We cannot get out of our own skin and, from a neutral standpoint, compare our idea about reality with reality as it is apart from our ideas about it.

It is instructive, we think, to ask what reality might be, "*in itself.*" What would be the way a thing is "under no description"—that is, *apart from any ideas about it*?

For example, if God looked at a tree and found it green-leaved and twenty feet tall—thereby putting it "under a description"— would God *not* know what the tree was "in itself" because God had an idea about it?

Lest the example seem circular, let us suggest why the claim that "things as they are in themselves cannot be known" (or "reality as it is in itself cannot be known") is *necessarily* wrong.

The heart of this doctrine is that the application of any descriptive term to things or "reality" negates the possibility of knowing what, in reality, it is like. Yet, on the contrary, it is *only* the application of descriptive terms to reality that makes possible knowing what reality is like. Consider:

Something that would *necessarily* be unknowable by *any* description must, necessarily, have *no* description. But to have no possible description is to have no properties, attributes, or characteristics— nothing even God could correctly state about it. Being *nothing in particular*—reality, as it is in itself, would be *no thing*, that is, *nothing*.

Indeed, to use the term *reality* to refer to that which would be unknowable by any description not only differs from what anyone means by "reality" but denies absolutely the whole point of talking about "reality" in the all the uses of practical life—for, every type of practice has, as a central concern, *the way things ineluctably are*. (And this is merely to suggest the mischief in informing laypersons that reality has only a speculative content—that it might be, well, *anything*.)

In effect, the perspectivist arguments of Rorty, Nietzsche, certain cultural relativists—and even Kant—entail that we cannot know what things are really like because we use our minds to do it.

The incoherence of the doctrine extends to its use of the phrase "external world" (or to phrases like "external" or "independent" reality). For, it is not possible to assert *anything at all* about an "external world" (or reality, etc.) if one cannot know that world *"as it is in itself."* Merely to describe it as *"external"* is to assert at least one way that the world *is* in itself. And to deny this one would have to say (absurdly), "the world is external but is not *in itself* external."

Indeed, it is impossible *to have the concept* of anything's existing "externally" or constituting a "world"—without ever having encountered properties that are not properties of one's mind (like sensations). One might as well suppose that a color-blind race would use the words *green* and *red* as we do in the language of seeing.

Finally, if the *evidence* postmoderns use to justify their references to an *external* world or "reality" (the world or reality they say can't be known *in itself*) does not represent the way the external world *actually is*, then that evidence is false. And if it is not false, then it must represent the world as it really is. Otherwise their evidence and "world" would be mere *appearance* returning it to the "in our heads" status to which Hume (and Locke) admitted they had to assign it.

I conclude, therefore, that the view in which we cannot know the world as it is in itself is *internally inconsistent*. To escape contradiction the position would, presumably, have to retreat to Hellenic skepticism, saying, "we cannot know whether *anything* exists outside our own awareness or consciousness.

The secular miraculous

When gods become humans, or humans become gods, the incarnation brings authority to whatever is said.

For this reason, we say that if we have knowledge, the divine is in us—*is incarnate*—and creates us human. More exactly, when we attain knowledge, the divine and the human are one. *The existence of knowledge is, in this sense, God's humanity.*

These statements are, of course, no explanation of knowledge. They offer a suggestion of the religious significance of knowledge and, at the same time, an interpretation of the Holy, or of "God." We say knowledge is itself the presence of God in us, for *only in knowledge is the truth guaranteed and the physicality of nature overcome.*

The hubris of interpreting "God" in this way is tempered—indeed, we hope, dissolved—by the fact that what we say, we say by way of arguments specific enough to be criticized.

We have tried to show, on the negative side, that the traditional understanding of God is inconsistent with convictions we cannot do without in the conduct of responsible life (for example, convictions about "will" and "person" and "beginning").

On the positive side, we have tried to understand what it is about "God," "Creation," "Miracle" and other theistic terms that makes them "religious" rather than, say, moral, magical, or scientific.

By means of these arguments, and those that claim the bankruptcy of both philosophic doubt and scientistic reductionism, we have sought to cast light on the miraculous nature of everyday life.

A note: probability is not enough

It is sometimes said that all we can justifiably claim is probability. (Knowledge claims are held to be both unjustifiable and unnecessary.) This position is untenable. It is logically impossible to make claims about the world if all the claims we make are *only probable*.[174]

Consider, first, a claim that something is probable, for example: "it will probably rain." This claim is not an isolated and arbitrary assertion. Probability claims are based on evidence of some sort.

But if we follow the thesis that claims about the world can only be probable, then the evidence for concluding "it will probably rain" is itself only probable. Instead of saying, "since a cold front is approaching, it will probably rain," we must now say: since a cold front is *probably* approaching, it will probably rain."

But there is no way to know what the probability of the cold front approaching is, unless we know the evidence for concluding "a cold front is probably approaching."

But that evidence can itself only be probable, and how probably true the evidence is will depend on the evidence for that degree of probability.

One can begin to see that the probability of an event can never be determined if the evidence (or "grounds" on which the probability rests can only be probable.

At some point we must categorically state the evidence. And this we can legitimately do only if claim to know what it is. Only if we *know* that a cold front is approaching, can we (from other situations like it) determine "it will probably rain."

The short form of the argument: It is suggested that the denial of knowledge is no problem since the claim that *P* is probable can rest on grounds *that are themselves only probable*. But in fact this situation entails *denying* "*P* is probable."

Consider that "*P* is probable" is inconsistent with "*P* may not be probable." (You can't say "*P* is probable," and at the same time say, "*P* may not be probable.")

But, in a world in which *evidence* is only probable, the *probability of P* (which is a function of that evidence) can only be *probable*.

But "*probably* P is probable" *entails* "*P may not* be probable." So, the idea of wholly probable world leads, ironically, to the demise of probability as a concept.

BELIEF

Psychology, anthropology, biology—the scientific naturalism characteristic of our time—has, in partnership with philosophic skepticism, made it plausible to view the mind as a structure founded on *beliefs*. Thus, the mind becomes a "belief-system."

But belief can never be foundational.

"Belief" presupposes knowledge

A belief is always a belief that something is *true*. We believe *that* evolutionary theory is true, *that* war is probable, *that* an argument is sound, *that* an action is right, that a picture is aesthetically good. The very idea of a belief *means* "a conviction that something is true." It is not simply "an emotional state" or a "disposition to behave" or "a habitual response"—it is not merely a "psychological" or "behavioral" phenomenon. Truth is unavoidably *part of the meaning* of "belief."

Even where our belief is expressed as a belief *in* something, which is to say, a *trust* in something (say, the police), the *sense* of our having trust lies in our believing it *is true that* the police can and will help us. Similarly, "I trust in God" entails, "I believe that the proposition, 'God will help me' is *true*."

But the claim of *belief-system "theory"* is that in the absence of knowledge—that is, without truth—one can nonetheless profess beliefs. Knowledge is deemed unnecessary.

However if, in fact, we have never experienced (nor could ever experience) something's being *true*, then what meaning could there be to "belief" (when belief is always the belief that something is *true*—or likely true?[175]

So, it becomes impossible—within a belief-system theory of the human mind—to understand what we are *saying* when we say we "believe."

In saying for belief we *must* be acquainted with knowledge, we do not argue that one can have no conception of *anything* that we have not encountered. (We can certainly conceive of a blue unicorn though are acquainted with none.) But being true is like being colored; neither truth nor color is composed of other, different, properties the way an "atom," for example, is composed of mass and electrical energy and motion.

Color and truth are *unitary* notions. What they mean is not *definable* in terms of other properties. It is as impossible for beings that have never encountered anything's being true to believe that a proposition is true, as it would be for beings without sight to believe that something is colored.

In sum, if the concept of "belief" includes as *part of its meaning* an assent to a proposition's truth, the very idea of a belief could not have arisen unless we were already acquainted with truth.

Belief-system advocates might respond: "No doubt we were brought up in a world committed to notions of truth, goodness, and beauty as if these things could be known and could serve as higher goals than mere belief. Perhaps the masses need such beliefs to feel secure. And, if we were raised to seek 'truth' and are uncomfortable trashing it, why not take our cue from commercial and traditional cultures? Why not encourage people to *believe* that their belief systems are ultimate considerations—that they *do* produce the justified certainty we happen to give the name, 'truths?'"

Well, why not? Isn't this what *myths* do for people?—give their lives seemingly valuable purposes and truths? Did not the French mathematician Blaise Pascal recommend to doubters that they engineer their own belief in God, since (to foreshorten his argument) if eternal bliss is real it comes only to those who believe?

So let us follow Pascal. Let us forget the implications of belief-system theory and embrace our illusory, but natural, feeling that we really can achieve that state of mental and emotional repose we call *truth.* (We have seen that David Hume was willing to do this by letting "Nature," not skeptical philosophy, resume control of his everyday beliefs.)

Surely Western "supremacy" owes much to intellectual legerdemain—having thrived on the belief that its moral and religious conclusions, whatever they were, were always based on God's Word.

But at this point we stop and ask why we ought to maintain any system of belief at all?

Why bother with assumptions, methods, and inferential arguments if belief-system theory has shown that our belief-system rests, ultimately, on beliefs? If *systems* of belief have as their basis mere conviction, they have no advantage over *single* beliefs that also are nothing but conviction.

The fact that people continue to lavish honor and attention on systems of thought such as theologies, logics, sciences, and ethical studies while agreeing (or even arguing) that all systems rest on belief becomes inexplicable.[176]

Why (come to think of it) do humans bother to have "ideas" at all; why do we attend to things called "propositions" or "statements" like "this is a tree" or "God exists"? Why believe *that*. . . (anything at all)?

We cannot explain our attention to ideas by saying (in today's popular fashion) that having ideas—propositions about things—helps us to survive as a species.

For, on belief-system theory *itself,* "evolution" is nothing but a *belief,* as is the rationality or credibility of the scientific method. On belief-system theory, evolutionary science cannot be accorded either truth or objective validity.

And since mindless organisms, like viruses and insects, seem not to have ideas or descriptive knowledge, it cannot be argued that species need ideas to survive.

The conceptual failure that allows belief to be *basic* to all rational thought is more than a technical mishap. It fundamentally misdirects our appreciation of belief. It suggests that belief can be sufficient unto itself and that our dispositions—our behavioral tendencies—can and must be formed apart from any basis in the real.

This—when *the importance of belief is that it constitutes humanity's attempt to live, so far as possible, by what is true!*

In making belief basic, civilized life becomes a form of sleep-walking and mind little more than an emotional playpen.

Believing what is true is essential to the *point* of believing. Without the possibility of knowledge, believing would have no success-criterion—no way to know whether the belief was right.

Entering the realm of beliefs would be like entering an archery event with invisible targets. (Even fictional characters are "believable" depending on how close their characters are to the way living persons might be in truth).

That is why we do not believe "just anything." That is why we do not believe that a capuchin monkey appeared to Thomas Jefferson and dictated the Declaration of Independence.

The importance of belief derives from knowledge

Even in cases where we try to believe what may *comfort* us—that is, even in cases of *faith*—we cannot profit from electing a *belief* unless we have internalized the *intellectual* concept of believing (believing something *true*).

To believe something for its therapeutic effect on us rather than because it is warranted by the evidence is *effective* only because we are already acquainted with what it is to have believed something we later found to be true (or false).

The link holds as well (as we have noted) for fiction. The thought of "Alice" being "in Wonderland," which can please both child and adult, is not the passive contemplation of images. It involves letting oneself, at some level, *believe* Alice is in Wonderland; it requires some notion of Alice's *really being there* (the truth of it) to enjoy the pretense. So, even the non-intellectual or "suspended" belief of literary enjoyment *presupposes* the intellectual nature of "belief"—the conviction that something is true.

Again: we could not find comfort in believing if it was impossible to have knowledge and thus impossible to have confirmed for ourselves the meaning and worth of something's being true.

For instance, we could not be comforted by believing that a loved one is still alive after thirty days lost at sea, unless it was possible to know whether someone was alive or dead, or to know whether the person we wanted to find is the person we may find and not a look-alike or impostor.

What we strive to make indelibly plain is that the *whole point of the stance we call "believing"* rests on our ability to know things that are so. Before taking up the views of philosophers who (nonetheless) think rational thought can rightly rest on belief, it may be well further to cement the conceptual link between justification and belief, for we wish to maintain that belief rests on justification—*never* justification on belief, and that therefore, belief can never be foundational for the rational mind.

Belief is intellectual

We have claimed that the concept of belief makes no sense unless we have encountered knowledge. This is because belief is our attempt to *live* in the light of the truth whenever knowledge of a particular truth cannot be achieved. *Belief* has an *essentially* intellectual character.

So essential to belief is truth that we aim to believe what is true even when belief *makes no practical difference*—that is, when no action or responsibility depends on what we believe.

For example, people who have no intention to navigate by the stars may excitedly believe the constellation they see is "Pegasus." But this exercise in "pure" pleasure ordinarily involves consulting a star map or text to insure that their belief that Pegasus is what they saw is likely true.

The assiduous research of bird-watchers and other hobbyists— even when they cannot be sure of their identifications—amply attests to belief's *essential* interest in truth. These familiar facts help confirm our view that belief is essentially an intellectual act. It aims at living in the light of truth—a point confirmed by our readiness to replace belief with knowledge whenever knowledge can be had.

Our claim is that the intention to assert what is true is *internal to the concept* of belief. But what of someone who believes something which they admit is unlikely?

We point out that such a person will never say "it isn't likely *so* I believe it." Rather, they would say, "it's unlikely *but* I believe it," the cautionary "but" acknowledging that belief in the unlikely goes against the grain, against the primary logic of belief. In saying "*but* I believe it," they understand themselves to be open to the question "why believe the unlikely?"

The crucial point is that they acknowledge having departed from belief's *conceptually* required justification. Of course, people believe the unlikely when they "have a hunch"—which is to say when *they have reason to believe* that their feel for things is, in this case, a good enough indicator that something may well supersede the evidence presently available.

Such a case does not contradict the link between belief and the intention to assent to truth because "but" implies the (eventual) need for justification even at the moment it puts it off.

On the other hand, saying "it's unlikely but I believe it" may represent a violation of the point of belief that most would reject as *willfulness* or as the well-known practice—"wishful thinking."

"It's unlikely but I believe it" might also express the need to believe despite or against the evidence because the aim is *not* a belief but a practical outcome that is served by having a certain belief (as in: "maybe this operation fails more often than it succeeds, but I'm better off going into it believing it will work for me." (This, we shall argue, is the situation of faith.)[177]

All uses of "belief" that ignore or defy the need for evidential justification are parasitic on the value we attach to the term in its standard or proper use. They make sense *only by trading on its name.* They depend on it; it does not depend on them.

Unjustifiable believing is rather like writing a bad check. Whatever credibility checks have derives from their success in drawing funds from a bank. Write enough bad checks and the checks become worthless. Believe whatever you wish and soon believing loses its meaningfulness.

For example, in the context of competition, we sometimes detach belief from evidence and "psych" ourselves into believing we can win a tough game. But the psychological state of believing the proposition "we can win" would be of no help were it not that *normally* (or paradigmatically) what we believe is justifiable and aimed at approaching the *truth*.

The same relationship holds between communication and truth-telling. If communication were not essentially (or paradigmatically) used to convey what we truly think, lying would have no power. If normal communication did not adhere to the success-criterion of honest speech, communication would cease to have an effect. Since we would no longer listen, dishonest talk would lose its utility.

And, analogously, if belief were not essentially directed toward truth (and therefore normally proportional to the evidence), false or dubious belief could have no utility.

For example, if we have to pass by a dog which we believe to be dangerous, we strive to have the belief that it is actually harmless, so that our having this belief (our making it a *psychological* fact) will prevent us from being fearful, from sweating or otherwise betraying our fear to the dog. Nothing could be plainer here than that the utility of purely practical belief (*psychologically* induced belief) depends on the *prior* idea of justifiable belief.

Justification is the bridge between bare conviction (a psychological phenomenon) and a commitment to *truth* (which is an extra-psychological phenomenon). Justification is what links the *dispositional* aspect of belief and its *intellectual* aspect.

When a justification fails egregiously, when it plainly does not link a disposition to the grounds (or evidence) on which it is purportedly based, the failure may be seen as constituting loss of mind—or even of self.

That is why the beliefs of those we call "brainwashed" are never thought to be *genuine* beliefs (never *their* beliefs, their *personal* beliefs) even though—as a *psychological* fact—the brainwashed *do* have the beliefs.[178]

A sustained, unjustified belief may thus be a kind of fixation, a thought cut off from the processes of justification and "covered" by such anti-intellectual excuses as "statistics can lie (so I never believe them)" or "science can be wrong, (so I needn't pay heed)" or the disingenuously heroic, "I don't care what anyone says."

Indeed, in our everyday, non-philosophical approach to the awful condition of insanity, it is plain that persistent belief *for no reason whatever* (or for a reason too implausible to be the *actual* or *justifying* reason) is paradigmatic of mental impairment. Surely, persistence in commitment without any justification suggests a clinically assignable breakdown which no "belief-system" philosophy can plausibly dismiss.

Because wanting to know what to believe is, fundamentally, wanting to assent to what is true, we claim that to believe without reasonable justification is incoherent—rather than *unethical*, as W. K. Clifford famously claimed in "The Ethics of Belief."

We agree that, in general, it is unethical to assent to beliefs with little or no justification when those beliefs may make a difference in one's actions. But our interest is theological, and so we are concerned with the role of belief in creating the *human situation*. Our interest is "metaphysical." And the *very idea* of believing makes sense only if truth is the goal and knowledge is real.

By now the reader will not be surprised to find us saying that without justification—without reason—believing reduces to a brain-disposition or organic proclivity; that is, it falls from the domain of the human into the domain of the organism.

The theory of properly basic beliefs

Among those who would have us rest mind on belief are the theistic philosopher Alvin Plantinga, the agnostic Anthony Kenny, and Dewey Hoitinga Jr. (a philosophical theist supportive of Plantinga's work). Though they pursue diverse arguments, all conclude that rational thought may *rightly* have belief as its foundation. For them, beliefs that are justified *neither by knowledge nor by other beliefs* can be properly *basic* to the structure of one's thought.

If we are right in saying that only knowledge can be foundational, these writers will be found assigning belief a foundational position by implicitly conflating it with knowledge or by arguing, directly, that knowledge is a form of belief.

Hoitinga, for example, argues that knowledge can be defined as a form of belief (and also that the terms *knowledge* and *belief* have a dual usage).

(Clearly, if knowledge *were* a form of belief, most of what we have argued would have to be rejected.)

Since theists commonly describe themselves a believers, the concept of belief must occupy a critical role in any theological inquiry. According to Alvin Plantinga, "a very large number of philosophers take it that a central question—perhaps *the* central question—of philosophy of religion is the question whether religious belief in general and belief in God in particular is rationally acceptable."[179]

Of course, theism has much to gain if it can be shown that a belief in God can be basic in one's thought and at the same time rational.

Plantinga's view is that this can be done, and that belief in God can be what he calls, "properly basic." That is, one can properly believe "God exists" *apart from any other beliefs*—that is, without depending on any other beliefs.

It is, we think, no accident, that a belief whose credibility is, thus, entirely self-sufficient, is, by definition, a belief that cannot possibly be criticized.

The idea that knowledge is a kind of belief

Dewey Hoitinga Jr. fields several arguments aimed at concluding that knowledge is "justified true belief"—and not a unique and indefinable "mental attitude" (as we have said, save for using the descriptive, "attitude").[180]

Hoitinga sets the stage for his argument by claiming that the relationship between knowledge and belief is marked by *ambivalence*. According to one linguistic usage, knowledge and belief are very different in that knowledge is infallible where belief is not so that. . . . knowledge and belief must be two different and incompatible states of mind, the one irreducible to the other. For if knowledge cannot err, how can knowledge be a form of belief?"[181] (This, of course, is our view.)

By way of illustration, Hoitinga tells us that if he were asked "do you believe the Earth is round?" he "might well respond, with what he himself terms the "appropriate emphasis": "I don't *believe* it, I *know* it."[182]

Hoitinga moves, however, to another example of usage, one that contradicts the first by treating knowledge and belief as *compatible*— and proceeds to argue from this example that knowledge is a *form* of *belief*, contending that

> unless there is some special point to be made that reflects the difference between knowledge and belief, I can quite correctly say that I believe the things that I know. I know that twice two is four. Do I believe it? Of course I do. I could also say that if I did not believe it, I could *not* know it. Thus to know something is also to believe it. No one can know what he does not believe. From this it follows that knowledge and belief are not different states of mind; quite the contrary, it looks very much as if knowledge is a form of belief itself. Instead of being a unique and indefinable state of mind, knowledge appears to be definable as a form of belief.[183]

Among the difficulties of Hoitinga's monologue is its abnormal linguistic character. If I know a thing I never ask myself if I believe it. And if I tell someone I know a thing, that person will not ask if I believe it. Nor does one ever ask of oneself "I know it, but do I believe it?"

The reason is that if one knows something, belief in that thing is unnecessary; we believe when we cannot know, not when we know.

Hoitinga's argument reveals no "ambivalent" relationship between belief and knowledge. If one says "I know it" and someone asks "do you believe it?" one can only be puzzled as to what they might mean. And if, like Hoitinga, one nonetheless attempts to answer this out-of-place question, "belief" is forced to to mean what it does not normally mean.

A simple substitution shows that in Hoitinga's monologue, "belief" has become equivalent to *having the thought that*, or perhaps, *taking the stand that*. To wit:

I can quite correctly say that I *have the thought of* the things that I know. I know that twice two is four. Do I think it? Of course I do. Thus to know something is also to have the thought of it. No one can know what he does not have a thought of. From this it follows that knowledge and having thoughts are not different states of mind . . . it looks very much as if knowledge is a form of having thoughts [so] . . . knowledge appears to be definable as a form of *having thoughts* [or, employing other substitutions, a form of asserting, a form of claiming, a form of assenting, etc.].

Indeed *everyone understands* that in such an abnormal conversation, if we say "yes, of course I believe it" or "yes, of course I think so," we do not thereby retract that we *know* it in favor of saying we *believe* it or merely *think* it—so that knowledge is a form of belief or knowledge is a form of having-the-thought-that.

It is because "I know" and "I believe" both entail *having a thought about* or *taking a stand on* (the truth or falsity of some statement), that if we answer Hoitinga's peculiar question by saying "I know it, but I *don't* believe it" we seem to deny or take back saying we know it.

But the fact of the matter is that if you *know* a thing, you cannot possibly believe it. *The logic of the usage is definitive*: If you know, you *can't* be wrong. But, if you believe, you *can* be wrong. Therefore, to say, "I know it so I believe it," is to say, "I can't be wrong about it so I might be wrong about it." The idea that knowledge is a form of belief is self-contradictory.

Indeed, the very point of describing one's conclusion as " belief" is to signal that what one says is conditionally asserted, is dependent on the speaker's judgment of the evidence.

The point of saying "I know . . . " is just the opposite. It is to signal that the proposition's intellectual *status* is entirely separate from one's own judgment; it is declared out of the nest of the mind, flying (or falling) entirely on its own.

Even the non-philosophical commuter knows that "this is my parking spot" differs critically from "I believe this is my parking spot." A surgeon about to be sued emphatically tells an insurance company "but, I knew the artery was blocked"; if the company lawyer *then* asks "isn't it true, doctor, that it's being blocked was something you believed?" the doctor would not then answer, "yes, I believed it." He would of course insist that he knew it.

There is no ambivalence in our ordinary senses of "know" and "believe." Only in contexts where the intellectual status of an assertion is not in question can "believe" be used, loosely, to mean the same as "affirms that," or "holds that," or "thinks that." But where truth is a matter of importance, "knowing" never means the same as holding, thinking, or asserting *or* believing; it means knowing.

Knowing and believing entail different commitments and actions. When I know a thing I may *rightly* not listen to counter-evidence! This is perhaps the chief reason intellectuals would like to do away with "I know it" and "true." But it is also the reason people who plant vines in their garden will never check to see if they have produced replicas of Rembrandt or Donatello.

If there is an overlapping of knowledge and belief it resides in the fact that the *behaviors* that follow from believing or knowing are often the same. If I believe a street is dangerous, I will avoid it. If I know it is dangerous I will avoid it.

But suppose a belief is fully justified and what it asserts happens to be true. Might it not, then, be the same as knowledge? Hoitinga suggests it is:

> When a true belief is justified, the combination may produce the knowledge that cannot be mistaken. . . . When belief is combined with truth and justification, something is created that makes the resulting *state of mind* infallible, even though belief by itself is not [the latter emphasis added].[184]

The reader may notice that when knowledge is reduced to a form of belief it becomes in some part psychological—a "state of mind"—whereas we have argued that knowledge is not a state of mind (not simply internal) but the state in which mind is joined with reality.

In any case, the idea that "knowledge" can be "*justified, true belief*," is a reduction of knowledge to an assertion "within one's head." A situation in which something that one *thinks* true happens also to *be* true can of course be nothing more than coincidence. And the same supposition, even if well-founded, does not become knowledge.

For example, suppose a person exhaustively studies airline safety records, knows the most respected pilots, calls the airport to investigate its physical condition, and acquires the latest weather information, elects to fly the safest airline, and then arrives safely. Should that person claim "I had knowledge of my safe arrival"? Foreknowledge may confidently be left to psychics—or to philosophers who believe that you have knowledge when you have justified belief in propositions that are true.

The point remains that belief can be wrong and knowledge cannot. The combination of *justification* and *coincidence with reality* cannot change that. Belief, even when justified and true, falls below the metaphysical status of knowledge.

Knowledge is categorical

The religiously significant character of knowledge lies in part in its distance from bodily influences. Its purity as union with the world depends on its transcendence of psychology. Belief, being dispositional or behavioral, and being a response to evidence that fails to produce knowledge, has always a gray area of psychological influence. It is not tied to evidence by logical certainty; evidence *indicates* and must be *weighed*.

That is why belief is a matter of degree while knowledge is never a matter of degree—one more proof that "knowledge" and "belief" mean incompatible things.

So we say that an assertion's being "justified" is *inconsistent* with its being "known." Knowing a thing is *more* than having the intellectual right to assert its truth. Thus "I know X is true" is, in effect, to *deny* that "X is true" is *justified* just as it is to deny that X is *believable* or *believed*.

If a foreman read the jury's verdict and said, "we find the defendant guilty and we find that 'the defendant is guilty' is a justifiable conclusion," the judge would ask, "which is it?" The court needs to know, categorically, "is the defendant guilty?" The judge would *not* ask, "why did you say the same thing twice?" Similarly, a corporation would not be satisfied with lawyers who, having been asked whether a certain contract must be honored, reported that "it is justifiable to say the contract is valid."

Saying that you know a thing and adding that the proposition you assert is justified is like saying, "It will rain," and adding, "rain is very probable." Which are you saying?

You cannot say both. If it *will* rain, then rain is more than *probable*. That is why if you say "it will rain" you cannot with consistency add that "there is a one hundred percent probability of rain." The latter claim is consistent with it not raining, while the former is not.

Knowledge is categorical, justified statements are conditional, having only the weight of their evidence. When we say we are justified, we say that we *have reason* to make an assertion; we make reference to our grounds. When we say a proposition is true we make no reference whatever to our grounds.

What may sometimes confuse is the verbal closeness between being justified in claiming knowledge, and claiming that a *statement is justified.* The difference is between saying "I am justified in saying 'I *know the cup is on the table'"* and saying *"'the cup is on the table'* is a justified assertion."

Considered as *actions*, knowledge-claims may be justified. It is the *content* of knowledge-claims that are true, not justified.

Perhaps it is useful to think of justification as granting a proposition the intellectual *right* to be accepted, and knowing as bestowing on a proposition the intellectual *duty* to be accepted; one does not have to agree to a justified thing, but one has to agree to a known thing (which, again, is why, if you say that what you assert is a *known* thing, saying *also* that it is a justified thing contradicts its being a known thing).

If "justified" propositions are not "known" propositions, and if "known" propositions are not "justified" propositions, knowledge cannot be defined as "justified true belief." And that (again) is because knowledge is not a form of belief.

Alvin Plantinga's "properly basic" belief

Alvin Plantinga claims that some beliefs are "properly basic." For Plantinga, a belief is "basic" when "it is perfectly rational to accept belief in . . . [a proposition] . . . without accepting it on the basis of any other beliefs or propositions at all."[185] His program of "reformed foundationalism" describes the structure of rational thought as a belief-system—a building made of rationally justifiable claims, a "noetic" strutcture—in which certain beliefs are the intellectual foundation on which all others depend.

Plantinga's position is puzzling. If a belief is to be accepted "without accepting it on the basis of any other beliefs or propositions at all" then how—without consulting other beliefs or propositions—can it be determined to be *properly* basic (rather than *merely* basic)?

Unless a "basic" belief is *self-evident*, its status as "proper" must rest on considerations other than itself. To rule upon the belief's propriety, those considerations must be more basic than the putatively "basic" belief. It appears, then, that the idea of a belief that depends on no other belief to be believed is inconsistent with the requirement that it be "proper" (or "rational") since that determination depends on other things we believe (as well as know).

There is also a problem in *identifying* a belief as "basic." Plantinga describes a basic belief as something one believes "without basing it on other propositions one believes." The bland technicality of this requirement belies the enormous, we think insuperable, difficulty of isolating something you believe that is believed *no matter what else you may believe.*

Consider the matter practically: If anything else Plantinga believes were inconsistent with Plantinga's presumably basic belief, then it would not be true that all his thought rested on that putatively basic belief. In order for his basic belief to be "basic" to all his thought, one of the beliefs would have to be relinquished. But which one?

And, as soon as he *passes judgment* on either belief, then the position in his noetic structure (his rational edifice) of those beliefs "depends on other beliefs"—*the ones used to consider it*—and neither can then be "basic," according to his own definition of "basic."

In addition, to successfully identify a belief as "properly basic," one must know—in advance of all possible new beliefs (or experiences)—that none of these beliefs or experiences can have negative implications for the basic belief. And the idea that one holds to a *belief* no matter what new ideas, beliefs, or experiences may come to pass is surely paradigmatic of dogmatic belief, not rational belief. Such a position can only be rational if one is God, that is, if one knows the future absolutely.

Locating one's basic belief

Hoitinga is aware that there is something problematic in locating a basic belief. He agrees that one can be mistaken about a belief's dependence on other beliefs.[186] (Indeed, Plantinga himself, during a discussion of self-evidence, serves up several instances in which we are often mistaken as to the dependence or independence of what we believe about our propositions).

Everyday experience tells us that it is not always easy to determine that a belief like "God exists" has no dependence whatever on believing that a certain religious tradition, religious official, or parental believer is credible. It is not uncommon to be surprised that what you firmly believe "for itself" depends on the truth of another conviction you reject.

Since we can be mistaken about the interdependence of *propositions,* Hoitinga says we should take the view that a belief is not a proposition but that "a belief is an attitude"; "otherwise," he says, "we would have the unacceptable position that propositions . . . are *taken* to be based on others . . . [when] . . . this may be mistaken"

To avoid being *mistaken* about a belief's being basic, Hoitinga says we must treat it as an *attitude of assent*: "beliefs . . . [are] . . . attitudes toward propositions."[187] But how does Hoitinga know that our attitudes of assent do not depend on other attitudes of assent?

Nothing is surer than that we ourselves can be mistaken about the source or cause or even the reason for our attitudes of assent. The problem of something's being "basic" because it is (absolutely) self-dependent remains.

Plantinga's idea that a belief can be basic is wrong at its root. Either we accept a belief as basic for no reason whatever or we accept it for some reason. And if we accept it for a reason, that reason (in which we must at least *believe*) becomes more basic than the belief seeking basic status.

In sum, to assert that a belief is basic requires that we *not* select it *rationally* (for some *reason* other than itself) but absolutely *arbitrarily*—not rationally. Plantinga is left saying, "It is basic if I say it is basic." This seems a very bad way to determine the acceptability of important propositions such as "God exists."

Conflating belief and knowledge

Plantinga's difficulties result from a failure to see that the only propositions on which a rational mind can finally rest are those that are known. He fails to see that conditional statements (like "rain is probable") must be asserted on the basis of unconditional statements (like "those are cumulus clouds" or "a cold front is moving toward us")—that is, on the basis of knowledge.

Without some foundation in knowledge, statements of belief and probability function like promissory notes in a bankrupt world. It is simply irrational to insist on holding to a proposition *no matter what else you may think* unless it is something you *know*.

One finds, therefore, that Plantinga's *examples* of basic beliefs are not beliefs at all. They are examples of knowledge.

In "Coherentism and the Evidentialist Objection," Plantinga's "properly basic beliefs" include the following: "I am feeling tired" and "*modus ponens* and the other truths of logic and mathematics," as well as (that traditional chestnut of skeptical empiricist thought) "I am being appeared to greenly."[188] ("being appeared to greenly" is the modern way of talking about Hume's sensations in awareness—sensations that purportedly are basic because they cannot be doubted.)

But these are not examples of belief. "Modus ponens" is a valid argument within logic ("If P, then Q"; "P" "Therefore Q"). ; Its validity is something we *know*. If we are aware that we are feeling tired we do not *believe* we are feeling tired, we *know* it. We might look at our behavior to see whether we are, in fact, tired, but not to know whether we *feel* tired. Emergency room patients never cry out, "I believe I'm in terrible pain."

The same is true of how things *appear* to us. Assuming that I know about colors and what it is to see "green," if I can say, "I am aware of green-ness" or "I am aware of a green area" then I can and must say "I know I am seeing an area of green" (I cannot say "I don't know whether I am aware of green coloration or not.") Sense-awareness is not a matter of *belief.*

None of Plantinga's "beliefs" are examples of belief. They are examples of knowledge. The only way such examples can be spoken of as belief is in that style of genteel good manners which leads the unfortunate who has just spilled a glass of Chianti on the rug to say "I *believe* I've spilled my wine!"

Despite these fairly plain considerations, Plantinga (speaking of *candidates* for "properly basic belief") conflates knowledge with belief at nearly every opportunity:

> Many of these propositions will be *apparently self-evident for me;* they will display the "evident luster" of which Locke speaks in this connection; a self-evident proposition, he says, displays a kind of "clarity and brightness to the attentive mind." Descartes speaks here of "clarity and distinctness"; each, I think, is referring to the same phenomenal feature. And indeed there is a phenomenal, experiential aspect to our apprehension of self-evident truths; but ordinarily, at least, *such truths are not believed on the evidential basis of other beliefs* detailing this phenomenal aspect [emphasis added].[189]

The phrase "apparently self-evident for me" reveals Plantinga's tendency to conflate knowledge and belief. The qualifier, "apparently," in "apparently self-evident," is oxymoronic, for a thing which is *apparently* self-evident—which is *believed* self-evident—is for that very reason *not* self-evident![190]

That which is self-evident cannot be a belief. It is nonsense to say, "this is self-evident, but it may not be true," and equally incoherent to say, "this is *evident*, but it may not be true." That which is *evident* is *known.*

Plantinga's flirtation with self-evidence, and *criteria for knowledge* of the sort Descartes and Locke suggested, only betray the need to give beliefs the status of knowledge in order that they may be "properly" basic.

Plantinga's aim is to justify being a believer. He seeks a way that belief in God can be foundational for rational thought and thereby secure from rational critique. If our noetic structures—our systems of inquiry into the world—all rest on basic beliefs, then each of our systems of thought is immune to criticism from anyone else. Everyone's thought would rest on basic beliefs—beliefs independent of any

other beliefs—so that no one's mind or noetic structure has a more credible foundation than any other. Perspectivism again rears one of its many heads.

Can circumstances justify belief?

We have mounted three internal arguments against Plantinga's version of rational belief: First, a belief cannot be both basic and "proper" since our belief in the standard for "propriety" must be more basic than the "basic" belief; second, there is no certain way to identify a "basic" belief, since there is no way to determine that we believe a thing completely apart from anything else we believe.

Third, we have noted that to avoid using other beliefs to choose one as basic, a basic belief must be chosen *for no reason at all*—making the belief, on which one's rational system is based, unjustifiable. And, since the point of belief is to assent to what is true, it requires being open to evidentiary considerations. Therefore no belief can be basic to our system of rational thought because no belief can be more basic (more foundational) than its own evidence.

In any case, one must not confuse *willfulness* with finding a basis for rational thought. And determining a belief absolutely independently—apart from anything else one believes—is, even were it possible, an act of willful disregard. A belief one *positions* so as not to be given up *no matter what* is a dogma; it treats belief as if it owed nothing to evidence. The only thing one ought not relinquish *no matter what* is something one *knows*, not something that is possibly not true. (And this is terrible burden of knowing.)

Plantinga's final argument for properly basic beliefs disputes our argument that for a basic belief to be "proper" we must have (contradictorily) a *more* basic belief in some standard for "propriety." To do this, he argues that basic beliefs can be "justified" (deemed "proper") by conditions or circumstances (facts of the world) rather than by anything we *believe*. Thus, the *propriety* of basic beliefs can be established without the use of other beliefs:

> It is sometimes claimed that if I have no evidence for the existence of God, then if I accept that proposition my belief will be groundless, or gratuitous, or arbitrary. I think this is an error; let me explain. Suppose we consider perceptual beliefs, memory beliefs and beliefs ascribing mental states to other persons: such beliefs as . . . I see a tree. . . . I had breakfast this morning, and. . . . That person is angry. Although beliefs of this sort are typically and properly taken as basic, it would be a mistake to describe them as *groundless*. In the typical case, I do not hold

this belief on the basis of other beliefs; it is nonetheless not groundless. My having that characteristic sort of experience— to use Professor Chisholm's language, my being appeared treely to—plays a crucial role in the formation and justification of that belief.[191] We might say this experience, together, per- haps, with other circumstances is what *justifies* me in holding it; this is the *ground* of my justification, and, by extension, the ground of the belief itself.[192]

Once more, beliefs are made basic by describing the kinds of things we *know* as things we *believe*—confirming, again, that only knowledge can be basic. "Perceptual beliefs, memory beliefs " and "such beliefs as . . . I see a tree. . . . I had breakfast this morning" are not normally what we "believe" at all.

When we perceive the breakfast table we do not *believe* we see breakfast table. It would be grounds for serious worry if we looked at the breakfast table and said "I believe I see a breakfast table." Nor do we say or think, "I believe I was in bed before I came to breakfast." We know very well we are looking at the breakfast table and that we were in bed before breakfast. And, of course, we do not hold such "beliefs" (as Plantinga calls them) "on the basis of other beliefs" and of course what we know is not "groundless" ("groundless being equivalent to "baseless" and implying "arbitrary").

The point is that if we did not know such things as that we see our breakfast table and that we were recently in bed, we could not know *anything*. That is why knowledge is basic.

The case of someone else's pain is unimportant; it can be a matter of belief or of knowledge, depending on the circumstances. The fail- ure of Plantinga's argument is that even if certain circumstances *could* justify calling a belief "basic," we could not recognize that a belief was "basic" unless (using *Plantinga's* terminology) we *believed* that the necessary circumstances were present. "Circumstance" and "grounds" are useless conditions unless we know or believe they exist. In and of themselves, they do not avoid the need for "belief."

Belief and responsibility

Plantinga is aware of Clifford's view (echoed by philosophers Brand Blanshard and Michael Scriven) that belief without justifica- tion is a failure of "*duty* or *obligation*."[193] Having attempted to shield belief in God from *intellectual* criticism by making it a "properly basic belief," Plantinga attempts to shield the concept of a properly basic belief from *moral* criticism. He rejects the idea that the justification of belief is a moral obligation because "belief is not for the most part directly within our voluntary control."[194]

"My belief in God," he says

> is . . . no more in my direct control than is my belief that I have a
> social security number; how therefore could I fulfill this moral
> obligation to withhold belief if I have no evidence? Can I have a
> duty—intellectual or otherwise—to do what it is not within my
> power to do? I should think not.[195]

Plantinga's rejoinder trades too heavily on what we have called
the "bodily" aspect of belief—the acquisition of feelings about things
and dispositions to think and act in certain ways. For, if the adoption
of "morally proper" beliefs is "not within my power"—if it is a matter
beyond our control—then the adoption of "rationally proper" or
"theistically proper" beliefs is also beyond our control.

If believing were entirely involuntary, God could not condemn
us for atheism or approve us for theism. Nor would electorates be responsible for the political beliefs whose consequences they inflict on
each other as well as themselves.

If, however, all Plantinga means is that we cannot alter what we
believe *directly*—that is, by a *direct* act of will rather than by considering evidence or argument—it is inconceivable that this patently impossible demand was ever the demand of Clifford, Blanshard, or
Scriven.

Belief is corrigible. That is why we are responsible for our beliefs.
Beliefs may be changed through a variety of activities and investigations. Belief is a feature of our mental being which we can affect, and
which reflects other decisions we have made that pose issues of honesty and truth. Believing is surely no *less* a moral responsibility than
getting angry or being passive or even sneezing in company—which
(despite being *almost* paradigmatically involuntary) can often be
managed better or worse.

The justification of belief is a moral issue because of the practical
and social effects of what we believe.

But because the whole idea (or point) of belief is to believe what is
true, the justification of belief is *conceptually* necessitated if believing
is to retain its *sense*. Unjustified belief is conceptually defective; it is
senseless.

Belief and believing

We have spoken of belief as an essentially intellectual conception. But, almost in passing, we have distinguished belief from *believing*, that is, from the psychological condition of *holding* a belief. We

wish to be clear, in preparation for discussing *faith*, that the justification for inducing the psychological state of *believing* is different from the justification of *belief* which always involves asserting some proposition ("I believe that the fire is out.")

If I, as a criminal, need to pass a lie detector test, it is *rational*—justifiable—to produce in myself a state of believing that I know to be *false*—namely, that I am innocent. (Perhaps I use self-hypnosis or drugs.)

So, when a state of belief is justified by *purely practical considerations*, a belief one knows is false can be rationally *believed* by one who knows it false.

Still, belief for *practical* reasons is parasitic on what belief fundamentally, or "by its nature" is, just as lying is parasitic upon *truthful* communicating (what communication, fundamentally is). Each departure from the point of the activity gets its utility from what is essential to the existence of the activity.

There would be no value in *mere states of believing* if believing had no *standard* connection with truth. (The specialist in lie detection would have no job if beliefs were not essentially aimed at assenting to what is true.)

Without knowledge—that is, without knowledge of the evidence that justifies holding a belief—belief would be as unintelligible as "news" in a world where no statements were ever true.

Convenient believing—*practical* believing—is derivate believing, and is effective only because believing reflects humanity's need for truth. And surely, religious belief must be belief in what is so, not in what is practical.

If belief can be basic, then the *standards* for belief cannot be basic. And when there is no *right* way to believe—no governance of belief—then you can believe anything—and then *believing becomes a senseless act* (and any standards, pointless). Indeed, if it is rationally possible to believe *anything*, then it is *easier*—and thus more reasonable—to believe nothing.

Belief for no reason

In *What is Faith?*, the secular British philosopher, Anthony Kenny, attempts to improve on Plantinga's criteria for properly basic beliefs:

> My complaint with Plantinga is that one must go much further than he has done if one is to make any substantial contribution to answering the question, "Is belief in God rational?" . . . Plantinga has not shown us why what goes for belief in the proposi-

tion "there is a God" may not go for belief in any proposition whatever. For all he has shown there would be nothing irrational in a noetic [knowledge or "cognitive"] structure which included among its foundations "there is no God."[196]

Like Plantinga, Kenny thinks beliefs can be foundational, and, like Plantinga, Kenny aims to prove there *can* be beliefs basic to our system of ideas which are *rationally* held to basic—yet for which *we have no reasons.*

Kenny's arguments for rationally fundamental ("properly basic") beliefs are several and are, as he says, aimed at *limiting* the kinds of belief that can be properly basic.

Thus, Kenny disputes the "many distinguished philosophers [who] have said, that the mark of rationality is the proportioning of one's belief to the evidence." He wants, therefore, to ask "whether a person can believe something rationally without having evidence for that belief. Can there be rational beliefs for which there is no evidence at all?"[197]

Like Plantinga and Hoitinga (and as we contend, *unavoidably*), Kenny's affirmative answer achieves plausibility by offering—as examples of foundational beliefs—contentions that are not beliefs "for which there is no evidence at all" but, rather, *knowledge*:

> There are many such propositions that I hold myself such as, that I am awake, that human beings sleep and die, that there is a continent called Australia where I have never been; that there have been Christians for about two thousand years. I claim that I am rational in accepting all these propositions and in no way guilty of credulity.[198]

These are statements ("I am awake," "Australia exists") that cannot possibly be wrong. That is, Kenny knows (as we know) they are true. They are not beliefs. And it is only because these are things we *know* that Kenny can convincingly assert, "I am rational in accepting all these propositions and in no way guilty of credulity."

If they *were* beliefs—if they *could* possibly be wrong—then Kenny would be in the untenable position of claiming that one's system of rational inquiry (one's "noetic structure") can *properly* rest on statements that can be wrong.

It is of course strange, if not oddly defiant, to say, as Kenny does, that there are rational beliefs for which we have no evidence. However, once his reason for saying this is understood, we will find it aids our case for the religious significance of knowledge.

The role of evidence

When do our assertions require no evidence? Kenny has many examples: There is, for instance, a *mathematical* case, "2+2=4," and a *factual* case "[it is] evident to the senses . . . that it is snowing as I write this."[199]

From these and like examples ("If I press my palm against my chest it will not pass through to my back"), Kenny concludes "things that are *evident* may be said to be *believed* without evidence [emphasis added]" because "it is clearly rational to *believe* what is self-evident or evident to the senses [emphasis added]."[200]

Two issues arise. The first is that these are examples of things we know, not things we believe. Second—and a matter of importance for Kenny's "criteria" for basic beliefs—is that something that is "evident" is not something "believed." It is self-contradictory to say, "The answer is evident but it may not be right" or "It's evident that you are tired but I don't know whether you are tired."

As for stating propositions without evidence, the contention is in a sense true and in a sense not. The sense in which we state things "without" evidence is the sense in which we state things without *indicating* that what we state *relies on* certain evidence. That is, to *say* a thing is "evident" is to give others to understand that it is no longer something you infer from evidence.

This no doubt seems an academic technicality, but at bottom it is not. Let us flesh out the "technical" point with an example.

If one comes home and enters the kitchen, it will be *evident* that there are several persons sitting at the kitchen table.

If it is evident, it would be *wrong* to say, "I *infer* that there are several people at the table from the evidence: the numbers of heads and shoulders, the movements of bodies, the positions of the chairs and the sounds of voices." One does not *infer* the existence of these people around the kitchen table—one *perceives* their presence there. And perception presupposes knowledge, not belief.

So does inference from evidence. For one must *perceive* the evidence. One must *know* what it is. If one did not perceive it, one would have to have *inferred* its existence and character from *other* evidence. And the character of that "other" evidence would have to have been inferred from still other evidence.

We must be able *not always to rely on inference* if are to make statements about the world. And that is what human beings are able *rightly* to do when they *know*.

Either we stop the endless progression of inferences by making things up (believe traditional ideas, consult our inner self, daydream, think what pleases us) or we stop by making use of what we know. If all our contentions are made up, the whole enterprise of rational argument and rational questing is absurd. But it isn't.

The deep issue here—why knowledge must be basic—surfaced on empiricism's "garden path." The observer's seeing a tree could not be explained as a process of physical causes and effects (light waves, nerve impulses, brain synapses). That is why Hume could not see the tree either, so to speak—why he admitted he could not "rationally" assert the existence of an external source for our "impressions" and their corresponding "ideas."

There is simply no way to make the leap from fantasizing, imagining, or dreaming to *perception* without having knowledge. To know one perceives a tree, one's "inner" statements must correspond to the way something is ("in reality"). And one cannot provide *an argument or proof*—something in one's head—that allows one to conclude that what one *thinks* describes something outside one's head—something *independent*, something "out there," something real (the point on which skepticisms depend).

So knowledge exists—somehow.

That is why, after saying "[it is] evident to the senses . . . that it is snowing as I write this," Kenny can conclude: "To this extent, therefore it is rational to *accept* propositions without evidence [emphasis added]."

Even so, Kenny should have said it is rational to *assert* propositions without (*making use* of) evidence. It is rational to *assert*, "there are several persons seated here." But when Kenny concludes that we can *accept* a proposition unconditionally, he uses a verb—*accept*—that is suited not to knowing but believing. One can *assert* or state a proposition without *implying* one is (currently) depending on evidence (for one may know the proposition is true).

But to *accept* a proposition implies a *decision* to hold it. It isn't just *evident*—one doesn't *accept* that there are people sitting at the table. And it isn't just an idea found in one's consciousness. So one cannot be said rationally to *accept* a proposition (*intellectually*, not practically) without having done so because of the evidence, or reasons.

Only a philosopher would maintain a way of speaking that departs so wildly from ordinary usage with respect to major issues. No sane speaker of English would ever say (following Kenny's way of talking) "it is snowing here but there is no evidence that it is snowing *because* I'm standing in middle of it." What one *could* say without misleading is "I don't need evidence that it's snowing; I'm standing here in the middle of it."

Something has gone radically wrong when absolutely conclusive evidence is said to entail the absence of evidence or reasons. Yet Kenny holds that matters evident to the senses lack evidence and that we have no reasons for concluding "four" when asked for "the sum of two plus two."

Foundational propositions can only be things we know, and things that are "evident" are things we know. If I hit my thumb with a hammer, it would be *droll* to say "one thing I shall always believe— one foundational belief for me—is that I hit myself with a hammer."

And it would be *absurd* to say, "I believe I hit myself with a hammer but have no evidence that this happened"—and *insane* to say "I believe I hit myself with a hammer, but because I saw it happen and felt it, I believe it for no reason at all."

The problem for religion and culture however, is that academic language often seeps into everyday approaches to reflection, so that, with the aid of skeptical and traditionally religious writers, it may one day be mooted that "respected" philosophers say, "basic beliefs can be rationally held on no evidence at all."

"Like Plantinga," Kenny announces, "we have rejected the classical definition of rationality as the proportioning of one's belief to the evidence."[201] Not to put to fine a point on it, it is a motto to delight the heart of school-averse juveniles and unregenerate dogmatists everywhere.

Fear of knowledge

Kenny's aim is to supply *criteria* for those "beliefs" (so-called) that can *properly* be considered basic (foundational for all our thought). If our own arguments are correct, his effort can only result in another failed attempt to supply criteria for knowledge—here wrongly cast as a discussion of "belief."

So, Kenny: "a belief is properly basic . . . if and only if it is
- Self-evident or fundamental
- Evident to the senses or memory
- Defensible by argument, inquiry, or performance. "[202]

Kenny admits "this is a complicated criterion" but says its advantage is that it is not subject to Plantinga's criticism that a "self-evident and incorrigible" standard for basic beliefs refutes itself (since is not, itself, "self-evident and incorrigible" and so not foundational).

The writer pleads puzzlement here. Kenny's escape, he says, lies in the "defensibility" criterion because then "it is not necessarily impossible (logically incoherent) to defend it by argument and inquiry."

But if a so-called "properly basic" belief were to be defended "by argument, inquiry, or performance" it would not be basic but *dependent* on the credibility of whatever was offered in defense of it. And if, on the other hand, it could be properly basic in the absence of such a defense, then the criterion would be useless.

As for the other two criteria, which require a proposition to be either "self-evident" or "evident," they can only be met by things we know. And it is tautological to say that anything we know is foundational (within a rational system of thought) since it is irrational to deny the truth of that which cannot possibly be wrong.

Fundamentally, Kenny's criteria for foundational propositions or beliefs cannot possibly work, for the general reason that no criteria can possibly be given for *identifying* true statements (or "knowledge"). And since beliefs rest on knowledge (on evidence, or "things we know"), there can be no criterion for guaranteeing credible beliefs (beliefs that could be foundational in the sense that they must be included in one's thought until supplanted by knowledge).

All the talk of "beliefs," of being "foundational," of being "properly foundational" "acceptable" and "acceptable without evidence" remind one of attempts to talk about sex in polite company. Apparently, one can speak of "foundational beliefs" but not knowledge, or truth—just as one can speak of "sleeping with" but not "having intercourse with." Knowledge seems now "the K word"—with a status reminiscent of "the F word." It is as if skepticism had so frightened philosophy that the mind's relation with the world could only be described in a manner unimpeachably behavioral or psychological, a manner that avoided any suggestion of "metaphysics."

Knowledge and "noetic structure"

In keeping with avoidance of terms like "knowledge" and "truth" that raise the specter of metaphysics, Kenny offers an argument for foundational propositions that relies on a rule of reason and (at least on the surface) an argument about the need for an intellectual *structure*—a "noetic" structure of ideas and beliefs and ways of reasoning that constitutes our way of acquiring ideas about the world. (We say "on the surface" because it is not a psychological mind-picture but a *conceptual* one we need not parse to make our points.)

How can it be that "Australia exists" or "humans sleep" are rightly held as basic beliefs and accepted without reasons or evidence? Such so-called "beliefs," are, Kenny says,

> incontrovertible examples of propositions that are rationally believed without evidence, while being neither-self-evident nor

evident to the senses. Some of these, such as the proposition that human beings sleep, are believed without evidence by everybody who believes them; the difficulty of providing evidence for them arises not from their obscurity but from their *obviousness; there is nothing more certain which could be offered in support of them* [emphasis added]. Other propositions, which I instanced . . . by the proposition that there is an Australia, may be believed by some people on the basis of evidence or testimony, but *can rationally be believed by others without evidence, because of the fundamental role they play in an individual's noetic structure* [emphasis added].[203]

By now we are alerted. Kenny says Australia-like propositions use no evidence because of their "obviousness." But "obvious" is plainly another way of saying "evident" or, simply, "known." But for Australia, "obvious" will not do; if its existence had been obvious, exploration would have been unnecessary.

Therefore the only new criteria for properly basic beliefs are two: that "nothing more certain can support them" and "they play a fundamental role in one's noetic structure."

Consider, first, the idea that belief can be foundational if nothing more certain can be offered in support of it.

According to Kenny, this is a rule Aristotle propounded when he said that

"the premises of an informative piece of reasoning had to be 'better known than the conclusion.' So too in my own case: p can only be the reason, or a reason, why I hold q if p is in a more basic position in my noetic structure than q. It is because of this that I maintain that there are no reasons on the basis of which I believe such propositions as that "there is an Australia."[204]

If one knows a thing—if one knows Australia exists—then, of course, no other reasons you could possibly muster "could be offered in support" of what one *already* knows. That would be like looking at your own hand and supporting the proposition that you are looking at it by looking at your other hand—or at a towel . . . or at your face in the mirror. So, once more, a foundational proposition is one you *know*, and that is what entails that nothing can support it, since no case of knowledge is more intellectually compelling than any other.

We come, finally, to noetic structure. "Australia may be believed by some people on the basis of evidence or testimony, but can rationally be believed by others without evidence, because of the fundamental role they play in an individual's noetic structure."

Kenny allows that if he were asked for reasons he could give some: "I have seen the continent on maps," "I have friends who have lived there, I have had letters from there, seen planes depart thither, seen pictures of Australian cities and deserts, drunk Australian wine, seen Australian animals in zoos, and so on."[205] He proceeds to argue that even if all such evidences for belief in Australia "turned out to be false, even if *all* the considerations I could mention proved illusory, much less of my noetic structure would collapse than if it turned out that Australia did not exist."[206] That is: All these evidences, taken together are not more believed by Kenny than "Australia exists."

But, this way of arguing is an example of the (G. E. Moore's) "naturalistic fallacy." For it posits a *factual* structure (not an argument) called a "noetic structure" or "*system* of ideas or propositions" and argues that a belief is foundational (*ought rightly* be held) if it supports more of *the structure*—more of one's other beliefs—than the all the pieces of evidence in support of that belief. But one ought not believe a thing true because believing it supports a system of beliefs—a *psychological* structure. It is an argument that defines right or good belief with belief with factually supportive belief. It is an argument that justifies remaining ignorant.

For example, those who believed the earth flat and those who thought the sun and planets and stars revolved around it could then, *rationally*, have maintained their flat-earth and geocentric beliefs, since less of their noetic structure would have collapsed had they rejected evidence against those beliefs. They could have denied that the top of the mast of an approaching ship is really the first part of the ship to appear—and other arguments such as about the shape of the shadow on the moon, etc.

Kenny's argument from "noetic structure" entails that the more profoundly wrong you are, the more rational it is to remain that way, for less of what you basically believe has to change. And this unacceptable implication results from making a *non*-normative or *factual* criterion—*the maintenance of one's system of beliefs*—a norm of rational belief. (We encountered this when Plantinga turned to such criteria for foundational belief as [the factual]"luminousness").

But Kenny soon abandons "noetic structure" as a criterion. Thus: "Though a belief may be basic for one person and not for another, *there are some beliefs which must be basic for everyone.* Among my basic beliefs is the belief that other human beings sleep. If this is false, then my whole noetic structure collapses," says Kenny—before continuing, immediately, to negate the whole theory of noetic structure and all talk of *belief*, proper or otherwise: "[that other human beings sleep] . . . is something I *know* if I *know* anything at all [emphasis added]."[207] ("Know"—oh dreaded word!)

The needless model of noetic structure and the profoundly misleading talk of belief is again put forward but retracted in the very next sentence:

> This, which I can say of myself, all other sane human beings can say also of themselves. If a belief of this kind were to be mistaken, one's entire noetic structure, including the whole methodology of distinguishing true from false, would completely collapse. If any beliefs deserve to be called *the foundations of knowledge*, these surely do.[208]

But, of course, *no* beliefs can be the foundation of knowledge. "I know that's a storm cloud so I believe it will rain" makes sense. "I believe that's a storm cloud so I know it will rain," does not.

The mind at risk

Kenny's emphasis on noetic structure underplays the metaphysical and epistemological centrality of knowledge—the fact that *knowledge* is one with *mind*. We say this even as we acknowledge that civilized life provides the web of knowledge, belief, and methodologies that make knowledge possible. What F. L. Will refers to as the great array of social practices concerning inquiry and what Kenny has in mind as our "noetic *structure*" is woefully under-appreciated.

But what philosophy resists is direct confrontation with the phenomenon that is knowing, for knowing is what creates not "just" civilization but *another order of being*.

One is supposed to be philosophically embarrassed by saying knowledge is the transforming miracle. And, indeed, one might be, were it not for the fact that so many philosophies have washed up, expired, on the beach of epistemology trying to avoid its mystery.

To illustrate: Kenny's account of knowledge and mind is expressed in his account of the difference in foundational character between knowing there is a fly walking up one's window and knowing there is an Australia.

Kenny argues that "the belief that there is a fly walking up the window pane is basic for me as I write this"—it is manifest to my senses." However, it does not, he continues, "serve as a foundation for any significant part of my noetic structure, and if it turned out false, little damage would be done to the web of my beliefs."[209]

But if Kenny had picked up a magnifying glass and followed the fly up the window, watching its movements, and had opened the window and heard it buzz and saw it land on the window but was told by several family members who were closely watching him and the window that there had never been a fly there, that there was *nothing* on the window, not a raindrop, not a piece of dirt, not a feather—the idea that he had *not* perceived a fly on the window would be as disorienting as being mistaken about Australia.

Perhaps a more persuasive case would be one in which one comes home, hangs one's coat in the closet, and then, looking around, sees oneself standing in the middle of a golf course; a phone call home brings the response that one has not been home today at all.

The point here is that any *bona fide* instance of failed *knowing* (not failed believing) can call into question one's power to know. (Here we must distinguish between "know" loosely used, as in saying "I know this my key!" Oh, wait a minute, no it isn't.")

Anything that we responsibly approach as a matter of knowing would, if it tuned out to be false, put our mind at risk—and with it the noetic structure that mind has developed.

Kenny's emphasis in explaining what makes for a *basic* (foundational) belief has to do with degree of disruption its negation would bring to one's system of rational thought—one's noetic structure or basic perspective.

Kenny says if he were wrong about the fly, "little damage would be done to the web of my beliefs" [but] "propositions which are universally basic are fundamental in a different way, in that they could not be given up without causing havoc in a our noetic structures."[210]

Quoting the twentieth century's most influential philosopher, Ludwig Wittgenstein, Kenny urges the point that foundational propositions are not simply premises from which we deduce other truths; rather, "a proposition such as 'the earth has existed for many years'" has a foundational place; "in the entire system of our language-games it belongs to the foundations. . . . it is the inherited background against which I distinguish true and false."

If I regard some proposition as being at the rock bottom of my conviction, "one might almost say that these foundation walls are carried by the whole house."[211]

The extent of the damage is truly described, but the missing piece is, once again, *knowledge*. For there would be no way to hold, contrary to all we have thought, that the Earth has existed only for a few years, save on the basis of knowledge to that effect.

We differ, then, from Kenny's theory that *some* knowledge is foundational. We say all knowledge is foundational *because nothing else is.* (Even *logical consistency*—the ability to state things in such a way that they *could* be found true, false, relevant, or irrelevant depends on our knowledge of a language).

If we and Kenny were ever to find that Australia's existence was a hoax beyond our wildest imaginings, it could only be on the basis of *knowledge,* however unexpected or astounding.[212] Our noetic structure would have changed, not "collapsed"—save in the tautological sense that we no longer assert the *particulars* that we now deny.

The absolutely basic point is not (as Kenny contends) that if "Australia exists" is false, and if "this is my hand" is false, then we can't know anything, but that it would be self-contradictory ever to say (if—*somehow*—we came to know there is "no Australia" and this is "not my hand") "now we *know* we *cannot* know." That we hadn't really known has to be determined by what we now know. Thus it is our ability to know that is foundational.

Of course, it is *true*, specifically, empirically, that if we are wrong about our hand and about Australia, it is *inconceivable* that we could have knowledge of this. But the reason it is inconceivable is because we know these things. We know we cannot possibly be wrong.

FAITH

"Now faith is the assurance of things hoped for, the conviction of things that are not seen."
—Hebrews 11:1

"One is not a Christian without having faith that certain beliefs are true."
—Kenneth Konyndynk, "Faith and Evidentialism"[213]

"There is hardly a word . . . subject to more misunderstandings . . . and questionable definitions than . . . 'faith.'. . . . Indeeed, one is tempted to suggest that the word "faith" should be dropped completely."
—Paul Tillich, *Dynamics of Faith*[214]

The term *faith* is often used to mean "religion." Islam and Christianity are, in this sense, *faiths*. But this usage is not always fitting.

Indeed it is misleading.

If, by one's "faith," one means the doctrinal and narrative content of a religion, then one refers to what the religion believes to be proper and true. And since the belief *that* something is right or true is an intellectual claim—a truth claim—it must, to be rational, have sufficient grounds and be open to public scrutiny.

But if "faith" means the *manner by which* beliefs come to be held, then the beliefs or "content" of the religion are, explicitly, not held on the basis of evidence. One *resolves* to belief them. They are not advertised as products of intellect or evidence but as the beliefs of "the faithful."

So there is an ambiguity about the status of "beliefs" inherent in using the term *faith* to mean "religion." It may not be too much to say that it affords religious beliefs the cachet of cognitive status (with its implication of having evidential grounds) while retaining the option, when attacked, of declaring them off limits as faith.

In any case, "faiths" suggests a special *way* that beliefs are held. After all, historical explanations are largely, if not entirely, matters of belief, but schools of history are not called "faiths." Even political systems in which people believe are not referred to as "faiths."

But when it comes to *religious* believing, faith, belief, and knowledge are tendentiously conflated. For example the same religions that call themselves "faiths" also claim knowledge of God's existence, when *knowledge* that something exists *precludes* having faith that it exists. (No one would say, "I see it's true and I believe it on faith.")

There is also the matter of effort. Because faith is said to require commitment, the maintenance of faith is considered a religious virtue. But knowledge is not effected by commitment and so cannot be a moral virtue (one does not have it by *resolving* to get it or by believing one has it).

For such reasons as these, it seems important to find solid ground—to consider faith in its standard sense as a kind of *commitment to believe* before appropriating the term for special (here, theological) ends.

The standard or everyday sense of "faith" is not irrelevant to religion, but neither does it mean "religion." If it did, people would not say their religion was a matter of faith, for that would be to say, "my religion is a matter of religion."

Finally, as the writings of Paul Tillich and John Hick testify, the term *faith* has been given specialized definitions within religion.[215] We will not chase all these programmatic definitions. When definitions are so specialized that, in them, faith does not aim at belief, they become irrelevant to the concerns of ordinary people whose concern is whether or not to have faith.

Faith and belief are different ideas

It is true that in the forgiving marketplace of conversational exchanges we will sometimes speak of belief when in fact we mean faith and vice-versa. Yet we all possess an understanding of faith such that we can all distinguish between it and belief. The difference is embedded in our language.

Suppose a woman was asked, "how can you believe your husband is still alive in that awful wreckage?" She might answer, "because I have faith that he is."

But if "faith" meant the same as "belief," her answer would have meant, "I believe he is alive because I have the belief that he is alive." (And we all know that, "I believe it because I have faith that it is so," is not a redundancy.)

The difference between faith and belief—*a difference crucial for religion*—emerges if we now suppose that that the wife loathed her husband.

In that circumstance she would never say, "I have faith that he is still alive." However, if asked what she *believed*, she might well say, "I believe that he is still alive."

From this we see that faith *presupposes* that *its object of belief is hoped for or desired*, while belief has no such presupposition.

Like *trust*—with which religionists sometimes identify it—faith always presupposes that what it believes in is pressingly desirable.[216]

No doubt the devil *trusts* or has *faith* that something evil will happen even as he *believes* God is likely to prevent it. We may *believe* our child will lose a match, but as long as the loss is not certain, we will try to give our child *faith* in a possible win.

So faith and trust differ from belief in that belief presupposes no particular attitude toward the truth of the proposition believed, while faith and trust presuppose a positive attitude toward the truth of the proposition believed.

Faith is the act of believing a proposition one hopes, wants, or needs to be true. Belief is the act of believing a proposition because it is likely true—whether or not its being true is good or bad.

Faith is therefore *tendentious with respect to truth*—a fact guilelessly enshrined in the adage, "faith is the assurance of things hoped for."

Faith as practical

Faith is the resolve to believe what we think we must believe to negotiate the trials and obstacles of living.

This account of faith as a *practical approach to believing* fits the facts. We need no explanation of what a person is trying to accomplish when, facing a necessary operation whose success is *known* improbable, that person says, "I have faith in this surgeon's skill." And we know why the person does not say, "Since success is improbable, I will let myself believe I am likely to die, for after all, that is the only rational approach to believing." Feeling hopeful rather than fearful may improve the person's chances for survival.

Therefore, *before* an operation, there may be *practical* value in believing what is unlikely, and practical disvalue in believing what is likely. *Believing*, considered as a psychological fact, can—like any other factual state (resting, walking, napping) be justified for *practical* rather than intellectual, reasons.

That is how believing can be justified apart from evidence. ("Believe in yourself and you can win!" or "We're the greatest!") One has need or desire to believe a thing. One uses a belief for the *effect* of its content, not the *truth* of its content. And that is why the concept of faith is entirely different from the concept of belief.

The *logic* of the situation is rather like the difference between looking at the painting of a hero so that one will believe one will soon be victorious and looking at the same painting to see whether or not it embodies invincibility and integrity.

The first kind of looking is practical, and is successful if it leads to victory even if the painting is mediocre. But the second is investigative and is successful only if it rightly assesses the evidence of heroic attributes.

The confusion engendered by specialized approaches to "faith" is epitomized in the Catholic approach to faith as described by John Hick in his *Philosophy of Religion*. Hick refers to such faith as "man's obedient acceptance of . . . divinely revealed truths."[217] But if a truth is *revealed* to someone, it is believed because it is *known* to be true and so it *cannot possibly* believed out of "obedience."

Meanwhile, Hick tells us, the, Vatican Council of 1870 defines faith as "a supernatural virtue whereby, inspired and assisted by the grace of God, we believe that things which He has revealed are true."[218] Here it is *not* obedience but the result of God's influence that produces "belief." (Although, again, if things are "revealed" they are known and therefore *cannot* be believed on faith.) But, in either case the belief is not achieved by evidence or argument.

Unfortunately, it seems a theological habit to define what it is to have *faith* in such a way that what is believed on faith achieves the status of *knowledge*—and therefore can be *neither* belief *nor* faith!

For example, (explicating Catholic doctrine), Nicholas Wolterstorff speaks of "that knowledge of God we obtain by faith."[219] If faith in "revelations" yields truth *because* we know that their content (being God's Word) is *true*, then we cannot hold them as either faith or belief. We can only *know* them. (If you *know* you are eating you cannot *believe* you are eating or have *faith* you are eating.)

Thus is faith wrongly assimilated to knowledge—one more lesson in undervaluing the context of daily life and standard usage.

(And, if faith in God is said to be the religious *precondition* for receiving revelation, then faith is not the *basis* of one's convictions regarding revelations—any more than one's theater ticket is the *basis* of one's convictions regarding a play.)

The tendentiousness of faith is implied by the idea that faith is a religious *virtue*. If the *believing* that occurs in *having faith* were not the result of an *elective* act, then believing in God could not be a *virtue*. If the believing, in *faith*, came not out of choice but out of *evidence*, then right or wrong belief would have none of the moral implications that theists commonly assign to it (lack of faith would not deserve eternal punishment).

It is true that one can *find* oneself believing in God (or even in one's future, worldly success) without having *consciously* chosen the belief. But one may or may not *acquiesce* in this belief. One is not powerless critically to reflect on it. One is not helpless before it. To live by it is therefore a *choice*. One is *morally responsible* for holding the belief.

It is true that scientific researchers sometimes have faith in theories for which there is scant, or even countervailing, evidence (Einstein's fruitless search for a unifying theory being a case in point). But, unlike traditional religionists, they do not use faith as the basis or "method" for *concluding* something is true.

Scientific faith in a theory abides by the rational standard that what follows from the theory be true. Therefore the *resolve* to believe in a theory is always conditional upon its consistency with further findings and not just on how much the theory *could* explain *were* it true (how wonderful it would be were it true). Thus, in science, believing, in the end, is never a matter of faith.

The tendentiousness of faith is well understood *when religion is not the subject*. (People viscerally grasp that faith does not begin with the question, "what is true?") In almost all walks of life, beliefs held on faith are suspect. When a parent has faith in a child's innocence, we credit the parent's belief in the child's alibi less, on the whole, than when an investigating officer believes it. When people advise us to buy a car in whose brand name they place much faith, we are appropriately cautious.

In each case, the more powerful the motivation for faith, the more we wonder how carefully the virtues and faults of the belief have been investigated. And this heightened concern for additional assessment exists even when we think that the one who has faith has no *intention* to mislead. Need, desire, and hope skew judgment. "Conflict of interest" laws are rooted in this commonplace knowledge.

Nor do we exempt ourselves. If, shopping for a house, we find what looks like the house of our dreams, we might well consult an expert on structural soundness to keep us from having faith in its structural soundness out of our desire to possess it.

When it is *important* that what we believe be *true*, we well understand the heightened need for independent checks on beliefs we urgently desire to be true.

Faith and religion

Religions understand they cannot be founded on what is false. And if religion cannot be based on what is false—*if* religion requires belief in what is true—then the *fundamental* way of coming to believe cannot be *intrinsically* tendentious. That is, it ought not be founded on faith.

It may seem we impugn the rationality of faith—that we say faith is merely wishful thinking. But the phrase "wishful thinking" presupposes a negative judgment.

It would, for example, be a cruel caricature of the person about to undergo the dangerous operation to say the person's faith in its success was "just wishful thinking." The phrase demeans by suggesting there is no rationality undergirding an act of faith—that its *practical value* must be nil or merely frivolous.

If faith were, inherently, just wishful thinking, it would never command the respect or recognition that in fact it does. This suggests faith is, *in general*, the act of resolving to believe true that which we *justifiably* need or desire to believe true. Indeed, life is fraught with hardship and uncertainty, so that there are likely many times faith can have a justifiable purpose.

There is, as well, a more positive reason. People find themselves unable, by demonstration or clinching argument, to confirm the rightness of actions and to argue for decency and the good in a world of familial and local allegiances that have no *essential* connection with either. Hence (as discussed in Chapter 2), the role of God as guarantor of objectivity and truth.

But this kind of justifiability poses less an *opportunity* for religion than a *danger*. For, religion cannot be pragmatic, and faith is, if we are right, pragmatically justified belief, belief in what "works" for us.

Internal to religion is the notion that God speaks truth. And equally internal to religion is that we must listen to God. But if we believe in that which we desire or that which we think we need, we listen to the source we prefer, that is (in effect) to *ourselves*, not God.

Thus understood, religions, when they are, *literally*, "faiths" have, ironically, the *form* of blasphemy—an unexpected judgment that does not please this writer, since startling conclusions are usually a sign of misguided reasoning. In any event, the reader has the arguments before him or her, and the writer throws himself on the mercy of the court.

Frederick Ferré sees the same pragmatic believing in a positive light. Thus, "the activities of the Church in worship and speech is impelled by man's powerful need to find a place for himself within a coherent concept of the universe which does not violate his deepest sense of value."[220]

But problems abound. A coherent place is not necessarily a true place; and the sense of value that must not be "violated" is in part dependent on the place we *already* take to be ours in the universe and thus cannot be *foundational* for religion (knowledge alone being foundational—not the projection of ourselves on reality or God).

As we write, an Islamic minority finds a coherent place for itself in the universe such that killing infidels is religious. And a minority of well-off American Christians, on the basis of deeply felt views of self and universe, support the Israeli occupation of Palestinian territory, with its consequent endless killings and retributions, so that the Jews may hold Jerusalem and permit the second coming of Christ.

Even if, on the whole, "the masses" needed institutional religion to maintain a workable level of morality, turning to religious persuasion in lieu of moral education and rightly educative institutions is rolling dice with the devil.

If our analysis is correct, religion, like every other attempt at understanding, must be rooted in knowledge, and therefore committed to well-grounded belief, not to faith. If faith *seeks* belief, faith must *value* belief, for it is senseless to pursue something (belief) one thinks of lesser value than what one possesses (faith).

The rationality of faith is thus parasitic on the rationality of belief. When we simply "allow ourselves" to believe or "feel we must" believe, we write a check on the bank of credibility. And if we write checks heedlessly they will soon be worthless. As we have argued, we could gain nothing from *believing* if beliefs *as a rule didn't turn out true*.

Above all, we underline this: faith is not a sub-category of belief. It is not a "form of belief" since it is not a form of truth-finding. It is not an *extension* of belief—not a generous expansion of *belief* from probability to certainty.

Objections to faith as practical: Kenny

The divorce between faith and belief is obscured by the counsels of Anthony Kenny, whose advocacy of "basic beliefs" muddied the waters of the belief-knowledge relation and now muddles the belief-faith relation. The complexities of his approach forbid extensive discussion here. Two points, however:

Kenny tries to defuse our objection to faith as knowledge (wherein we insist it is illegitimate for faith to claim the *intellectual* certainty that belongs only to knowledge).

Hewing to the theory of properly basic beliefs, Kenny says that "fundamental propositions" (basic beliefs) "are all held with a degree of commitment as strong as any knowledge claim could carry with it.[221] "So the beliefs of faith can be as foundational as any belief and as foundational as what we call "knowledge." In fine, Kenny places faith in the same intellectual or cognitive space as belief and knowledge.

The conflation of faith and belief and knowledge is clearer, still, when he declares that "faith, is, by definition, a belief in something *for a particular reason*: namely, that God has revealed it [emphasis added]."[222] First, belief "for a reason" is vague. It could be a *practical* reason or a *cognitive* (truth–dependent) reason. But Kenny throws the definition to the cognitive, treating faith as having a reason—nothing less than that is *God's revelation*. But if God is thought to have *revealed* it, the reason must be considered as *knowledge*—and faith is certainly not belief on the basis of knowledge.

Objections: Tillich

Although Paul Tillich's introduction to his *Dynamics of Faith* tells us "faith" has so many definitions the term is almost hopeless, he nonetheless manages to title sections of his *Dynamics of Faith*, "What Faith is," and "What faith is not."

(The same movement from the surface of language to its depth occurs in William James' *Varieties of Religious Experience*; there James says so many definitions abound, there can be no one definition of religion—proceeding, however, to give fairly specific criteria for what is, or is not, "religious.")

Tillich defines faith as a *concern*, and this seems quite simply, wrong. "Faith is the state of being ultimately concerned."[223] In Tillich's case, however, we take the liberty of seeing something deeper than can be captured by criticizing his use of the term *faith*.

Tillich recognizes the traditional view of faith as elective belief or belief as a matter of will (the will being employed in lieu of adequate evidence for belief). "Faith is understood as an act of knowledge with limited evidence and that the lack of evidence is made up by an act of will."[224]

This "Catholic" idea of faith is "voluntaristic" or will-involved because it begins as *intellectual*, that is, with the idea that something is *true*. Without this idea of a truth, "without a theoretically formulated content the 'will to believe' would be empty. . . . But the content which is meant in the will to believe is given by the *intellect* [emphasis added]."[225]

Tillich rightly criticizes this *intellectual* interpretation of faith, saying "such belief, as the *basis* of the will to believe, is not faith [emphasis added]."[226]

But faith is still a kind of resolve or choosing or willing. Thus, in departing from will and opting for "concern," Tillich campaigns, in our view, for a definition of "faith" that while wrong, eschews the dogmatic and self-serving character of faith in favor of an "open" more fruitful approach to the divine or the deliverances of "God."

Why not call Tillich's "ultimate concern" *faith*?

We think it too far from what "faith" means. To call it "faith" lessens the life-determining seriousness of an ultimate *concern* (which is something to be *pursued* not decided), giving it instead the aura of something that might well be hopefully or opportunely believed.

On the other side of the matter, this book's concern with reality— with the imperatives revealed in experience as independently real, with the awful responsibility of knowing, and the life-robbing horror of living by fictions—is, we think, an "ultimate concern" that does not rest on more ultimate "evidence" and in that respect, at least, is like faith.

The reality of God understood as *the law-giving character of reality* is not something one can stand outside and confirm from a third-person vantage point. It is therefore *understandable* that an ultimate concern with such a God-Reality might be termed a matter of *"faith."* (Recall that evidence, to avoid circularity, would have to come—impossibly—from *outside* normative reality, that is, *independently of* reality or of human experience.)

In our view, Tillich's "ultimate concern" cannot reduce to *faith* in (what we describe as) a law-giving reality (whose laws are discerned through knowing). It emerges, *if answered*, in the form of a *realization* or *insight*, and thus can be *religiously foundational*.

It is closest in character to Kenny's and Plantinga's notion that one can hold a proposition as foundational without *inferring* it from evidence It is *categorically*—not conditionally or probably—true that there is a law-giving reality (for to support it by evidence is to use it to prove itself).

Some will justifiably complain, "well you just *believe* there is a law-giving reality" or "independent imperatives" (the good, the true, and the beautiful)—or perhaps, "you *want* to believe it so it is *faith* (in the sense of "faith" that even Tillich wants to reject).

But by now the reader can see that the whole of this work is devoted to *reminding* us what we say and do and *cannot but* say and do in the corridors of responsible activity. The existence of rationality and sense is not provable by something neither rational nor sensible. A normative reality is evident or there is none—and that is why we lock up people who in "real life" have no realization of the fact. So one is left with the bluntness of the real in which God says, "I am." The goodness of peace and the badness of war are both evident (war, when elected, being at best a "necessary evil")—and no amount of philosophy or religion can help those who do not see it.

Objections: Kierkegaard

We have already discussed Kierkegaard's rejection of cognition or *mind* in favor of believing in a "God-man" (Jesus)—an idea he himself called "insane" and a "leap of faith." The religious center of this faith lay, we argued, in the passion of believing the miraculous—of transcending physical law and the limits of human rationality.

Kierkegaard's flinging of himself over the edge of reason has kinship with Tillich's idea of faith and religion as an *"ultimate concern"* and with our own notion of an ultimate reality of the normative which is akin to tradition's "God." Such ultimate concerns posit ultimate objects that as *ultimate* cannot be confirmed in their properties by independent evidence.

But, against Kierkegaard, neither we, nor Tillich, allow that it makes religious sense not to make sense.

Religion's requirement of mystery, finality, and miracle do not entail self-contradiction. The miraculous and the mysterious are (as we argued) about the emergence, in an otherwise natural (physically determined) world, of beings whose non-natural (undetermined) *perception* of what *ought* to be can change what happens in the (physical) world that gave it life. This, in our view, is the miracle of incarnation in which spirit and body become a single (*human*) being.

Certainly, if mystery, miracle, and finality are internally contradictory or imply that which is impossible, they will have to be given up—and religion with them (save for the poesy of wonder and acceptance).

We are left speculating as to what insights concerning religion may lie beneath the unacceptable self-contradictoriness of Kierkegaard's faith. In any case, the fever of his faith comports in broad outline with the logic of faith as we understand it, namely the *will to believe what we think it desirable be true.*

What Kierkegaard attempted, it seems, was to make the will to believe (faith) purely *religious by* stripping it, entirely, of reason and making it existentially self-sacrificial. His first-person emphasis on confronting Jesus (the God-man) was an attempt, existentially, to realize a uniquely religious stance.

As the visual life is seeing, it seems that for Kierkegaard, the religious life was faith-ing.

One senses this in his confession of faith's enormous effortfulness: "If I wish to preserve myself in faith I must constantly be intent upon holding fast to the objective uncertainty, so as to remain out upon the deep, over seventy thousand fathoms of water, still preserving my faith."[227]

Of great interest to us is Kierkegaard's view that faith is the necessary criterion of a religious attitude. For this is to say religion is a certain viewpoint taken toward existence.

Looked at this way, Kierkegaard might be read as telling us that religious insight is like aesthetic insight and moral insight. Only if one resolves, elects, to look at existence a certain way can its aesthetic or its moral characteristics enter into one's life.

If a person is single-mindedly scientific (as Hume resolved to be when he looked for beauty in a painting), then he will not experience or find or see any aesthetic quality. The same may be said of empiricists like Edwards and Hare who, as scientistically committed thinkers, could perceive or experience no moral realities. (Again, we feel we must insist that if they said, in court, that rape or torture were not in reality wrong, but just thought repugnant by most everyone, they would be regarded as physiologically deficient, as sociopaths.)

Kierkegaard insisted that the religious must be encountered in first-person experience of the miraculous. Speaking of belief in Jesus, he admonished a bookish, philosophical approach:

> It is eighteen hundred years and more since Jesus Christ walked here on earth . . . but . . . a believer must continue to be as contemporary with His presence on earth as were those first contemporaries. This contemporaneousness is the condition of faith, *and more closely defined it is faith* [italics added].[228]

It is in this spirit that we endeavored to put before the reader the baffling fact of knowledge, the inexplicable union of a physical creature with the world through the medium of mind—a union which is at once physical and non-physical and—when confronted squarely for the incredible thing it is—hardly less awesome than confronting God as man.

Indeed, it may be fairly suggested that in seeing *what must be, what could be, and what ought to be* it is we who are God as man, in the Kantian sense that we can perceive and give ourselves the law.

But while we represent "God's humanity," we are not God, for (in keeping with theistic logic), the law we give ourselves is seen within what is not ourselves.

No doubt talk of this kind will either amuse or repel many excellent minds, and rightly where our arguments fail. But what we say about religion's object is, we think, warranted by taking, as foundational, the metaphysics of responsible, civilized life. And if there is anything sacred in the brief life of our race, then the boundary-line or "borderline" rhetoric of religious language seems required to say what must be said.

Indeed, Tillich was never able to satisfy critics with respect to religion's proper object. His definition of it (and faith) as "ultimate concern" seemed psychological, and his insistence on God as the ultimate ground of being, and thus the object of our ultimate concern, never achieved a conceptual wholeness that satisfied critics and inquirers.[229] Language withers at the edge of understanding. But this means inferences from such language must be equally unstable and tentative: call them intimations, suggestions; never orders or doctrines.

Objections: John Henry Newman

The distinction between belief and faith cannot be maintained if all forms of inquiry rest at bottom on faith. Anthony Kenny quotes elements of John Henry Newman's University Sermons (preached before Oxford University in the first half of the nineteenth century) in which a man's faith in Jesus' message is resolved "Because he has a love for it, his love being strong though the testimony is weak. . . . Faith . . . does not demand evidence so strong as is necessary for. . . . belief on the ground of Reason."

But while this small portion of Newman's quite varied arguments comports with the view that faith is a resolve to believe out of desire or need, another of his arguments defends faith along familiar perspectivist lines.

Paraphrased by Kenny, Newman claims that "However systematically we ague on any topic, there must ever be something assumed ultimately which is incapable of proof, and without which our conclusion will be as illogical as faith is apt to seem to men of the world. We trust our sense without proof . . . " (and so on).[230] And, quoting Newman directly, "It may be said that without such assumptions the world could not go on: true, and in the same way the Church could not go on without Faith."[231] (An argument of despair or pragmatic acceptance?)

We saw the same argument from Alan Isaacs when we dealt with skepticism. The problem in this direction, of course, is that if all thought is at bottom a matter of faith—is intellectually unjustifiable—then the faith that there will be no judgment by God is as justifiable as the faith that there will be.

Faith as knowledge

To avoid the inherent conflict between believing on faith while insisting on knowledge (on knowing the truth), John Hick attempts to show that faith is a form of knowledge.

This can only be a case of linguistic politicking, for faith, by definition, is not knowledge—and indeed, involves believing with little or with contrary evidence. As one might suspect, this equivalence will be managed by demoting knowledge rather than by promoting faith.

Hick proposes to analyze "faith" in that "sense or use of the word . . . which occurs when the religious man, and more specifically the Christian believer, speaks of 'knowing God,' and goes on to explain that this is a knowing of God by faith."[232]

But Hick's analysis is not intended to be uniquely theological. It is offered as a "descriptive (or, if you like phenomenological)" analysis that "could be acceptable to both believers and non-believers."[233] "A Christian and an atheist or agnostic should equally be able to say, Yes, that is what, phenomenologically, faith is—though they would of course then go on to say radically different things about its value."

A religious foundation in knowledge is as important for Hick as for Karl Bath:

> Church proclamation is language. . . . which comes forward with the claim to be true and to uphold itself against the lie. . . . You have probably also suffered from a certain kind of preaching and edifying talk . . . which does not however stand up to this simple question as to the truth of what is said. The Christian faith rests upon knowledge.[234]

Hick subdivides knowing or "cognition" into two categories—"cognition in presence and cognition in absence." Faith falls under the first heading; it is a form of "cognition in presence" or "perception."

Hick holds that biblical accounts support the notion that faith is a mode of perceptual knowing. Biblical narratives "confidently presuppose a knowledge of God by acquaintance" while "our theological literature recognizes for the most part only cognition in absence."

This biblical emphasis on knowing God through some sort of perception is said to contrast with Catholic emphasis on faith as belief in the authoritativeness of theological propositions in that

> the Bible itself, and other writings directly expressing the life of faith, are full of men's encounters with God and men's personal dealings with the divine Thou, [but] the dominant systems of Christian theology nevertheless treat faith as belief, as a propositional attitude. . . . Thus faith, instead of being seen as a religious response to God's redemptive action in the life of Jesus of Nazareth, has been seen instead as primarily an assent to theological truths.[235]

Hick's search for uniquely religious knowledge "by acquaintance" finds itself required first to clarify perceptual experience (biblical people having perceived God or known God by acquaintance).

It will have to be less than what it is. That is, perception will have to be re-described so as to more "accurately" reflect what it "*really* is" is to perceive anything visually. Slipping into an observer's or "third person" viewpoint Hick begins an explication of seeing as a sequence of happenings rather than as something we *do*.

He tells us straightaway that "today" it requires no "elaborate argumentation" to hold that "seeing . . . is not a simple straightforward matter of physical objects registering themselves on our retinas and thence in our conscious visual fields."[236] (It will be shown to involve *interpretation*, seeing things as this or that.)

The inadequacy of the retinal-registering view has been amply shown, Hick claims, by Ludwig Wittgenstein in *Philosophical Investigations*. There, Wittgenstein refers to familiar, optically illusory drawings which look to us first one way, then another.

Most readers will have see a line-drawing of a cube which sometimes we seem to be seeing from the top and other times from the bottom. Many have see Kohler's goblet-faces diagram which looks like a goblet standing in the middle of the page but then like two faces in profile looking at each other. So, says Hick, we find in perception "that the mind switches back and forth between the alternate ways of *seeing-as* [emphasis added]."[237]

That is, the events or happenings that take place in visual perceiving when we say "I see" always involve making interpretations of what lies before our eyes. (The case of the optical illusion throws this presumably constant fact of mental processing into high relief.)

Already language has taken a holiday. If we spoke precisely, then instead of saying, "I see my hand" we would say, "I *interpret* what I see before me *as* my hand." But, for Hick, making the interpretive factor *explicit* no longer "misconceives" the nature of "seeing" and (by extension) the nature of all "experiencing." "Let us, he says, "at this point expand the notion of seeing-as into that of experiencing-as."[238]

Before the confusion accumulates unmanageably, the fallacy in this must be brought out. The very act of saying that we see something *as* something *entails* that we do not see it as it *is*. To see a thing *as* something is to see it as something *other than what is seen*. I see the dunce cap as a mountain; I see the bowling alley as a gangplank; I see your face as my grandfather's face.

Once Hick leads us to understand "seeing" or experiencing" as "seeing-as" and "experiencing-as" things as they themselves are become *unknown* because not (simply) *seen* or *experienced*. Instead of "cognition by presence" or biblical "encounters with God," we have "cognition by interpretation" of "what we don't directly see" and biblical encounters not with God but what biblical characters experience-*as* God.

Hick trots out the whole panoply of perspectivism, revisiting Rorty and anthropology to cut *knowing* down to faith-supportive size. Thus: "To recognize or identify [anything at all] is to be experiencing-as in terms of a concept; and our concepts are social products having their life within a particular environment."[239]

Hick acknowledges our complaint that "to recognize" entails seeing a thing as it is, and recognizing-*as* does not.[240] He claims we lack a term to cover cases where we don't know whether there is or is not recognition (and more). But this is nonsense. If "Myrna *recognizes* her coat," then it is her coat. That's what the statement *means*. If we are not sure, then "Myrna thinks she recognizes her coat" or "Myrna perhaps recognizes her coat" or "Myrna recognizes what seems to be her coat," and so on, *ad infinitum*.

No, the English language is not missing a verb. Hick is not, as he claims, therefore "driven to use 'recognition' generically, as 'knowledge,' in 'theory of knowledge' is used to cover error as well as knowledge. . . ."[241]

Indeed, the "theory of knowledge" does *not* mean "the theory of what may or may not be knowledge" (so it could be the theory of belief or the theory of daydreaming or the theory of fancies).

The whole point of Hick's excursion into subjectivist language is to lower the bar for knowledge—or more exactly, to lower the boom. Hick: "The conclusion that *all* experiencing is experiencing-as enables us to meet a fundamental objection between experiencing-as in ordinary life and in religious awareness." That objection rests on the fact that we can see something *as* a rabbit if we are *acquainted* with rabbits, but if we have never seen God, how can we experience something *as* God?[242]

We have already made this argument, above, and Hick admits it might be conclusive except, he says, "we can learn to recognize," that is, "we can learn to *use the concept* 'act of God.' As we learned to use other concepts, and acquire the capacity to recognize exemplifying instances."[243]

But learning to use the *concept* of God only solves the problem of experiencing or recognizing God, if the concept of God (like the concept of "color" or "rabbit") comes into the language *by having encountered* or *experienced* God (as we have encountered or experience colors or rabbits). And the claim to experience God is precisely what is at issue!

If learning to use *a concept* called "God" is all one needs for God to be something known, or to be "cognized by presence" or even have a purchase on reality, then every child that knows how to use the concept *superman* or *the boogie man* has "encountered," as biblical persons are said to have encountered, "God."

Responsible faith

Faith is the great internal contradiction of traditional theism. For a life of faith (based on hope and need) is a life based on what the individual wants to be true, while a genuinely religious life can be founded only on what God wants to be true.[244]

Faith is therefore intellectually or spiritually self-serving, being the expression of what is desired or wished for or needed (no matter how *morally* justifiable the desired content, as in "let me serve others, always"). For traditional religion, the content of faith must in fact be God's decree (or law), not one's own—even if one thinks one's own idea of the good is right.

Nor can faith, like belief, ever be foundational, for both are dependent on the reality of truth and therefore subject to confirmation as truth.

That is why, once faith attaches to particular factual, moral, or religious propositions, it has the proverbial tiger by the tail. Faith that the Earth was created in seven days will in time be brought down by the falsity of the belief it affirms. The idea that God approves of slavery had, similarly, to be given up.

More important, however, from the viewpoint of traditional religions, is that their own statements and behavior belie any claim that what they believe by faith is at bottom anything more than a matter of faith.

Both the leaders and the followers of major religions have disdained, denounced, attacked, and killed not only opponents who stated that some (or all) religious beliefs were false but also those who simply refused to acknowledge they were *true*.

This well-documented intolerance for dissent shows that however much a faith may meet felt needs or express great hopes, the entailment of certain beliefs by that faith inescapably yokes the faithful to the requirement that what is believed be true.

In the words of, John Hick, "If the Christian message presents itself as poetry, or . . . analogous to poetry . . . it will no longer be entitled to be listened to as an alleged news abut a transcendent order of *fact* . . . significant for human life."[245]

And so faith tends, illegitimately, to transmute into knowledge—typically by "God's direct revelation." What is begotten by hope becomes truth without meeting the requirements for claiming truth.

It follows that religious faith must in the end prove true, and this, in turn, means that it cannot—indeed, cannot, because of what religion itself demands—remain belief in isolation from what non-religious inquiry can tell us.

If someone wants to believe that we are not descended from animals, then they want to believe something to which non-religious inquiry has shown indubitably false. The denial of evolution is the hubris of faith above evidence, of desire above truth, or—as we think it better put—of self-satisfaction above God.

Quite simply, *faith, like any other human choice, must be responsible*. And it speaks volumes on the state of religion that this injunction is *entirely absent* from our expressed social and cultural concerns.

If I treat what I *like* to be true as what is *likely* to be true, or as what is *true*, I will be conflating *my desires* for what is *desirable*—with respect to actions, relationships, policies—in short, for what affects my fellow human beings.

In thinking they hear God, faith-based believers treat their own wills as God's will; this, from a religious standpoint is blasphemy.

REVELATION

The theological answer to skepticism is the doctrine of revelation. God's Word is truth. The fallible human mind must therefore know God's Word if it is to have knowledge. A recent book on Karl Barth paraphrased the problem as Barth saw it: "Can we do nothing but give voice to our experience? If so, what help is there for us?"[246]

Barth's answer (as we saw in Chapter 2, "God's Authority") was the revelation of God's Word. Revelation avoided the taint of human fallibility or *mind* because "knowledge of God is a knowledge *completely effected and determined from the side of its object, from the side of God* [emphasis added]."[247]

But of course there was a problem. The Protestant theologian Emil Brunner was well aware of it: "The presupposition of all valid speech or teaching of the Church about God is the self-revelation of God. . . . But there is still a final step to be taken: the question still remains: How can human *doctrine* spring from divine revelation?"[248]

The answer we offered in Chapter 2, "God's Authority" was that immaculate (uninterpreted, unjudged) revelation cannot, *as a matter of logic*, be available to humankind.

The obviousness of the problem was worrisome, since so many brilliant and sincere theologians have not been troubled by it. The point was not that human beings cannot know God's Word or what God intends. Maybe, if miracles occur, they can.[249] The point was that such knowledge must be humanly proclaimed and can be *no more authoritative* than a human mind (which theology itself does not trust).

As for the argument that God has unfathomable ways to inform us, such that we engage in no knowing of our own, we argued that *this* claim, too, is unavoidably a human claim—and so can have no more authority than the human mind can supply.

When the *Catholic Encyclopedia* says, "Revelation may be defined as the communication of some truth by God to a rational creature through means which are beyond the ordinary course of nature" that is a claim, a theory, for which the Catholic Church is responsible and is the authority, not God.

Nothing else is logically possible. *Our* knowledge of God's Word is not *God's* knowledge of God's Word. Whatever we say of God's Word is something for which *we* are responsible. Anything less makes the refusal to accept responsibility for one's claims a necessary condition for religious correctness!

Insofar as the lives of other human beings are affected by claimed revelations—biblical, mystical, or otherwise—the idea that those who announce these revelations and urge that they be acted on *have no responsibility whatever* for them, is simply morally intolerable. (And this we conclude in sorrow when we think of men like Paul Tillich and Karl Barth who drew upon their sense of God's Word to fight tyranny and poverty.)

Revelation through mystical experience

In the revelatory power of its transport, mystical experience seems akin to aesthetic and sexual experience. But whatever neighborhood it occupies, mystical experience stands as a citadel of religious truth, deflecting questions from anyr realm of intellect. Whether challenges are scientific, philosophic, psychological, logical, or theological, it matters not. All are useless. What mystical experience reveals cannot possibly be false and the way it shows truth cannot possibly be described. Or so its advocates say:

> We are rejecting logical argument of any kind as the first chapter of our theology or as representing the process by which God comes to be known. We are holding that our knowledge of God rests rather on the revelation of His personal Presence as Father, Son, and Holy Spirit. . . . Of such a Presence it must be true that to those who have never been confronted with it, argument is useless, while to those that have it it is superfluous.[250]

Mystical knowledge of God, moreover, is "like our knowledge of tri-dimensional space, and all other primary modes of knowledge, something that cannot be imagined by one who does not already possess it, since it cannot be described . . . in terms of anything else than itself."[251]

> It will not be possible to describe the compelling touch of God otherwise than as the compelling touch of God. To anyone who has no such awareness of God . . . it will be quite impossible to indicate what is *meant* one can only hope to evoke it, on the assumption that the capacity to become aware of God is part of normal human nature like the capacity to see light or to hear sound.[252]

Not only is mystical revelation self-contained and its content evidently true, but it is "ineffable." That is, it cannot be described: "mystical experiences, unlike all other types of experience, are completely ineffable, or non-conceptualizable."[253]

Let us take up, first, the claim of "ineffability"—the idea that mystical experience is uniquely indescribable. This claim of unique ineffability is indefensible.

In fact, ineffability is claimed for many types of experience. Haven't we heard, or ourselves said, "if you haven't experienced love, no one can describe it to you," or "if you haven't experienced the wonder of wilderness, there's no use trying to explain it to you" or "only if you have experienced beauty can you know what beauty is?"

And don't we think that if people cannot experience color there's no way to describe color to them? So the fact that mystics say mystical experiences "can't be described," doesn't in itself suggest that mystical experiences are *in principle* conceptually distinct from other, non-mystical experiences.

In addition, the many experiences we say "can't be described" are in fact described by us quite often and by some of us quite well.

Indeed, the special virtue of poetry lies precisely in describing such "indescribables" as love, compassion, beauty, color, and music—and even mystical experience itself—as we can see in this passage from Saint John of the Cross:

> In this knowledge, since the senses and the imagination are not employed, we get neither form nor impression, nor can we give any account or furnish any likeness, although the mysterious and sweet-tasting wisdom comes home so clearly to the inmost parts of our soul.[254]

So, we know that *wisdom* is part of the content of this putatively *indescribable* experience, and that the wisdom is pleasing (sweet-tasting) to hear and that it is not about finance or carpentry but about topics that relate to "the soul."

But the claim of ineffability is problematic also, in that it has religious, and eventually, moral implications. If mystical experiences had no implications for religion, they would be nothing more than excitements. They would be of no religious importance.

And if mystical experiences have implications, then they cannot possibly be *conceptually empty*. They must present standards or propositions or imperatives. Saint Theresa was strengthened in her religious beliefs by mystical experiences, as was St. John of the cross. But how is this so if what they experienced was conceptually empty?

It is perhaps instructive here to recall the empiricists' problem with "sensations." The reason Locke and Hume and the Greek skeptics could not attest to the existence of an external world was because sensations are without concepts—they have nothing to do with *ideas*; they are brute happenings and therefore can imply nothing at all.

If mystical experiences are like looking at a color or having an aesthetic feeling—and are therefore, simply, sensations of a certain "feel"—then they cannot possibly confirm or disconfirm, direct or re-strain, the mystic's thought or action. Being without any proposi-tional or conceptual content, they can have no implications—for reli-gion of anything else.

But, if, for whatever reason, they *do* have implications, then they are open to critical evaluation. For the ideas or events or actions they *imply* are not *themselves* mystical experiences. They are open to inves-tigation. And if something entails something else which is false, then that thing cannot be true.

This means that mystical experiences are not immune to inquiry, even though—like someone's experiencing of color or of love or of beauty—they cannot be inquired into *directly*. Once cannot experi-ence someone else's experience, but since this is true of all human ex-perience, it obviously does not prevent us from discussing the same issues and having the same subject matters into which we may jointly inquire.

The attempts to sequester the implications of mystical experience from critical inquiry by such claims as that "to those who have never been confronted with it, argument is useless, while to those that have it, it is superfluous" and that it "cannot be imagined by one who does not already possess it, since it cannot be described to him in term of anything else than itself" are, likewise, fallacious.

For what is said is *true of all experiences*: the experiencing of color, love, brightness, darkness, lyricism, beauty, moral obligation, and of course *knowing*, to name several of several million. One who has never known anything, seen any color, felt any love, experienced any brightness—and so on—cannot be enlightened as to what these things are by *an argument*, nor can such things be *imagined*, since they, *no less than* mystical experience, "cannot be described to him in term of anything else than itself."

What is curious, indeed, about the comparison of mystical expe-rience of God (or any experience of God) with our experience of color or light or beauty (and so on) is how *utterly unlike* our primary knowledge of light, color, sound, three-dimensional space, or other minds is our experience of God—or any other of the objects sought by mystical engagement, such as a Hidden Reality, The Spirit of Nature, Complete Union with What Is, and so on.

No sane person doubts the existence of light, color, sound, space, or other minds. But many sane people doubt the existence of God.

And many, having experienced what they took to be God, have later changed their minds as to what it was they experienced. And this is no small matter. For no one, having experienced light, color, love, or aesthetic characteristics, ever changes one's mind as to the reality of the content of these experiences, or their status as "basic" or "primary" modes of knowing.

Moreover, anyone who cannot experience space, light, color, sound, or other minds is considered impaired, either physiologically or psychologically. Indeed, the inability to experience these "primary" modes of knowing is paradigmatic of "impairment."

"Color-blindness," "deafness," and "brain damage" are the operative diagnoses. But few are those who regard a failure to experience God or Transcendent Unity as impairment.

God-blindness or transcendental deprivation are non-existent diagnostic categories both popularly and academically.

Finally, traditional Judeo-Christian and Islamic religionists have in the main argued that God will punish or at least not reward nonbelievers. But *if the inability to experience God were truly analogous to the inability to experience sound or color or space or other minds, then it could not be the fault of those who do not experience God that they do not.*

Since—if God is just—people who never experience God or have God revealed to them would never be punished, then either God is held to punish the impaired for their impairment (God is unjust), or mystical experience of God is not a "primary mode" or "basic way" of knowing but the fruit of a freely chosen effort.

Insofar as "revelation" is understood to mean knowledge ineffably given, the doctrine is insupportable.

Revelation and discrimination

The idea that God speaks to us would be more plausible, in our view, if God spoke to all of us.

Somehow, it is supposed, God speaks only to an extraordinarily limited number of us. Even Protestantism cites a Bible whose inspired creation was not a worldwide phenomenon.

(The latter point cannot be explained as flowing from the limits of literacy, since, if the message was, in truth, *essential* both to a good life and to eternal life, God could have made everyone literate. Such an act would have been no more miraculous than enabling simple people to write a record of religious and moral truths.)

It may be claimed that only those sufficiently pure of heart are vouchsafed God's direct address. But then, the unclean are those most needy of hearing God in the indubitable way that God purportedly addresses those who claim to have heard him.

Of course there is always the "argument" that God has his reasons—and that his reasons are unfathomable to us.

But remarkably, those who use this argument do not keep silent about the statements or communications of a Being whose reasons they "cannot possibly understand."

Are God's communications instances of testing, playing, torturing, teaching, telling, ordering? *One cannot understand a communication's import without knowing the reasons behind it.* (One who denies this may someday leap on the stage to pummel an adult actor who bullies a juvenile actor.)

So, although God's Word is said to be what it is for unknowable reasons, those who use the "He has his reasons" argument as explanation or defense seem, nonetheless, to know enough of God's reasons to construct a life around their interpretation of his word—and to urge (or compel) others to do the same. Moreover, it is hard to make sense of the idea that God has his (unknowable) reasons since not knowing God's "mind" it cannot be known by humans that God has "reasons" at all.

We cannot address all the counter-arguments. (We refer to such arguments as that God informs a few to test the desire of everyone else to know him—an argument so cruel it is hard even to recount it.)

What we suggest is that there can be found no good reason why God could not speak his word directly to the members of each generation. Then, surely, each human being would have a fair and equal chance to follow God's Word, and the failure of any could not be excused by the conditions of his or her background.

This is not to "presume to speak for God." It is only to infer from the claimed absolute goodness of God what might reasonably be done consistently with the absolute goodness *attributed* to God. On that basis, it is hard to see why God would discriminate against tribes living out of the mainstream, or against illiterate peoples, or those who are already self-centered or heedless.

The morality of the situation is familiar. If a teacher helps one, but not another, the teacher needs a very good reason to avoid the charge of unethical (indeed, unloving) behavior.

In sum, the idea of revelation as it has historically emerged seems seriously inconsistent with the notion that God loves us, or is good, and is all-powerful. For it is not what good teachers or parents would do to bring their word to some, but not all, their children—and, in the bargain, bring it *so unclearly* that its content would be endlessly disputed by those who received it.

The counter is that God's Word comes to all, as, perhaps, "conscience" or in answer to prayers for guidance. Thus it is humanity's fault for not understanding God's Word.

But this is awkward, indeed, when one considers that God is the all-powerful teacher or communicator yet is somehow unable to formulate a message that cannot be mistaken.

Nor can it be argued, against the latter point, that to protect our free will it must be possible that when God tells us or attempts to persuade us of something, *it must be the case* that some (perhaps many) will refuse to attend to or comply with God's message.

For if someone is successfully persuaded that something is true or good or right, we neither conclude, nor commonly suspect, that their free will must have been violated or suspended. So successful persuasion—even universally successful persuasion—is consistent with the free will of the persuaded. (Surely no theologian will argue that God can fail to be successfully persuasive.)

Knowledge as revelation

It seems clear that where there is knowledge there can be no conflict with God's Word as traditionally understood. Furthermore, the fact that knowledge "appears" in the universe—that it appears in evolved animals become, by virtue of that knowledge, "human"—is as unfathomable, as monumental, as miraculous as any voice in the ear of Mohammed or Moses or Saint John of the Cross.

We find in this incarnation of truth, this *understanding* of what reality permits, demands, and enables, an analogue—if not an analysis—of what Brunner describes as that "toward which all the teaching and witness of [the New Testament's] original witness is directed," namely, "the Word become flesh."[255]

We have striven concretely to argue that knowledge is a metaphysical bafflement of fundamental religious significance.

And while, in the nature of the case, neither we nor anyone can give evidence that we *know* what we *know* (it being an absurdly circular project), we have pointed out that the mere fact of rational discourse on the subject presupposes the existence of knowledge. Moreover, it is impossible to argue against the rationality of discourse since any such argument is itself a rational discourse. Therefore the *philosophical* basis for claiming that knowledge exists does not require a separate (and therefore circular) claim of knowledge.

By contrast, the idea of revelation does exactly that, claiming to have *knowledge* because God grants us knowledge. This, we found unconvincing: It founds its explanation on an explanatory force or entity—God—that the explainers themselves find more unfathomable than what it (God) purports to explain. And, last but hardly least, it claims knowledge in order to claim knowledge.

Revelation as openness

Whether one looks at knowing from the theistic viewpoint or the one advanced here, there is an emphasis on reception. One must be open to what is. This is a requirement, not a method. We do not suggest that knowledge is gained passively. Being open is being ready to receive, and one need only step into a lecture on string theory to know one is not "ready to receive" without having engaged in an enormous amount of active inquiry.

Perhaps, having said so much about faith as will, and having now emphasized openness, the best thing we can do is let the art historian, Edgar Wind, say something about the latter virtue:

> In turning to the experience of art, we may find that here the role of the will is exactly the same as in the pursuit of knowledge. Whether we go to the theatre or not, depends on our will; and whether on leaving the theatre we declare our feelings about the play ... these are matters in which our will is involved. However, in the presence of the play itself, our response would not be genuine and right unless our will were temporarily suspended. Persons who can never forget what they want, and exert their own will in the presence of a work of art, are debarred from authentic artistic experience. The work of art, no less than a truth, demands a genuine and complete oblivion of the self.[256]

Revelation and reality

But what is it we are open to when we know? What is "out there" to be known, indeed, what is it for something to *be* out there, to be "real?" We have focused on the knower and on the known only insofar as critics of knowledge have by implication or direct statement tailored reality to meet their epistemological theories. The time has come to discuss what it is that, from outside us, creates us what we are. It is the very structure and substance of things independent. It is what Baruch Spinoza called "God."

NOTES

1. Frederick L. Will, *Pragmatism and Realism*, ed. Kenneth R. Westphal (New York: Rowman and Littlefield Publishers, Inc., 1997) p. 37.

2. Ibid.

3. The idea of an "independent" reality is, these days, anathema; we discuss it later. The philosophical reader may, here, recall Spinoza's "God"; but his God or reality was *physical determined*.

4. We have in Chapter 2 examined feeling as implying mind; later, in discussing the fields of morality and aesthetics we will maintain that mind re-

quires feelings for truth.

5. This follows Ch. 2, where feeling depends on idea, e.g., creating profound or superficial feeling.

6. This view departs from most philosophy in seeing the mind-body problem not as a false problem but as a genuine confrontation of unlike substances whose degree of unification is presupposed in any action that correctly claims to be based on reasons and is chosen not caused; we say, in effect, it is a miracle that a system of molecular causes can formulate an uncaused molecular theory.

7. See Kenneth Hamilton, *The Promise of Kiekegaard* (Philadelphia: J. B. Lippincott Company, 1969), p. 56; Kierkegaard, the believer, admits Christ as "God-man" to be "humanly speaking . . . an insane combination."

8. This is not an oxymoron. If God visibly healed someone every day, the act would miraculous and commonplace.

9. Yes, there are mystical views which say all is illusion, but none of their proponents think they are talking to no one or do not know whether they are meditating or drinking Coca-Cola.

10. We understand that not every use of "knowledge" is quite serious. All statements in a "Book of Knowledge" sold door to door are not expected to be infallibly true. But there would be no skeptics if knowledge did not centrally mean a witting grasp of things such that what is grasped cannot possibly be wrong.

11. The view of certain "conventionalist" philosophers. See Leszek Kolakowski, *The Alienationof Reason* (New York: Doubleday & Company, Inc., Anchor Books,1969; orig. pub. Poland, 1966), pp. 129-30.

12. Knowledge as "justified *true* belief" will be considered later.

13. The complexity of "rationality," its rootedness in the life of feeling and active experience, is developed in a major and comprehensive way in Frederick Will's *Pragmatism and Realism*.

14. F. L. Will, *Pragmatism and Realism*, p. 65.

15. See Ch. 2, "Skepticism and Scientism vs the Person."

16. Paul Tillich, *My Search for Absolutes* (New York: Simon and Schuster, Inc.; a Touchstone Book, 1967), p. 64.

17. There is a certain irony in the support by modern empiricisms of medieval claims regarding a "finite," self-deceptive human mind.

18. The power of unnoticed learning is referred to in educational circles as "concomitant" learning. Its power is acknowledged when parents demand, in frustration, "do as I say, not as I do."

19. We begin with empiricism's simplest form, though we think it represents the spirit of all later forms.

20. The reader should know that the most complete, brilliant, and amusing critique of the British empirical tradition—the empiricist understanding of terms like "appearances" or "sensations"—is to be found in a brief, eminently readable book by J. L. Austin (entitled, with characteristic Austinian wit, *Sense and Sensibilia*).

21. John Locke, *Essay Concerning Human Understanding*, Book IV.

22. David Hume, *A Treatise of Human Nature* (1739), Book III, Section VI.

23. Long, *Hellenistic Philosophy*, 2nd. ed. (Berkeley: University of California Press, 1986), pp. 81-82.

24. Ibid., p. 83.

25. We cannot do justice to Kant's struggle here. See, for example Roger Scruton, *Kant* (Oxford: Oxford University Press, 1982), pp. 32ff.; and Immanuel Kant, *Critique of Pure Reason*, 2nd. ed., trans. Norman Kemp-Smith (Hampshire, UK: Palgrave Macmillan, 1920) ,p. 275.

26. Kolakowski, *The Alienation of Reason*, pp. 114-117.

27. In fact, into *all* subjects, as, for example, natural science, aesthetics, and religion.

28. Hume seems to have thought he could start from the premises of Hellenic skepticism and not himself end as a skeptic!

29. Hume, *A Treatise of Human Nature*, Part I, Section I, "Of the Origin of Our Ideas."

30. In the words of Polish philosopher Leszek Kolakowski: "Intended to provide science with unshakeable foundations, Hume's analysis deprived it of any possible foundation." Leszek Kolakowski, *The Alienation of Reason*, trans. Norbert Guterman (Garden City, N.Y.: Anchor Books/ Doubleday & Company, Inc., 1969), p. 38.

31. Ibid., Part III, Section II

32. Ibid., Part III, Section XIV.

33. Kolakowski, p. 132.

34. Ibid.

35. William James, *Pragmatism* (New York: Longmans, Green and Co., 1949) p. 57. (We note that if, in the end, only truth can "satisfy" us, any talk of "satisfactory relations" will return us to *intellectual* justification, thus negating any difference between truth-seeking and pragmatic satisfactions.)

36. Kolakowski, pp. 134-135.

37. The Crosman and the Fish excerpts are found in John M. Ellis, *Against Deconstruction*, pp. 116-117.

38. These "evolutionary" explanations of our judgments are akin pragmatic redefinitions of truth.

39. Kai Nielsen, *After the Demise of the Tradition: Rorty. Critical Theory, and the Fate of Philosophy* (Boulder, Colo.: Westview Press, 1991), p. 57.

40. Alan Isaacs, *The Survival of God in a Scientific Age* (Baltimore: Penguin Books, 1968) p. 169.

41. In *New Studies in Berkeley's Philosophy*, ed. Warren E. Steinkraus (New York: Holt, Rinehart and Winston, Inc., 1966), p. 47.

42. Donald Fiske and Richard Shweder, eds. *Metatheory*, p.173. For a difficult but trenchant critique of Kuhn, see Frederick L. Will, *Pragmatism and Realism*, essay 4, "The Rational Governance of Practice," esp. p. 71.

43. Ibid., p. 173.

44. Ibid.

45. How many times has the reader heard or read that "reporters never report" because they are always selective or simply, "human."

46. 48. Friedrich Nietzsche, *Beyond Good and Evil.* trans. Walter Kaufman (New York: Random House, Inc. Vintage Books, 1966), p. 16.

47. See John Richardson, *Nietzsche's System* (New York: Oxford University Press, 1996), p. 230. "Nietzsche is very seldom satisfied with . . . doubt] . . . that attacks the truth of our beliefs. . . . he says not that our beliefs might be false, but that they are."

48. Nietzsche, *Beyond Good and Evil*, p. 11.

49. Friedrich Nietzsche, *The Will to Power*, trans. Kaufman and Hollingdale (New York: Viking Press, 1968), p.522.

50. Richardson, p. 228.

51. Edward Sapir, "Linguistics as a Science," *Language* 5.4 (Dec. 1929), pp. 207-214.

52. Richardson, p. 225.

53. Richard Rorty, *Objectivity, Relativism and Truth* (Cambridge: Cambridge University Press. 1991) pp. 148-9.

54. Norman Geras, *Solidarity in the Conversation of Humankind: The Ungroundable Liberalism of Richard Rorty* (London: Verso Publishing, 1995), p. 111,

55. Ibid.

56. Richard Rorty, *Contingency, Irony and Solidarity* (Cambridge: Cambridge University Press, 1989), p. 5.

57. Ibid., p. 6. Rorty's view is akin to Kuhn's which said basic changes in physics are not driven by truths but by changes in the outlook of physicists.

58. Ibid.

59. Ibid., p. 6.

60. Ibid., p. 7.

61. Ibid., p. 5.

62. Ibid., p. 48.

63. Ibid., p. 49.

64. Ibid., p. 48.

65. As we shall see, the same is said of evaulative terms like "good" and "ought" in moral skepticism.

66. Rorty, *Contingency*, p. 8.

67. For an extensive discussion favoring the reality of the good, see Robert Peter Sylvester, in *The Moral Philosophy of G. E. Moore,* ed. Ray Jenkins Jr. and R. W. Sleeper (Philadelphia: Temple University Press, 1990), especially pp. 131ff.

68. We omit idealist (non-empiricist) conceptions such as Bradley's "self-realization" (F. H. Bradley, *Ethical Studies*) because they covertly made use of "good" when they defined, say, "realization," to differentiate it from mere factual change.

69. Mill did not always hold to this simple definition as chapter 2, "God's Meaning" points out.

70. For a detailed discussion of the naturalistic fallacy, see Robert Peter Sylvester, *The Moral Philosophy of G.E. Moore* (Philadelphia: Temple University Press, 1990), pp. 158-68.

71. The example is drawn from Robert Peter Sylvester, *The Moral Philosophy of G. E. Moore*, p. 135.

72. Sylvester, *The Moral Philosophy of G.E. Moore*, pp. 138-40.

73. David Hume, *Treatise of Human Nature*, Book III, Part I, section I in *Hume's Moral and Political Philosophy*, ed. Henry D. Aiken (New York: Hafner Publishing Company, 1948).

74. Peter Conradi and Iris Murdoch, eds., *Existentialists and Mystics* (New York: Penguin Books, 1997), p. 380.

75. G. E. Moore, *Ethics* (New York: Oxford University Press, 1965; orig. pub. 1912), p.43.

76. Simon Blackburn, *Truth: a Guide*, p. 43.

77. For an intelligible account of Stevenson's (and A. J. Ayer's) emotivist theory see Mary Warnock, *Ethics Since 1900* (Oxford: Oxford University Press, 1960) chapter four, "The Emotive Theory," esp. pp. 92-106, since those pages also include a reference to A. J. Ayer's (early form of) emotivism.

78. Mary Warnock, *Ethics Since 1900*, p. 92.

79. Paul Edwards, *The Logic of Moral Discourse* (New York: The Free Press, 1955), p. 221.

80. Ibid. p. 221.

81. Edwards analyzes "ought" in the same way: the statement that "a euthanasia bill *ought* to be passed" is analyzed into this "objective" statement: "If euthanasia is legalized . . . suffering . . . will cease . . . without bringing about further suffering." (Edwards, p. 216).

82. Ibid., p. 211.

83. Ibid.

84. Ibid., p. 189.

85. Ibid.

86. Ibid., p.189.

87. Ibid., p. 221.

88. R. M. Hare, *The Language of Morals* (New York: Oxford University Press, 1964; orig. pub. 1952), p. 1.

89. Ibid., p. 15.

90. Hare does affirm the intertwining of description and evaluation in the vast sea of terms like "tyranny" or "courage" that indicate factual behavior and evaluate it at the same time. But this is like the intertwining of an telephone cable with the current it carries; they remain two functionally different things

91. Ibid., p. 164.

92. Ibid., p. 195.

93. Ibid., p. 165.

94. Ibid.

95. Ibid., p. 146.

96. Ibid., p. 91. This logical point is Hare's version of Moore's "naturalistic fallacy"; "good" can't be defined by physical or psychological properties *only because* "good" *commends*—it doesn't *refer* at all. (Moore thought "good" *did* refer but to a special, non-natural property of "good.")

97. Ibid., p. 149.

98. Ibid., pp. 95-6.

99. Ibid., p. 103; see ch. 6, "Meaning and Criteria" on this issue.

100. Ibid., p. 130.

101. Ibid., *The Language of Morals*, p. 146.

102. George I. Mavrodes, "Religion and the Queerness of Morality" in Robert Audi and William J. Wainright, *Rationality, Religious Belief, and Moral Commitment* (Ithaca: Cornell University Press, 1986), p. 216 (see the entire article for a discussion of the conflict between an empirical reality and a moral reality).

103. George I. Mavrodes, "Religion and the Queerness of Morality," p. 226.

104. Hare, *The Language of Morals*, p. 164.

105. Ibid., pp. 168-169.

106. Ibid., pp. 168-169.

107. Ibid., p. 55.

108. Ch. 2 argued that the will of God cannot explain moral obligation; it makes being a *person* impossible.

109. Students of philosophy may sense our implicit contention, that terms like "ought" and "should" when used to make moral statements, are simply not *definable* in any informative way, They cannot be analyzed into parts (like "imperatives" and "rules") and retain their specifically moral implications (meanings).

110. We understand this view opens the door to fabulists; but so does freedom of speech.

111. Sally Quinn, "The Least Immoral Choice," Op Ed, *The Washington Post,* January 9, 2007.

112. There is surely an irony here, the irony that skeptical theories drive us toward seeking help from the least empirical, least skeptical domain, namely religion.

113. Hare, p. 69.

114. Ibid.

115. Ibid.

116. Ibid.

117. Bernard Williams, *Ethics and the Limits of Philosophy* (Cambridge, Mass.: Harvard University Press, 1985), pp. 82-89.

118. The idea that rationality is far broader than deductive reasoning is a central theme in Frederick L. Will's later essays. These are collected in Kenneth R. Westphal, ed., *Pragmatism and Realism* New York: (Rowman & Littlefield Publishers, Inc., 1997). See esp. Chapter 4, "The Rational Governance of Practice" and Chapter 5, "Reason, Social Practice and Scientific Realism."

119. Hare, p. 1.

120. John R. Searle, *Mind, Language, and Society* (New York: Basic Books, 1998), pp. 28-29.

121. See, for example, in Robert P. Sylvester, *The Moral Philosophy of G. E.Moore*, p. 64, Moore's point that "concepts (logical ideas) are what we properly make use of in judgments, *not* psychological ideas."

122. Which is why we so often rail against *identifying* mind with psychological events. *Identifying* aside, we agree that much thinking is in fact shaped or "over-determined" by psychological forces.

123. Cannot be deduced from "initial conditions" of the brain and covering "psychological" or "physiological laws (as a projectile's trajectory can be deduced from initial conditions and laws like the law of gravity).

124. The conditions necessary and perhaps sufficient for the emergence of witting rationality might be specifiable, but would no more "explain" it than an explanation of they way light waves reach our eyes can explain the aesthetic character of a painting.

125. "Free" as "uncoerced" (by someone or some group) is about political or social freedom, not "freedom of the will." No one is less free than an uncoerced, thoroughly indoctrinated, happy, cult member.

126. See for example, Brand Blanshard, "The Case for Determinism," pp. 19-30, in *Determinism and Freedom,* ed. Sidney Hooke (New York: Collier Books, 1961) or Philipa Foot, "Free Will as Involving Determinism," pp. 71-

80, in *Free Will*, ed. Sidney Morganbesser and James Walsh (Englewood Cliffs, N.J.: Prentice-Hall, Inc. , 1962).

127. J. L. Austin, "If's and Can's" in *Philosophical Papers*, ed. J. O. Urmson and Geoffrey Warnock (London: Oxford University Press, 1961).

128. Sam Harris, *The End of Faith* (New York: W. W. Norton & Company, 2004), p. 273.

129. Ibid., p. 273.

130. Ibid., p. 274.

131. This is the same tactic used by the unnamed protagonist in Dostoevsky's novel, *Notes from Underground*, in which the central character makes unpredictable choices for the purpose of showing he is free.

132. Immanuel Kant, *Groundwork of the Metaphysic of Morals*, trans. H. J. Paton (New York: Harper & Row, 1964), p. 114.

133. John 8:31-32.

134. This is what troubled Sam Harris.

135. Kant, *Groundwork of the Metaphysic of Morals*, p. 126; see especially pp. 125-6.

136. Iris Murdoch, "Metaphysics and Ethics," *Existentialists and Mystics*, ed. Iris Murdoch and Peter Conradi (New York: Penguin Putnam Inc., 1998), p. 65.

137. The idea that physical laws can have exceptions yet be laws is propounded by Roger Scruton in *The Intelligent Person's Guide to Philosophy*, (New York: Penhuin Books, 1999), pp. 97-98; we deal with this in Chapter 4.

138. C. S. Lewis, *Miracles* (New York: Macmillan Publishing Co., Inc., 1960 [orig. pub. 1947]), p. 46.

139. Ibid., p. 47.

140. Ibid., p. 48. See also p. 102: miracles are the most "improbable" events.

141. Ibid., pp. 48, 58-59, 101.

142. Ibid., p. 62.

143. Ibid., *ch.* 4, "Nature and Supernature," pp. 25ff.

144. Ibid., p. 35.

145. Ibid., ch. 4, "Nature and Supernature." pp. 25ff.

146. Ibid., p. 28.

147. Jerome. B. Schneewind, *Moral Philosophy from Montaigne to Kant* (Cambridge, UK: Cambridge University Press, 2003), p. 8.

148. Lewis, p. 98.

149. Richard Purtill, *Thinking About Religion* (Englewood Cliffs, N.J.: Prentice-Hall, Inc. 1978) p. 79.

150. Whether our view of knowledge as miraculous is implicitly self-contradictory we leave for Chapter 4.

151. Søren Kierkegaard, *Training in Christianity*, as quoted in Kenneth Hamilton, *The Promise of Kierkegaard* (Philadelphia: J. B. Lippincott Company, 1969).

152. William James considered a kind of knowing acceptance of life to be the *religious* attitude.

153. We have previously remarked on the covert narcissism of those who think that if they inflict pain and suffering on themselves they are not according themselves prime importance; but in finding salvation in their own, particular pain, they are.

154. The argument is recounted in George Chatalian, *Epistemology and Skepticism: An Enquiry into the Nature of Epistemology* (Carbondale, Ill.: Southern Illinois University Press, 1991), p. 23.

155. And saying we are genetically "programmed" for knowledge is a claim that rests on knowledge.

156. John Dewey, *Logic: The Theory of Inquiry* (New York: Henry Holt and Company, 1938), p. 66.

157. Frederick L. Will, *Pragmatism and Realism*, pp. 99-100; see especially p. 103.

158. So, the failure to find foundations should never have cast doubt on its existence.

159. It may even be the case that the word *is* could not arise without knowledge of factual existence.

160. Will, *Pragmatism and Realism*, pp. 1-19.

161. Ibid., p. 14.

162. Ibid., p. 9.

163. Ibid., p. 18.

164. The reader may recall the "garden path" in which "seeing" was stripped of knowledge by reducing it to physiological facts—the outcome being that one could see nothing at all!

165. Will, p. 19.

166. It is interesting, we think, that a reality looked at with no interpretation or surmise at all would be, if one could "see" it nothing other than a Humean "impression"—a blank, brute *sensation*. So early empiricism lives beneath perspectivist "conceptual" skepticism.

167. E. O. Wilson, The Biological Basis of Morality," *The Atlantic Monthly* 281.4 (April 1998), 53-70, 57.

168. Rene Descartes, *Discourse on Method*, trans. Arthur Wollaston (Baltimore: Penguin Books, 1960), p. 61.

169. Perhaps the most generally unappreciated contribution to the theory of knowledge is John Dewey's explication of "the situation." See his *Logic: The Theory of Inquiry*.

170. Will, p. 148.

171. David Hume, *A Treatise of Human Nature*, Part IV, Sect. II in Robert Paul Wolff, ed. *The Essential David Hume* (New York: The New American Library; a Mentor Book, 1969, p. 105. See also an extended discussion of the conflict between Reason and ordinary life experience in Part IV, Section VII of the Treatise, "Conclusion of This Book."

172. Norman Geras, *Solidarity in the Conversation of Humankind: The Ungroundable Liberalism of Richard Rorty* (London: Verso Publishing, 1995), p. 111.

173. Norman Geras, *loc. cit.*

174. Or only tentative—and for the same reasons we now offer.

175. Believing that something is likely makes no difference. It has to be *true* that it is likely.

176. One is reminded of deconstructionists writing texts on deconstruction that claim texts have no meaning that can be called their own.

177. See the section "Faith."

178. No *behavioral* distinction can be made between real and "brainwashed" or "indoctrinated" belief since the latter can last as long or longer

than the former.

179. Alvin Plantinga, "Rationality and Religious Belief," in *Contemporary Philosophy of Religion*, ed. Steven M. Cahn and David Shatz (Oxford: Oxford University Press, 1982), p. 255.

180. Dewey J. Hoitinga, Jr., *Faith and Reason from Plato to Plantinga: An Introduction to a Reformed Epistemology* (Albany, N.Y.: State University of New York Press, 1991).

181. Ibid., p. 5.

182. Ibid.

183. Ibid., pp. 5-6.

184. Ibid.

185. Alvin Plantinga, "Rationality and Religious Belief," in *Contemporary Philosophy of Religion*, p. 270.

186. Hoitinga, p. 178.

187. Ibid., p. 178.

188. Plantinga, "Coherentism and the Evidentialist Objection," in *Rationality, Religious Belief and Moral Committment*, ed. Robert Audi and William J. Wainright (Ithaca, N.Y.: Cornell University Press, 1986), p. 113.

189. Plantinga, "Coherentism and the Evidentialist Objection," in *Rationality, Religious Belief and Moral Commitment*, p. 113.

190. The job of "self-evident" is to leave no room for doubt or mere *seeming*.

191. Few tortured locutions such as "seeing treely" more aptly make the point that in straying from ordinary language we are bereft of implications and thus easy prey to arbitrary conclusions.

192. Plantinga, "Coherentism and the Evidentialist Objection, pp. 270-271.

193. Ibid., p. 111, n.6.

194. Ibid., p. 111.

195. Ibid.

196. Anthony Kenny, *What is Faith?* (New York: Oxford University Press, 1992), p. 13.

197. Ibid., pp. 8-9.

198. Ibid., p. 13

199. Ibid, p. 9

200. Ibid., p. 9.

201. Ibid., p. 18.

202. Ibid., p. 20.

203. Ibid., p. 19.

204. Ibid., p. 14.

205. Ibid., pp. 14-15.

206. Ibid., p. 15

207. Ibid., p. 16.

208. Ibid., pp. 16-17.

209. Ibid., p. 22.

210. Ibid., pp. 21-22.

211. Ibid., p. 22.

212. See Paul Dietl's "On Miracles" in *Contemporary Philosophy of Religion*, pp. 146-153, in which Dietl shows that even the revolution in thought that miracle requires can be something a secularist could know.

213. In *Rationality, Religious Belief, and Moral Commitment: New Essays in the Philosophy of Religion*.

214. Paul Tillich, "Introductory Remarks," *Dynamics of Faith* (New York: Harper & Row, Publishers, Inc., 1957; Harper Torchbooks, 1958).

215. John Hick, *Philosophy of Religion* (Englewood Cliffs, N.J.: Prentice-Hall, Inc.; Foundations of Philosophy Series, 1963), see pp. 61-73.

216. See John D. Godsey, *The Promise of Richard Niebuhr* (Phildelphia: The J. P. Lippincott Company, 1970), esp. p. 22, e.g., "faith is not . . . intellectual assent to propositions . . . but . . . ersonal trust . . . also . . . loyalty." Since trust and loyalty presuppose the belief that something is true, what we say of faith and belief applies also to trust.

217. Hick, *Philosophy of Religion*, p. 62.

218. Ibid.

219. See, this conflation extensively demonstrated in Nicholas Wolterstorff's "The Migration of Theistic Arguments: From Natural Theology to Evidentialist Apologetics," in *Rationality, Religious Belief, and Moral Commitment*, pp. 62-70.

220. Frederick Ferré, *Language, Logic and God* (Chicago: University of Chicago Press, 1961), p. 159.

221. Kenny, *What is Faith?* p. 53.

222. Ibid., p. 54.

223. Tillich, *Dynamics of Faith?* p. 4.

224. Ibid., pp. 35.

225. Ibid., pp. 35-36.

226. Ibid., pp. 36

227. Søren Kierkegaard, *Philosophical Fragments*, trans. David Swenson (Princeton: Princeton University Press, 1962), p. 182.

228. Søren Kierkegaard, *Training in Christianity*, trans. Walter Lowrie (Princeton: Princeton University Press, 1944), p. 84.

229. See, for example, D. Mackenzie Brown, *Ultimate Concern; Tillich in Dialogue* (New York: Harper & Row, 1965).

230. Kenny, *What is Faith?*, p. 93.

231. Ibid., p. 93.

232. Hick, *God and the Universe of Faiths*, p. 37.

233. Ibid.

234. Karl Barth, *Dogmatics in Outline* (New York: Harper's & Row, 1959), pp. 22-23.

235. Hick, *God and the Universe of Faiths*, pp. 37-38.

236. Ibid., p. 39.

237. Ibid., p. 39.

238. Ibid., pp. 39-40.

239. Ibid., pp. 41-42.

240. Ibid., p. 42.

241. Ibid.

242. See Ibid. p. 43.

243. Ibid.

244. And by "wanting," so to speak, makes true.

245. Hick, p. 10.

246. Timothy Gorringe, *Karl Barth: Against Hegemony* (Oxford: Oxford Uni-

versity Press, 1999), p. 102

247. Barth, *Dogmatics in Outline*, p. 23.

248. Emil Brunner, *The Christian Doctrine of God*, trans. Olive Wyon (Philadelphia: Westminster Press, 1950), p. 22.

249. See Paul Dietl, "On Miracles," *American Philosophical Quarterly* 5.2 (April 1968).

250. J. Baillie, "Our Knowledge of God" in *New Essays in Philosophical Theology*, ed. Antony Flew and Alisdair MacIntyre (New York: The Macmillan Company. 1955), p. 132.

251. Ibid., p. 82.

252. Farmer, "Towards Belief in God," p. 40.

253. Walter Stace, *Time and Eternity.*

254. Saint John of the Cross, as quoted in William James, *The Varieties of Religious Experience*, p. 132.

255. Emil Brunner, *The Christian Doctrine of God*, p. 15.

256. Edgar Wind, *Art and Anarchy* (London: Faber & Faber Limited, 1963), p. 88.

Chapter 4

GOD'S BODY

"I understand Substance to be that which is of itself and is conceived through itself; I mean that the conception of which does not depend on the conception of another thing from which it must be formed."
—Baruch Spinoza, Ethics Book I, Part I.

"There is one lawgiver. . . . "
—James 4: 12

"We hold these truths to be self-evident, that all men . . . are endowed by their Creator with certain unalienable Rights. . . . "
—Thomas Jefferson, "American Declaration of Independence"

INTRODUCTION TO CHAPTER FOUR

I cannot adequately communicate how far this journey toward a vision of God has taken me from my scientifically naturalist roots. I can only hope to convey how close—as well as how far—my final understanding of divinity is to the traditional idea of God.

In keeping with the aim of prior chapters, this chapter, "God's Body," is less a dismissal of "God" than a reconstruction. As the culmination of a theological journey, it will, if successful, have shown that "transcendence" and "miracle" still have an application, and that God can be understood as "the necessary being" albeit in a transformed sense. Indeed, what I have to say about "God" may lie close to what Paul Tillich had in mind when he described God as the "ground of being."

Because this chapter finds "God" in all things, its conception of God comports with the not uncommon feeling that God is *present* or *immanent*. What that conception is, I hesitate, bluntly, to say. This is not because ideas about God are over-freighted with emotion. It is because this most important conclusion, if baldly stated, must surely seem inappropriately abstract to those for whom God has always had a name or been referred to by a personal pronoun.

I am emboldened, however, by the equally impersonal descriptions of God offered by believing theologians. A work on Aquinas, for instance, describes "the absolute transcendence of God as Being itself beyond that-which-is," and finds "God alone the transcendent cause beyond Being . . . the unique and universal cause of all," concluding, "he is thus, moreover, the immediate cause of everything."

Against this magisterial, yet abstract, conception, the thesis of this chapter has, on the surface, only the virtue of simplicity to offer. It contends that religious preeminence of "God" derives from that about God which is God's *inexplicable necessity*. I am led to say that necessity is God's very substance, so that, simply: *"God is necessity."* Whatever theological justification or weight this conception may have depends, of course, on the reasons that stand behind it—the reasons that comprise this chapter.

I find it difficult to say I clearly understand descriptions of God's nature such as the one I quote above. I sense (as you, perhaps do) that there is "something" true in saying God is a "transcendent cause beyond Being . . . the unique and universal cause of all that is." But to serve as truth rather than excitement, the description must, in the end, say something one can *live by* or "live in the light of"—something that can shape the practices of daily life. This is, to me, the "existentialist" standard implicit in the Socratic dialogues and honored by Søren Kierkegaard who, in his saner moments, knew where reason must be anchored.

So, what I say of God—as to in what sense God *exists* (or has real "substance")—must be rooted in what lay theists find essential in their idea of God (*religiously* essential, not *psychologically* essential, as in, "God brings me peace"). Guiding this chapter (as it has influenced the others) is the thought that theists, when pressed, will agree that God's *essential* role is as source of final and authoritative direction.

If God were not the maker of laws, God would not be the object of religious awe. True, God is often identified with love, but a god without directive implications would be a god with no implications for the meaning of life. A God that caused us to *be*, that loved us—but had *nothing to say* regarding what we must or ought do would not be the *God, Lord, Father/Mother,* or *Intelligence* that is the object of popular and institutional devotion.

This is not to dismiss the religious significance of love. Chapter 5 attempts to place it in the context of a reconceived ultimate reality. It is just that love depends on "principles" such as *selflessness* and *openness* to the other, so that love, too, becomes what it is—becomes more than an inner sensation—by embodying the principles or "laws" that are, in my view, aspects of the "God" theism always sought.

I speak of making "laws." But the laws I refer to are not just "physical laws" or "moral laws," or "logical laws" but all that is law-like. I refer to the "unbreakable" characteristics and relationships that over time and in the course of diverse practices we find holding fast as a matter of experience. I refer to the *obdurateness* of the world. And, what I propose is that it is in this obdurateness that, in actual practice, we first recognize "reality."

For example: The poet tries a word and it "doesn't work"; the philosopher argues but finds his conclusion doesn't follow; the painter applies a color and finds the painting loses strength; the mathematician essays a proof but sees it is incomplete; the astronomer's prediction fails; the engineer's bridge sways fatally; the moralist feels the chill of insensitive judgment. All these things involve the recognition of relationships and qualities that are what they are despite wish, will, hope, preference, and desire. All involve doing to the world or speaking to the world, and getting something back from the world.

But, faced with an untoward result, none of the practitioners, above, speak with the voice of science to dissolve their problems. None invokes neurology or psychology. None say standards of truth, right and wrong, qualities of goodness or badness are only "in our heads" so that our "problems," so-called, are only what we ourselves *project* onto the world.

None say, "well, what I get back is only the way things *seem* to me; it's all a matter of *belief*." And so the philosopher doesn't seek people who will make him *feel* his conclusion "follows." The painter doesn't look for critics who will persuade her the painting is stronger. The mathematician doesn't look for looser rules. The astronomer does not accept it when his friends insist his prediction was successful. The engineer doesn't find a way to explain the bridge's collapse by reference to traffic. The moralist doesn't take a drink to feel her judgment wasn't so bad.

Moreover, as Plato taught us, if they *did* do those things, the philosopher wouldn't be a philosopher, the painter wouldn't be a painter (the mathematician not a mathematician, the engineer not

an engineer, and the moralist not a moralist). Plato's point, my point, and the point of ordinary people, is that a *vocation* (read: "*any* form of action—including reasoning") is *identifiable* because of its intention to realize the *best outcome* of *certain kinds* of encounters with "the world." But this intention would be nonsensical if there were no *objective* "best," no ways that things *obdurately* are—no *necessary* features of rational inference, of physicality, or of worldly qualities.

The recognition of various kinds of *necessity* is the recognition of things that in various ways are *real*. This is something we all know implicitly. When we advise the young to "face reality," we are warning them that there are things in life that can neither be changed nor rightly denied. Some things *must be*; the world has a law-like structure.

The *religious* importance of things having necessary characteristics shows in the repugnance theists feel for an "accidental" universe. Many say this is *only* the demand that the universe be *intentional*. But I think not: if God gave us, by *intent*, an environment of pure chance, the world would have no more meaning than it would as "an accident."

No. What "God" gives is *necessity*—the principle, or "ground" of the real in all domains—rational, physical, moral, aesthetic. No accident that, in Genesis, the world *comes into being* when "the Lord" transforms chaos into *order*. The world gains *requirements*—becomes lawful. (These are reasons why the main philosophical work of this chapter is an analysis of "reality." There is another. Empirical philosophies deny we can *know* worldly necessities—a position made famous by the father of modern empiricism, David Hume.)

God, I suggest, is the necessity of things. Hence God is always present, immanent, in the real. Necessity is invisible (as Hume pointed out), so God does not appear by way of the (physical) "five senses." The fact that things have *one character and not another* is alone what permits us to "learn"—to transcend our physiology by *knowing*—by *non-physically* incorporating in ourselves the necessities that form the world; hence, *incarnation*.

When Galileo's experiments uncovered what, *physically, must be* with respect to the rate that things fall, Galileo learned something, in this sense, of God. When the character of what we saw in medieval times led us, in the Enlightenment to realize that certain rights, morally, *must be*, I say "we came into the presence of God." And so the law is "given unto us"—(more literally), *present* to us—when we find what *must be*.

This idea of God shares much with the theistic God. It shares *in-*

explicability. It shares *non-corporeality* (for it is an active *principle* and not a "thing.") It also shares *universality* and *ultimateness.* It is *sustaining* of all things and thus is, as the Aquinas reference stated, "the transcendent cause beyond Being . . . the unique and universal cause of all. . . . the immediate cause of everything." And since necessity is not *visible*, "one cannot see the face of God." Finally, the existence of necessity is as *miraculous* as the existence of tradition's "God," particularly in presenting *normative* as well as physical *necessities* (the standards and laws of rationality, morality, and aesthetics.) It echoes the requirement that God be a "*necessary* being."

To realize the immense strangeness, the mystery, of a *physical* universe in which there exist *evaluative norms* (guidance and law) is not accomplished in a single act of thought. Empiricists will insist the idea is a "category error"—a belief in the truth of metaphor! To accept it one must *live* the arguments through. (Does not "conversion" require disciplined reflection?)

My thought—my hope—has been that in facing down the scientistic and skeptical attacks on rationality and knowledge, the reader may come, viscerally, to feel the "ground of being" which is God—necessity in all its forms. I suspect that only through such active engagement can the immanence of the necessary touch one's emotional life. Only then can one feel the miracle of the law. Only then can God be *known* as that which lies within "the world."

In the vastness of a voiceless realm of energy, *necessities* physically support us, physically destroy us, yet give us, for a moment, light to see that realm for what it is—to know the fact of it, the good of it, the bad of it *and of ourselves.* May not this reality be the God we always sought but feared to realize was *present*?

No doubt the absence of an indubitably "parental" "God" presents a new, less "forgiving" conception of life, but to (once more) quote Paul Tillich, "Being religious means asking passionately the question of the meaning of our existence and being willing to receive answers, even if the answers hurt."

A great deal has, of course, been left unsaid, not least the way this chapter draws implications from its conception of God to the irreligiousness of materialism and orthodoxy.

In this search for a defensible, awesome, and mysterious God, reinforcement is given the hope that we can live in terms of the good, the true, and the right. And, on the basis of our perception of immanent lawfulness, implications are drawn for the meaning of human life that return us to ancient times. For it was Plato who thought that in seeing the Good we perceived so concretely what we *ought* to do, that we could not fail to do it without denying *ourselves.* Thus this "God" is one with humanity.

GOD AND REALITY

"God's body" is a strange phrase. This is particularly true since, in traditional terms, God "is a spirit" (John 4:24), or, as an orthodox Jewish source puts it, "no carnal attributes may be assigned to Him."

But it is hard to think oneself created, ruled and observed by something bodiless—by not even a voice in space.

Surely God has some kind of substance. Theologians disparage the idea that God is "an old man with a beard," but while the image embarrasses serious theologians it is seldom successfully dispelled. What, essentially, is God? What is the substance of divinity?

Puzzlement accumulates with Spinoza, where "there is but one substance—God or nature—[so] that distinct bodies are merely modes of this one substance, considered as extended."[1]

Things become more specific and but remain elusive in the theology of Paul Tillich, where God is *"being-itself,* the creative ground of essence and existence and beyond both."[2] (Is "being-itself" *non-corporeal*; is it "spirit"?)

It seems agreed that God is not made up of parts. God is one "thing" not many. God is, to be sure, a "mystery"—beyond human conception. Yet we suppose God specifically to be (to put it in Tillich-like terms), the ultimate ground of being and that which expresses itself through everything that exists.

What is the thing, the "being-in-itself," the single "substance" that is not physical, the "transcendent cause beyond Being," yet is God?

It seems advisable to step back from descriptions of God and ask on what grounds they are inferred, since God does not greet us in the street or sit down with us in council. Without parsing our way step by step from one theological formulation to another, it seems the case that God is, on the one hand, (roughly) the explanation of all things and in some way, also, the body of all things—*the immanent sustaining force of what is ultimately real or existent.*

The universal, sustaining presence or "immanence" of God, is a speculative theme that made sense to thinkers as far apart as the theist Eckhart and the atheist Spinoza. Eckhart saw a manifold reality as the manifestation of *willing*; Spinoza saw it as the manifestation of *physical causation.* Pointedly, both were looking for what *makes* the world what it is, that is, for what *necessitated* a many-faceted reality.

The operating notion was that God *explains* the world, not only (in the case of Eckhart) as stuff coming-into-being, but—also in the case of Eckhart and Spinoza, both—the necessitation of being-the-way-it-is.

Central to God's religious meaning is that God explains the nature of the world we face. It is common to consider, as religion's basic question, "why is there anything at all?"

But, if that remains religion's basic question, then religion has no basic question. For, as Chapter Two pointed out, the question is incoherent. It cannot be answered, not because the human mind is limited, but because the question itself is internally contradictory (there being no explanatory bridge from nothing-at-all to something).

The only *ultimate* and *universal* question about existence that remains to be asked is not what explains the fact that things *exist* but what rather what *constitutes* something we are, or can be, aware of as "real." If there be some such factor or form of the real (and here language falters, the subject being too rarely visited to have spawned standard usage), then perhaps that factor is the creative principle, "the sustaining ground of being." Surely, that which is constitutive of the real may with justification be understood as reality's creator, or "God."

(Note: by "reality" we mean, here, all that can in principle be recognized as *existing*, so dreams exist in their way, rivers in their way, arguments in their way, qualities in their way, rationality and irrationality in their way, and so on—all aspects of reality, all in one way or another capable of *existing*.)

So the question, "why is there anything at all?" becomes "what is it that makes for things being *as* they are?" What is there about *anything* we regard as in some respect "real" that is essential to our declaring it so? Is there one constituting principle? This is the question whose answer we pursue.

Since real things can be utterly different in *type* (dreams, stars, energy, persons, obligations, arguments)—whatever might constitute them real cannot be native in type to one of them. It cannot, for example, be a *corporeal* phenomenon like electricity or energy or magnetism or a corporeal principle (as in scientism, where "rational judgment" is reduced to a physical or "psycho-physical" process because *only physical processes are "real"*).

The search for what is essential to *the way things exist*—to the *character* of existence—is an ancient one. Anaximander looked for that which was essential to all *physical* existence. He rejected Thales' notion that water (or fluidity) underlay all that was physically real. It was too particular. Any universally constituting feature would have to be, as it were, *abstract*, if it was to underlie all physical forms and transformations. Hence, Anaximander hypothesized that the physical world is grounded in "laws."[3]

Since religion seeks God in all that exists or is real, "God" would have to be similarly "abstract." Hence, God is "incorporeal" or "other-worldly." Tillich, in his search for God, opined that there must be a "creative" ground both of "essence" and existence" and that God was our "ultimate concern" or the "ground of being." And, perhaps there *is* something essential to the *existence* of every "essence, that is, to every *type* of thing" (be it an *inference* or an *ocean*).

If there was such a constant, then the vast panoply of diverse, incommensurable things that can in various ways be "real"—might be understood as the various "modes" (to use Spinoza's term) in which *creation* (reality) expresses itself.

In sum, it is hardly novel to think, as this chapter does, that the idea of God may be the idea of an active principle (a term, admittedly vague) that constitutes things "real."

It is a line of speculation that made sense both to the theist, Eckhart and the atheist, Spinoza. Eckhart saw reality as the manifestation of *willing*; Spinoza saw it as the manifestation of *physical causation*. Pointedly, both sought to explain what *made* the world be the way it was, that is, what *necessitated* the way things existed. What was at stake was the idea that God (in some sense) *explains* the world—an idea essential to "God's" religious meaning.

(Spinoza, of course, called a *physically* determined reality, "God," since "God" is the "power" that stands between ourselves and chaos. God is the something *within all things* by virtue of which realities can be distinguished. Otherwise we would have only what we would call "sensations" in awareness with no basis *even for imagining* the idea of "real" as opposed to "unreal." Our lives would be like living in a dream. We would have no occasion to contrast an unreal or *dreamt* threat with a threat not "in the head"; we could identify no "*real*" threat. Strictly, even the idea of a "threat" would be unintelligible.)

What remains, then, to be in some sense "explained" is not the *presence* of reality but the *nature* of it, and the possibility of describing something within it which, being *constitutive* of it, may with reason be understood as its Creator or as "God."

The key to its recognition will lie in whatever—in *experience*—allows us to see a thing as in some way *real*—as independent of will, wish, desire, need, or hope. What we call "real" is something that in some way we must take into account.

Though we cannot *define* "existence," we *can* recognize when something has features beyond our control—when it is in some way "real." We do not *make* the reality we use and with which we must contend. Something not ourselves is responsible for, is constitutive of, the real. And is such a feature to be thought of as less than "God" (at least when God has not already been conceived in the form of a *person*)?

So we say—as we have said in other places—our idea of the greatness of God derives from our idea of the greatness of reality. And if reality has a universal, essential character or form (incorporeal and perhaps, properly, the *spirit* of it), then we are glad for that form or spirit. We are grateful that by its presence we *exist* (even for a while) as sentient beings. And so, in that gladness, what should we call that which constitutes things *real*—"the Creator?" "God"?

The attempt to find the ground of "God's" status as religion's object takes us far from everyday language—especially when one rejects the everyday language in which God acts as a kind of *absolute magician*. Decisions as to proper descriptive terms become, no doubt, contestable in the domain of theological inquiry where God is, already, an incorporeal will or inscrutably all-determining power.

Nonetheless, we think there is present—in all that is real (or, as we shall sometimes say "exists")—one essential and protean "force" that has a kinship with theology's "God." It is therefore a "force," "form," "principle," or "spirit"—which every serious seeker quests to know. And though we shall attempt to name it and justify its role, yet it is a "force" that many who philosophize would consider bogus or "rationally unjustifiable."

A CLOSER LOOK
AT NECESSITY AND EXISTENCE

What we refer to is *necessity*—the protean and essential condition of *whatever* is real in the *way* it is real.[4] It will be our argument that the substance (substantiality) of reality is one with the presence of necessity. Necessity is the inexplicable, hence ultimate, *law-like* character that is the substance of *anything*'s "reality." In this way, it is the ground of all "Creation."

As we are now in a conceptually unfamiliar place, a bit of "technical" tightening and a connection with the familiar, is in order.

The fact that things "exist" in very different ways—that, for example a *logical implications* and *sailboats* both "exist"—does not mean that "exists" or "is real" changes *meaning* when used for qualitatively

different objects.[5] (A mirage is not really the *thing* that it looks like to the observer. The "lake" is not real. But the mirage—the illusion of the lake—is, in *its* way, real enough.)

Courtroom behavior exists and self-contradictions exist, but if evidence is self-contradictory it can *affect* courtroom decisions, showing that very different types of things (logical contradictions and judges' decisions) can and do exist in the same "world" (share the same Existence).

So, it may be that whatever *exists*—be it an idea, a dog, a color, an imagined object, a person, a mind, a nation—can share a characteristic unique to *existing* (to being *in its own way* "real"). That characteristic, we contend, is *necessity*.

"Necessity" must be present, we argue, if a thing is to be found *in some way* to exist or be "real." "Necessity" and "existence" do not *mean* the same thing. Thus, as independent terms, they can be found *related* to one another. So, we can intelligibly argue that necessity is *conceptually required* for existence—that is: "existence presupposes necessity."

The wording is "technical," but it specifies a relationship that is readily exemplified by the relation between color and area. For example, "color and "area" (or "extension") are—like "necessity" and "existence"—terms with different meanings. But you can't have a color that occupies *no area* (that has no "extension"). This is not a *physical* truth. (It makes no sense to doubt it and *search* for a color that is present but occupies *no area at all*.) We know that a color requires an area. So we say it is *conceptually* necessary that there be an area ("extension") for there to be a color. Color presupposes extension, just as *existence presupposes necessity*.[6]

A clarification: If dreams can be said to exist (and they do), are we not saying "everything exists" or "there is nothing that does not exist"? Not quite. In ordinary situations, if someone says, "Valhalla doesn't exist; you just dreamed it," they are saying that Valhalla doesn't exist *the way places exist*. They are not denying that the *dream* of Valhalla existed (that's what they're commenting on). Nor are they denying that that *idea* of Valhalla exists in one's imagination. The *context* of speech steers us to the *type* of existence in question. Our selves and our lives are of *reality*. An odd but accurate way of making the point it is that we never concern ourselves with that-which-has-no-kind-of-existence—with *nothing-at-all*.

NO GOD WITHOUT NECESSITY

If we say the idea of "God" is the idea of *what must be*—of necessity—we do not claim that "necessity" is what people "really mean" by "God." We do, however, think necessity is part of what they mean and further: *that necessity is the part that makes God "religious."* (How this comports with God's *intending* is discussed further on.)

Neither what God intends nor what God must be is something we derive from experience. God is not an agent whom people come across in daily life; God is not observed but imagined.[7]

What we *do* confront is a world that has a character of its own.

In the course of active experience, we find a separately empowered "other." Things have properties—a rather simple, obvious point whose very ordinariness hinders a religious perspective on it. We encounter an ever-present "otherness" that presents itself as (in one respect or another) not subject to what we will, desire, need, hope, or wish for. The necessity of things or aspects is their character as law and, like the laws of justice about which we typically speak, may be so consequential as to demand, on pain of death, *obedience*—just as their *acceptance* guarantees all *possibilities* (mountain climbing can kill you or fulfill you). Necessities are the complement of genius and character.

Around us, as in us, there is an evident, multi-faceted, and (*finally*) inexplicable structure of necessities. And it is the presence of this ineluctable necessitation, we suggest, that constitutes the religious component of what people mean by "God." (Baldly stated: we are aware there is something else that has it its own way.")

"God" is *religious*, on this view, because the mystery of a law-governed existence is awesome and—as "ultimate"—beyond any possible explanation. Necessitation, understood as law or that which—in the various domains—is *normative*, seems, in theism, crucial to the religious sensibility.

One need only bring to mind the vehemence with which theists reject "scientific" or *non-intentional* descriptions of the universe as reducing life to "an accident." That is, without law, without objective *requirements*, there is chaos, hence meaninglessness—the rule of no rule at all (which is what the perennial, pejorative employment of "accident" is meant to convey). The implication is that even if our "ordered" world were accidentally patterned it would still be a meaningless arrangement.

In theism "God" explains world's necessities—either by being *behind* them as their maker (the clockmaker *theory*) or by, directly, *being* them as "pure, irresistible will" (the preference of mystics like the Sufi, Al Ghazzali, who said cotton does not darken because of the flame but because God wills it thus to darken).[8] And this universal reign of unfathomable law or "what must be" inclines those who reflect on life as a *total situation* to make their peace with the idea that life requires things of us. The acceptance, with equanimity, of necessity in the sense of "what must be" is an expression of obedience that, according to William James, defines the *religious* attitude.[9]

We do not offer a "technical" doctrine of necessity. We are interested in it as in experience we find it. Necessity is the condition of whatever we think real *in the way that we find it* to be real. So, simply, and by way of introduction:

If one cannot breathe water, water is *physically* real, and if one cannot say yes-and-no to the same thing, then *meaning and logic* are real, and if one cannot deny the power of a painting, then *aesthetic* properties are real, and if torture is repugnant to feeling then *moral* "ought" and "ought not" are likewise real. (Not by virtue of single, isolated instances, of course, but experienced over time, action, and circumstance as "the way of the world.")

As the necessity presupposed by anything that in some way exists or is "real," "God's body" is the incorporeal substance of all realities. It is the protean necessity that in active experience we find but cannot *see* (as Hume was at pains to remind us).

BARRIERS AND CLARIFICATIONS

The greatest obstacle to conceiving God as necessity is not, in our view, theism's "personal" conception of God. That at least perceives God as the giver of laws. The real impediment is the tendency in philosophy to deny that *necessity* can justifiably be said to exist as an aspect of the world—that is, to exist *outside* purely definitional domains such as logic and mathematics.

For that reason, it is theologically important to examine the arguments against worldly necessitation (or the reality of laws). (It is always allowed that *logical* necessity is real enough—that if P is Q then if not Q, [necessarily] not P.)

Our main contention is that, as matter of experience, when we find that something is in some way real—that it, in some way, exists—we discover what there is about it that we *cannot change*. And since the limits on possibility (the necessities) surface in different ways—logically, physically, morally, aesthetically—necessitation proves to be the unifying principle (form, or spirit) of *all* that is manifestly real.

In this way, necessity is—like tradition's "God—*invisible, world-shaping*, and *immanent*.

As noted, above, necessity is not "existence" itself. Existence is existence and is not made up of parts. That is why we say necessity is the *form* or *spirit* of existence. Necessity cannot *explain* existence (any more than extension or area can explain the reality of color). Any attempt to explain existence is incoherent. Necessity would have to (already) *exist* to explain how come there is existence.

Crucial for our argument is that the traditional idea of God is not just the idea of existence, of what (merely) *is*. God is in all ways the idea of *what must be*. Necessity is the very substance of God, *even in traditional terms*.

God wills, but purportedly only in terms of the *necessities* of his nature—the goodness, the rightness that God cannot but express (it not being "in God's nature" to be evil or mistaken).

What human beings consider real are "things" that exhibit necessitation—the characteristic that, in our terms, is the substance of the divine, or "God's body" (necessity being consonant with tradition's claim that God is not physical is not *corporeal*).

Even imaginary demons and "spirits" are *real* (to those who believe in them) because they have *ways* and *requirements* that human wishing, willing, wanting cannot, *alone* change; to affect demons or spirits in any way means taking account of conditions, spells, chants that are *necessary*.

What we must show, philosophically, is that it is justifiable to say that the *condition* of anything's being *real is that its properties exhibit necessity*. What we must show, theologically, is that God is necessity—an identification circumstantially supported by the penchant of religions for instituting beliefs and practices as absolute *requirements*—pure necessities—in honor of, or devotion to, God. From theistic orthodoxy to Confucian ceremony, religion thrives on *what must be done*. Indeed, we suggest this feeling for the *required* is an attempt to *incorporate* God (as the non-corporeal necessity of whatever is real).

Indeed, it seems no great stretch to see the biblical focus on God's "word" or "logos" as an effort to state the principle that necessity defines the real, since *logical* or *linguistic* necessity is, perhaps, paradigmatic of necessity.

DIVINE NECESSITY AND DIVINE INTENTION

A comment is, however, in order on the issue of divine *intention* or "will." Our identification of the God-idea with a non-supernatural sense of necessity leaves out the element of *intentionality* that is part of Creation narratives. One may well consider this difference great enough to render our analysis theologically irrelevant.

But we think this conclusion must ignore the fact that the idea of a creator's "intent" is *already* deeply problematic—not in *popular* religion (where God is treated as a *person*) but in theology (where the use of "intent" runs up against descriptions of God's *necessary nature*—for example, God's omniscient, timeless, effortless "making" or having happen).

There really is no normal sense of "intent" possible when speaking of God in a theologically careful way. God doesn't have to *try* to do anything (doesn't have to imagine and execute, plan or craft, consider what is right or wrong, or "*get the idea* of doing a thing."

We "intend" only because it takes time and effort to do what we want to do—especially to bring something into being. But if, like God, we never *wanted* for anything, never had to *try*, we would never be able to *intend*—for it is logically impossible intend to do the specific thing you have already done. For God, whatever needs to be accomplished has been "already," *timelessly*, accomplished (it being God's nature to be one with *Being*).

For this reason, it is deeply problematic, if not conceptually impossible, to attribute "intentionality" to an all-creating entity that requires no time to act and that cannot have left anything out of existence that ought to have been in it.

For these reasons, the traditional picture of God as *agent*-creator—as *intending* reality—may, *upon analysis*, not differ greatly—if at all—from understanding God simply as the existence of necessity. Nor can the popular view be reinstated by saying talk of God *intending* things is "analogical" (the standard, "saving" retort not dealt with in this book). And even if the claim of "analogical" language about God could be made plausible, few are the believers (including theologians) who *really do* think of God's *intending* things as something very different from what is meant when we speak of people intending things.

Of course, the idea that God "loves" us is out of step with our claim that God is "necessity" (unless it be pointed out that the necessitations comprising our physical universe have in fact brought forth and (for a while) sustained this strange, thoughtful race). But God's outright love for us (and for Creation)—apart from being a deeply psychological and mundane attribution to an unfathomable force—has always been maintained by means of arguments strained to the point of self-deception. Such explanations as that God's plan *requires* horrors to complete reality's perfect goodness [etc.] cannot, by wearing the badge of *logical* consistency, justify or make *good* the agonies that plague the innocent. They cannot make terror, fear, and pain "really" part of "perfection." They cannot euphemize (as necessary for "perfect goodness"), the pain of blameless animals continually torn apart by other animals, the awful illnesses inflicted upon innocent children and adults, the biologically driven doom of over-population, and the final destruction of humanity by the sun.[10]

(Indeed, this kind of arguing—coupled with the need to rely on faith rather than publicly accessible argument—illustrates, sadly, how religion is made vulnerable by insisting on a *literal* understanding of humanity's earliest intellectual speculations.)

THINGS IN THEMSELVES: REALITY

We have all along insisted that religion sees the meaningfulness of human life as coming from "outside" it—from something *independent* of it—as in the quest for God's Word or revelation.

And this independent source, must under any definition, be *reality*, since, from a religious standpoint, life's *meaningfulness* cannot be fabricated. It cannot be the psychological projection of worth, truth, or obligation onto the muteness of space, time, matter, and energy.

But, as we have seen, it is often argued that we cannot know reality at all—much less its ultimate character. For that reason, our discussion cannot proceed without revisiting the claim that reality (the way things are in themselves) cannot possibly be known.

The argument made by many (e.g., Kant, Nietzsche, Rorty, and Shweder) is that we cannot know what things are like *in themselves*. We cannot know things as they "really" are apart from what our minds contribute to our conception of it.

As Shweder said, "the mind has no way of getting beyond the skin. . . . " ; "*It becomes impossible, in principle, to separate what is mind and what is reality, to say how things would look from 'nowhere in particular.'*"[11]

To know reality as it is in itself we must see it "from nowhere in particular"—free of any particular perspective or "language"—that is, free of our ideas as to the way things really are.

But suppose we could get out of our skin? Suppose we could take leave of ourselves (our minds contaminated with ideas about the way things are) and, like cinematic ghosts of ourselves, detach from our thinking bodies and see reality as it is—as God might see it. What would we see *"free" of any ideas at all* about what we are looking at?

Plainly, *nothing*. Even if we saw a mere "point," that would be seeing something framed by an idea. For, a point entails that it is not a "square" or a "color"—which shows that to see a point is to see something in terms of an idea. (We saw in the case of empiricism's "garden path" that perception requires ideas.) Even were God to have no ideas about what it was he saw, he would have to be looking at *nothing*. (Whatever exists, as Aristotle said, exists in a certain way.)[12]

So, rather than being a barrier to seeing reality as it is, having ideas about reality is a *necessary condition* for seeing it *as it really is*. Indeed, the only way the fact of using ideas could *negate* the possibility of seeing reality would be if reality had no properties or qualities to describe. But if it had no properties or qualities of any kind it would not be anything. There would be no reality—no way things in themselves really are.

Thus, skepticism has stood truth on its head. In its search for immaculate conceptions—for ideas that are pure because untainted by the human mind—skeptics passively await sensations while, nearby, theists passively await God's Word.

REALITY, ROUGHLY

When, in everyday, civilized life, we speak of "facing reality," we mean there are things and relationships and conditions whose characteristics one *has to* take into account.

"Reality" refers to things that are *obdurate*. What people call "realities" are things that cannot be changed merely by wanting, hoping, desiring, wishing, imagining, dreaming, or mentally striving ("willing"). Thus we can say of "the threat of war" (something that is not physical) that it must be taken into account—that it is real, indeed, "very real."

The recent penchant of sophisticates for asserting the possibility of "multiple realities" defeats the very idea of reality. If one cannot accomplish something in one reality (in the face of its resistance), there is always another that may accommodate one's desire. And if our differing perspectives entail different "realities" (not just *ideas of* different realities) then we can all have, or believe, *whatever we desire*, undeterred by a world that might otherwise force us to grow up.

But the very idea of different realities (of unfettered acts and thoughts) calls the question, "what constitutes 'reality?'"

NECESSITY AND REALITY: LOGIC AND IDEAS

Reality is *constituted* by necessity. That is our principal and final "metaphysical" theme. Wherever something is found to be *necessarily the way it is*—that thing has a status *of some sort* "in reality."

Animals explore their world to discover what they have to deal with. We do the same. We find out what can be moved, so to speak, and what cannot be moved. The difference is that we find many more *kinds* of things in our world than animals can find. We have a richer realm of Being.

Consider logic. Logic is not imaginary. Logic is not physical. Logic is, however, real. It is real enough to be studied, real enough to be wrong about, real enough not to conform to will, wish, want, whim, urge, imagining, or desire.

Logic is consistency among statements. You cannot wish consistency into being; you cannot wish inconsistency out of being. The *necessity* that is part of the meaning of "consistency" is not fabricated, fictional, or a matter of preference. Its obdurateness is not physical; its reality is *independent of psychology*, and thus is independent of our particular self. Its character is "its own." It is a reality.

Logic is real even though it is not real *the way* a tree is real. It is not "physically" real. But it is independent of our wish and whim. *It is must be reckoned with.*

The reality of logic is not found merely in sentences or letters. "P and or maybe so Q and X so why not if not Y mostly then perhaps P but not, but then again Z," has no logic. But if we state: "If P, then Q," then we *must* agree that "if not Q, therefore not P" is entailed by (contained in) what we said. For, if P *necessitates* Q, (if, when P, there *must* be Q) then, if there is no Q, there *necessarily* can be no P.

So logic is a domain, a department of reality by virtue of a certain kind of necessity.[13]

A note: it is sometimes said that our ideas exist neither in space nor time since they are not physical, but this will come as rude shock to historians whose specialty is intellectual history and who locate the origin and spread of ideas in such three-dimensional and chronologically specific realities as, say, Florence, in the fifteenth century, or Switzerland in the first half of the twentieth. The unreality of ideas is also a mark against the professorial class who sometimes advertise their classrooms as places of ideas. (And brain events are not ideas.)

NECESSITY AND REALITY:
THE PHYSICAL WORLD

There are necessary relations among meanings, and thus a domain called "logic." There is also a domain—a kind of reality—called
"the physical world." This, we shall argue, must have its own necessity or else it is no domain at all. Without its *own* kind of necessity, the
physical world would not be a department of reality.

It is, in our view, a standing condemnation of philosophy that so
many philosophers who extol experience show such disdain for its
deliverances. For, only an *ideologically* narrowed definition of "experience" could allow so many to follow Hume and deny finding physical necessitation an aspect of what they experience.

On this score, one imagines a philosopher who has been falsely
accused of a murder confidently providing evidence that he was a
thousand miles away at the time of the stabbing—only to be told that
nothing is *impossible* by citing his own writings. And one could smile
or weep were he to explain, "well, to stab someone from a thousand
miles away is extraordinarily *improbable*"—to which the prosecutor
would rightly respond, "but then it is *possible* that you did it."

The denial of physical necessity by many philosophers of science
stunningly discounts the experience of science's practitioners. It is a
glaring example of crediting third-person experience more than first-
person experience.

A recent article on the Large Hadron Collider, being completed
near Geneva, Switzerland, makes plain that *in the experience of scientists doing science*, some things are *responsible* for other things happening—that they *make* or *necessitate* their happening (or not happening).

For example, the Collider may reveal the existence of the "Higgs
particle":

> Its discovery would have many fantastic implications, one of
> which is that the void of space is not really void but is perme-
> ated by an invisible field that *acts* a bit like cosmic molasses.
> This Higgs field, if it exists, *exerts a drag* on matter passing
> through it, *lending* mass to particles that *otherwise wouldn't* have
> any [emphasis added].[14]

In an aside, the same article speaks of necessities. We are told that
"to get from one side of [the collider] to the other, it is *necessary* to
drive through several towns, and then descend three hundred feet in
an elevator," (one can't possibly pull the towns toward one and bur-

row down with one's hands)—and that one can bicycle through the tunnel, "but in that case a supply of emergency oxygen is *required*."[15]

When we read that the collider "will *unlock the secrets* of the universe or . . . prove this ambition to be hopeless," we have to ask why, if the things we see in the world just *regularly*—not *necessarily*—occur the way they occur, then why would *regular patterns* shown by the collider constitute "secrets?" Plainly, they are called "secrets" because scientists suppose them to *operate* behind the scenes—they are what *make* other things happen.

Only a philosopher could hear a *working* physicist say, "The more energetic the particles are, the more force you *need* to keep them on orbit" and then tell the physicist that nothing *makes, forces, or necessitates* anything else to happen because there is no way, by argument, to *prove* physical necessitation exists. Only a philosopher could say we don't know that the atomic bomb destroyed Hiroshima because all we can rationally assert is a great cloud arose and at the same time Hiroshima's buildings burned and shattered.

Bringing the issue back to the simple reality of civilized experience: If a safe falls on one's toe, and the toe flattens, splits and bleeds, not only is it not brilliant, it is not *rational* to *deny* that given the fall of the safe on it, the toe *necessarily* suffered damage.

Physical necessity is a basic revelation of experience (as Kant in a way, insisted, though he unfortunately attributed its *source* to the mind not the world). In *Experience and Nature*, John Dewey makes the point that *causality* is understood—we would say "revealed"—when we try to do bodily things. One has only to dig a hole in the ground, to push and twist and pause and move dirt again, to understand that one thing can *make* another thing happen.

In sum, a child that does not come to understand that flames cause a heating of the finger would be thought not a philosopher but a victim of retardation.

PHYSICAL NECESSITY DENIED

We shall not replay the whole exciting story of Hume's "destruction" of physical necessity (the idea that because we have no *sensation* of necessity like the sensation of *warmth*, we have no *experience* of necessity—as if "experience" consisted of sensations—*a lifetime of experience being a lifetime of sensations!*).

We have also previously alluded to "conventionalists" who said physical laws didn't refer to worldly necessities but were only convenient rules for drawing conclusions or making predications. All this to deny physical necessitation, even to the point of saying science doesn't yield knowledge but is simply a practical way to think.

We dwell on this matter because even contemporary philosophers such as Stephen Toulmin and Roger Scruton cannot admit the existence of physical necessity.

Toulmin, a philosopher of science, denied necessity was real by denying that physical laws are true of the world. According to Toulmin, a law of nature is something of which we ask not, "is it true?" but "when does it hold?"[16] Toulmin claimed that "the logical opposition 'holds/does not hold' is as fundamental as the opposition 'true/untrue,' and cannot be resolved into it."[17]

""Laws of nature are not the sort of things we can speak of as true, false or probable at all. Yet [they] can reasonably be called empirical."[18] Apparently, "this law holds but doesn't exist" is sensible within Toulmin's scheme.

It is, we think, important to see the subtlety with which necessity is these days denied. So let us examine Toulmin's handling of the matter:

Toulmin eliminates the necessity we find when doing science (or digging holes) as a first-person inquirer by adopting a third-person interpretation of the scientist's first-person thinking.

What one can see of that thinking from outside it will, of course! be more "objective." Toulmin begins by casting doubt on the scientist's first-person way of stating what is going on:

The "error" of interpreting laws as if they described worldly necessities is, according to Toulmin, "made easier by the scientist's customary idioms; "If the wall is 16 feet high and the sun is at 30 degrees, the shadow *must* be 10 ½ feet deep." The shadow *must* be a certain length under those conditions, says the scientist—whose language or "idiom" is leading him astray (rather as moralists are led astray, according to Hare, by the idiom of *descriptive* language that they wrongly think describes good and bad acts).

Toulmin explains that the scientist's statement is just the application of currently accepted theories of optics. For Toulmin, the scientist's talk about what *must* in fact happen, is *(when looked at from outside the scientist's own experience)* nothing more than *someone applying a theory* into which factual statements like "16 feet high" have been plugged.

Looking at scientist's mind *from outside*, Toulmin can see only the scientist's "argument" (which is why *we* have emphasized that *knowing* is only a first-person phenomenon).

Since doing science is making arguments, Toulmin concludes that *logicians* can afford to say *the same thing* less compactly but *more explicitly*: "If the wall is 6 feet high, and the sun is at 30 degrees, then a proper application of the theories of optics which have been found reliable in such circumstances as these will *necessarily* lead us to the conclusion that the shadow will be 10 ½ feet deep."[19]

But, in fact, the scientist's statement and the hypothetical "logician's" statement do not state the same thing. They are not even *about* the same thing. The scientist says the *shadow* must be a certain length; he is referring to the world. Toulmin's logician says the *shadow's length must be asserted from the premises*; he is referring not to the *must be* of world but to the "must be" of a logical argument.

The fallacious result is that logic can have necessity but the physical world cannot.

The British philosopher, Roger Scruton also denies the reality of physical necessity but by means of a different argument. Scruton's idea is that a physical law states a probability, not a necessity.

He is led to this approach by attempting to explain how a physical being can have a will that is not physically determined (necessitated) and can therefore be a "free" will.

Free will cannot remain a mystery! Here Scruton and Toulmin exemplify philosophy's drive to *demystify* reality whatever the cost to common sense and the language that embodies it. (It is, we think, the reigning ideology of "Anglo-American" philosophy.)

To be sure, one ought always attempt to explain what ignorance or confusion proclaims mysterious or miraculous. But the desire to make things comprehensible turns ideological when comprehension is "achieved" by denying what cannot reasonably be denied—for example (and roughly, of course), the standard sense of basic concepts, or the things we all know. It is this Faustian insistence on explanation that makes much philosophy the enemy of religion.

So, Scruton sets out to explain how free will is possible even though we are dependent on a physical brain. The price of his explanation is of course the rejection of physical necessity, that is, the empirical reality of physical laws.

The deterministic view of physicality is, he says, that "one event causes another only if there is a law connecting them. And laws have no exceptions."[20] Thus, "the way the world is at any future time is fully determined by the way the world is now. That goes for my actions too. . . . so how can I be free?"[21]

Scruton says this account of cause and effect is "very old-fashioned." He tells us that "scientific laws have exceptions" and that "they tell us, as a rule, what is probable under certain conditions."[22]

Scruton references quantum mechanics, saying "even the ultimate laws of the universe must be phrased in terms of probabilities."[23] Scruton concludes, "It is therefore never true that the effect *must* follow, given the cause; only, at best, that it is likely to follow."[24]

So if one jumps from the window of a twenty story building it is likely one will fall, but not certain. Or if one tries to lift a railroad engine with a feather, one is likely, but not certain, to fail. Thus: ideology.

Even at the linguistic level, Scruton's translation from law to probability fails. Start with the fact that the statement of a physical law: "masses mutually attract" *is inconsistent with* the statement, "masses *may not* mutually attract."

But Scruton's substitute statement, "masses will probably attract" entails the statement "masses may *not* mutually attract." (Whatever is *probable* is not *certain*.) Hence, the statement of physical law, "masses attract," cannot be equated with the probability statement, "masses probably attract"

Hume's shadow still darkens the field of philosophy. "From him," says Iris Murdoch,

> more than anyone else . . . we have derived a philosophic tendency, which is still with us, to see the world in terms of contingently conjoined simples, to see it as a totality of ultimate simple facts which have no necessary connection with each other.[25]

(In a world of contingently joined simples, there can be no more connection between the nucleus of an atom and its electrons than between the colors of marbles in a bag.)

Not all philosophers deny necessity. Among the finest exponents of the idea that physical laws describe physical or "natural" necessity is William Kneale.

Against Hume, Kneale points out the peculiarity of Hume's ever thinking that *necessity* could be sensed or "observed" as a kind of visible condition, for

> necessary connexion is thinkable, but certainly not imaginable; and there is no reason to suppose that, because it is thinkable, it must also be sensible. On the contrary the supposition that it might be sensed is clearly mistaken. When we say that *a*-ness necessitates *b*-ness, we mean that it is impossible for an *a* thing not to be *b*. Our idea of necessitation, is therefore, the notion of a boundary to possibility. How could such notion be a copy [Hume's "idea"] of anything contained as an element in actual experience?[26]

THE MYTH OF "REGULAR CONNECTIONS"

The denial of necessity leaves us with *chance* connections between events or conditions or *regular* connections between them. Hume, of course insisted all we ever observe are regular connections between one event or condition and another.

The idea that connections between events are "chance" connections says that there exist no *actual* or "physical" connections between events. "Regular connections"—connections that have no causal linkage—are, at bottom, only chance connections by another name. Indeed, *purposeful* connections would be the only contrasting type of connection in a world of "regular connections."

Begin with one billiard ball striking another. The first ball (A) causes the second ball (B) to move.

We might suppose this situation covered by Newton's Laws of Motion. But if there are no necessities—only *observed regularities*—Newton's "laws" can be dismissed. So can the idea of "striking." (Indeed what we call "the world" is also about to be dismissed.)

If the motion of ball A (above) has *always been observed* to precede the motion of ball B (above)—*and that is all*—we have a chronicle of events. When this is chronicle is "explained" in the language of "regular connection," an ambiguity is introduced.

The statement, "I see A then I always see B" tells us little. We don't know whether it reports a recurring hallucination or a series of happening in the world. But when phrased, "A is regularly connected with B" the talk seems to be of the world, and suggests that between A and B there is something called a *connection*. But if things *don't* make other things happen, then between A and B there can be no third thing—no "C"—no force that might constitute a *connection*.

If we strive for clarity and say "regular connection" *only* means (unambiguously) "I see A and then I see B, always," then "regularly connected" must mean "regularly sequenced *in my awareness*." Now we must question the reference to "ball" A and "ball" B.

We spoke of billiard balls A and B. How can we speak of "balls?" We see a yellow circular object in motion (ball A) and we see a green circular object in motion (ball B). But are these "things" or just colors moving in my awareness?

I reach out to touch "ball" A. I feel pressure in my fingertip. Ordinarily we would say that is evidence of a solid object contacting my finger. Yes, there is an object there—a ball. But we can't say that. We are in a world, now, in which nothing *makes* anything happen. Nothing *has to be* this way or not this way.

So I cannot *explain* the pressure as *caused* by the solidity of the ball. *Now* all I can say is that when I see my arm and finger extending, what happens, regularly, is that there comes a time when I feel "pressure" and cannot move my fingertip further toward the yellow circle in my field of vision.

If all we ever experience are regular connections, there can be no *explanation* of why the pressure conjoined with stopping my finger regularly occurs when I move it toward the yellow circle; nothing *makes* anything else happen and therefore nothing can *account for* what happens. The result is that I cannot say there is a yellow *ball* (A) before me but only that movement toward the yellow circle is regularly followed by pressure in my finger and the cessation of movement in my arm.

It now becomes clear that a three-dimensional world containing *things* or *objects* can never be rationally claimed. There is no way to *find out*—to *test for*—anything we call the "properties" of what we perceive.

Every test of the character of a putative "thing" involves doing something that is supposed to have an *effect* on what is tested—a consequence of action that that will reveal its properties or character. For example: "Is this a glass window?" I try to put my hand through it and my hand is stopped; "yes it's not just an opening in the wall it's a pane of very clean glass or plastic."

But in a world of "only regular connections and no *causation*, no *physical necessitation*, all we find out is that someone's hand, when moved toward what looks like the outside world, regularly stops moving. And there can be *no explanation*—no "glass," no "plastic"—for that would require claiming that the glass or the plastic *prevented* the movement—*made it* impossible, *necessitated* greater pressure to make it possible. ("Prevent," "make," "necessitate," have no application in a world composed only of regular—and irregular—phenomena.)

The conclusion we reach is that our idea of a world and the theory of regular connections but-no-necessities are incompatible. Either we are living solipsistically—within our own awarenesses—or we are not.[27]

(We shall not expand the discussion into the area of chance. Chance or *probability* will not save regular connections. Probability is based on object knowledge or else pure mathematics.)

(A note of explanation: we have spent some time on regular connections in part because *it has a bearing on whether science and religion are compatible worldviews*.)

NECESSITY REVISITED

Talk about *reality* and *existence* is freighted with logical subtleties too numerous to explore.[28] Our hope is to confine what we say to those notions of reality and existence which reflect their use in actual pursuits. That, of course, is why we made reference to the Collider.

What we have so far argued with respect to logic and the physical world is that they would not be considered realities—would not be distinguished from dreams or hallucinations—were it not for the necessities we encounter in these very different domains of linguistic communication and bodily activities.

Now what we wish to emphasize is that, in fact, *logic* may be said to *exist* only because of the necessities we encounter in *forming ideas* (the "necessities" being what is *required* to state a proposition or make a proposal)—and the physical world may be said to exist only because of the necessities we encounter in attempting *bodily activities.*

It is not that necessities exist as one kind of thing while the logical and the physical exist as another kind of thing. We do not find one thing, necessity, and then observe that it is *paired* with the logical and the physical. Necessity is the *mode* of anything that exists so that to find necessity in experience is to know that *something* (of some sort) *exists.*

This is not a crystal clear claim; "mode" may even mask something the writer has missed. But these matters are difficult to state familiarly, since ordinary language does not develop around issues of reflection at such a great remove from practical matters. Hence, something more concrete is in order.

Whatever exists, exists by virtue of some kind of necessity—just as a color exists by virtue of there being an area. (A point is dimensionless and can have no color.)

Color and area (like "existence" and necessity") have different meanings, but the very idea of a color involves the very idea of area. One cannot conceptually separate the color, say, *green* (not the wavelength *of* green) from an area that it occupies. So, to say something exists (in some manner) is to say that something is necessary (in some manner).

Similarly "believing" and "being awake" are not the same thing, but believing *cannot* be said to occur unless one is awake.

What we claim is that if anything of an identifiable kind *exists*, then some appropriate *kind of necessity* must be found *inherent* in it— unavoidably *belonging* to it.

For example, suppose one were told that a force-field has been created through which one cannot thrust one's hand. Suppose one found, upon trying, that one's hand was indeed stopped at the point where force-field was said to begin. One might well conclude that the force-field *existed*.

But if one were later to learn that a master hypnotist had, by suggestion and the use of covert techniques, made it impossible for one to move one's hand beyond the indicated point of the force-field—and *that* was why the force-field "worked"—then one would conclude that the force-field *did not exist* (but that the power of hypnosis did).

The *way in which* the reality of a thing is discovered is by the necessity inherent in *it* and *not* by the necessity of something *else*.

That is how a child learns that *wanting* has no physical power in the world; the ball will not roll toward it just by wishing hard that it would. It is not possible to attract it by wanting or wishing. The reality of the mind differs from the reality of the arm.

The reality that we classify as "physical" is determined on the basis of such bodily actions as are described, above—from finding out why one's hand was stopped, to coming to know what makes a ball roll, to knowing whether the Higgs particle is a physical reality.

The very *conception* of the "physical" or—"physical world"—is learned through active encounters with what is *required, bodily,* for ends to be achieved. The world of dreams is a realm where nothing is impossible, so nothing is physically real.

And the way we understand and thus, through experience, *define* what is "physical" has a deeply metaphysical bearing on the much mooted question of the compatibility of science with "religion."

THE INCOMPATIBILITY OF SCIENCE AND THEISM

Science claims that physical necessities (laws) exist and that it is these that account for such things as the way wood resists the passage through it of our hands and the fact that we cannot fly by waving our arms.

For theism, the behavior of whatever we can sense or whatever affects our bodily selves or world is the direct effect of God's will.

C. S. Lewis understood that for miracles to be possible nature could not have its own necessities; a miracle cannot violate a necessity, for that would be to do what is impossible—a self-contradictory notion. Hence he denied there were physical laws.

Rather than fall into describing nature as *insubstantial* (as noted: a realm "observed" to have no impossibilities is a dream), Lewis sug-

gested the physical world be thought of as a book authored by God—
an analogy which is relevant in that a book is, in a sense, willed by its
author, but irrelevant in that the physical book is not the result of any
author's will but of a printing press.

More consistent with a "God's will" explanation of the physical
world, and therefore more startling, are the views of the medieval
mystic Meister Eckhart and the creators of the Hindu Upanishads.
Like Lewis, they understood that miracles could not contradict *actual*
necessities ("physical laws"). But they took the incompatibility between laws and miracles to its logical conclusion. For them, what we
call 'nature" or "the physical world" is not the independent reality
(the "book") we suppose it to be.

The *only* necessity is God's will. Thus, Eckhart explained that "if
God turned away from his creatures for one moment, they would be
reduced to nothing.'"[29] Similarly, the Upanishads proclaimed the
world absolutely dependent on a "permanent [process of] creation."[30] As framed in Dvaita tradition, "this creation . . . [the natural
or perceptible world] . . . boils down to the constant intervention of
Brahman, who can *at will reshape even the very structure of the initial material*. Brahman can change the very nature of worldly things [empha-
sis added]."[31]

Physical reality thus becomes nothing other than will—*God's*
will. That is, there is no force-field stopping one's hand, there is no
granite wall stopping one's hand, there is no steel barrier stopping
one's hand, for the stopping is *entirely* up to the hypnotist's—or
God's—will.

The walls don't have their own (*inherent*) necessity that accounts
for the stopping of one's hand. The proof of this, in theism, is that if
God stopped willing that the steely looking surface in front of one resist the passage of one's hand, one's hand *could* pass through it.

And if one's hand could pass through it because God changed
what God wills, then there no more exists what we would call a "steel
wall" (or "physical wall") than there exists a "force-field" when the
hypnotist entirely determines what is possible for the movement of
one's hand.

Thus, science, which depends on the actuality or efficacy of physical necessities, is contradicted by a theism which says there are no actual necessities other than God's will. One or both views cannot be
true.

Ironies, as usual, abound: In the "war" that is a family quarrel,
"God's will" theists and their empiricist opponents agree: There is no
such thing as *physical* necessity. And the hard-headed philosophers

who maintain we can find no physical necessities treat the universe like a dream, for it precisely because "anything can happen" that we call the mind's content a "dream."

EXAMPLES OF INCOMPATIBILITY

When someone crashes a car in a videogame it isn't reported to the insurance company. It isn't a real crash. A car crash didn't exist.

One day we will have fully electronic simulations in which holographically, three-dimensional cars crash and molecules of burn-smell and perfect fidelity audio are produced and sensations of pain are transmitted to the brain. It will look and feel to the driver or observer just as it looks and feels being in a car crash.

Still, we will not report it to the insurance compan; it is not a real crash. The crash does not exist (except as a simulacrum). Why? The content of the experience is determined by an electronic program, not by the physical necessities of metal, rubber, gasoline, glass, momentum, human flesh, muscles, or whatever makes up the necessary and sufficient conditions of a car crash. If it *had been* constituted by those necessities, it would have been a real car crash. The crash would exist.

Because the necessities of electronic interaction and transmission determine the content of the experience, not the physical necessities of the car—its composition, mass, and momentum—the crash is not real, does not exist.

Hence, if the content of our experience of the physical world is determined not by the necessities of that world but by the necessities of an agent's will (God's will), then the physical world is no more real, no more *exists*, than the car and the crash in the videogame.

We are walking in, as it were, God's imagination—which, as poetics, may have a certain glow. But if it were true, then the world in which we walk, the sea upon which we gaze, the stars that inspire us, the forests that sober us, the flowers that delight us, the animals that fascinate us, the sunsets that enthrall us (even our own bodies)—have only the substance of "special effects"—for if God should think something else or should sleep, they would, in the word's of the Bard, "vanish into air, into thin air."

A lexicographer might counter that "'real' just means what the content of experience normally is—even if it is a function of God's will."[32] But "real" is not a proper name for *whatever it is* on which we build and risk our very lives.

"Real" is a conception, it is the idea that something has its own character, its own being, its own necessity—that it is a genuine "other" to which we relate and which fills our lives. And if it were *possible* for it to vanish or entirely change at any time then what else would it have been but something entirely without substance? If a mountain could change to a low wall and back, again, to a mountain, and back to a low wall, the way images change in a slide show, it could not, in any conception of reality by which we live, be a real mountain.

If the trees of the great forest do not stand but are *held up* by the self-executing will of a non-corporeal agent—a Master Magician— then the *trees* of the great forest—like the force-field—are not *at all* what we thought they were. Not trees, not *things* at all, but looks and feels and smells which, *themselves*, as looks, feels, and smells are expressions of that same will—for what we call "our bodies" are not held together by "muscles" or "cells" but by a will that is not a property of muscles or cells.

And if our bodies are only ideas, as it were, in a mind not our own, what then is left that is "us?" No wonder we were given "free will"—though our will must contend with real things, with the necessities of the world. But no! Not so! "Things" being only *willed appearances*, our will must contend only with another will, which, being "stronger" controls—"at the end of the day"—the entire contest of human and world.

So, there is literally no *sense* to a "reality" which has none of its *own* requirements, and no sense in speaking of physical "laws" that have not their *own* necessity—for what happens in a God-willed world is entirely up to God and therefore not predictable on the basis of any "law" that, being independently necessary, could differ in its effects from his will.

Indeed, the Creator-god cannot create a "world" because a world can be a world only if it has *its own* rule. And if it had a rule that was its *own* and not just the same thing as God's rule, God could not overrule it. That is what "having its *own* properties, its own *laws* or necessities" means! (For God to create a separate or independent *world* is for God to create the famous "stone so heavy God could not lift it.")

One must be clear about what one is asserting when one asserts that a thing has a power of "its own"—as when a world is created that is a "world" because it has its own powers (which is why we marvel at it). It is a difficult issue on which to reflect because it asks us to understand our basic notion of reality, which is nothing less than the foundation of our sanity.

We revert to a mundane example in hopes of striking the right spark. Think of the automobile (that which is *auto* mobile). Think of the child's automobile which, to move, must be pushed by an adult or another child. It is not a real automobile for the reason that it does not move itself. Suppose the automobiles of the adult world moved *only* because they were "pushed" by something outside themselves. They would not be what we thought they were. They would not be "automobile" but dependently mobile. They would not be real automobiles. And so it is with a world that has no movements of its own. It would be no real world.

A final thought-experiment: If things are what they are by the will of God and on no other basis, then it is *possible* that a person could become a bird. But would that be a bird? (And if that *were* a bird, was that a *person*?)

For the bird could become a stone and (now we embark): the stone becomes a fly, the fly a tower, the tower a ball, the ball a rope, the rope an ocean, the ocean a stringy clump, the clump an antelope, the antelope a pie, the pie a steamship , the steamship a parsnip, the parsnip a planet, the planet an all-redness, the all-redness a lightning bolt, the bolt a bird and the bird a person. A "bird?" A "person?" We are at a loss. How can these be "things" of any kind?

They cannot. Whatever can be *anything* is no *thing* (is nothing). There are no *things* unless they have (they own or necessarily possess) properties—and to have *any* possible property at any time is to have no properties at all. No properties, then no "things." And so we do not know what to think or say about the kaleidoscopic procession we have just described. Indeed, we can't even *think* about them.

This is the point of Frederick Will's "Thoughts and Things." Our very minds depend on the condition that *not* "anything can happen."

Let us understand we are not saying that things *will* change. That is not the point. The point is that *if* what we think of as "things" *could* change "at will" then they couldn't be the *sort* of thing we think they are—believe they are, are utterly convinced they are (enough to live and die by what we think they are).

Things that *could* suddenly be otherwise—even if they *never* demonstrate that they could—are not the "things" we think they are. For example: If a person one knew all one's life were, very late in that life, to walk through a wall without disturbing either the person's body or the wall, you would suddenly realize that this person wasn't a "person" but had been something else *all along* (perhaps a ghost, or an alien, or an imaginary friend you had imagined all these years, or perhaps God). In any case, a "person" capable of doing that was *never* a *real* person, and, similarly, a world capable of being *any way at all* has never been a *real* world.

Let us close with a summarizing thought experiment: You buy an unbreakable chain. A month later it breaks. You return it for a refund. The seller refuses, telling you it was an unbreakable chain—up to the moment you broke it. He adds that unbreakable chains break many times but between each break they are unbreakable. Do you accept his reasoning?

The seller becomes a scientist. He tells you there is a law of gravity. You say, "do you mean that masses have, so far, been found to move toward one another?" He says, "no, the attraction is *necessary*. That's why we call it a physical *law* and not just a physical happening." "But didn't God will the Red Sea to defy gravity?" "Yes." "But, if gravity can be suspended, it can't be *necessary*; so it can't be a physical *law*."" "Of course it can," he says, "it's necessary up to the point that it isn't necessary. You see, no matter how many times God wills things to happen that contradict physical laws, they are laws in between the times they are broken."

If you reject the seller-scientist's reasoning, then you reject the contention that science and Creator-God theism are compatible. The theological idea that accommodates science by acknowledging that there are physical laws, but insists that physical laws exist because God wills them is implicitly self-contradictory. That which is dependent on *will* is dependent on choice, not on any purportedly "physical" nature.

A COUNTER-ARGUMENT

A colleague of the writer suggested an argument that might be raised against the idea the existence of physical laws is inconsistent with a "physical" world effected by God's will.

This argument rests on the fact that physical laws are said to hold only on the basis of certain initial conditions. If the initial condition is a "black hole," the laws of gravitation and other laws holding outside a black hole may not hold. A less cataclysmic initial condition is "the absence of friction": thus only "in the absence of friction" will the law "a body in motion tends to stay in motion" be observed to hold. (We disregard questions about degrees of friction and whether the law really continues to hold.)

Hence, in sum, the counter-argument for theism is that "for any law, the initial condition of its operation is always that God wills it."

The problem here is that the *initial condition*, "God wills it" renders the law otiose. If the initial condition for physical laws is that God wills what the laws say must happen (that A must produce B), then what happens is explained by the initial condition of God's having willed it. Physical laws would always be irrelevant since God's will (the "initial condition") is always sufficient to bring about the "effect."

The idea that God would create physical laws that "work" because God *wills* that they work supposes God to create an instrument that has no more effect than can be achieved without it.

Another path of objection to this counter-argument is that there is no independent way to know what God wills, so if physical laws hold only when God wills, scientists could never determine when physical laws exist.

From these considerations we can see that the "clockmaker theory" of Creation is incoherent (*pace* the political brilliance of the Founding Fathers). The universe—the will-driven clock—is not an independent world operating *by its own laws*. There are no *independent* powers, no independent laws effective *independently* of God's will and thereby constitutive of another world than God's—a physical world called "the *natural* world."

NECESSITY AND MORAL REALITY

If God's substance is identical with undifferentiated necessitation, then the *reality* of moral requirements—the fact of moral necessities—is one facet of the reality of God.

Theologians and philosophers agree that religion is not the same thing as morality, but the way in which morality might be said to depend on religion has remained an area of dispute.

With respect only to the *logic* of the relationship, our position is that necessitation—logical, physical, moral, esthetic—is what gives form to what would otherwise be chaos, chance, "accident," "stuff."[33] It is the reality of necessity that makes the reality of morality possible.[34]

(And because there is form or necessity, there can be "mind"; for if the world could be *any way, at any time*, there would be no *things* to be known—and if nothing is known there is no "mind.")

But, of course, the mystery of moral necessity is a bitter pill to those whose laudable attempts to explain it pass from rational doubting to ideological refusal. (Harsh, perhaps, but it is hard to understand how the reality of good and evil, beauty and ugliness, can be denied by anyone who has faced decisions regarding a child, a lover, a parent, a legal case, a political struggle, or a war—or has heard Bach's B-Minor Mass, Beethoven's quartets, authentic gospel music, certain jazz solos; or spent time in the Louvre or the Metropolitan Museum; or simply gazed at a mountain range at sunset.)

Just as the domain of *logic* is real (and not just a pattern of sentences) only if there is logical necessity, and the domain of the *physical* is real only if there exist non-intentional necessities, so the domain of moral obligation is real only if there *exist* moral necessities.

All these descriptions are, to be sure, circular since to recognize a type of necessity is to recognize a domain—the domain of which it is the constituting principle or "spine." But the salient point, for us, is that these are not domains created by "definition" or "social convention." They are not "games," not even "language games."

Logic, physicality, morality, aesthetics are domains forced upon us through active experience. As outgrowths of civilizing activities, they are not arbitrary or "conventional." Their character represents what we find *obdurately present within our experience*. ("Experience" does not mean "sense-experience" or "sensation" as empiricists assume.)

Let us recall how Edwards and Hare denied the reality—the factuality, the worldly actuality—of moral obligation or moral *necessity*.

For these empirically minded philosophers, the *necessity* of a moral principle was merely *intentional*. On the basis of "experience" (sense-experience) moral obligation cannot be inferred. Necessity lay only in a person's *decision* to treat a moral principle or "rule" as necessary for all.

A moral principle could not be derived from contemplation of the actual qualities of actions and relationships—from any goodness or badness revealed in experience. Thus, incredibly, there can be *no such thing as moral insight*.

How could there be (for the scientistically minded), if there were no factual truths with moral implications into which an insight might be had? Indeed, *insight is never significant* (if mentioned at all) in *empirical* epistemologies because *seeing reality*—knowing—cannot be *explained* empirically.

Therefore, for empiricist theorists, moral necessity can only be *made up*. To be morally necessary a principle had only to meet *formal* requirements. It had to be a principle honestly intended to prescribe the conduct of all human beings; it had to be based on criteria for application; and it had to be freely chosen.

Hare adopted the Kantian requirement that in formulating a moral law, one must consider whether one would accept the principle if someone else applied it to one. But this, as we have argued, could only lead (within the view that good and bad, right and wrong are not factual) to the acquisition of psychological information as to how one feels, but not to morally probative information.

For empiricists, like Hare, agree that one cannot conclude what *ought* to be from what *is*. In short there is no such thing, for them, as information or worldly experience from which goodness or badness, rightness or wrongness can be *inferred*.

Fundamentally, then, the *existence* of moral law—and therefore the existence of a moral domain—depended entirely on *the manner in which* something called a "moral law" or "moral principle" was formulated.

A moral law exists, on this scheme, if a universal law is freely formulated and based on empirical *criteria*. Moral rules have the same overall logic as the rules of a game, save for the fact that those who formulate moral "laws" insist that everyone is in the game whether they choose to be or not.

But this kind of existence accords morality no necessity other than *logical* necessity and *lexical* necessity. So *logically*, "if I *decide* a principle for behavior is necessary, it is by definition necessary," and, most importantly, *lexically*, "being decided as *necessary for all human beings to follow* is what the *word* morality *means*.

But *why* does it mean that? If we have no insight into uniquely *moral* necessities, why is it we go about formulating universal rules in this way? Why, indeed, when there is absolutely *no necessity for them to do this*—or for the rules to be followed by others—save for the decision of the decision-makers that everyone do so and the decision of everyone else to comply.

Of course the utilitarians and sociobiologists say the necessity comes from the desire to survive, for that requires people follow certain rules of behavior. But this is practical necessity, not moral necessity. To make it a moral matter, it has to be *morally* necessary that people aim at human survival. This possibility has, of course, been "cut off at the pass" since *survival* is a fact and therefore cannot imply an *ought*.

Empirically viewed, moral behavior becomes an absurdity. (Which is why George Mavrodes thought it had to come from God, and why scientists can hopefully offer to explain it neurologically, biologically, and sociologically.)

The failure to admit a domain constituted by the "obduracy" or *undeniability* of moral necessity as a *type* of necessity stems from a narrow epistemology. In accordance with the logic of David Hume, no matter how much *experience* one has with the way life *is*, one can discover nothing that would allow one to *infer* or rationally *conclude* that an action ought or ought not be done, ought or ought not be preferred, or is good or bad.[35]

Rational thinking ("reason") can avail morality no basis in reality, so that, "Tis not contrary to reason to prefer the destruction of the whole world to the scratching of my finger."[36] (Hume developed a *scientific* account of morality in which *sympathy* becomes the engine of compassion. But this is all drives and associations that are part of our physical nature, not a matter of knowledge. It is all behavior and internal "sentiment.")

As we early on suggested, this is the same denial that plagued the philosophy of science and effectively unhinged the physical world. There it was said that from observing what, "physically," *is*, one cannot rationally conclude what *must* be.

In short, empiricist thinking denies the reality of *worldly necessity*—whether physical or moral or aesthetic—as a consequence of its view of human experience.

William Kneale, writing about Hume, remarks on this narrow, quasi-photographic idea of "experience":

> The question "How do we obtain the idea of necessary connexion?" can be answered only by the statement that we know the incompatibility of certain items such as redness and greenness which we have met in experience. The empiricists are right in saying that there can be no thought without experience, *but they are wrong in saying (or implying) that thought is the reproduction, or anticipation, of experience in imagination* [emphasis added].[37]

In the corridors of actual practice, rational thought about existence is not limited to what one can see before one—to "experience" viewed as a *snapshot*.

The fact that one "gave the law to oneself" was supposed to legitimize the attribution of *necessity* to a moral principle. But of course all it did was deem it "moral" in *form* while denying any knowledge of good and bad by which its putative moral force might be supported.

For most people endeavoring to live within the arena of consequences—for every society that is literate, and many that are not—morally necessary actions do not exist just *because* someone (even an entire society) decides to call a principle "moral." Morally necessary actions do not exist just because someone intends that all follow it (monarchy, inherited social status, and slavery being examples).

The chief concern of morality is that an *accepted* morality be the *right* morality. We seek to know what is necessary. In this work's sense of what makes things ultimate or sacred, we seek the assurance of God.

FEELINGS AND NECESSITY

We have, throughout, argued against the idea that we are merely physical beings to be understood the way physical things are understood.

One great danger in this is the suggestion that we are bodiless creatures. Moses Mendelssohn, for example, held that "since the faculty of thought cannot be explained as a product of material combination, the soul must be immaterial, and, as such, must be imperishable."[38]

But we do not think the graveyard is a transfer point from one railway line to another. The body is essential for the mind, but the mind somehow "cooperates" with the body to know the world on non-physical (rational) principles. "Somehow" is the operative word. It is the word that points to an ultimate mystery.

Human feelings are a critical aspect of this fusion that knowing requires. Without them, the morally and aesthetically normative aspects of reality cannot be known. One who feels nothing can evaluate nothing.

Yet, they confound description. They are bodily yet not exactly so. They are an aspect of awareness, yet not completely so. There will always be philosophers "dissolving" this "only apparent" puzzle, but never successfully, for no self-respecting intellectual ever rests confounded.

Feeling, because it is in some sense bodily, is, we shall argue, the *incarnation* of necessity. It is the body's side of that union with what *must be*—with "God"—that we have previously referred to, generically, as "knowing." Specifically, our feelings are crucial to knowing what is worthy in itself. Only in the medium of feeling can those *qualities* of life be apprehended that, as truths, *inform* us with respect to what ought or ought not be done.

So, we say feeling has necessary role in the cognition of "the good." Without it there can be no "empirical" or "worldly" basis for moral necessity. That is, there can be no worldly truths upon which a moral system can claim to rest. Nor can there be worldly truths on which the necessities of art may be said to rest.

Without a cognitive role for feeling, moral systems and aesthetic judgment are myths gullibly accepted as appreciations of what must be or "what is right" in each illusory domain. Either that, or they are rules for the most comprehensive engagements on the most comprehensive playing field, with newborns carried into the stadium as the dead are carried out.

FEELINGS REVISITED

Chapter 2, "God's Meaning" took up the subject of feeling for two reasons: The first was to argue that the nature of human feelings cannot be understood on a mechanical or cause-effect model: Feelings arise from one's understanding of an object. The second reason was to conclude that the worthiness of the object determined the worthiness of the feeling that arose from its contemplation.

This conception of feelings found support in the fact that people commonly speak of various feelings as appropriate or inappropriate, justifiable or unjustifiable.

We said the fact that people *evaluate* feelings showed they do not regard them simply as psychological facts caused by other facts. Were a fragrance to produce a feeling associated with a past event, it would be absurd to ask whether the evocation of that feeling was "justifiable" or "appropriate." The associated feeling just "happens." It is something *caused*; it is a psychological phenomenon.

By contrast, if one feels excitement or pleasure at hearing a political speech, one would not be surprised to be asked whether that feeling was justifiable or appropriate. The feeling is *about* the speech. It is not *caused* by or "triggered" by the speech (although, of course, there are cases where it *is* "triggered").

Similarly, our feelings regarding religion and art are subject to evaluation. They can be superficial, profound, appropriate. But, if they are discovered to have the character of mere *association* with an object, they will be considered irrelevant either to religion or art.

So, if I feel devotion to a religion because I associate it with an author I admire, my feeing of "religious" devotion is suspect at best.

And if I feel pleasure looking at Rembrandt's painting, "The Staalmeesters," because it reminds me of the cigar box favored by my father whom I loved, my pleasure in looking at the painting is *irrelevant* to its aesthetic character.

And in the domain of morality, too, feelings are judged with respect to their object. To enjoy the discomfort of others is "sadistic." To feel little or nothing about the situation of others is not just a psychological fact. Clinical definitions of sociopathy, like that of the World Health Organization, speak of "*callous* unconcern for the feelings of others [emphasis added]" while "psychopathy" involves, among other things, "*shallow* emotions [emphasis added]" (Cleckley 1976; Hare 1993). Terms like "callous" and "shallow" are evaluative and reflect standards of *appropriateness* to their object.

And who would not ask of someone unmoved by starving children, "how can you look at them and feel nothing about it?"

Indeed, it is evident that the judgment of how people feel about things, and *why*, is a foremost concern of human life.

Once we let go of a mechanical model of feelings and rely, instead, on the understanding of feelings on which we build a life, we are forced to confront things we cannot explain on the basis of third-person, scientific interpretations of experience.

Furthermore, a scientific reconstruction of what we experience when we evaluate persons, things, and relations rests on no *scientific* argument for doing so. The urge to *explain* evaluations as psychological phenomena stems, rather, from the puzzlingly intractable character of evaluative disagreements.

But the fact that we *bother* to *argue* matters of value, and that argument generates conclusions that determine the direction of whole peoples, forces us to say either that evaluations must be *systemically rooted and physiologically embedded* knowledge-claims, or that no knowledge is involved and that we *stake our lives on a shared delusion* concerning the reality of values.

To opt for the latter position, to say that civilized understanding is metaphysically deluded is to claim a view of reality better grounded than the one that has commended itself, through experience, to practitioners in all the institutions of life—from politics, through the arts, familial relations, and across the entire range of self-described "professions."

External, third-person reinterpretations of experience are in no position to have priority over first-person experience of normative matters. It is only within that experience that values are commonly seen as aspects of reality whose assessment requires appropriate feeling (or "sensitivity").

Scientistic reductions are a skepticism. They decide upon the nature of (first-person) moral experience from a third-person viewpoint. But, of course, in so doing, they prefer their *own* (typically unnoticed and unacknowledged) first-person experience of other people's *arguments* to any first-person experience of moral *situations*. Thus, they are distanced from feeling with respect to the elements of moral judgment.

To prefer theorists' *existentially removed* conception of *reality* over conceptions of reality that have emerged from centuries of engagement with life is strangely disingenuous when that conception itself can *only* be established through experience. The strategy ignores the warning to philosophers urged by Charles Sanders Peirce, that one should "never doubt in one's philosophy what one does not doubt in one's heart."

FEELINGS AND NORMATIVE REALITY

Our view of feelings harbors a problem. The problem is that we have said the evaluation of feelings depends on the evaluation of feeling's *object*, but now we say that the object must be judged, in part, by our *feelings*.

To deal with this apparent contradiction, we need first to agree that feelings are in some way foundational to evaluation.

We must agree that someone who feels nothing in particular about forests and beaches and mountains cannot possibly see why natural environments ought not be treated solely from the point of view of profit—and that a person who feels nothing in particular about the fate of anyone but his or her own family cannot be expected to formulate sound moral judgments.

And this is true even if such persons know "the right answers." For one can be "socialized" and understand that people almost universally find forests beautiful and inspiring—or even come on that basis to *believe* it, without a basis in feeling for their belief. (Without feeling one can believe a forest is inspiring—sort of "see it"—but be easily swayed to put it to practical uses that would destroy its inspiring character.)[39]

The relationships between feeling, rationality, and the objectivity of values pose immense problems of explication. Language is really not well suited to expressing whatever truths there may be in these matters. The issues are knottier, in our view, than the issues surrounding physical necessity. But if feeling is essential for aesthetic and knowledge, there is nothing for it but to state our position and to do so more didactically than we would like.[40]

So, we state our conclusion: *feeling is the medium of evaluative judgment*.

We therefore assert the oft-ridiculed idea of feeling as a "sixth sense"—but we mean by "sixth sense" a *necessary medium* of perception, *not* an infallible pathway to truth. And, in any case, this is how it is with the sensory mediums of "the five senses." For they, too, are essential for knowing the physical world and yet, *of themselves*, do not deliver the truth. So, the medium of feeling may plausibly be said to operate in a manner analogous to the *sensory* mediums within which we perceive *physical* reality.

That is, through *the way things feel to us* (as in, *look* to us, *taste* to us, *sound* to us) we discern those qualitative properties of reality necessary to aesthetic and moral assessments. Without them, those evaluative "assessments" are not really assessments but express only social *conventions* (agreed upon rules) or else mindless *phenomena*—that is, psycho-physical "reactions" triggered by sense-perceived events that can have no more credibility or cognitive status than a headache.

So, if aesthetic judgments and moral judgments rest only on social convention or brain-conditions, they have no necessity *in reality* and therefore no uniquely compelling claim on our decisions to act. There would be no objective moral or aesthetic *oughts* to conflict with will or desire or urge. As if, for example, there were no *objective* grounds (no truths about value) on which the Taliban's destruction of Afghanistan's third-century statues of Bhudda could be contested.

Still, we must ask how a medium of perception (feelings or "sensing") can be judged against its object—and yet be the judge, in some way, *of* its object? This appears to be *self-contradictory*. It is, however, the situation of all self-correcting perceptions,

Consider what in fact we do. Take vision: the medium of vision is judged by its object—the optometrist's eye chart. Yet, there is no way to judge what is relevantly true about the eye chart without looking at it, that is, without relying on *seeing*—on the visual *medium*. So while the eye chart is the object for evaluating seeing, the characteristics proper for the eye chart are established on the basis, in essential part, of seeing itself.

Even though we depend upon a fallible instrument, like vision, we can, by applying it to different objects in different ways under different conditions, improve its objectivity. And these activities do more than merely change what we see. They make our vision more accurate—something that is possible only because there is something "out there" that can break in upon the experience we bring to it. That is, the work of our sensory mediums can be improved because there are necessities in the world (things that are their own way and not just any-way-at-all).

The self-correction that improves a fallible mind occurs only through further use of the mind. This point is often made about the scientific method; it is "self-correcting (even though perspectivists insist it is self-enclosed and therefore circular and based on "faith").

The way we better our perceptions and our theories is by using them under intelligently varied conditions and in the light of challenges to what we conclude by means of them.

The situation is, of course, the same with respect to hearing. When we listen to music, we judge our hearing against the sounds of the orchestral recording. But judging the sounds of the recording depends upon the quality of our hearing.

When we listen to the music from the aesthetic standpoint, what we feel in the music—its ethereal quality or its fiery quality or its contemplative quality or its sadness—may be modified through extended listening or re-hearing of the piece, until we determine what qualities are really in it.

The almost unbelievable failure to acknowledge the cognitive role of feeling is made clear when we bring to mind the incredible refinements of sensibility that make up the fields of aesthetic criticism.

In this regard, it is appropriate to quote a genuine madman, Vincent van Gogh, saying against the counsel of his academic simulacra that

> the . . . drawing has to be a drawing of the figure for the sake of the figure and the inexpressibly harmonious form of the human body, but at the same time a pulling of carrots in the snow. . . . Tell Serret that *I should be desperate if my figures were* correct. . . . I adore the figures by Michelangelo though the legs are undoubtedly too long. . . . Tell him for me that Millet and Lhermitte are the real artists, for the very reason that they do not paint things as they are, traced in a dry, analytical way, but as *they . . .* feel them. Tell him that my great longing is to learn to make those very incorrectnesses . . . those changes of reality, so that they may become, yes, untruth if you like—but more truth than the literal truth.[41]

But perhaps feeling's perceptual role can be best assessed on occasions of our own response. Consider a portion of an eighth century poem by Ch'ang Chien: ". . . the mind of man touches peace in a pool/ And a thousand sounds are quieted/ By the breathing of a temple-bell."[42] Or respond to Shakespeare's meditation on the human situation in *The Tempest*: "we are such stuff as dreams are made on, and our little life is rounded with a sleep." Or, consider the plainspoken "Daniel Boone" of Stephen Vincent Benét:

> When Daniel Boone goes by, at night,
> The phantom deer arise,
> And all lost, wild America
> Is burning in their eyes.

In the absence of feeling one is "blind" to what *exists* in such words.

So, there is an auditory medium, a visual medium, a tactile medium, an olfactory medium, a medium of taste *and a medium of feeling*. By means of these, employed singly or in combination, we so approach the world that by their varied, intelligent, and repeated use we render more objective our perception of reality's normatively qualitative aspects.

What we contend is that there are at least two conceptually different paths to perceiving the *normative qualities* of reality. One, aesthetics, is in the interest of valuable perceptions, the other, morality, in the interest of obligatory actions. In *aesthetic* perception, one feels the aesthetic warmth of a painting—even though, in physical perception, the sensory *eye* sees, in the same paining, only orange and yellow (and the skin feels only a cool surface).

In moral perception, one *feels* what estrangement is, or love, or challenge or what it is to face danger. But the qualities of existence that have normative implications are beyond enumeration.

Of course the perception of these qualities depends, as we early on said, on our *understanding* of the object. It is just that without a tether to reality—without palpable experience—*evaluations* would be nothing more than arbitrary assessments made to *seem* reality-based by sheer familiarity, or the weight of social opinion (as Hare suggested all evaluative principles were).

We have, however briefly, considered aesthetic judgment. Let us reflect on what we do when a moral judgment is called for:

Suppose we feel uncomfortable to criticize a certain person (we feel it somehow "wrong"). Someone recounts to us in detail what this person has done. We have feelings about this. The quality of the person's actions feel, as it were, darker, more ugly than when we brushed some of them aside.

Someone else reminds us of the person's unfortunate upbringing. We empathize and then sympathize. We feel the person as a victim; we feel something about the helplessness of the young. Now we must act. We mull the situation over. Scenarios pass through our mind, and always with feelings about what we consider. We decide that when we think about (feel about) what the person has done, the other things we thought about, and had feelings about, do not outweigh the hardness, the callousness of what the person has done. Our feeling for justice contributes to our resolve. We ought to confront and not let this go. We feel criticism is right in the sense that we *conclude* it is right because, in essential part, of the *feel* of it.

(Aside: there are many senses of "feel"; we think our example doesn't trade on one or another meaning of "feel" misleadingly, and we think, in this context, the non-philosopher knows very well what is meant by how things feel to one.)

We insist that—although feeling is the *medium* of evaluations—aesthetic, moral, and other evaluations arise out of knowledge and warranted beliefs that do not depend upon normative qualities. Sophistication determines feelings and feelings are essential for sophistication.

Evaluations are dependent on assessments of physical fact, historical fact, likely consequences, theoretical frameworks, and, above all, the discipline of attempting to evaluate *consistently*. As Chapter 2 argued, feeling is not *sufficient* for evaluation.

Without feelings (in the case, above) where the question was whether or not to criticize someone, we would not have bothered to reflect on hearing what the person had done.

We would merely have consulted a rule (the cruelty of the petty bureaucrat), or acted out of habit (the morality of the dullard), or thoughtlessly responded (the sangfroid of the irresponsible). We would have had sociopathy's or psychopathy's "*callous* unconcern for the feelings of others" or "*shallow* emotions."

Indeed, the tendency for emotional waywardness to be regarded as a *medical* problem suggests that in the non-philosophical world, feelings are regarded as not radically different from visual or auditory senses. A radical departure from the norm is treated as a failure of one's physiological *equipment*. The body has failed the mind it normally supports.

The dispute at hand is essentially one as to how "experience" is to be understood—for worldly reality can be known only through experience.

Our own view is that there exists no more authoritative a basis for determining the categories of reality (factual, moral, aesthetic, logical) than first-person experience in a civilized, educated world of consequential activities. (Here, we offer no *criterion* of truth, but rather a practical rule for finding it.)

If it be true that everyone—amid "real life"—is convinced that goodness and badness and rightness and wrongness and appropriateness and beauty and ugliness and gracefulness are all features of reality that *cannot be denied*, then philosophers can have no *stronger* or more credible basis for denying the reality of what everyone finds real in experience.

The absence of a stronger ground in theory than in the making of life choices makes scientism, ironically, more a *faith* than a rational determination. We must concur with Paul Tillich's observation that "if representatives of modern physics reduce the whole of reality to the . . . movement of . . . particles of matter, denying the really real quality of life and mind, they express a faith. . . ."[43]

That normative qualities exist—and are *evidence* for concluding what is good or bad, right or wrong *in itself*—is in effect, the idea behind Erich Maria Remarque's antiwar novel, *All Quiet on the Western Front*.

Remarque crafted a scene that allows us to perceive qualities available only to those who can feel, and which—if *factual*—provide *evidence* as to the goodness or badness of war.

We are all conversant with wartime deaths as expressed in numbers. But numbers, no matter how large, do not present the qualitative truths on the basis of which one can evaluate what it *is* to kill, even for one's country, even in self-defense. (Our excerpt describes but one situation of war; we do not offer it as a comprehensive account of war's moral significance.)

The setting of *All Quiet* is the First World War. Remarque's soldier-protagonist, a German, huddles in a shell-hole, avoiding bullets and shrapnel, hoping to survive. Suddenly a French soldier falls headlong into the hole. In fear, and almost by reflex, Remarque's protagonist stabs him. The soldier dies slowly, over some days. The protagonist must watch his dying, hear the gurgling in his throat. At the Frenchman's death he pours out his sorrow and guilt:

> "I will write to your wife," I say hastily to the dead man, "I will write to her, she must hear it from me, I will tell her everything I have told you, she shall not suffer, I will help her, and your parents too, and your child—"[44]
>
> His tunic is half open. The pocketbook is easy to find. But I hesitate to open it. In it is the book with his name. So long as I do not know his name perhaps I may still forget him, time will obliterate it, this picture. But his name, it is a nail that will be hammered into me and never come out again. . . .[45]
>
> Irresolutely I take the wallet in my hand. It slips out of my hand and falls open. Some pictures and letters drop out. . . . There are portraits of a woman and a little girl, small amateur photographs taken against an ivyclad wall. Along with them are letters. I take them out and try to read them. Most of it I do not understand, it is so hard to decipher and I know scarcely any French. But each word I translate pierces me like a shot in the chest;—like a stab in the chest.[46]
>
> I have killed the printer, Gérard Duval.[47]

We contend that our perception of a situation's qualities—what we feel these events to *be*—is an instance of evaluative knowing, and, since we realize the events as described can be real, an instance of worldly knowing.

And if it is *true* that description tells us things that are true-of-the-world with respect to what is good and what is bad, then it is also true that we *can* infer (not "deduce") what *ought* to be from what *is*! And so we reject the empiricist shibboleth, "no ought from is."

The idea that feelings permit *knowledge* of what is normatively real represents the judgment of the working world. *It is the idea on which human life is based.*

Hardly an action is taken, hardly a decision is reached or a reflection registered, that doesn't involve an evaluation of *something* in the world. We breathe *feelings* about things as constantly as we breathe the (equally invisible) *air*.

Iris Murdoch and others make a point about evaluative language that supports our insistence on the ubiquity of evaluations that find "facts" or "behaviors" to have specific normative *qualities*. They point out that there exist legions of evaluative terms that combine fairly specific *normative qualities* with patterns of behavior in a single concept.

Murdoch says philosophy has focused too much on the one term, *good* and ignored such common combined fact-value terms as "'brave', 'free', 'sincere', which are the bearers of crucial ideas."[48] Bernard Williams supplies other evaluative, yet behaviorally delimiting terms, that he refers to as "thick" concepts; for example, "malicious, brutal, inconsiderate, self-indulgent, greedy."[49]

A brief passage from Max Lerner's introduction to the work of Thorstein Veblen illustrates the way moral discourse weaves behaviors and specific normative qualities together:

> For he [Veblen] was analyzing an America in the *sleaziest* decades of its civilization—an America of *crassness* and *money-lust*, of *boodle* and *greed*, of men of power whose *garish* pecuniary values were made the subject of emulation by the whole people.[50]

The importance of such terms is that they point to the way qualities and behaviors are commonly tied together in our evaluational practices—in such terms, for example, as "spendthrift" and "miser." Evaluation is constant. It is the ever-present evidence of life's meaningfulness. "What did you think of those people we just met?" is not usually about physical fact—about how tall they are or how much money they have or the color of their hair—but about good or bad qualities.

Is the rug looking too dark, the pictures not straight, the closet in disarray? Are not the flowers cheerful? Is one's skin looking sallow, one's activities becoming dull—too much TV, not enough reading? And what of the garden? Is it lush, lively? And the sky . . . such wondrous blue today and magnificence of the clouds and the lovely lilt of the Irish neighbor's speech and the look of our table setting which is a bit shopworn.

Evaluation is the very substance of our talk and attention. And all this is done as it can only be done, within the medium of feeling, in terms of which we gather in the reality around us.

Hume spoke implicitly on this point when he declared, "Tis not contrary to reason to prefer the destruction of the whole world to the scratching of my finger."[51] For if "reason" is understood as Hume understood it—as logical, scientific, or utilitarian inquiry—then inquiry into the word can yield no conclusion regarding the worth of anything.

On a Humean view, there is no qualitative knowledge of the world and thus no basis in *knowledge* that might suggest the end of human civilization is worse than a scratch on one's finger. (Hume explained morality as caused by *sympathy*, but not because sympathy opened the window to the quality of others' lives; sympathy caused other sentiments to arise, it was not a gateway to moral *knowledge*.)

Feelings are what allow *knowledge* of the good. We repeat: without the perception of qualities through the medium of feeling one can have knowledge only of what is *considered* good. And if it were true that we had no actual knowledge of the good, then what is *considered* good would be nothing more or less than what is *approved* of. "Good" would mean only "I (or we) approve of it."

Of course this leaves unexamined what "approval" is. Hare saw that it approval involved making use of standard for judgments. But if there is no knowledge of the good, the standard can bring us no closer to a (non-extent) moral or aesthetic truth than we would be without a standard.

Without an ability to perceive the good in reality, standards of the good are not supported by *knowledge* of the good. The whole enterprise of living is then completely made up as to purpose or worth.

This predicament leads, of course, to the search for God's Word. But because God's Word (as claimed) must always be evaluated to distinguish the genuine from the imagined, we cannot benefit from seeking God's Word on the theory that we ourselves cannot know the good. We would have no *objectively compelling* basis on which to judge the genuineness of any putative divine "word."

The phrase *objectively compelling* is of course a reference to necessity—to what is *required* with respect to the good. Without this necessity there is no domain of the good and so no domain of morals, aesthetics—indeed—of actions or things objectively significant in any way.

FEELING, NECESSITY, AND ART

Morality and art are both domains at the heart of human life, for both are concerned with what *must* be done to realize objects and actions that are good *in themselves* and, for that reason, make life lived in terms of them good in itself.

But art may inform us more clearly, perhaps, than morality with respect to whether qualities exist that have normative implications perceptible only in a medium of feeling. Art is less entangled in consequences, theories, and practical interests.

For example, the reality of aesthetic "tension" in music or painting challenges an empirical view of experience. In the latter, "tension" can only refer to a psychological or bodily state. And to say work has tension is to say it makes the viewer tense. But the idea of *aesthetic* tension denies that the tension in an art work refers to the work's capacity to cause the perceiver's psychological or bodily tension.

(Of course, the whole business of feelings, qualities, and normative implications calls for a separate work. Our discussion will be confined to a few points in support of aesthetic necessity.)

Beethoven rather straightforwardly expressed the idea that an artwork's elements cannot be altered without destroying the identity or integrity of the work. "*Muss es sein*? (must it be [just this way]?" he rhetorically asked, concerning the finale of his String Quartet in F Major (Op. 135). His answer was clear: "*Es muss sein! Es muss sein!* (It must be! It must be!)"

For us, the crucial point is that the creation of art objects is—for all its emotional "freedom"—a discipline. That is, art can succeed only when it perceives what is aesthetically *necessary*.

The twentieth century saw an outcropping of "aleatoric" art. But *avant garde* outbursts that seek to *found* art on chance (not *use* chance) are fundamentally absurd, since chance organizations are compatible with the total absence of an artist.

Art is a matter of embodying qualities for *perceptual understanding* (not for mere "fun" or "thrills"—a roller coaster can better guarantee one or both).

Art requires the artist to discern what the addition, subtraction, and alteration of elements causes *aesthetically* to happen, not *physically* to happen. And the necessity of additions, subtractions, and changes is as much a matter controlled by what one quality *does* to another as the addition of weights or springs in building a clock is controlled by what one physical property *does* to another.

Necessity plays no less a role in creating an aesthetic domain than in creating a physical domain. It is a matter of the artist's perceiving what each element of the work *requires* (given the other elements and the work's dominant theme—whether verbal or non-verbal).

Art has, of course, been used for practical ends from supporting religious institutions and attitudes to enhancing the effectiveness of salesmanship. But, even so, if it is nonetheless art, its materials have been organized in terms of their aesthetic qualities to maximally realize an aesthetically concrete theme. If the presentation of that realized theme has practical values as well, so be it.

But once *practical* necessity overrules *aesthetic* necessity in deciding on the features of the object, the object enters another domain and requires another rubric such as "commercial art" or "illustration" or perhaps "propaganda."

The chief point is that art is the exploration and use of *aesthetic* causality (within an individual work in a historical context of aesthetic learning); it is not a search for *physical* (psychological) causality.

So, contemplating genuine art, one's breath is caught by the beauty of a moment or gesture, but contemplating a practical object one's breath is caught by sudden and egregious nudity or by the shock of an unexpected "special effect" like a wave washing over a city or a man being made to melt.

"Commercialism" and much (though not all) of Soviet "social realism" is the organization of perceptual object for its psychological effects more than for its aesthetic qualities.

Past religious art was typically beholden first to aesthetic necessity and secondarily (if effectively) to religious purposes. This was readily achievable, in our view, because religion is an appreciation of Being in itself and thus requires the ability to perceive a thing as it is in itself, much as one perceives an art object or a moral dilemma.[52]

The idea that aesthetic objects are successful *as art* only when the experience of them is valuable apart from practical ends, was apparent to the British philosopher, G. E. Moore who defined "beauty" as "that of which the admiring contemplation is good in itself."[53]

So, the question is, what are we doing when we spend time looking at a painting or, even more strangely, listening for over an hour to a musical composition?

It is clear we are not having *the kind of experience empiricism defines as "experience."* We are not looking at colors and lines, and we are not listening to sounds. Neither of these sense-perceptible phenomena is the focus of our attention though both are essential for the existence of what it is we *are* focused on. We see warmth, strength, movement, harmony, radiance, sorrow, joy in the painting and we hear the same sorts of thing in the music.

None of these aesthetic properties (qualities) is perceived by the senses. And much effort has been wasted attempting to explain how the sense-perception of art objects stimulates or triggers emotional states in us that we (self-deluded, as always) project onto the art works themselves. In a *scientifically* defined world it is impossible to perceive worldly facts that are there—when not *sensibly* there.

The existence of aesthetic qualities, like morally relevant qualities, is yet another *defining* feature of *human* experience that lies outside scientific observation. For that reason the empirical or "scientistic" philosopher must insist that the "perception" of art is simply *sense-perception* that stimulates emotions by virtue of *associations*. (Of course some make the case by defining "aesthetic perception" as stimulation by objects hung or placed in museums—in other words "art" is a *conventional* term for psychologically stimulated under certain social conditions.)

But if the safety pin that we used to pin the diapers of our only child (now fifty years old) makes us weep when found, we do not for a moment think it an example of *art* (even if we had crafted it ourselves out of spring steel).

Perception (of non-physical reality), not *association*, defines our relation to art. "There is one—and only one—test for the aesthetic relevance of an interpretation [of an art object]: it must heighten our perception of the object and thereby increase our aesthetic delight."[54] Clearly, the "heightening" of perception is not seeing the colors and lines better, as if one were looking at a meter in a laboratory.

It is seeing, but seeing qualities and relationships visible only through the medium of feeling. "Heightened" perception in art cannot be obtained by cleaning one's glasses or moving closer to the object. It is a matter of getting hold of how the qualities embody a theme or notion or emotional state. It is a matter of feeling or "sensibility." (If "aesthetic delight" were nothing more than "delight," *period*, then interpretations of art would not have to be "right" but only *effective* in heightening pleasure. This would allow delight to come from the way one thinks about the art and not, necessarily, by way of perception at all.)

So, when we love to contemplate a still life because it reminds us of Grandmother's table-setting we are not appreciating it as art. Our

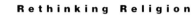

emotions are then not essentially derived from perception; they are essentially derived from association.

The American philosopher, O. K. Bouwsma, pithily and pointedly noted that when it comes to an aesthetic property like the quality of sadness, "the sadness is to the music rather like the redness to the apple, than it is like the burp to the cider."[55] (The sadness is not something *caused* in us by music.) The proof, of course (against the "association" or "psychological" theory of art), is that we can perceive sadness in music, painting, sculpture, dance, or poetry without becoming sad.

As for *necessity*, the painter will find that the painting "needs" (must have) some orange over here, the playwright that some additional action is *necessary*, and the director that film *ought to be* shorter.

We see an indirect recognition of necessity in certain common critical phrases. For example, when we say a work is "self-indulgent," we do not mean that making it was a matter of unalloyed enjoyment for the artist. Rather ,we say it, first, because the film's content and organization is not self-justifying. It does not convince perception that the way it is, is the way it *ought* to be. The flagrancy of its arbitrariness must be explained. And that "self-indulgence" explains it psychologically, as the product of a will not concerned with what, aesthetically, was *required*.

The whole ethos of art, like the ethos of science, is to have in one's "work" all that is needed and nothing in excess of what is needed. Art, no less than science, requires a grasp of what is *necessary* in the hope of finding the *sufficient*.

NECESSITY AND POSSIBILITY

Necessities tell us what cannot be done. This suggests nothing more than restriction, particularly if one's idea of a law-giving derives from the Old Testament's demands or from the New Testament's equally unyielding "Revelations."

But in fact, necessity is the complement of liberation. It is the condition of meaningful action. For, without necessity, what is possible would be—always—a matter of *chance*. If the physical world were not a domain of necessities, there could be no reliable prediction and therefore no way to develop scientific knowledge. Indeed, necessities (as we have argued) are what constitute "worlds" of any kind.

And even if the physical world could (in some sense) exist, it would be without value. Mountains and deserts and forests and seas would have no character other than fickleness if properties came and went as a matter of chance. Words like "mountain"—*object* words, *thing* words—would never exist.

The implications of necessity for meaning and creativity is a commonplace in the arts. An artist who could not count on blue staying blue, or on the effect of its being placed near green couldn't create art. And a poet who cared little for the absolutely right—the essential—word or phrase would be no poet at all. If anything can be, nothing matters.

Human relations without the inertia of habits and of coherence of psychological "identity" would be utterly impossible. If psychological inertia were not provided by the brain's organic necessities and all our choices were equipossible, we could never say who we were (or who those around us were) in respect of *character*, *personality*, likes or dislikes. Societies could have no dependable expectations.

In sum, freedom would be valueless without necessities. Actions could not be distinguished from accidents. We could count on nothing. Further—as we have been arguing—without *aesthetic* or *moral* necessity, the actions we undertook would be meaningless, for if nothing is *required* of action, then acts may be preferred, but none can be *preferable* to any other.

In fine, it wouldn't *matter* what we thought or did. And when what we do "doesn't matter," we face less a philosophical impasse than a clinical depression.

Necessity is the essential condition of actual and possible worlds and therefore of meaning. And if this is true, then being *human* is a function of knowing what *needs* to be done with respect to both ends and means. Physical, moral, and aesthetic necessities tell us what the right action is, what the best action is, and what actions ought (rightly) be done to arrive at that which it is right or best to brought into being.

Action in the light of what independent necessities demand makes human activity—and thus human *being*—worthy of the "gift" of consciousness. This inexplicably obdurate "other," this necessity that is, and has always been, is the law-like character of the real to which we owe what we are and to which we owe the possibility of increasing its worthiness. The awareness of inexplicably sovereign and immanent norms (physical and rational) may constitute what it is we are in awe of—and yet love. Necessitation is the awesome-yet-magnetic in experience that is humankind's sense of "divinity." The forms of necessity are the facets of God—the substance of the "numinous."

NECESSITY AND IRRELIGIOUSNESS:
MATERIALISM

It is characteristic of religions to reject worldly acquisitiveness— better known, perhaps as *materialism*.

But why is it one "cannot serve God and mammon"?[56] Perhaps the issue is *distraction*. Love is supposed to be toward God above all else: "For where your treasure is, there will your heart be also."[57]

But one finds no admonitions against loving the beauties and respites of nature more than God. Perhaps "the outdoor life" is considered no distraction from God because nature is so often regarded as a manifestation of God. And here lies a clue. For, the materialistic way of life seems as incompatible with the love of nature as with the love of God.

Rather than being a mere *distraction*, the materialistic way of living is a force against the given—in theistic terms, against the world that is given to us.

There is, we think, a deep, if veiled, insight in the common understanding, that materialistic living is as *incompatible* with loving and respecting nature, as it is with loving and respecting "God," so that "he that layeth up treasure for himself . . . is not rich toward God."[58]

The insight we speak of is the perception that materialism is not just a *moral* fault. The reason "it is easier for a camel to go through a needle's eye, than for a rich man to enter into the kingdom of God"[59] may have more to do with the materialistic *Way of Being* as, *in itself*, ungodly. Rather than being a transgression of moral law, which is, in any case, not *directly* a religious matter, materialism may be, in essence, the denial of what is holy.

Interpretations always vary, to be sure, but as we shall see, there is the notion in Buddhism and Confucianism as well, that the incompatibility of religious and materialistic life is *irreligion*.

It has been a feature of our argument that love and respect for the divine is love and respect for the nature of things, for their necessity—for the "es muss sein" of the world's physical ways, aesthetic ways, moral ways, and the ways of understanding and knowing.[60]

To love and respect the necessities (things beyond our power to change) is to love and respect "god" or the "gift" that we find existence, in the final analysis, to be.

As the aim of our philosophizing is religious understanding, it may be useful, before offering specific arguments, to suggest, *metaphorically*, or in terms of the feeling-tone, what it means to love and respect necessity:

It is with full awareness to pass one's hand over the rough, sun-warmed surface of a great boulder, or to feel the rush of water around one's fingers in a stream, or to caress the body of a loved one, or in silence, to let oneself hear nothing but the wind—all things that must be or ought to be.

Philosophically speaking, it is *willingly* to follow out the *normative* import of things—their requirements or *imperative* character——and thus the possibilities as well as the impossibilities that create the physical, aesthetic, moral, and rational domains.

So, a more specific example of what it can mean to honor the necessities of rationality (outside the obvious example of formal logic) may be found in the notion of "economy of explanation."

The most rational explanation makes use of the fewest possible explanatory principles. For, it makes no *sense* to use *more than* one needs and no *sense* to use *less than* one needs. By rejecting the irrelevant, the former respects necessity, just as by rejecting insufficiency, the latter likewise respects what is rationally necessary. Not to follow either principle is not to respect mind.

The love and respect for necessity can be found in love and respect for language. To respect its rules (not mindlessly to follow them) is to respect implications among words that have been found *necessary* for conceptualizing reality. Language is the vessel of our learning. More than a tool, it is the necessary medium of a civilized human community.

And language carries also what is necessary in the matter of identity or "tradition," for a stable, precise, and comprehensive language is the mind of our forbears held in trust for our use.

This vision of a language whose necessities are one with our own intersects with the Confucian religious outlook as reported by Philip Ivanhoe. Rejecting the anti-Confucian, *empiricist* view he says that

> within an empiricist's worldview, one acquires language purely as a tool in the service of one's basic needs and desires.
>
> But, as one is led to see and understand certain features about oneself and the world, instead of using language . . . purely as a means to satisfy basic needs and desires—one may come to see it as intrinsically valuable, and as a new source of satisfaction.

Thus, a poet

> who regards the right kind of language as life itself . . . [can] . . . achieve the literary equivalent of the Confucian sage; her love

of and devotion to her art would mirror the sage's delight in and dedication to the Way"—the way of living that is right in itself.[61]

History, too is beholden to necessity. It does not chronicle events but attempts to unearth whatever *necessities* may have helped shape their course. And science, in loving and respecting the physical world, seeks to ferret out its laws. For science, far more often than not, is done for the sake of knowing the laws and not for the sake of using them. Indeed, the fields of astronomy and cosmology and archeology amply testify to the primacy of the urge to know what made *this* happen rather than that.

And, in assimilating of this love of knowledge to the love of God, we reconceive, in our own plodding way, the theologian, Jonathan Edwards' view that to find out "the reasons for things in natural philosophy is only to find out the proportion of God's acting."

But love and respect for the *unchangeable*—the necessities that *constitute* the human situation—implies not only *reading* the book of life but learning from it how to *write* in it.

For, the ability to create, produce, and even sensibly consume involves being guided by reality's *normative* character. Metaphorically speaking, the true maker of things listens first to God's Word.

We must be brief in sketching this point, for the world's *imperatives* teach us in ways that are numberless. That is to say, the way the world works thrusts itself in upon us, impresses us, fills us, prepares us, "stimulates" us.

The creations of equatorial peoples are often rich with bright, sometimes clashing, color; one who has seen the birds and the flowers of tropical climes can understand why. The world's colors enter into us, teach us, and we make things of them that never existed.

Here, a small myth of invention: The creation of the wheel likely involved seeing, in the light of physical necessities, what *must be done*. People need to move things. While things can be carried, slid, or floated, they can also be seen to slide more easily over small logs than on the ground. Round cross-sections can act as "bearings." Irregular rocks do not roll well. Logs do. Sections of logs do so better. Small sections of log linked by a pole are "wheels." Whatever the *particular* truth of inventing the wheel, *the many kinds of ways that things work* in the world are the ground for insight, imagination, and invention.

In a real, non-metaphorical, sense, the necessities of the world reveal themselves to us—and in informing us (through our actions) as to what *cannot* happen, they allow us to determine what *can* happen (re: the discussion of necessity and possibility above).

So, the craftsperson or artisan respects his or her material by studying it, working with it, finding out what can be done with it and finding out *from it* what new forms and uses a material might have. The carpenter seeks to understand the wood, physically and aesthetically. The carpenter respects what it offers and imagines how to form it into an object no less valuable in itself than the wood from which it was made.

The "true" craftsman, like the hobbyist (who represents the perfect relation between actor and world) loves and respects what is given and because of that is, even in a small way, ennobled. For the craftsman is not limited by appreciating the given but is enabled to extrapolate from the natural good what must be done do create a cultural good—something good in the human situation.

Part of everyday wisdom is to be relieved to see beautiful wood grain reappear after yellowing paint has been removed from antique furniture. In a sense, the entire argument against materialism can grow from this simple understanding.

The world helps us to see aesthetic or moral ends that—through our imagination and knowledge—we might, with effort, reach. Michelangelo gave expression to this idea when he said, "Every block of stone has a statue inside it and it is the task of the sculptor to discover it." August Rodin had the same understanding: "There are unknown forces in nature; when we give ourselves wholly to her, without reserve, she lends them to us; she shows us these forms, which our watching eyes do not see, which our intelligence does not understand or suspect." (Of course scientism will see such talk as "poetic," as "psychological projection" rather than as a description of how the human mind is *informed* through contact with the world.)

Literary artists, similarly, wait for imperatives that are not arbitrary or calculated dictates of will when they speak of waiting to see what the characters they have created will do. It is not that the characters have wills or are "persons." Rather, the many imperatives latent in the language of the story, the plot, the rhythm, the prior actions of characters have an aesthetic impetus that cannot be rightly determined outside the medium of feeling. They cannot be determined by "theory" or calculation—which is perhaps why works that survive on "plot" tend to be entertainment rather than art.

The same is true of "practical" creations—ships, engines, pulleys, levers, trains, automobiles, radio, airplanes, computers. Those who tinker, reflect, hypothesize, pursue, build are persons taught by the very materials they reshape into the tools and conditions of cultural life.

So, however briefly and crudely, we have sketched a way of living that loves and respects and takes its inspiration from the necessities that define what is real. And this we exemplified in only a few of life's departments; we spoke of rationality, invention, science, history and art but did not, for example, mention sport.

In a religious approach to life, one loves, respects, and is guided by what natural norms demand of us—by imperatives into which we have insight by virtue of the social, intellectual, productive, and artistic activities into which we enter.

Necessity is the mother of possibility and of rightness.

In what way, then is *materialism* irreligious? Is not *materiality* another name for what is physically real?

No doubt *materialism* is sometimes thought of as concern with physical objects. So considered, it is, as a failing, an *over-concern* with physical things. But this is a "sin" of excess. It surely falls short of any *fundamental* conflict with religion. That is why religions seldom condemn those who too many times build shelters, fashion roads, collect antiques, invent devices, or build walls. Inventors who have spent years developing airplanes, radio, radar, sonar, the telephone, and television have not been accused of *ungodliness*—nor could they plausibly be so chastised.

True, some Amish sects abjure the later accoutrements of technology, but their view seems not quite on the mark, since few other religious groups so severely reject human invention to honor God or live in a "spiritual" manner.

Of course there is a religious insight behind their resistance to the "advantages" of industrial and post-industrial society. We think it has to do in part with an insight into the irreligion of materialism, but also, on the positive side, with a feeling for the sacred in nature that one finds in Confucianism and in many Native American religions (a topic we consider separately).

Let us now try to make conscious precisely what it is that makes a way of living" materialistic." To that end, we ask which of the following persons is "materialistic" and which (other things being equal) is not?

Two wealthy persons each buy an extremely expensive sports car. It is a well-known make that many wish they could own. The first person knows little or nothing about the history of car design or about auto engineering, knows it is a desirable and much-desired car, drives the car to stores, theaters and, in general, around town and has it serviced at a dealership. The second person is knowledgeable with respect to car design and automobile engineering, chooses the car because it meets the highest aesthetic and engineering standards, participates in the tuning and care of the engine, races the car in local and regional events, and seldom drives it around town.

Two people buy land. The first puts ostriches, llamas and other less ordinary animals on the land and hires someone to take care of them; the land and the animals are shown to visitors and friends. The second works to insure that the land continues to support the flora and fauna that it did originally, walks the land for its beauty, and bequeaths it to the county as permanent open space.

Two women habitually purchase expensive clothing. One wears a thing once or twice then gives it away. The other is a style expert who uses the clothing to instruct budding designers—professional and amateur.

Two men purchase expensive media equipment. One knows little about it and orders the most impressive-looking object he can get. The other orders what happens to be the same object, but because it is the most natural reproducer of visual and auditory material he can afford.

In each scenario, people acquire the same material objects (or money as power to possess them), but only the first person in each example could be considered "materialistic," while the second person would not.

What the materialists share is that the motive for possessing material objects has nothing *essentially* to do with the properties essential to those objects. In effect, the *materiality* of objects does not exist; their inherent properties have no bearing on what is done with them.

The materialistic person doesn't give a damn about the material world. And this is why the carpenter who daily acquires and shapes wood and the painter who daily acquires and uses paints and the engineer who acquires materials and makes models and the computer programmer who acquires electrical components and plastic discs are none of them *materialistic*—even though their lives are concerned with acquisition and thought about *materials*.

Such people love and respect materiality's necessities—physical and aesthetic. It is they who are instructed and guided by that which is *outside* themselves. Not so, the materialist who would subject the whole material world to what is *within us*.

It is the materialist to whom possessing and selling the giant redwood tree is a matter merely of "personal choice." Unmindful of materials' possibilities, they are neither prepared nor inclined to consider how the material world might bear upon the "oughts" or "the good" of the world.

Not "God's law"—not the whole range of physical and evaluative imperatives—but *what we will* or *want* is sovereign in materialism. If the principle were applied in a Catholic setting, the wafer would be ingested not as God but as a snack.

So, the materialistic car manufacturer will make of steel and rubber and plastic and glass whatever will garner him the greatest return over a given time. Materials will not be shaped by what the engineer or the artist see in the materials, or by what the materials suggest for the construction of a more ideal life (unless those standards, by good fortune are, in a given case, advantageous for marketing).

The materialistic consumer will, as a way of living, buy the car that that makes him or her feel important or powerful. For him or her as well, the design, the engineering, the ecological effect, and effect on one's neighbors and community are irrelevant.

Neither will understand the appositeness of Louis Sullivan's dictum "that form ever follows function" because neither pays attention to the relationship between engineering, utility, and beauty.

Together, they create a world based on power and status in which the heedless consumption of the world can only accelerate. Where comparisons are constant and invidious, status is never secure; acquisition must be endless. If the internalization of reality is growing up, then materialism means never growing up—mundanely or religiously.

It is a life in which liberal arts graduates can enter advertising agencies and comfortably counsel the public that in the acquisition of objects, you can "be the envy of your friends!"

Materialism has no love or respect for that which is "other" than self. *It requires that one not love the world, but possess it.* It is, therefore a genuine evil, more comprehensively and deeply irreligious than the moral failure it undoubtedly is.

The simplicity of Amish life guards against the allure of materialism's undeniable bounty and thus against the self-aggrandizing system and symbols that drive its ever-changing, ever-expanding, heedlessness. In respecting the essential, it has much in common with early Chinese thought and the closeness to nature that characterizes Native American religions.

RESPECTING NECESSITY: CONFUCIANISM AND NATIVE AMERICAN RELIGION

The irreligiousness of materialism need not be fought by a swing of the pendulum. To reject it is not to adopt asceticism. For, a decision to ignore the possibilities of the material and social world is, equally, to make one's "inner self" sovereign over the normative demands and possibilities of reality.

If materialism dishonors the "gift" of the world by indiscriminately acquiring it, asceticism dishonors the world by indiscriminately rejecting it. One employs the world to impress others, the other uses it to ignore them.

Each, in its way, seeks to create an impregnable self rather than a self risked in service to the world.

While theistic religions reject materialism and often (but not always) asceticism, Native American and Confucian religions oppose both. However, the latter two oppose materialism and asceticism in ways more closely linked to the notion that "God's" substance is nothing other than what the world requires of us and makes possible for us.

For them, this world is holy, not *essentially* because a different kind of world—a supernatural world—has been *revealed*. It is rather, that an appreciation of the physical, aesthetic, and moral nature of the world is an appreciation of what is holy.

This world—the natural world—is found holy through an understanding of its ways. There is overlap, of course, in Native American religions, with the supernaturalism of Judeo-Christian-Islamic theism, but there is a noticeable and notable difference in emphasis. What is sacred for Native Americans is, as it were, visible, in the immutable ways of nature that together enable and guide the human way of being.

What is sacred for Confucianism is the immutable nature of what is, uniquely, the human *way of being* in the world—which, stated more mundanely, is the way only humans can bring things about; and stated more religiously, is a way that is as *inexplicably* powerful as it is inexplicably given.

Herbert Fingarette's account of Confucian thought finds its focus in the "magical quality" of "distinctively human powers."[62] Like our own essay into secular theology, Confucius' way of thinking sees this power in everyday life, so that, he, as we, must attempt to "reveal" as remarkable (even sacred) things we all do that are "already so familiar and universal as to be unnoticed."

It is not our intent to dwell at length on Fingarette's analysis. The relevant feature for us in Confucius' account of distinctively *human* interaction is its basis in knowledge of the necessary.

The Confucian emphasis on "*li*," which means "holy ritual" or "sacred ceremony" seems at first removed from the everyday. But its

link to quotidian human life is that civilized life (like ceremony) achieves success only through willing cooperation in the performance of actions understand by the participants to be right.

Its "magic" lies in the fact that when human beings understand what *must* be done, things are accomplished by virtue of what we *say* to each other—as opposed to how we might bribe each other or threaten each other or manipulate each other psychologically. Thus, Confucius contrasts the ruler who uses *li* with the ruler who seeks to attain his ends by means of commands, threats, regulations, punishments, and force.[63]

Fingarette uses the simple example of two people who, meeting on the street, shake hands. This unselfconscious act of recognition and equal respect takes place "without any command, stratagem, force, tricks, or tools, without any effort . . . [to make one or the other] . . . do so."[64]

It is "magical" (we might say "miraculous") because things are effected—changed, accomplished—in the world on the basis of mind or understanding and not causality.[65] "We are least like anything else in the world when we do not treat each other as physical objects, as animals or even as subhuman creatures to be driven, threatened, forced, maneuvered."[66]

As *li* is, "for Confucius . . . the explicit and detailed pattern of that great ceremony which is . . . the humane life," we can, according to Fingarette, think of *li* "as the map" of the *Tao*—which is, in ancient China, the "Way" or "right path" or "right Way of life."[67] (*Li* is what we might term the "mode" or "way" of walking the right path.)

The point is that there is a right way.

Against modern thinking, there are no choices here; one comes to know what is necessary for human beings to do or one fails. "To take any other 'route' than the Way is not a genuine road but a failure through weakness to follow *the* route. Neither the doctrine nor the imagery allows for a choice, if we mean by choice a selection, by virtue of the agent's powers, of one out of several equally real options."[68]

Still, "one can be truly following the Way . . . whatever the level of one's learning—for a wholehearted commitment to learning the Way is itself the Way for those who are not yet perfected in the Way."[69]

Indeed, for Confucius, the study of "literature, music and the civilizing arts" is learning the codes of the *li*. Finally but importantly, through learning one comes to see "the intrinsic nobility of the goal that provides the 'pull' [on one's behavior and thought]. . . . It is the Way that has power, and this power is effortless, invisible, magical."[70]

Like the Platonic idea that virtue comes from knowledge (and can be taught), and our own insistence on reasons empirically *grounded* in perception of life's qualities, the Confucian "Way" is directed by knowledge of what ought to be, that is, knowledge of nature's imperatives or normative implications.

In sum, the Way is as removed from a self-aggrandizing principle for living as the Sermon on the Mount.

Native American religions, unlike Confucianism, attempt to explain nature's ways anthropomorphically, thus allying them with the Judeo-Christian-Islamic tradition. But the theme of natural ways as the touchstone of the holy returns them to Confucian thought. Both honor an idea of the naturally *given*—what in terms of our thesis are the necessities, normative and physical—that constitutes the various aspects of reality.

Native peoples, like disciples of Confucius, are enjoined "' to walk in the sacred way'—that is, to live in balance and harmony with the universe," and, for American religions, "the spirit world."[71]

Like Confucianism, these religions are, despite voluminous references to spirits and the spirit world, very much of the earth. When the Native American scholar and poet, N. Scott Momaday, says "We Americans must come again to a moral comprehension of the earth and air. We must live according to the principle of a land ethic," he commends to his readers the understanding of Native Religions, for "if there is one thing which truly distinguishes . . . [the Indian] . . . it is surely his regard of and for the natural world."[72]

The element in Confucian and Native American insight that we find important is not a strict philosophical principle but rather an attitude—what we have called a love and respect for the substance of things, their way of being as we find that to be in experience. And this way of being, as the way that is unchangeable, is the ultimate in law and thus, as we have argued, that which we feel as "God."

That is why the way humans live, if understood as ineluctably a certain way, takes on sacred character beyond the mere factuality of that way. Seen as a way or as a whole it is a vision of the ultimate not foreign to "Indian" thought: "The holistic character of traditional American cultures shows through clearly in the inability of natives to distinguish thoroughly between nature and divinity," notes a recent work on *Native American Religions*.[73]

(Even "the Great Spirit," while responsible for existence is not a personal God—utterly *other* in respect of nature and society—and so is more an aspect of what we experience than the remote or radically "other" God of Judeo-Christian-Islamic theology.)

In any event, the "inability" to distinguish between nature and divinity may not be quite the deficit suggested. Because we argue that *knowing* is a humanity-creating union with reality—a part of "God's" *religious* meaning—we find it no encumbrance that for Native Americans, "the line between the self and 'outside' realities has not been as sharp or rigid as it became for Europeans after the Enlightenment."[74]

As the authors point out, "Native Americans were not schooled to . . . skepticism, the way that Europeans have been. . . . They did not bring to their culture the "hermeneutic of suspicion . . . "[75] Because "the ordinary rule among native Americans has been . . . [to make] . . . no rigid separation between secular affairs and sacred," native American religions resemble Confucian religion more than popular theistic religion which tends sharply to distinguish the sacred and the secular.

When we learn that, for example, among the Wintu people, "the individual is a delimited part of society"—that "it is society that is basic, not a plurality of individuals," we see the closeness of some Native American religions to the Confucian idea that social life is intrinsically religious, being, in its unforced, non-mechanical way of operating, a *sacred ceremony*.[76]

And when we learn that "Native peoples . . . did not understand the European notion that land could be parceled out and owned," because land was "a living spirit"; and that the idea of owning it "sounded as foolish as owning the rain or the sunshine," we are brought face to face with the difference between a utilitarian view of nature and sacred one.[77]

The Native American attitude is summed up as an "attitude of humility and respect toward reality." The author of an article on the Wintu people "cannot find an adequate English term to apply to a habit of thought which is so alien to our culture. We are aggressive toward reality. . . . Our attitude toward nature is colored by a desire to control and exploit."[78]

Importantly, we are dealing here with religion, not morality, with love and respect for a given order. The Wintu hunter's "relationship with nature is one of intimacy and mutual courtesy."[79] If a deer is killed, no part is wasted, "not because he believes in the intrinsic value of thrift, but because the deer had died for him."[80]

This "courtesy" reflects the view that what nature has made necessary must be honored. And this approach seems only a logician's step away from the love of God.

Remarking on the plaint of an elderly, Oklahoma Indian, mourn-

ful over the loss of trees and animals so abundant in his youth, the authors of *Native American Religions* speak of "senses formed by a natural landscape, one largely unaltered by human interventions" and
make the claim that "their beauty was a mark of their holiness, their
divinity. That they came from Wakananda, the ultimate creative
power that was both beautiful and divine, meant that they mediated
ultimate reality.[81]

They may have come from "a creative power," but it is clear that
what warranted the explanatory thought was not an independent
revelation from Wakananda but the inexplicably beautiful character
of nature as the Oklahoman Indian had found it.

ORTHODOXY, MODERNITY, AND MEANING

Orthodoxy is perhaps the most desperate effort to identify with
God as the giver of laws. Modernity is perhaps the most self-con-
scious effort to deny the existence of laws. Each, in its extremity, mis-
shapes life's meaning.

By orthodoxy we do not mean, simply, "adherence to God's law"
(though we mean at least that). Rather, by "orthodoxy" we connote a
life-encompassing adherence to highly *specified* doctrine and performance—to *particulars*, not the law-like relations that make particular things possible. Orthodoxy calls for absolutely specified obedience to God's law in matters of belief, morality, familial and gender
relationships, dress, eating, and the scheduling of all actions.

Logically speaking, orthodoxy is the carrying out of God's commands; it is living in accord with God's Word. Metaphorically speaking, it is living as close to God as earthly life permits. A life lived by divinely authoritative prescriptions is a "godly" life.

In this, orthodoxy represents the extreme embodiment of both
misunderstanding and understanding.

On the side of misunderstanding, there are two elements. The
first is the matter discussed in chapter 2 under the heading of "God's
Authority." The requirements of Orthodoxy cannot possibly be justified on God's authority, but must, as a matter of conceptual necessity,
be justified on "man's" authority to claim God's authority.[82]

It is therefore on the authority of the orthodox, *themselves*, that
godly requirements are specified. And, it is quite a different matter
for the plan of one's life to be required on the authority of oneself and
others than for it to be required on the authority of God.

The second misunderstanding is equally deep, but perhaps more
egregious. Reality is constituted by *diverse* necessities, among which

are logical, conceptual, moral, and aesthetic necessities. (That at least is the theme of this chapter.)

The modes within which necessities appear range enormously. Necessities (rational, physical, moral and aesthetic) structure philosophy, theology, science, the arts, nature, societal situations, interpersonal relations, recreation, sports and intercultural issues. In the light of these manifold forms of necessity, the subsumption of *all* manifestations of what *must be* and what *ought to be* under *a single type of necessity* is most profoundly to beggar "God's world."

To do this is to do in theology what scientism does in philosophy; it is to beggar the world by reducing all worldly necessity to a single kind—for scientism, physical causation.

It is, after, all the great diversity and subtlety of things that constitute humanity's situation from which life's meaning is derived. The subjection of life's normative diversity to a single, normative standard for meaningful thought and action is, in effect, to render life itself *meaningless*.

That is, by insisting that all of life's characteristics and possibilities must be tested against the standard of *doctrine*, one *says* that life has no religiously significant meaning *of its own*.

(An example might be the denial of funds for stem cell research. Let a million reasons be offered that bear on health and the alleviation of human suffering; none will be heard. The doctrine is that in an embryo, not taken from a fertilized egg, about four to five days old consisting of 50-150 cells, *the soul is present*. Since the soul cannot be empirically identified, the objection is a matter of *revelation* and is thus *doctrinal* and not a product of human experience, even in the broadly conceived sense advocated in these pages.)

Once orthodoxy is adopted, obedience is all, and an increase in meaningfulness can come only with an increase in the scope and intensity of specified obedience. (Even as this is written, orthodoxy is demanding orthodoxy in the political state, particularly in certain Middle Eastern Jewish and Islamic circles.)

If what humanity feels as God's presence are, in reality, the necessities that offer us challenge, growth, and fulfillment, then in turning away from what life has to teach us, orthodoxy turns both from the Word and the Substance of God. Orthodoxy is a tragic cessation of learning in the broadest sense—a rejection of the book of *life*.

Ironically, out of an *absolute insistence* on hearing God, it tragically and incorrigibly listens to itself—the authority of its voice thought, *per impossible,* to be that of a voice not its own.

On the side of *understanding*, however, orthodoxy is sensible of the fact that necessities are the *foundation* of a meaningful life. The Confucian ceremony, the Native American landscape represent what endures; they find sacredness in the permanently given, in nature of things. The Amish way of simplicity, like the way of the Shakers, recognizes the holiness of the enduring, for that is what we can see and touch of the necessary.

Even the urbane mind of William James acknowledged that the heart of the religious attitude lies in the willing acceptance of *what must be*. "Happiness in the absolute and everlasting is what we find nowhere but in religion."[83] Always at the heart of Tillich's "ultimate concern" is not what might be or what is now but what necessarily is.

Baldly stated, the love of nature is not the love of "this year's model."

The conflict between the Amish way and the modern way represents the conflict between religion's love and respect for necessity and modernity's assault upon it.

"To be modern," says Marshall Berman, "is to find ourselves in an environment that promises adventure, power, joy, growth, transformation of ourselves and the world—and at the same time threatens to destroy everything we have, everything we know, everything we are."[84] How can this be?

Modernity has in many ways fulfilled the dreams of humankind—advancing, from the nineteenth century through the early twenty-first in ways that make the previous eighty centuries seem a single, frozen moment. Stunning advances in knowledge, technique ,and in human affairs—from nuclear physics and space flight to the banishment of racism and the international acknowledgement of human rights—promised affluence, decency, and leisure, spiced with sport and entertainment.

Yet, with all it has achieved, modernity has fostered in moderns a sense that contemporary life lacks meaning. Religion offers a clue to this conundrum.

In pursuing the eternal, religion implies that life's meaningfulness is founded on that which abides. The sense in this is obvious. Meaningful lives require stable identities, and a stable identities are, by and large, formed only in a stable world.

This psychological observation has its non-psychological counterpart in the epistemology of Frederick Will whose essay, "Thoughts and Things" makes the point that we, quite literally, think by means of the how the world behaves around us (not causally determined by it, but instructed and guided by it).[85] If it is true that "we are what we eat," it is, perhaps, even more true that "we think what we see."

It follows that in a world continually changing "under our feet," the confusion and impermanence without us must engender confusion and shortsightedness within us.

Hence, the resistance to change and the quest for meaning become one. Eternal and immutable ways are offered by Confucianism, by Native American and other theistic traditions. For them, as for political ideologies and advocates of fixed life styles (e.g., the Amish), stability is *foundational* for meaningfulness. Resistance to change is not "stubbornness"; it is the nightmare of lostness.

Modernity, on the other hand, is the antithesis of stability. "To designate our age as modern," Reinart Kosellek has argued,

> is to designate ours as an age that lives for the future . . . that opens itself up to the novelty of the future. . . . suggesting a fundamental break with the past, in which the continuous encounter with "the new." . . . [with] . . . 'new experiences never before had. . . . is endowed with an epochal character.[86]

The point is emphatically seconded by the philosopher Charles Frankel, who claims that "in no other age have men lived with so dizzying a sense of change, or seen their basic material and social environment being made over, and made over again, so steadily."[87] But nothing gives us modernity better than a phrase one finds in the *Communist Manifesto* of Karl Marx and Friedrich Engels: "all that is solid melts into air."

The reason meaning is lost in modernity is because its continual, often unpredictable, changes alter the context of our actions and thoughts, and *context determines the meaning of our actions and thoughts.*

The absolutely fundamental role of context in determining what things mean was argued in chapter 2, as an aspect of "God's (religious) meaning." There, narrative of God's role as *purposeful Creator* was seen as providing the *ultimate* and unchanging (eternal) context for all actions. (That is why, we argued, the idea that "God is dead" seemed to many to entail the meaninglessness of life.)

Whatever "the meaning of life" may be, those who seek it hope that it shows life to be meaningful. For, in ordinary parlance, *what is meaningful is what is worth one's time* and, by extension, a *meaningful life is a life worth the living of it.*

But before life can be found meaningful, the meaning of what we do and think must be ascertained. For this, a context is required. For example, some who think the physical context of life is such that the human race is doomed may conclude that what we do and say is pointless, since it will all be swallowed up by an expanding sun. But whatever context turns out to be *true* and *relevant*, it can never be (usefully) either one if the context of our lives is always changing—not in minutely "technical" ways, but in the character of what is necessary.

So, the meaning of a dollar changes if the financial system collapses or if the earth is struck by an enormous asteroid. The meaning of a liberal education is different for someone who must work two jobs and on weekends than it is for someone who spends evenings and weekends in leisure. The meaning of large family is different (and birth announcements have different meaning) if families are already starving rather than living comfortably with little prospect of long-term starvation. The writing of a book is a lonely thing in an illiterate or functionally illiterate society, and an exciting, socially significant thing in a society that honors literacy.

To wax momentarily "sociological"—as one ought, at length, to do if modernity is properly to be anatomized—the invention of the automobile first meant freedom. But it played an essential role in the development of suburban sprawl, the end of the small town, and finally became not freedom but confinement and an ecological disaster as once sparsely traveled roads became jammed with commuters. The meaning of the automobile changed as the context of its use changed. (The reader may already have noted that automobile commercials typically show the owner driving in beautiful, wide-open spaces, through mountain passes, across deserts, or by the sea.)

Most importantly, the nature, hence meaning, of the city changed, and of the town, and of the phrase "going to work." Readers unacquainted with Thornton Wilder's play, *Out Town*, will, we think, find the heart and soul of the argument that God's substance lies in the fundamental necessities conveyed better in that work than in the logic of these pages.[88]

The point is not that any change is the enemy of meaning. It is that, despite many and important exceptions—as for example, the rejection of racial and religious discrimination and the exploration of space—an inverse relationship exists between the rapidity and ubiquity of change and the depth of meaning things and actions possess.

For example, the current "problem" of "gay marriage" which is commonly cast as a problem of "discrimination" may—even if it should involve discrimination in the moral sense—have much to do with a fundamental change in context.

Marriage has been the symbol of the ideal human union, and that union has incorporated a bodily reference connoted by the terms *man* and *woman*—which is to say, it has been the symbol of evolved, genital cooperation vital for the continuation of the race and for the generation of blood-connected families. In short, it has had, and still has, enormous meaning as one of life's central, ideal forms, having as much to do with the body and with "blood relations" as it has to do with love and commitment.

To sunder the connection between ideal love and the uniting of genital difference may be, in the end, good or bad. Our point is that an alteration in the concept of marriage is *mysteriously* upsetting when one asks "how does a homosexual marriage *interfere* with heterosexual marriage?"and is less mysterious when one appreciates the role of heterosexual marriage *defining the context* of human life.

"Meaning" is simply not possible in the absence of a context. Without the context of an entire financial and legal system, a thousand-dollar bill is a piece of green paper. The meaning of the cotton gin, once economic and social, is now historical, only. And so it goes.

Clearly, if the ideas, habits, objects, and physical surroundings that constitute one's context change, then the basis for determining the meaning of an idea, act, gesture, or production becomes indeterminate, impermanent or both.

The result is that the meaning of what one thinks or does becomes indeterminate, impermanent, or both—the word for this being *insubstantial*. That is why Native American religion has such substance, for the meaning of its thought and action is tied to the ineluctable forms of nature, to forms that have preceded, and will survive, us.

Surely no agnostic rejection of the Bible as "the Word of God" is half as powerful—religiously—as the following, oblique, Native American critique: "If you take the Christian Bible and put it out in the wind and the rain, soon the paper on which the words are printed will disintegrate and the words will be gone. Our Bible *is* the wind."[89]

The force of the closing sentence reflects our understanding that the wind is an expression of natural necessity. The power of its simple words supports the idea that necessity is central to a meaningful life. To worship "God" is to find wonder and beauty and power—challenge and possibility—in "the wind," in what *must be*.

From this we can, perhaps, see what it is that makes technology religiously problematic. The sailboat is challenged by the wind, moves by the wind, waits for the wind, is a partner of the wind. An Indian might say it dances with God. But the boat powered by a gasoline engine thinks nothing of the wind. And when the engine roars, and drives the boat, one cannot feel the wind as it comes of itself, nor hear the sighing of the sea.

Love and respect for natural physical properties is awakened, and seen as deeply right, when Westerners contemplate Japanese temple carpentry. The structure's relation to wood, like the sailboat's relation to the wind, depends upon the natural properties of wood, rather than nails or glue. Nails would tear through the wood as the outboard engine tears through the water. This, we think, is more than aesthetic appreciation; it has to do with loving the very *being* of wood—otherwise plastic Lego construction would be similarly moving, and it is not.

We do not mean by these examples to advocate a Luddite negation of technology. We mean only to indicate that a connection with what we cannot change, with the necessities definitive of nature, goodness, beauty, and truth, cannot be lost without losing the context of a meaningful life.

Religion is a matter of depth as well as comprehensiveness of meaning. Like responses to aesthetic features and to the morality of actions, religion's appreciation of *being* may at any time be called out of us. It is an unselfconscious response to what is given, whether a setting sun or the flow of wood grain.

So, for example even though the wood in a violin is glued and lacquered, its grain and shape are beautifully mated; the character of the wood is celebrated and respected, not only for its appearance but for its way of sounding music . The violin is treasured and its age is often part of its meaning (age turning thought toward eternity and the mortality of generations).

Contrast this with a rock band's guitar, whose plastic and metal form celebrates its distance from nature, and whose insubstantiality is asserted by smashing it before a delighted audience in a ritual display of disrespect—for the instrument, for the music it plays, and for the effort of its creation.

Perhaps the day will come when a violin soloist, having finished a performance of Prokofiev, Bach, or Mozart, stomps her seventeenth-century Guarneri instrument to pieces before leaving the stage.

And why not, in a context of continual change or *replacement*—the condition in which nothing counts. In an earlier stage of modernity, Sigmund Freud said, "Love and work are the cornerstones of our humanness," but somewhere between forty and fifty percent of "permanent" love relationships will become impermanent through divorce and work will be changed ten or so times making it, too, less of a commitment.[90] Change itself changes, becoming ever faster. Phones become handsets become cameras become writing devices become icons of exciting novelty; food becomes something pre-prepared by others, not for love but for money; appliances become quickly obsolete and can neither be fathomed nor repaired; in art and entertainment, sensation and shock replace narrative and form; and in the arena of notoriety, celebrity replaces accomplishment.

When action's context is artificiality and impermanence, it can be governed only by sheer *will* and pure *desire*. In consequence there is nothing to respect and nothing to worship. In turning from all that might be asked of us, and hiding from all that we cannot escape, we sacrifice the ideal to the arbitrary—and open our hands to find nothing.

The aim of all this is not to introduce a blueprint or a doctrine but to gesture toward the religious. We do not argue that *anything* necessary in nature—like a virus—is to be loved, nor do we maintain that simply being in nature is enough. We say only that to live mindful of the eternal is, in part, to live mindful of the laws that determine reality.

A separate volume would be required to uncover the engines that drive modernity. But it would be disingenuous, to say what we have said and not say, as well, that when the *necessity* of profit (in a business-oriented society) becomes the *reason* for work, then reality receives its walking papers.

To the extent that I do what I do not to realize the best possibilities of physical and cultural materials but to receive the personal advantages that come with money, then to that extent I will do (with the world) whatever I need to do. In a word, if I can profit by selling the lesser rather than the greater object, I will sell the lesser. The evaluative norms of the good have become irrelevant, and if what I profit by destroys the giant redwood, let it fall. That is what it means "to sell the sizzle (wink, wink; nod, nod) not the steak."

One sees the sacrifice of evaluative norms fairly clearly in the realm of sport where winning (profit) is proclaimed the *point* of sport. But even the adults who "educate" the young in this way would rather play against an opponent who will likely beat them rather than against someone hobbled by an injury. And this is *inconsistent* with the winning as the *point* of sport. The experience of competitive sport *requires* trying to win (to profit); it is not *identical with* winning (profiting).

In any case, religion, in asking that we seek the eternal, asks that we understand the norms that constitute not only the realities of nature but the realities definitive of the good, whether the goods we seek be vocational, recreational, or familial.

The eternal, the necessary, cannot be changed. The religion that brings us closer to God cannot do so on the wings of fantasy. Fantasies are human in origin. They change. As a result, religions follow religions, changing even as they lay claim to being "absolute"—or at least not "relative."

For they are rooted in a quest that popular thought has not been able to conceptualize save in the form of a historical narrative, that is, in the form of a myth. And though, as Mircea Eliade says, "myths are believed to be true," sooner or later they are not. Sooner or later the truth finds them out and they evolve, betraying their earthly origin.

But these myths are all, to be sure "on to something." And what we have striven to do is find that something. We have sought the idea of the holy that is true and thus able to invite and sustain critical reflection, needing never to be kept behind the high wall of faith or justified by its useful or pleasing consequences

In speaking as we have of necessity, we have (of necessity!) beggared the idea by not expansively describing the many ways necessities show themselves. The richness of the reality's normative ways, especially in matter aesthetic and religious, is, above all, what we have short-changed.

But a proper case for normative laws can only be made by great poetry and great sermons, philosophical theology being but the guardian at the gate—the defender of mind against phantasmagoric suppositions; the advocate of everyday experience against its impoverishment by scientistic and theistic attempts to explain the inexplicable.

NOTES

1. Stanford Encyclopedia of Philosophy, posted 2006, http://plato.stanford.edu/entries/spinoza-physics/

2. Bernard Martin, *The Existential Theology of Paul Tillich* (New York: Bookman Associates, 1963), pp. 142-43.

3. Discussed in Robert S. Brumbaugh, *The Philosophers of Ancient Greece* (New York: Thomas Y. Crowell Company, 1964), p. 18.

4. Whether we can more satisfactorily characterize the way necessity "exists" than by speaking of a "protean" existence is doubtful. The question of whether "redness" exists or whether only red things exist, for example, marks the entrance to what seems an interminable battle between Platonists, nominalists, paraphrase-nominalists, immanent realists, and other children of definitional exactitude—few, if any of whom we could ever expect to satisfy. What we say is, we hope, true enough to serve our subject.

5. For a demanding exploration of the meaning of "is," see G. E. L. Owen, "Aristotle on the Snares of Ontology" in *New Essays on Plato and Aristotle*, ed. Renford Bambrough (Oxford, UK: Routledge & Kegan Paul, Ltd., 1965), pp.

69-95.

6. See again the discussion of the meaning of "is" in G. E. L. Owen, "Aristotle on the Snares of Ontology," in *New Essays on Plato and Aristotle*, pp. 69-95.

7. Even those who *say* they find or meet God everyday, do not say, "I just saw God in supermarket" or "was talking with God during lunch, and God said...."

8. How ironic it is that people not given to theories, *insist* on being theoretical when it comes to existence. But how else to talk about necessity when one is not a professional theorist?—"will" is the necessitation everyone understands.

9. See in Wiliam James, *The Varieties of Religious Experience* (New York: The New American Libray, 1958), pp. 47-49.

10. Let the theologian who argues that, because there is a plan larger than we can see, the agony and death of innocents expresses God's love, deliver his lecture at the bedside of a child with terminal cancer.

11. In Donald Winslow Fiske and Richard A. Schweder, *Metatheory in Social Science: Pluralisms and Subjectivities* (Chicago: University of Chicago Press, 1986), 173.

12. "to be, then, is always to be something or other," in *New Essays on Plato and Aristotle*, p. 76.

13. This is a way of saying that the explanation of human reasoning by the physiology of cause and effect simply denies logical necessity and therefore "mind" and "rationality" as we understand those terms.

14. Elizabeth Colbert, "Crash Course," in *The New Yorker*, online only, July 20, 2007, "Annals of Science."

15. Ibid.

16. Stephen Toulmin, *The Philosophy of Science* (London: Hutchinson & Co., 4th. impression, 1958), p. 79.

17. Ibid.

18. Toulmin, *The Philosophy of Science*, p. 82.

19. Ibid. pp. 94-95.

20. Roger Scruton, *An Intelligent Person's Guide to Philosophy* (New York: Allen Lane the Penguin Press, 1998; orig. pub. London: Allen Lane the Penguin Press, 1996), pp. 97.

21. Ibid., pp. 97-98.

22. Ibid., p. 97.

23. Ibid., p. 98.

24. Ibid.; see for contrast William Kneale, *Probability and Induction* (London: Oxford University Press, 1949), p. 242: The most obvious peculiarity of a hypothesis of law is that they can be decisively refuted by experience."

25. Iris Murdoch, "Metaphysics and Ethics" in *Existentialists and Mystics: writings on philosophy and literature, Iris Murdoch*, ed. Peter Conradi (New York: Penguin Books, 1999; orig. pub. Great Britain: Chatto & Windus Limited, 1997). p. 68.

26. William Kneale, *Probability and Induction* (London: Oxford University Press, 1949), p. 78.

27. The unreality of regular connection in reducing to discrete (unconnected) phenomena or sensations is remarked in William Kneale's *Probability and Induction* when he says, "Whenever I use the word 'iron', I always mean

something more than is manifested to me at the moment." (For it is "iron" this *would* happen or *that* would happen if I did this or that to it.)

28. The logical and philosophic issues raised by the idea of existence are staggering in number and complexity. We suggest referencing a review of the issues in the online *Stanford Encyclopedia of Philosophy* at http://Plato.stanford.edu/entries/existence/. We hope to speak intelligibly and usefully of reality but acknowledge that there is more to the subject than we can fully comprehend.

29. F. C. Copleston, *Medieval Philosophy*, p. 156.

30. "Miracles" being *intermittently* apparent examples of Creation.

31. Natalie Isayeva, *Shankara and Indian Philosophy* (Albany, N.Y.: State University of New York Press, 1993), p. 251. Also known as a doctrine of Dvaita as propounded by Madhva (see dvaita.org).

32. This is very like the vision of Bishop Berkeley who declared that the world of our perception is in fact nothing more or less than the perceptions in the mind of God.

33. Remembering that as a matter of what can be *thought* nothing can explain "existence," not even a "God"

34. In addressing the *logic* of the relationship we do not speak about, but do not minimize, the *context* or "worldview" that favors morality without deductively implying it.

35. It doesn't matter whether "no ought from an is" is understood as a deductive doctrine or an inductive doctrine, the result is the same.

36. David Hume, *Treatise of Human Nature*, Book II, "Of the passions," Sect. III, "Of the influencing motives of the will."

37. William Kneale, *Probability and Induction*, p. 78.

38. Harold Hoffding, *A History of Modern Philosophy*, vol. II (New York: Dover Publications, Inc., 1955), pp. 13-14.

39. This echoes the Platonic view that virtue is knowledge. If one knows the good, in that sense of "know" which includes *appreciation*—the sense required for knowing the good—one believes in the good and not in opinions concerning the good.

40. We reserve the relation between feeling and religious reality for later discussion in order to simplify the discussion.

41. Vincent van Gogh, in *The Letters of Vincent Van Gogh*, ed. Mark Roskill (New York: Atheneum, 1984), p. 236.

42. Witter Bynner, ed., and trans., *The Chinese Translations* (New York: Farrar, Straus, Giroux, 1978), p. 65.

43. Paul Tillich, *Dynamics of Faith* (New York: Harper & Row, Publishers, Incorporated; Harper Torchbooks, 1957) p. 82.

44. Erich Maria Remarque, *All Quiet on the Western Front*, A. W. Wheen, trans. (Boston: Little, Brown, 1929), p. 227.

45. Ibid., p. 228.

46. Ibid.

47. Ibid., p. 229.

48. Iris Murdoch, *Existentialists and Mystics,* p. 72.

49. Bernard Williams, *Ethics and the Limits of Philosophy* (Cambridge, Mass.: Harvard University Press, 1985), p. 192.

50. Max Lerner, ed., *The Portable Veblen* (New York: The Viking Press, 1948),

"Editor's Introduction," p. 7.

51. Hume, *Treatise of Human Nature*, Book II, "Of the passions," Sect. III, "Of the influencing motives of the will."

52. To appreciate a thing "in itself" requires a context. Nothing is good in itself outside a context. So, hearing Beethoven's 3rd. Symphony having heard no music makes it impossible to perceive. Hearing it daily makes it impossible to perceive. Perceiving value requires context, as does perceiving physical fact.

53. G. E. Moore, *Principia Ethica* (Cambridge, UK: Cambridge University Press, 1903), p. 201.

54. Edgar Wind, *Art and Anarchy* (London: Faber and Faber, 1963), p. 66.

55. O.K. Bouwsma, "The Expression Theory of Art," in *Aesthetics and Language*, ed. William Elton (Oxford: Basil Blackwell, 1959), p. 73.

56. Matthew 6:24.

57. Matthew 6:21.

58. Luke 12:21.

59. Luke 18:25.

60. The "miracle and mystery" of necessity derives, of course from being inexplicable and invisible—from being within or "immanent"—even as it *constitutes* the many facets of whatever is real.

61. Philip J. Ivanhoe, *Confucian Moral Self-Cultivation* (Indianapolis: Hackett Publishing, 2000), p. 34.

62. Herbert Fingarette, *Confucius—the Secular as Sacred* (New York: Harper & Row, Publishers; Harper Torchbooks, 1972), p. 6.

63. Ibid., p. 8.

64. Ibid., p. 9.

65. Ibid., p. 11; Fingarette describes how, in the proper setting, the expression of a wish to someone ready to honor it accomplishes the end wished for. It is a matter of seeing what ought to be done, not a matter of force.

66. Ibid., p. 11.

67. Ibid., pp. 19-21.

68. Ibid., p. 21.

69. Ibid.

70. Ibid., p. 27.

71. Paula R. Hartz, *Native American Religion*, p. 12.

72. N. Scott Momaday, in *The Remembered Earth: An Anthology of Contemporary Native American Literature*, ed. Geary Hobson (Albuquerque: University of New Mexico Press, 1981), p. 162.

73. Denise Lardner Carmody and John Tully Carmody, *Native American Religions: An Introduction* (New York: Paulist Press, 1993), p. 9.

74. Carmody and Carmody, *Native American Religions*, p. 8.

75. Carmody and Carmody, *Native American Religions*, p. 8.

76. Dennis Tedlock and Barbara Tedlock, eds., *Teachings from the American Earth* (New York: Liveright Publishing Corporation; Liveright Paperback, 1992; orig. pub. 1975), p. 139.

77. Hartz, *Native American Religions* (USA: Facts on File, Inc. 1997), p. 92.

78. Dorothy Lee, "Linguistic Reflection of Wintu Thought," in *Teachings from the American Earth*, p. 140.

79. Lee, *Teachings from the American Earth*, p. 140.

80. Ibid.

81. Carmody and Carmody, *Native American Religions*, p. 65.

82. A reader unacquainted with chapter 2 can there find the argument against all "saving" considerations such as deriving God's authority through *faith*, *revelation* or *mystical experience*.

83. William James, *The Varieties of Religious Experience*, p. 54.

84. Marshall Berman, *All That is Solid Melts Into Air* (New York: Simon and Schuster, 1982), p.15.

85. As we, in agreement, have said "mind" is an unintelligible idea in the absence of "worldly knowledge."

86. Loralea Michaelis, "The Wisdom of Prometheus: Kant, Marx, and Holderlin on Politics, Disappointment and the Limits of Modernity, *Polity* 31. 4 (1999): 537.

87. Charles Frankel, *The Case for Modern Man* (Boston: Beacon Press, 1971; orig. pub. Harper & Brother, 1955), pp. 197-8.

88. The 1940 film version with William Holden and Martha Scott has the essential mood and therefore the essential message, though in some versions. Wilder's powerful ending was changed to make it "happy."

A too cool, but more accurate version is the 2003 film with Paul Newman. But the play requires a genuinely "rural" interlocutor in order to be fully realized.

89. Commonly attributed to an anonymous Native American woman.

90. By 1996, median tenure (with the same employer) stood at ten years.

Chapter 5

Concluding Unscientific Postscript: Truth, Love, Death

TRUTH

In the light of all that has been argued, "God's Word" is but a single word, and that word is "truth."

What is normally called "the word of God" is a series of commands, doctrines and visions of the good to which the claim of God's authority—not man's—is ascribed. The internal inconsistency of this idea has already been discussed in Chapter 2, under the heading "God's Authority." We will not address it here.

That which makes whatever God has been *thought* to say "religious" is, nonetheless, its status as "the last word"—its unchallengeable claim on us.

And if no coherent case can be made for a supernatural Creator, the only *other* way commands, doctrines, and visions of the good can rightly call for our obeisance is by their evident rightness, that is, by the truth of their imperative character. For, surely, it is no part of religion for one human's way of life to be under the authority of another.

As we have said, God's meaning is that of the ultimate and true context for determining what to do and think. And the mystery of it, we have also said, lies in the fact that we encounter—in the experience of active social life—standards for thought and action and feeling that stand opposed to what we *prefer* to be right, good or true.

That such *independent* standards—which are the basis of civilized, indeed, of *human* life—exist in a universe that shows no sign of *intending* their existence or the existence of anything else is, of course "impossible" ("impossible but true").

We have, throughout these pages, taken to task those who assume that for such standards there *must be* an explanation. To wit: either there is a supernatural agent who created reality and its standards or there is a brain process that gives us the feeling that there is a reality with its own standards! In either case we stand forever barred from confronting *ultimate* reality (theism saying, "wait for heaven"; scientism: "it's all in our heads").

Our message has been that if, in theistic thought, confronting that which creates us human and gives us the law would be confronting God, then confronting the rational and physical norms that, in experience, we cannot deny, is confronting an (appropriately) incorporeal "God"—a "God" whose substance—*necessity*—is the form of what we find real.

Enter, truth:

Truth, like existence itself, is indefinable. The idea that what is true is what corresponds to reality is but a metaphor in the garb of a straightforward factual claim. But if what we say about independent standards is correct, seeing and appreciating what is true is hearing "God's" word. Logos—"God's Word"—creates the human world; *seeing truth is coming into our being as human.*

How is this to be clearly understood?—by means of life examples:

Consider a loving union. Forty years of family life, of memories housed in attic trunks, of raising children in a small town. How saccharine, yet thunderously right. And then, the surviving spouse, sifting through old documents now that death has ended living love, finds a small sheaf of letters. And these letters—unbelievable—written between the dead spouse and a lover, tell, irrefutably, of a love that bound the dead spouse to another all those many years.

What of the old photographs now? The wedding, the apartments lived in, the interplay of friends, the smiles, the kisses, and the faces looking directly into the camera? The children. What do they mean? And what of the few years now remaining?

But this is to forget the "facts"—the *empirical* facts. Surely the surviving spouse can remember *the facts*. Empirically defined facts cannot change. The sensations of loving and being loved were what they were. The lovemaking was what it was—the procreation, the cooperation, the sharing, the physical helping, the sense of being cared about were all what they were, In no way are the *facts of experience* no longer the facts of experience. Any surviving spouse capable of the simplest cost/benefit analysis would see that, *empirically* speaking, only a very small portion of life's span has been, *empirically*, soured.

Why then, do we all understand that the facts of *experience* have been changed, that much of life has been shown intractably wasted and barren? Is it not because the experiences, though wonderful, were not founded on truth?

And what is this but to say that the surviving spouse—and all of us—can live meaningfully only if what we think so "corresponds to reality." Our idea of things must be what is so of things.

What possible difference can this distinction between the "phenomenally" experienced and the truth make—to an animal? What sense can we make of this abstract notion that things must be "so," that we must live not in terms of psychological experience alone (like the animals) but *absolutely*, in terms of the relation between what we suppose and what holds for the universe outside. This: *human* experience is not a set of wholly *internal* facts!

We are linked to the universe by mind. (If this were not so there would be no "mind" at all—only a chamber full of "sensations" and shapes.) The idea of truth is, as Chapter 3 said, unintelligible in terms of world described from outside first-person experience and, insanely, apotheosized as "the *objective* facts."

The fact of feeling love, the fact of working out a life together, of being held, of seeing another's smile—all these facts add up to nothing—are merely *phenomena*—fantasmagoric—unless they are *in truth* what they seem. To be meaningful, what we think and feel of life must be so. Our very lives hang on what we really know.

The history we have learned, the history of our nation, if found to be false becomes ashes—our political identity a kind of nightmare. No matter the thrills of political rallies and commitments, if based on falsehood.

One may experience joy and inspiration reading a biography, but if one learns it is false, one does not total up fifteen hours of empirical joy and one minute of empirical horror and conclude it was—nine hundred to one—a joy to have read it. There is no joy finding oneself pleasantly duped.

Deceived. About the past, the present, and the probable future. This is our hell, to be unknowing—like the cow, the chicken, moving upon the earth without a concept of truth. This is why the lie is a serious flaw, and self-deception, spiritual suicide. And it all turns on things being so and not so.

Truth is not an academic matter, and no neurological, psychological, or biological causal theories can undermine its role in creating and sustaining a *human way of being* (since all inquiries, as we have argued in Chapter 3, presuppose the attainability of truth). Indeed, what irony it is to have the offspring of our union with the universe—those thinkers whose badge is knowledge—turn upon that union to deny its truth—*on grounds of knowing what is so!*

When physical and social science are permitted to define our nature they tell us what an autopsy can tell us about the human character.

The ceremonies of truth are everywhere. What, save the love of truth, of the world, is signaled when we seek out the name of a bird we have just seen, or a flower that attracted us during a walk in the woods? The name doesn't sharpen what we recollect or what we will see, should we see the bird or the flower again. *Naming* is a *getting hold*, it is a completion of *a union*. So far is it from seeking a merely lexical completeness!

And what is it to *know* how the earth was formed, or how we evolved, or what Jefferson said, or whether Plato soured in his old age? For, this knowledge is not sought for its practical value. It is, save for odd chance, without utility. It is good in itself to know. And what is this but to confirm that our lives are uniquely human insofar as we are one with the real. It creates us, as God is said to have done.

The truth is God's Word.

LOVE

This work has said little about love. Yet did not the New Testament say "God is love" (John 4:8)? And is not "love thy neighbor as thyself" regarded as a religious injunction?

Moreover, *agape*—God's love for humanity—is a major theme in theology, though perhaps not in popular thought, since, in agape, God loves us for nothing about us but by loving us creates whatever worth we have. Such love is rather like the sun's relation to the moon, wherein the moon shines only by reflected light.

Then there is "human" or quotidian love in which the object is loved for certain characteristics, however real or imaginary those may be. As earthly or "secular" love, it can have effects. The basically decent person who is loved may well become an even better person, and a "bad actor" may be moved by love toward a more decent life. Neither effect is guaranteed.

But what is *religious* love as the attitude of a human, not a God?

To be religious in character, love must have to do with what is ultimate. The famous injunction, "love thine enemy," makes love an *ul-*

timate requirement. As "ultimate" it cannot be made dependent on conditions. And as an injunction to love one's enemy, it cannot intelligibly be understood to speak about earthly or "secular" love.

This is so for two different reasons: First, it is psychologically impossible; no one can actually love a cruel jailer or the soldier who destroys one's home and family—unless one is a masochist or in some other way neurotic.

Second, it makes the standard sense of the term *love* senseless. To say to someone one has fallen in love with, "I love you just as I also love strangers and enemies," is absurd. In fact, it demeans the person to whom it is offered, since it is available, indiscriminately, to anyone.

In the words of Sigmund Freud: "A love that does not discriminate . . . [forfeits] . . . a part of its own value, by doing an injustice to its object; and secondly, not all men are worthy of love."[1]

So religious love, if it is to make sense, yet include loving "thine enemy," must have a meaning that cannot be discerned simply on the basis of the language in which it is couched.

We suggest it is best understood as caring about, seeking what good there can be, in the "other," and by "the other" we mean all that exists. To "love" thine enemy is not to hate but to seek the possibility of good, even in the presence of evil. It is not to give up the religiously essential goal of maximizing the good. To love "God" is to be open to all that may be good in reality or that might, in reality, be *made* good.

Religious love is Platonic in its attempt to realize, to bring into being, the ideal type of any object. It is a way of being-in-the-world and so constitutes an approach to all existence. It therefore seeks to identify the moral and aesthetic necessities that, in combination with knowledge of physical necessities, make possible the betterment of *the smallest as well as the largest thing*.

The beauty of the grasslands or the garden may call equally for management. A population fallen upon dark days of violence and hatred must be brought back to its humanity, just as a child, psychically wounded or misguidedly indoctrinated, must be enabled to uncover truths and be guided by them,

There is, in this, nothing new, save for the notion that in caring for the good of the world we are responsive to something inexplicably ultimate and demanding. We respond to independent standards—standards that are, when we think and act in relation to them, *obdurate*. Whatever we may want or will be so, it is a fact of our experience that some things, over time, are evidently obligating. They define what is real, normatively—what is rational, moral, aesthetic, relevant, appropriate, and so on.

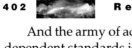

And the army of academic arguments against the existence of independent standards is, ironically, entirely dependent on them. Academic arguments are forged in accordance with the strictest standards—of evidence, logic, plausibility, style—and for the purpose of "maintaining standards" when it comes to validity and truth. If, indeed, academics do not think those standards ought compel the *rational* assent of their audience, the whole idea of a "university" will clearly have to be revisited.

So what we argue is that in seeking, finding, and obeying the normative aspects of reality, we obey, and appreciate being shown, the way—which is what "God" is traditionally supposed to do.

We are *lovers of the world* in that we are open to the world—are eager to learn—and *stewards of the good* in that we ought recognize, maintain, or realize what in the world is good.

We do not *love* disease or deadly physical events. Love is openness to the other, and a giving of oneself to the good of the other, but while it sets the self aside, it does not go so far as to deny the self.

Mature love is not blind. And if it is not "blind," it is open to what or who the other really is. Love may at first be blind, but if it stays blind, it denies the self, making all decisions of the self dependent on the needs or direction of the "other" and can only be regarded as "infatuation."

Indeed, to exist this way is to become a "nothing" so that one has nothing in the way of a "self" to give as a gift to the loved one. It cancels out the possibility of a loving *union*.

So it follows that to love the world one must not accept it completely as given, and that is why, religiously, *we lovers of the world must be stewards of the Good*.

Curiously, it has never seemed plausible to this writer that the traditional, omniscient, omnipotent, omnipresent, necessarily existing *being* could ever have an interest in—and certainly not a great concern for—such limited, puny beings (comparatively) as ourselves. The various arguments that such a God *needs* us have always seemed nothing more than attempts to "save" the God concept from impersonality (the remote king in the remote castle really loves us).

Even more curiously, then, the idea of religious love as a love of the world that implies *stewardship of the good* gives sense to the idea that "God" needs us. For all that might—with understanding and work—be good, and that now simply exists as *possibility*, falls to us as those alone able to *realize* it.

We are, thus, able—not by fantasy but by reason—to be at home in the universe. We are not orphaned because we have work to do—

work inexplicably given—and which, if not done, guarantees the death of *human* life. *We humans have a life whose ultimate or "religious" meaning lies in the recognition, appreciation, and realization of the good of existence.*

DEATH

The following essay, "The Religious Meaning of Death" is the text of a lecture delivered by the writer at the Tubac Center of the Arts in Tubac, Arizona. The occasion was an exhibition of twenty-eight photographs and associated text whose subject was a small, Mexican-American cemetery at Tubac. The exhibit, which the writer termed a "meditation," had as its theme the shared mystery of human existence beneath all theological and philosophical differences.

The lecture is as homiletic as it is philosophical. But it has been a theme of this work that philosophy is rooted in the existential. First-person judgments made within the practices of responsible living are foundational to philosophy that is more than formal logic. Otherwise, like formal logic, philosophy can have nothing directly to say on what is important in life.

THE RELIGIOUS MEANING OF DEATH

Doing art and doing philosophy

During many wonderful years in Arizona, I found myself repeatedly drawn to the small cemetery on the outskirts of Tubac. The photographic and textual work "In a Believer's Graveyard" is the outcome of that attraction.

For a photographer, the graveyard's lively presence in a vast and silent landscape cried out to be preserved. Yet, early on, I found myself aware of something else—something more than its flowers and personal remembrances—something of religious import deeper even than its heartfelt doctrines. It was the call of this underlying "something" that returned a non-believer every year to a believer's graveyard.

For I was also a philosopher—one whose notion of ultimate reality conflicted with the worldview that informed the graveyard's prayers. Indeed, it was the very starkness of this difference that forced into my consciousness the fundamental sameness of our mortal circumstance.

We desire that death be overcome, that love should have no end. Death speaks to the mystery of our existence, to the famous—or infamous—"meaning of it all." There, in the graveyard, in the presence of such palpable yearning and sorrow, love and hope, I could not help but be moved, camera in hand, beyond the critical responses of philosophy.

Yet a response that suffices for art may not suffice for religion. For, religion demands more than emotions, affinities, or wishes. Religion is an attempt to understand the meaning—if any—of human life. And, as a form of understanding, it requires truth. ("Thou shall not worship false gods.")

Even the supernatural—even God—must be a fact. Indeed, so religiously fundamental is truth that Mahatma Ghandi thought it "more correct to say that Truth is God than to say God is truth."

There is, however, a contrary view, one concerned more with *utility* than truth. On this view, religious beliefs are justifiable if they ease sorrow or lead us to help others. Belief is justified by its effects. It is right to believe a thing true if it helps us reform, or creates community, or aids us in becoming "successful."

Of course, some link this position to truth. They say that if a belief is morally effective or psychologically useful it is likely true. But this makes religious truth pragmatic—a status no believer will accept once so baldly stated. The sacred is not sacred on the basis of *results*—as the story of Job seems designed to show. Indeed, a pragmatic or utilitarian approach to the sacred seems *definitive* of irreligion.

Often, people hold both pragmatic and realist views at once. Even Saint Augustine was not always clear, saying, in *The City of God*, for example, that the Christian religion "is the one salutary and true religion"—that is, the one religion good for you and also true—which is different from claiming it is good for you simply in *being* true (that is, good for you *spiritually*—not *mundanely*).[2]

So, when we wonder how, religiously, to think of death—that is, in terms not of need but of religious truth—we must be guided by our religious sensibility. We must be genuinely open to the question whether a given understanding of death's significance is *religious* in character rather than therapeutic, poetic, or merely traditional. As justice is not the same thing as what is legal, the religious, I suggest, is not the same thing as what is doctrinal.

It is not easy to look afresh at doctrine, which is why, perhaps, the Psalm says only "the upright shall behold His face" (Ps. 11:7) and, in Plato's parable of the cave, why only those who truly seek can endure looking into the sun.

Without further prologue, then, let us, journey into that realm of extreme ideas called "religion" where nothing less than what is eternal and ultimate will do.

"If I never live again . . . "

The subject of religion and death was first broached for me in a serious way by Peter Berger's *A Rumor of Angels*. Berger (a sociologist and lay theologian) made the claim that a religious viewpoint demands faith in the possibility of life after death. Though the idea was hardly unfamiliar, the religious necessity of resurrection suddenly struck me as not merely dubious but positively *counter-religious*.

This reaction was troubling. When millions celebrate the promise of immortality as *religious*, the philosopher who demurs is very likely mistaken. But I could not shake my doubt, and there was nothing for it but to think the matter through.

I cannot here recount the whole of Berger's case—particularly the idea that we experience "signals of transcendence," but I can, with fairness, present its logic.

Berger claims that behind "all quests for redemption" is "the reality of suffering, evil, and death."[3]

Against these dark aspects of earthly life, there stands another empirical fact—humanity's natural proclivity for faith. In fact, so important is our "experience of trust in the order of reality," that it lies "at the very center of the process of becoming fully human."[4]

Berger then claims that this natural, human-making, *faith in reality's order* would be undermined were we to understand death entirely from within a scientific perspective, that is, as the end of us. For then "the experience [of trust] is an illusion and the role that it embodies is a *lie*."[5]

It becomes

> perfectly obvious that everything is *not* in order, is *not* all right. The world that the child is . . . told to trust is the same world in which he will eventually die. If there is no other world, then the ultimate truth about this one is that eventually it will kill the child as it will kill his mother. . . . the final truth would be not love, but terror, not light but darkness. The nightmare of chaos, not the transitory safety of order, would be the final reality of the human situation.[6]

I must note that Berger describes the natural death of children and mothers as "killing." This step in his argument is illegitimate. We only speak of "killing" when a death is in some sense *unnecessary*.

When people die natural deaths, we do not say they have been *killed*. By applying a term to natural death that only applies to *unnecessary* death, Berger loads the dice in favor of thinking natural death is unnecessary—a breaking of life's order—and thus to be thought of as (to say the least) unloving.

But, tendentiousness aside, Berger's *religious* conclusion remains. If death is final, *this world* is "not love, but terror" and "the *final reality* of the human situation" is a "nightmare of chaos." A finite life is a pointless life.

Berger is hardly alone in concluding that life is ultimately meaningful only if it never ends. The eighteenth-century German philosopher, Immanuel Kant, argued that eternal life was required to make sense of morality. Over-simply: moral action makes no sense if it does not yield happiness. Since, in a finite, earthly life it does not and cannot, there must be an eternal life in which the conjunction of virtue and happiness *can* be achieved.[7] Thus, death's finality drains life of moral significance—which surely undercuts its religious significance.

In a similar vein, the contemporary British theologian, John Hick, argued that a finite life violates the ideal of human development. According to Hick, it would be "an intolerable contradiction" to affirm that God loves everyone and "evokes in them the desire to reach the highest potentialities of their nature" yet "has ordained their extinction when they have only just begun to fulfill the divine purpose which has endowed them with those potentialities and aspirations."[8]

The result of such arguments is to find death a kind of mistake. It is a betrayal—of trust, of morality, of love, of human development. In arguing that a *finite earthly life* is pointless—and thus without *religious* meaning—all justify the same rueful (if not bitter) plaint: *"If I never live again, I will have lived in vain."* It is a sentiment seldom baldly stated—perhaps because one could not comfortably say it to God. And in this embarrassment lies our first critical observation.

One could not comfortably say it because it is a purely human—or God-independent—argument which entails that if there is a God, and God has given us a finite earthly life, we must conclude God has not done the right thing.

That is, speaking entirely from *within* the same theistic framework that supports an eternal after-life, we must allow that God's creatures can rightly and independently decide what God *must* do to do the right thing. Since it is—for theism—irreligious for humans to set standards for God, we see that by insisting on ideal factual conditions for religious significance, a mistake has been made.

Sacredness: the self and the good-in-itself.

So we look again at finite earthly life: Can it possibly be *religious* to say that *my personal existence* is the necessary condition of the *ultimate meaningfulness* of my life? What of those whom I touched, those whom I remembered, and those to whom I gave what I could? Does my passing *retroactively* render past love and kindness pointless and my existence meaningless with it?

In fine, if we say life is sacred does its cessation mean we were wrong—that we now see it was *never* sacred?

And if, instead, we affirm that life *can* be sacred, surely death cannot render it pointless. For, from a *religious* point of view, what is sacred is never pointless.

Indeed, can it possibly be religious to evaluate the whole of civilized life from the viewpoint of our own participation? Is it *religious* to say that the meaningfulness of knowledge, sentience, love, ethics, art, friendship, communion, creation, appreciation, insight, and discovery—is "illusory" because my own participation in these things cannot last *forever*?

Of course the practical or *empirical* mind will say that when I die, life's content becomes *pointless for me*. But, for the religious mind to say, "if pointless *for me*, then *pointless*," is to make what happens to *me* the test of all meaningfulness and thus to negate a religious attitude absolutely—whether there is God or no God.

Indeed, strictly speaking, the rule, "meaningful only so long as I am alive" accords to oneself the status theologians reserve for God as the source of all meaning.

The religious lies outside time

Let us apply Berger's dictum to the race as a whole: if all humanity perishes and is unremembered, then the human race was pointless. Again, to the practical mind, this may seem self-evident: a few billion years of effortful creation, of civilized feeling, of devotions, learning, sorrow, laughter and then . . . eternal silence!

But what of the *religious* mind? Is it comfortably *religious* to say: "when the last voice is heard, the last Cezanne burns, the last notes of a Bach Toccata fade away, the last poem evaporates and the last child smiles" that humanity's moment was a waste? Or is it more plainly *religious* to say—even of a *doomed* humanity—that for a time, the universe knew itself, and had a voice, and that the centuries when dust could speak were times of genuine transcendence?

Did not the late theologian, Paul Tillich, think it essentially religious to speak of an "eternal which is present *in* a time"?[9] Indeed,

Confucianism's status as *religion* rests on the idea that sacredness lies *outside* time (is not a matter of time), for "it is the following of the Way itself that is of ultimate and absolute value."[10]

Surely religion's peculiar quest is for the *timeless* importance and meaning of what we do. It seeks things of meaning in themselves— like ritual or devotion—things whose meaningfulness is independent of future events and *in that sense*, "other-worldly" or *absolute*. Religious meaning *transcends* the context of practical living. If religion can find the eternal in the present moment, how could it be *religious* to say that if the human race ends, then its struggles, its love and its achievements must be (as Berger says) merely *illusory* goods?

The religious as the selfless

The idea that finite life negates life's religious meaning stands the significance of death on its head. It is not the denial of every available fact regarding death but (in devotion to truth) the acceptance of the facts, which comports with a religious attitude. *For only if we think death final can our lives be given as a gift. One cannot offer up what one continues to possess.*

To realize this is perhaps to be born again—not out from death but out from pointlessness. It is to emerge from the a-religious, animal self-interestedness of *survival* into the saved, uniquely human, disinterestedness of life understood and given over to the Good (or, in theistic terms, to God). Not lent—to be reclaimed when awakened from the grave—but given, absolutely, as the only life one has.

This is why the martyr has religious significance while the successful escapee does not. The religious meaning of giving one's life arises from narratives of final sacrifice—the story of Abraham's willingness to give the life of his son, and Socrates' self-sacrifice to justice.

A sacrifice loses *religious* depth when it lacks finality—like the donation of an organ we know will grow back. And this unconditional form of commitment seems essential to distinguishing a *religious* from a *practical*, or "worldly" perspective. As folk religion says, "virtue is its own reward"—to which these arguments add: "so is life."

A life religiously given is not interest paid to God on the condition that the principal be kept intact.

The discomfiting issue of Jesus

What about Jesus, then? For, Jesus' sacrifice is surely viewed as deep, even though his death was temporary. The idea conflicts with what I just argued. Time restricts me to two observations, which, as a devotee of religious sentiment and religious art, I do not make lightly.

First, I think my view of sacrifice and finality does reflect our root sense of religious depth and that the idea of resurrection makes the term "death" ambiguous. Consider that a child, innocent of doctrines, might well say, "he didn't *really* die" and that someone convicted of murder would pose a conceptual problem for us if the dead victim rose and lived a full life. So death and resurrection are not easy conceptual partners.

Second, one feature of resurrection bears upon the internal consistency of any theistic argument for the essential religiosity of an after-life. This feature is conflict of interest. If you love someone whom you know to be rich or able to make you successful, you quite literally cannot know to what degree your love is of the person or the prospect of reward. This psychological quandary we all recognize when we say that if the person became poor or ineffective and you felt the same love, you would then know, or as we say, could then be "absolutely certain," that your love had nothing to do with reward.

If this account is true, then if we are to love God purely and not for personal gain, the promise of eternal life makes this religious love impossible to assure. What sensible person would say, "love me and if you do, I'll make sure you'll get what you want"? The conflict of interest between love of God and fear of death makes it factually impossible to know whether one loves God religiously or practically.[11] In this way, the doctrine of eternal life is counter-religious.

Religion and the finite self

The controlling hope of the religious interest is to know and willingly accept what calls out to be done—not to know how to live forever.[12] (A witless or hurtful life gains no religious significance by going on forever.) And, if this is so, the highest act of commitment is the *unconditional* giving over of one's life to what the *Good, True, and Beautiful* (or God) demands—a commitment apart from any ancillary benefit.

So, religion is in this way "always a serious state of mind" as William James advised.[13] It is *seriousness* and what joy it may bring will likely depend on whether one can in fact love what is in itself good or whether, instead, one can only find satisfaction in comparative *advantage*—the great principle of worldliness.

In speaking this way, I take myself to be expounding the principle of selfless giving that every religion *professes*.

This selflessness is not the *literal* selflessness that offers the body because it does not know how to offer the soul. It does not flagellate, fast painfully, embrace terrible discomfort, and make of debilitating pain a virtue. Such "selfless" self-negation is merely disguised self-regard—as if one's bodily suffering were an object of ultimate concern (or worse: that regular bouts of self-affliction will pay off, in manageable installments, the one great sacrifice otherwise pending at the end).

The life we religiously commit, we commit not to this one or that one or to *us* ("our" people) nor even to all who live and who will come after—others no more deserving of the gift than you or I—but to God. Which is the popular way of saying—*to whatever is absolutely fundamental*—to whatever it is that brings humanity (or sentience) out of a *physical* world.

Religious selflessness does not demean or negate the self but gives it over to the truth in order that one have a self. For, without the truth what is in one's head is only in one's head; one might as well be dreaming. Without a basis in knowledge, one is not a self but a container of sensations, impulses and fantasies.

Ironically, self-possession is possible only when the self is also in possession of what ought to be done—when what is self and what is called for are one. So the specifically religious question, "can a *finite* life embody ultimate meaning?" may be *positively* answered in either of two ways that speak of what must be done.

Theists can say our lives are ultimately meaningful "*insofar* as we have followed God's *will*" and non-theists, "*insofar* as we have followed the *Good*. Although many are taught that *God*—as *will*—creates us human—few are encouraged to consider how *the Good*—as *evidence*—creates us human (how through knowing and appreciation, we express the universe—as suggested by Baruch Spinoza and G. F. Hegel in the seventeenth and nineteenth centuries).

As absolutely differing but basic narratives, these accounts of our creation and development lay claim to something *inexplicable in principle—yet true*. In thus affirming the reality of miracle, each validates the element of mystery essential to religious experience. These two views—each compatible with the religious significance of finite life—are the choices that constitute theology's fork in the road.

Meanwhile, outside, dusk approaches. The objects of remembrance that populate the graveyard will stand vigil through the night. In silence, they will grieve for "them that sleep." But in the morning, when the sun forgives the night, their very sorrow will celebrate life's wonder.

NOTES

1. Sigmund Freud, *Civilization and its Discontents*, James Strachey, trans. (New York: W. W. Norton, 1961; orig. pub. 1930), p. 49.

2. Saint Augustine, *The City of God,* Book IV, Chapter 1.

3. Peter L. Berger, *A Rumor of Angels: Modern Society and the Rediscovery of the Supernatural* (Garden City: Doubleday and Company, Inc., 1970), pp. 52-53.

4. Ibid., p. 56

5. Ibid.

6. Ibid.

7. Immanuel Kant, *The Critique of Practical Reason*, 2nd. ed., trans Abbott, p. 218; see discussion in Wilhelm Windelband, *A History of Philosophy, vol. II*, rev. ed., trans. James H. Tufts (New York: Harper and Brothers, Publishers, 1901), pp. 555-556.

8. John Hick, *God and the Universe of Faiths* (London: The Macmillan Press, Ltd., 1973), p. 185 *ff*.

9. Paul Tillich, *The Religious Situation*, trans. H. Richard Niebuhr (New York: Meridian Books, 1956), p. 37.

10. Herbert Fingarette, *Confucious:the Secular as Sacred* (New York: Harper Torchbooks; Harper & Row, Publishers, 1972), p. 20.

11. Did God not notice this?

12. I say "the controlling hope" not "the very character of," for religion is a stance toward the miraculous fact that good exists, not the moral stance itself (religion is not the same as morality).

13. William James, *The Varieties of Religious Experience* , p. 47. See esp. pp. 42-56, though on p. 55 James wobbles toward a pragmatic interpretation of religion's role in accepting necessity.

Chapter 6

Responses

A STEP NOT BEYOND:
RETHINKING GOD WITHOUT RELIGION

Ironically, given his critical evaluation of postmodern philosophy, Soffin's text brought to mind John D. Caputo's seminal and provocative thought in his most recent and profoundly theological work, *The Weakness of God*. Although they stare at each other from across the chasm separating analytical from continental philosophical traditions, both authors seek a move into the "beyond"—beyond scientific materialism, beyond superstition, beyond religion (as institutionalized strictures), and even beyond the classical God himself (gendered language intended). Both thinkers seek to understand the ultimate meaning of life, the ultimate meaning of "God" beyond religion—although in theory Caputo would contest any claims to ultimacy—and discover at the end of the path an ethics *sans* ethics.

Moreover, in taking a step beyond, both Caputo and Soffin demonstrate what Caputo, channeling Derrida, terms as *"un pas au-delà,"* a step beyond that is really a step *not* beyond—a step beyond the solely metaphysical *and* material that actually brings them a step closer toward the other, the neighbor, the thing itself, which is actually a step toward "God" (*Sovereignties in Question*, "Shibboleth: for Paul Celan," 51). If readers can wade through Soffin's analytical philosophical gyrations they will find that his conclusions are as seminal, provocative, and fruitful as Caputo's.

Soffin dismantles the religious notions of a personal creator God, whose will dictates the order and activity of the universe and the scientific materialistic notions of creation by "accident," in favor of third way—a way that steps beyond religion and science into the realm of necessity. Only through necessity can we know a thing exists in reality—no necessity, no real existence. Soffin says that "the substance (substantiality) of reality is one with the presence of necessity. Necessity is the inexplicable, hence ultimate, law-like character that is the substance of anything's 'reality'" (330). And for him, "God . . . is the necessity of things, present in 'the real' in all of its forms," and this necessity is eternal, unchanging, rational, physical, and beautiful (324-5; 390-1). Indeed, Soffin claims that "'God's body' is the incorporeal substance of all realities" (333). We comprehend and apprehend this "God" existentially, in the material reality of the world as it touches our emotional/perceptive life. Through this life we come to feel/perceive the immanence of God and the miracle of the laws of necessity that govern the world. In the realm of the religious, moral, physical, logical, and aesthetic, necessity gives form and order to what is otherwise chaos, chance, and accident (353).

While Soffin goes to great lengths to explain necessity as it pertains to logic and aesthetics, the brilliance of his thought shines most luminously in his exposition of the religious connection to reality in the realm of moral necessity. He argues that only through moral necessity (in tandem with the physical, logical, and aesthetic) can we know the right and the best actions to take in life. The acts demanded by necessity make human activity valuable, "God"-worthy. Consequently, his treatise, if taken to heart, profoundly affects how we live our lives in the world.

Because this necessity is inexplicable, ultimate, and awesome as the form or spirit of existence, it is also religious (325). Soffin expresses the religious sensibility in these terms: "The awareness of inexplicably sovereign and immanent norms," [laws] that "constitute what it is we are in awe of—and yet love" (371). This love and respect for what Soffin calls "the divine" realizes itself in the world as love and respect for things in nature—the things in the world that science and theism merely use as a possession or as a means to a "greater" end. He says that "to love and respect the necessities (things beyond our power to change) is to love and respect 'god' or 'the gift' that find existence, in the final analysis, to be" (373). In other words, if we love and respect a piece of wood used to craft a bench, rather than just using the bench for our own ends, we note the beauty of the wood grain, the browns and tans that give it color, the smoothness of its surface, and the strength of its substance. We appreciate things in themselves (including the human other) and treat them with love and respect.

In Soffin's step beyond scientism and theism, he ultimately takes a step *not* beyond the world of necessary things. In his exhortation to a new kind of religious consciousness, Soffin calls for a more Native American "attitude of humility and respect toward reality," a love and appreciation for the given (and necessary) order of things, because in that order of the ordinary we find the sacredness of the divine. For, "to worship 'God' is to find wonder and beauty and power—challenge and possibility—in 'the wind,' in what must be" (388).

While I believe that taking a step beyond scientism, theism, and materialism may provide a prophetic voice from which both traditions can benefit, I would argue that we take a step *not* beyond relational-ism, that we leave open the possibility of a relational God. Ironically, Soffin's "love" of the thing itself, the appreciation of the object rather than the mere utility of it smacks of relationship, the sort of relational theism he critiques. How do you love and appreciate an object *sans* relationship? Love, respect, appreciation—all relational words—necessitate some sort of relationship. If Soffin finds God in the necessary, in the world of unchanging things, the very things he exhorts us to love and respect and appreciate, are we not loving and respecting and appreciating God? If the thing we love, respect, and appreciate just happens to be another person, or even a beautiful sunset that brings us joy, or the bench that, in its sturdiness, keeps us from falling on our tail, is that not the divine somehow relating back to us by way of those necessary things?

In fine, I believe that in our "relationship of intimacy and mutual courtesy" with nature and with the world, we also embark on a relationship of mutual and somehow reciprocal intimacy, love, and respect with the divine—however one chooses to conceive it (380).
—*Sharon L. Baker teaches theology and religion at Messiah College.*

RATIONALIZING RELIGION
AND SPIRITUALIZING PHILOSOPHY

Alan Soffin and I have been back and forth on philosophy for fifty years. I've called him every nasty philosophical name I could think of—essentialist, rationalist, objectivist, foundationalist, anti-relativist—to no avail. Still he continues to pursue his quest for Truth and, in recent years, to encompass theology within the orbit of that quest.

Thank goodness for that because *Rethinking Religion* repays careful examination of its unfolding arguments and bursts forth repeatedly with powerful, memorable prose. For an essentialist, rationalist, objectivist, etc. Soffin is surprisingly open to life's mysteries—even its "miracles" (as he defines the term)—which provide a sense in which an atheist by conventional definitions of the term can find common cause with the religiously devout. He is open to mysteries in the sense of being moved by them, as in a twilight visit to a Latino cemetery or on listening to a Beethoven symphony in a Paris cathedral. It is in the tension between Soffin's rational sensibilities and his direct emotional experience that his dialectic begins. And it is from that dialectic that Soffin seeks to rationalize religion and spiritualize philosophy— not, as he points out (p. 34), for the first time:

> Theology's emphasis on the meaning of things and philosophy's on the truth of things creates a relationship much like that of rival siblings. The so-called "natural" theology of the Middle Ages was, after all, philosophy thought capable of marking the path to God. But when theological scholars found it wandering anywhere but to another world, it was superseded by faith and revelation—by a theology whose arguments remained heavily philosophical but whose advantage lay in knowing by divine grace where the other world lay. As Saint Anselm fatefully and philosophically announced in offering a rule for rational theology, "I do not seek to understand in order that I may believe; but I believe, that I may understand."

To those comfortable with what they take to be the complementarity (or ultimate unity) of conventional "theo-logics," Soffin provides reason for philosophical rethinking and spiritual reawakening. The ultimate paragraphs are for me the next to last two in Chapter 1:

> Indeed, religion—essential or useless, illusory or true—seems of all compelling human interests, the most internally conflicted. Its gods have been infinitely loving, infinitely punitive, or both; they have been multiple or single, bodied or spiritual, outside the universe or all that is the universe. Its selflessness has meant to some a life humbly offered to the needy, to others a life risked in war against the unconvinced. Thought lucid enough that we may know it "as a child," God's message has required special schooling, justified interpretive priesthoods, perpetual exegesis, and sectarian revisions without end. At its center lie mysteries "beyond human understanding" yet it reveals for humankind "the meaning of life." Deemed in fact inexpressible—mystical, ineffable—the nature of the Divine or the Holy has consistently generated works and preachments that explain it, describe it, and apply it to practical life. Though insisted on as truth, religion is defended as belief; it is the only professed truth that cleaves to proper nouns, so that we comfortably accept Hindu religion, Jewish religion, or Western religion but not

American physics, Mexican chemistry, or Canadian zoology.

Pronounced a matter of the most effortful faith (as in Kierkegaard's "infinite passion"), religion's truth is said also to be perfectly obvious (as in the conviction that "human life couldn't possibly have happened by accident"). Said by Judeo-Christians and Moslems to require belief in supernatural agency, religion is said by Confucians and Bhuddists to require none. Declared a creature of neurosis or merely an instrument of social control, it has nonetheless emerged and re-emerged as the avowed apex of spirit in societies of every kind and size. And in the final paroxysm of its own confusion, no message of love against hate has historically yielded so much of both.

This having been said, I remain critical of Soffin's disdain for what he calls "scientism," for what I take to be overreliance on ordinary language analysis, and for much else, that, God willing, will keep us arguing for the next fifty years. —*Herbert W. Simons, Emeritus Professor of Communication, Temple University*

JOINING THE GOD OF HISTORY AND OF THE PHILOSOPHERS?

I generally learn most from books written by those who dip into a very different pool of sources from mine. As I look over Alan Soffin's bibliography, I see mostly works I do not know and a smaller group of works with which I am just vaguely acquainted. And of even the very small number of works I know in depth, I soon learned that Soffin sees very different emphases there than I do. True to form, I learned much from reading this text, an erudite work of passion, sensitivity, and sharp-edged rationality.

Soffin's quest is to investigate and understand life's meaningfulness as richly as possible from the perspective of the two major and largely competing versions of existence in contemporary culture, that of theism and that of scientistic materialism. Unlike so many others, however, Soffin is not interested in contrasting these perspectives to demonstrate one or the other as superior. Soffin seeks genuine elucidation in each of the strengths and self-contradictions involved— how each finally undermine a full-orbed concept of meaningful personality—finally drawing from both to outline what he calls the "religious" life, formed as an expression of recognition, appreciation, and realization of the good of existence.

I very much appreciate what Alan Soffin has accomplished in this book. Though once I eagerly took every philosophy course available,

I since have grown quite tired of philosophers' discourse. Totally aside from the pervasive undercurrent of arrogant intellectual elitism, it often feels in this discourse that there is a willful reduction of its own potentiality by insistent habitation in the head, not the heart. For example, recently I was attracted by a notice of the campus philosophy club concerning a public lecture by a noted guest professor on the topic, "the social value of radical ontological skepticism." I didn't really understand that, but hoping, I suppose, for a whiff of academic political dissent following the November midterm elections, I decided to attend. It turned out to be mainly two hours of heated wrangling over whether or not there be any validity to the statement "this lemon is sour."

But if I cracked Soffin's text with an attitude of hesitant Muggeridgean world weariness inspired by such tests of attention endurance, I was very pleased to learn rather immediately that Soffin's work is anything but that kind of philosophical discourse. From his discussion contrasting God as Creator with that of cosmic first cause, to his highly stimulating presentation of knowledge as true incarnation, and much more, this has been a book worth reading. I hope that Soffin's discussion of the problems attentive to maintaining doctrinal orthodoxy receives the wide attention it deserves in Mennonite and Evangelical Christian circles and beyond.

Much as I would rather sit with Alan Soffin and discuss the guitar styles of Robert Johnson and Son House, I feel it is at least part of my assignment as a respondent here to voice some criticism. So, to begin with, I am inclined to think that Soffin overly stresses the role of rationality in human existence. Surely much of this difference is simply that between a social worker and a philosopher. Nevertheless, given that we are mortal beings driven by the same overriding survival instinct as other living creatures, it is not surprising (it is rational to assume . . .) that we are motivated at least as strongly by pure anxiety as by rationality. The urge for rationality (predictable order) may well itself be understood largely as a mechanism for quelling existential anxiety.

Soffin doesn't deny this, and in fact his final pages on death and meaning in life are a real treasure, which I intend to plunder liberally. But I do think there is enough of a shift in emphasis here between Soffin's understanding and mine (which I outlined in an earlier book in this same Cascadia Living Issues Discussion Series series) that it is worthy of mention. To sharpen the point here, I am not convinced that Soffin's approach is really adequate to account for radical personal and collective human evil. Of course such evil is irrational, and clearly overcoming such evil would entail becoming more rational. But I'm just not sure that recognition gets us very far.

Second, if the biblical tradition teaches anything at all, it is that God is a God of history, and that we hear the commanding voice of God in the movement of events in our time. Presently, many of us are hearing this commanding voice clearly saying at least two things: "Thou Shalt Learn to Share Thy Resources With All in Need" and "Thou Shalt Hastily Endeavor to Bring Thy Population Explosion Under Control." Obviously, most of those in theistic-based religions are not heeding these commands. They worship the market distribution of resources, all the while to continue being fruitful and multiplying. It would be worth discussion with Alan Soffin whether his emphasis on grateful acceptance of the laws governing our existence points in this same direction, and might even be, in fact, the means by which we again are able to hear this (still, small) commanding voice. If so, we would have here a case in point in which the biblical God of History and the God of the Philosophers might truly join as One!
—*Daniel Liechty, Associate Professor of Social Work, University of Illinois*

Passing

Not just the mountains sleep.
Existence, too;
Its galaxies and particles
Unruffled by destructions
That would terrify a Maker.
Within the whole,
But one eye blinks,
Reading,
If you please,
Until the light goes out.

Bibliography

Armstrong, Karen. *A History of God.* New York: Random House Publishing Group, 1994.

Audi, Robert and William J. Wainwright, eds. *Rationality, Religious Belief and Moral Commitment.* Ithaca: Cornell University Press, 1986.

Austin, J. L., J. O. Urmson, and Geoffrey Warnock, eds. *Philosophical Papers.* London: Oxford University Press, 1961.

Barth, Karl. *Dogmatics in Outline*, trans. G. T. Thomson. New York: Harper's Torchbooks, 1959.

Berger, Peter. *A Rumor of Angels.* Garden City, N.Y.: Anchor Books, Doubleday & Company, Inc., 1970.

Blackburn, Simon, *Truth: a Guide.* Oxford: Oxford University Press, 2005.

Bambrough, Renford, ed. *New Essays on Plato and Aristotle.* Oxford, England: Routledge & Kegan Paul, Ltd., 1965.

Brown, D. Mackenzie. *Ultimate Concern: Tillich in Dialogue.* New York: Harper & Row, Publishers, 1965.

Brunner, Emil. *The Christian Doctrine of God.* Trans. Wyon, Olive.. Philadelphia: Westminster Press, 1950.

Cahn, Steven M. and David Shatz. *Contemporary Philosophy of Religion.* Oxford: Oxford University Press, 1982.

Carmody, Denise Lardner and John Tully Carmody. *Native American Religions: An Introduction.* New York: Paulist Press, 1993.

Castelli, Jim. *A Plea for Common Sense.* San Francisco: Harper & Row Publishers, 1988.

Chapell, V. C., ed. *The Philosophy of Mind.* New Jersey: Prentice-Hall, 1962.

———. ed. *The Philosophy of David Hume.* New York: Random House, Inc. The Modern Library, 1963.

Chatalian, George. *Epistemology and Skepticism*: *An Enquiry into the Nature of Epistemology*. Carbondale, Ill.: Southern Illinois University Press, 1991.

Churchland, P. S. and T. J. Sejnowski. *The Computational Brain*. Cambridge, Mass.: MIT Press, 1994.

Copleston, F. C. *Medieval Philosophy*. New York and Evanston, Harper Torchbooks, 1961.

Dabney, D. Lyle and Hinze, Bradford E., eds. *Advents of the Spirit: An Introduction to the Current Study of Pneumatology*. Milwaukee: Marquette University Press, 2001.

Davies, Brian. *An Introduction to the Philosophy of Religion*. Oxford: Oxford University Press, 1993.

Dietl, Paul. "On Miracles," *American Philosophical Quarterly* 5.2 (April 1968).

Dray, William, *Laws and Explanation in History*. London: Oxford University Press, 1957.

Dewey, John. *A Common Faith*. New Haven. Yale University Press, 1934.

———. *Logic: The Theory of Inquiry*. New York: Henry Holt and Company, 1938.

Dobson, James. *When God Doesn't Make Sense*. Carol Stream, Ill.: Tyndale House Publishers, 1997.

Dulles, Avery, S. J. *Models of Revelation*. Garden City, N.Y.: Doubleday & Company, Inc., 1983.

Edwards, Paul. *The Logic of Moral Discourse*. New York: The Free Press, 1955.

Eliade, Mercea. *The Sacred and the Profane*, trans.Willard R. Trask. New York: Harcourt Brace Jovanovich, Publishers; a Harvest/HBJ Book, 1959.

———. Mercea Eliade, *Myth and Reality*, trans. Willard R. Trask. New York: Harper & Row, 1963.

Ellis, John M. *Against Deconstruction*. Princeton: Princeton University Press, 1989.

Elton, William, ed. *Aesthetics and Language*. Oxford, U.K.: Basil Blackwell, 1959.

Esslin, Martin. *The Theater of the Absurd*. New York: Vintage Books, 3rd. ed. 2004.

Farmer, H. H. *Towards Belief in God*. New York: Macmillan Publishing Co., 1947.

Feigl, Herbert and Michael Scriven, eds. *Minnesota Studies in the Philosophy of Science*, vol. 1. Minneapolis: University of Minnesota Press, 1956.

Ferré, Frederick. *Lamguage, Logic and God*. Chicago: University of Chicago Press, 1961.

Findlay, J.N. *Meinong's Theory of Objects and Values*. Oxford: The Clarendon Press, 1963).

Fingarette, Herbert. *The Secular as Sacred*. New York: Harper & Row Publishers, Harper Torchbooks, 1972.

Fisch, Max H., ed. *Classic American Philosophers*. Englewood Cliffs, N.J.: Prentice-Hall, Inc., 1951.

Fiske, Donald and Shweder Richard. eds. *Metatheory in Social Science: Pluralisms and Subjectivities*. Chicago: University of Chicago Press, 1986.

Flew, Antony and Alisdair MacIntyre, eds. *New Essays in Philosophical Theology*. New York: The Macmillan Company. 1955.

Freud, Sigmund. *The Future of an Illusion*. Garden City, N.Y.: Doubleday Anchor Books, 1957 [orig. 1927].

George Gallup Organization. "Basic Beliefs" 1991 for *Times Mirror*.

Gardiner, Patrick. *Kierkegaard*. Oxford: Oxford University Press, 1988.

Geras, Norman. *Solidarity in the Conversation of Humankind: The Ungroundable Liberalism of Richard Rorty*. London: Verso Publishing, 1995),

Godsey, John D. *The Promise of Richard Niebuhr*. Phildelphia: The J. P. Lippincott Company, 1970.

Gorringe Timothy. *Karl Barth: Against Hegemony*. Oxford: Oxford University Press, 1999.

Hamilton, Kenneth. *The Promise of Kierkegaard*. Philadelphia: J. B. Lippincott Company, 1969.

Hamlyn D. W. *Metaphysics*. Cambridge, U. K.: Cambridge University press, 1984.

Hare, R. M. *The Language of Morals*. New York: Oxford University Press, 1964; orig. pub. 1952.

Harris, Sam. *The End of Faith*. New York: W. W. Norton & Company, 2004.

Hartz, Paula R. *Native American Religions*. USA: Facts on File, Inc. 1997.

Hebblethwaite, Brian. *In Defense of Christianity*. Oxford, England: Oxford University Press, 2005.

Hick, John. *Philosophy of Religion*. Englewood Cliffs, N.J.: Prentice-Hall, Inc.; Foundations of Philosophy Series, 1963.

———. *God and the Universe of Faiths*, revised edition. Glasgow: William Collins Sons & Co., Ltd., 1977.

Hoitinga, Jr. Dewey J. *Faith and Reason from Plato to Plantinga: An Introduction to a Reformed Epistemology*. Albany, N.Y.: State University of New York Press, 1991.

Hume, David ed. Aiken, Henry D. *Hume's Moral and Political Philosophy*. New York: Hafner Publishing Company, 1948.

———. ed. Wolff, Robert Paul. *The Essential David Hume*. New York: A Mentor Book, The New American Library, 1969.

Hooke, Sidney ed., *Determinism and Freedom.* New York: Collier Books, 1961.

James, William. *The Varieties of Religious Experience.* New York: Mentor edition, The New American Library, 1958.

————. *Pragmatism.* New York: Longmans Green, 1908.

Joyce, James. *Portrait of the Artist as a Young Man.* New York: The Modern Library, 1928.

Kant, Immanuel. *Critique of Pure Reason,* 2nd. ed. Trans. Kemp-Smith, Norman. Hampshire, U.K.: Palgrave Macmillan, 1920.

Kant, Immanuel. *Groundwork of the Metaphysic of Morals.* Trans. Paton, H. J. New York: Harper & Row, 1964.

Kater, John L. *Christians on the Right.* New York: Seabury Press, 1982.

Kenny, Anthony. *Action, Emotion and Will.* London: Routledge & Kegan Paul, 1963.

————. *What is Faith?* New York: Oxford University Press, 1992.

Kierkegaard, Søren . *Philosophical Fragments.* Trans. David Swenson. Princeton, N.J.: Princeton University Press, 1962.

————. *Training in Christianity.* Trans. Lowrie, Walter.. Princeton: Princeton University Press, 1944.

Kneale, William. *Probability and Induction.* London: Oxford University Press, 1949.

Kolakowski, Leszek. *The Alienation of Reason.* Trans. Norman Guterman. Garden City, N.Y.: Doubleday & Company, Inc. 1969.

Kushner, Harold. *When Bad Things Happen to Good People.* New York: Avon Books, 1983.

Levy, Ian Christopher. *Scriptural Logic, Real Presence, and the Parameters of Orthodoxy.* Milwaukee: Marquette University Press, 2003

Lewis C.S. *Miracles.* New York: Macmillan Publishing Co., Inc., 1960 (orig. pub. 1947).

Locke, John. *Essay Concerning Human Understanding*, Book IV.

Long, A. A. *Hellenistic Philosophy*, 2nd. ed. Berkeley: University of California Press, 1986.

Mill, J. S. *Utilitarianism, Liberty, Representative Government.* London: E.P. Dutton & Co., 1910.

Moore, G. E. *Ethics.* New York: Oxford University Press, 1965 (orig. pub. 1912).

Morganbesser, Sydney and Walsh, James, eds. *Free Will.* Englewood Cliffs, N.J.: Prentice-Hall, Inc., 1962.

Murdoch, Iris. ed. Conradi, Peter *Existentialist and Mystics.* New York: Penguin Books, 1997.

Nielsen, Kai. *After the Demise of the Tradition: Rorty. Critical Theory, and the Fate of Philosophy.* Boulder, Colo.: Westview Press, 1991.

Nietzsche, Friedrich, *The Gay Science*, trans. Walter Kaufman. New York: Random House, 1974; Vintage Books, 1974.

———. *Beyond Good and Evil*. Trans. Walter Kaufman. New York: Random House, Inc. Vintage Books, 1966.

———. *The Will to Power*. Trans. Kaufman and Hollingdale.New York: Viking Press, 1968.

Norris, Kathleen. *Amazing Grace*. New York: Riverhead Books, 1998.

Novak, Michael *Belief and Unbelief*. New York: A Mentor Book, The New American Library, The Macmillan Company, 1965.

Oliker, Michael and Walter P. Kolakowski, eds. *Images of Youth*. New York: Peter Lang, 2001.

Otto, Rudolph. *The Idea of the Holy*. Trans. John W. Harvey. Oxford: Oxford University Press, 1967 (orig. pub. 1923).

Pagels, Elaine. *The Gnostic Gospels*. New York: Vintage Books, Random House, Inc., 1979.

Passmore, John. *Philosophical Reasoning*. New York: Charles Scribner's Sons, 1961.

———. *Recent Philosophers*. La Salle, Ill.: Open Court Publishing Company, 1985.

Pelikan, Jaroslav, ed. *The World Treasury of Religious Thought*. Boston: Little, Brown & Company, 1960.

Penelhum, Terence. *Survival and Disembodied Existence*. London: Routledge and Kegan Paul, 1970.

Purtill, Richard, *Thinking About Religion*. Englewood Cliffs, N.J.: Prentice-Hall, Inc. 1978.

Quine, Willard. *From a Logical Point of View*. New York: Harper & Row, 1963.

Remarque, Erich Maria. *All Quiet on the Western Front*. Trans. A. W. Wheen. Boston: Little, Brown, 1929.

Richardson, John. *Nietzsche's System*. New York: Oxford University Press, 1996.

Rorty, Richard. *Objectivity, Relativism and Truth*. Cambridge: Cambridge University Press. 1991.

Ryle, Gilbert. *The Concept of Mind*. Chicago: The University of Chicago Press, 1949.

Sapir, Edward, "Linguistics as a Science," *Language* 5, no. 4 (Dec. 1929).

Schneewind Jerome. B. *Moral Philosophy from Montaigne to Kant*. Cambridge, UK: Cambridge University Press, 2003.

Seabrook, John. *Nobrow*. New York: Vintage Books, 2001.

Searle, John R. *Mind, Language, and Society*. New York: Basic Books, 1998.

Scruton, Roger. *Kant , Kant*. Oxford: Oxford University Press, 1982.

———. *The Intelligent Person's Guide to Philosophy*. New York: Penguin Books, 1999.

Smith, John E. *Reason, Experience and God: John E. Smith in Dialogue*, ed. Vincent M. Colapietro. New York: Fordham University Press, 1997.

Sylvester, Robert Peter, Robert Jenkins, and R.W. Sleeper, eds. *The Moral Philosophy of G.E. Moore*. Philadelphia: Temple University Press, 1990.

Taylor, Charles. *The Explanation of Behavior*. London: Routledge & Kegan Paul.

Taylor, Richard. *Metaphysics*. Englewood-Cliffs, N.J.: Prentice-Hall Foundations of Philosophy Series, 1963.

Tedlock, Dennis and Barbara Tedlock. *Teachings from the American Earth: Indian Religion and Philosophy*. New York: Liveright Publishing Company, 1992.

Tillich, Paul. *Dynamics of Faith*. New York: Harper & Row Publishers, Inc.; Harper Torchbooks, 1957.

———. *The Religious Situation*. New York: Meridian Books, 1956.

———. *My Search for Absolutes*. New York: Simon and Schuster, Inc.; a Touchstone Book, 1967.

———. "The Lost Dimension in Religion," *The Saturday Evening Post*: June 14, 1958.

Toulmin, Stephen. *The Philosophy of Science*. London: Hutchinson & Co., 1958.

Ward, Keith. *Religion and Creation*. Oxford: Oxford University Press, 1996.

Warnock, Geoffrey. *English Philosophy Since 1900*. London: Oxford University Press, 1958).

Warnock, Mary. *Ethics Since 1900*. London: Oxford University Press, 1960.

Will, Frederick L. "Thoughts and Things," *Proceedings and Addresses of the American Philosophic Association*, 42, pp. 51-69.

———, *Pragmatism and Realism*; Westphal, Kenneth ed. *The Later Essays of Frederick Will*. Lanham, Md.: Rowman & Littlefield. 1997.

Williams, Bernard. *Ethics and the Limits of Philosophy*. Cambridge, Mass.: Harvard University Press, 1985.

Wilson, E. O., "The Biological Basis of Morality," *The Atlantic Monthly 28*, no. 4 (April 1998).

Wind, Edgar. *Art and Anarchy*. London: Faber & Faber Limited, 1963.

Windelband, Wilhelm. *A History of Philosophy*, 2 vols. New York: Harper & Brothers, Publishers, 1958.

Wolff, Robert Paul, ed. *The Essential David Hume*. New York: The New American Library, a Mentor Book, 1969.

Zaehner, R.C., ed. *The Concise Encyclopedia of Living Faiths*. Boston: Beacon Press, 1959.

The Index

The Author

Alan Soffin lives in Doylestown, Pennsylvania, with his wife Jean. He holds a Ph.D. in Philosophical and Social Foundations of Education from the University of Illinois. Although retired from teaching at both Michigan State and Temple University, he remains active in matters intellectual, educational, and artistic.

At Delaware Valley College's Center for Learning in Retirement, he teaches philosophy of religion, aesthetics, and epistemology. With the aid of his ex-students, he is restoring his feature film, *Confessor* (1968)—an experimental film funded in part by the American Film Institute. He is also preparing a web version of an art work in image and text, "In a Believer's Graveyard." A meditation on love and mortality, it has been twice shown at Tubac, Arizona's Center for the Arts.

He is regular contributor of poems, essays and memoir pieces to *DreamSeeker Magazine*. His essays have appeared in *Images of Youth* (Peter Lang, 2001), *Educational Theory,* and the journal of the Pennsylvania Modern Language Association.

He developed innovative programs for learning in the Wissahickon School District. Convinced that school reform requires reform in the *culture* of schooling, his "Videoexchange" (1974) pioneered the use of classroom-created video exchanges between foreign and American students. Languages were learned, friends were made, and cultures were shared. His "Community-School TV" partnered students and community members in the making of documentary video and slide shows that brought community and school together. (Both programs were recommended for dissemination by Pennsylvania's Department of Education.)

Rethinking Religion began in response to his first wife's death. He faced religion's defining question: "What is the meaning of our lives?" But there seemed no way forward. He had rejected both traditionally theistic and wholly scientific worldviews. Was there a third way? Could there be a conception of "God" as mysterious and guiding as that of traditional theism yet rooted in the structure of human experience? His answer was the ten-year effort of *Rethinking*—a philosophical theology that does not reduce religion to psychology, genetics, morals, or poetry. "It's demanding," he laments, "but the Mennonites were right—understanding before acceptance."

When not grappling with conceptual arguments, Soffin finds his truth in the desert Southwest, the B Minor Mass, and at times in the early Blues.

CPSIA information can be obtained at www.ICGtesting.com
Printed in the USA
BVOW030412261011

274493BV00007B/5/P

9 781931 038805